April 13, 2002

OAH - Washington D.C.

See America First

Mark —
for a fellow traveller.
Many thanks for your
thoughtful comments
early on.

Russ

See America First

TOURISM AND NATIONAL IDENTITY, 1880–1940

Marguerite S. Shaffer

SMITHSONIAN INSTITUTION PRESS
WASHINGTON AND LONDON

PRODUCTION EDITOR: Ruth G. Thomson
COPY EDITOR: Karin Kaufman
DESIGNER: Amber Frid-Jimenez

LIBRARY OF CONGRESS CATALOGING-IN-PUBLICATION DATA
Shaffer, Marguerite S.
   See America first : tourism and national identity, 1880–1940 /
Marguerite S. Shaffer.
      p.   cm.
   Includes bibliographical references and index.
   ISBN 1-56098-953-X (alk. paper) — ISBN 1-56098-976-9 (pbk. :
alk. paper)
      1. Heritage tourism—United States—Marketing—History.
   2. National characteristics, American—History. I. Title.
   G156.5.H47 S52   2001
   338.4′79173048—dc21   2001020921

BRITISH LIBRARY CATALOGING-IN-PUBLICATION DATA
AVAILABLE

Manufactured in the United States of America
08 07 06 05 04 03 02 01   5 4 3 2 1

⊖ The paper used in this publication meets the minimum require-
ments of the American National Standard for Information Sci-
ences—Permanence of Paper for Printed Library materials ANSI
Z39.48-1984.

For permission to reproduce illustrations appearing in this book,
please correspond directly with the owners of the works as listed in
the individual captions. The Smithsonian Institution Press does not
retain reproduction rights for these illustrations individually or
maintain a file of addresses for photo sources.

Frontispiece: Snapshot from "Trips to Colorado, Yosemite and
Throughout the Grand Canyon," anonymous photograph album,
c. 1921. (Reproduced by permission of the Huntington Library, San
Marino, California)

For Ben and Callie

CONTENTS

INTRODUCTION

*I*N LATE APRIL 1892, Stephen Merritt, a Methodist minister from New York City, boarded a train with his wife Mary Eliza to commence a Raymond and Whitcomb Company transcontinental tour to California and Alaska. "For many years," Merritt explained in the opening lines of his travel journal, "it has been my desire and design to see 'the land I fondly call my own.'"[1] Merritt also confessed his need for a vacation. He had not only been ministering his congregation but also managing a store and teaching at a missionary college. In addition, three deaths in his immediate family in the year prior to his travels had taken an emotional toll. So when a new pastor arrived and the chance came for Merritt to take time off, he set out to see America.

Merritt's two-month tour took him to a number of noted turn-of-the-century attractions: the Garden of the Gods in Colorado, Las Vegas Hot

Springs in New Mexico, Yosemite National Park, the Cliff House in San Francisco, the glaciers of Alaska, and Yellowstone National Park. He and his excursion party traveled in luxury, riding in private Pullman Palace cars secured by Raymond and Whitcomb and stopping at posh resort hotels such as the Raymond in Pasadena, the Hotel Del Monte in Monterey, and the Palace Hotel in San Francisco. Merritt marveled at the mountain scenery of Colorado, the lushness of California, the urbanity of San Francisco, and the sublimity of Yosemite and Yellowstone. He reveled in the diverse people and places he met along his journey and expressed a contagious enthusiasm for the sights and scenes of America. "Our dear home!" he wrote as he traveled through Colorado. "We are learning to love it more and more, and to rejoice that we live in this favored land. Blessed Country. How our hearts bound with joy under the dear Stars and Stripes!"[2] His personal musings, extensively chronicled in his journal, suggest that the spectacle of the American nation as it unrolled across the American landscape renewed his spirit.

In following the progress of Merritt's tour, one can't help but be captivated by his thick description of the tourist experience in fin de siècle America. Expressions of patriotic fervor and sublime transcendence, religious epiphany, and personal joy breathe new life into long-forgotten resort hotels and Pullman Palace cars and provide an alluring view of natural attractions now paved over with roads and trails or hemmed in by commercial sprawl. His journal has a dramatic appeal all its own, but it also offers an entrée into the larger messages and meanings embedded in the turn-of-the-century tourist experience. Merritt recounts his tour as a kind of voyage of American discovery, implicitly and explicitly linking his experience with the larger search for cultural and national identity. His narrative suggests a broader connection between tourism and nationalism, implying a more complicated link between the emergence of the United States as a modern urban-industrial nation-state and the search for American identity.

Half a century after Stephen Merritt chronicled his tour, a more famous American also left New York City to travel the country, taking the subway and then the trolley to Bearsville, New York, where Route 6 crossed the Hudson River. On a rainy day in mid-July 1947, Jack Kerouac stuck out his thumb in hopes of catching his first ride to California. As he wrote in the opening lines of *On the Road*, his novel chronicling his travels across America,

"I'd often dreamed of going West to see the country."[3] Embracing Walt Whitman's "Song of the Open Road," Kerouac traveled across America from east to west and north to south and back again, seeking to discover the "real" America of workers and farmers, cowboys and tramps. He hitched rides, rode Greyhound buses, and drove with friends. He stopped in seedy hotels, prowled pool rooms and bars, and worked odd jobs. Far removed from the posh Pullman Palace cars, the luxury resort hotels, and the scenic tourist attractions of the turn of the century, Kerouac's journeys were voyages of self-discovery, rites of passage in which he escaped mainstream America. In celebrating the freedom of the open road made accessible by the automobile, Kerouac articulated the desires of an alienated youth overwhelmed by both the possibilities and the predictability of widespread consumer abundance.

Although Kerouac avoided established tourist destinations—scenic landscapes, historic monuments, and roadside attractions—he embraced many of the desires that inspired the tourists who preceded him. He sought intense personal experience, an escape to liminal space where the self could be temporarily reimagined, an opportunity for physical, mental, and spiritual reinvigoration, a glimpse of "the good life"—all the promises of modern consumer culture. As such, *On the Road* came to embody a new permutation of the very consumer culture Kerouac sought to escape. In many ways, however, *On the Road* marked the end of a particular kind of tourism in the United States, reflecting in its opposition the culmination of a little over half a century of tourist development.

This book is about the moment in between these two journeys—a moment characterized by the rise of what I call national tourism. Distinguished from the resort vacations, the picturesque tours, and the literary pilgrimages of the early nineteenth century in which the genteel elite sought out the "sacred places" of America, national tourism extended from and depended on the infrastructure of the modern nation-state.[4] As a national transportation system and communication network spread a metropolitan corridor across America, as methods of mass production and mass distribution created a national market, as corporate capitalism begot an expanding middle class with time and money to spend on leisure, tourism emerged as a form of geographical consumption that centered on the sights and scenes of the American nation.

In other words, tourism was integrally connected to the emergence of the United States as a corporate, urban-industrial nation-state. Just as brand-name goods and mass circulation magazines along with mail-order catalogs and chain stores helped shape and define a national market and culture, tourism helped imbue the nation with form and substance.

Between 1880 and 1940 the emerging tourist industry in the United States actively promoted tourism as a ritual of American citizenship. Commercial clubs, railroad corporations, the National Park Service, good-roads advocates, guidebook publishers, and a wide array of tourist advocates and enthusiasts defined the tourist experience in national terms. Adopting and modifying the established elite tradition of secular pilgrimage to the demands of modern consumer culture, advocates promoted tourism as a patriotic duty. Tourist industries used the strategies of modern marketing to develop and promote brand-name tourist destinations that would attract a national clientele. In the process, they created and marketed tourist landscapes as quintessentially American places, consciously highlighting certain meanings and myths while ignoring others, deliberately arranging historical events and anecdotes, intentionally framing certain scenes and views into a coherent national whole. As the tourist infrastructure expanded, public and private tourist advocates worked together to develop a canon of American tourist attractions that manifested a distinct national identity. They encouraged white, native-born middle- and upper-class Americans to reaffirm their American-ness by following the footsteps of American history and seeing the nation firsthand. In teaching tourists what to see and how to see it, promoters invented and mapped an idealized American history and tradition across the American landscape, defining an organic nationalism that linked national identity to a shared territory and history.[5] And tourist interests insisted that by seeing the sights and scenes that embodied the essence of America, by consuming the nation through touring, tourists would become better Americans.[6]

Tourists increasingly responded to these promotional campaigns. Touring narratives, travel diaries, and scrapbooks of the time suggest that many tourists took to the road to discover the "real" America. Their responses to the marketed tourist experience range from trite notations to thoughtful meditations, but regardless of their form, the responses reveal that tourists made their journeys into stories, highlighting the sights and events that were most "memorable" and appropriating the marketed experience as their own. In consuming the marketed tourist spectacle, tourists consciously and unconsciously took part in a larger dialogue about personal and public memory as well as individual and national identity. They sought to position themselves as participants in the shifting cultural and social relations of the emerging urban-industrial nation-state.

Historian George Lipsitz has suggested that as the process of incorporation disrupted traditional forms of collective memory and identity, commercialized leisure "helped to reshape cultural memory and consciousness."[7] The development of national tourism was central to this process. As a national transportation and communications network broke down the barriers of distance and time, as mass production and mass distribution provided widespread access to standardized goods, as decisions made by corporations and a strong federal government impacted the everyday lives of people across the country, America emerged as a modern nation. Simultaneously, tourist industries manufactured and marketed America as "nature's nation," defining a shared history and tradition that manifested an indigenous national identity sanctioned by God and inscribed across the natural landscape.[8] Tourism, defined as a kind of virtuous consumption, promised to reconcile this national mythology, which celebrated nature, democracy, and liberty, with the realities of an urban-industrial nation-state dependent on extraction, consumption, and hierarchy.

However, this is not simply a supply side history. Tourist industries did not engage in a rhetorical, one-sided dialogue about American identity. Tourists, in consuming the nation, also participated in and shaped this search for national identity. Sociologist Dean MacCannell has defined the tourist landscape as a kind of stage set providing a backdrop for the production of social and cultural identities of the modern leisure class.[9] Tourism, as a form of consumption, allowed white, native-born middle- and upper-class Americans to escape the social and cultural confines of everyday life to liminal space where they could temporarily reimagine themselves as heroic or authentic figures. In doing so, tourists drew on and responded to the larger discourse of national identity that pervaded prescriptive tourist material. At multiple levels tourists engaged issues of identity and status that were central to the shifting notions of citizenship shaped by the emergence of America as an urban-industrial nation-state. Through this process, tourists helped affirm an ideal of mobile citizenship that redefined political rights in consumer terms, celebrating seeing over speaking, purchasing over voting, and traveling over participating.

Many scholarly works have focused on the topics that frame this study: the search for American identity, the development of a national consumer culture, and the solidification of the United States as an urban-industrial nation-state.[10] Building on a number of key questions, this study uses tourism to explore the ground in between these distinct disciplinary fields. What is the connection between tourism and the search for American identity? Why did tourism promoters encourage expanding numbers of white middle-class consumers to imagine and consume the nation in geographical terms? How did tourist industries seek to reconcile the mythology of America with the realities of the urban-industrial nation-state? And how did tourism promote and reflect the larger shift from public space to marketplace, from republican citizen to patriotic consumer?[11] This book argues that tourism—both the production of the tourist landscape and the consumption of the tourist experience—was central to the development of a nascent national culture in the United States. Tourism not only reshaped and redefined the built and natural environment of the United States, transforming the symbolic value of American landscape, but also influenced the way people defined and identified themselves as Americans. As such, national tourism, as it emerged between 1880 and 1940, was integrally involved in a larger cultural dialogue about shared national identity and an ideal of mobile citizenship that affirmed and legitimized the social, economic, and political relations of modern consumer culture.

I

THE CONTINENT SPANNED

Seven weeks of steady journeying, within hail of a single parallel line
from east to west, and still the Republic! Still the old flag, . . . still the
same Fourth of July;—better than all, still the same people with hearts
aglow with the same loyalty and pride in the American Union, and
the same purpose and faith for its future.
—Samuel Bowles, *Across the Continent*, 1865

CELEBRATING THE TRIUMPH OF the Union and anticipating the
completion of the transcontinental railroad, Samuel Bowles, editor of
the *Springfield Republican*, embarked in the summer of 1865 on a four-
month transcontinental journey to see America. Traveling with Schuyler
Colfax, Speaker of the House of Representatives and chairman of the
House Committee on Post Offices and Post Roads, Albert Dean Richardson, western correspondent for the *New York Tribune*, and Lieutenant
Governor William Bross, senior editor of the *Chicago Tribune*, the party
sought to promote the completion of the transcontinental railroad and in
the process direct the national gaze away from the carnage of the Civil
War and toward the expanding possibilities of the West. In a series of letters written to his home newspaper and later gathered in a book, Bowles
acquainted his readers with the people, places, and resources of the

nation. "The Continent is spanned, the national breadth is measured," he exclaimed in a burst of patriotic fervor. "How this republic, saved, reunited, bound together as never before, expands under such personal passage and footstep tread; how magnificent its domain; how far-reaching and uprising its material, moral, and political possibilities and promises!" Extolling the virtues of the expanding railroad system and expressing a shift in national focus, he concluded, "There is no such knowledge of the nation as comes of traveling it, of seeing eye to eye its vast extent, its various and teeming wealth, and above all its purpose-filled people."[1] Clearly, Bowles's travel narrative, *Across the Continent: A Summer's Journey to the Rocky Mountains, the Mormons, and the Pacific States,* reflected a turn from the sectional animosity between North and South and a shift toward the West and the expanding nation. But more important, the narrative gave new meaning to the development of tourism in the United States.

Although hundreds of people had traveled cross-continent over the very route traversed by Bowles, *Across the Continent* envisioned a new kind of travel.[2] As he explained in the preface, "There will be many to come after us in this Summer's Journey, partly inspired by the pleasure of our experience, chiefly incited by the increased smoothness of the ways . . . . I anticipate such facilities for the Overland Passage, as will invite hundreds where one has heretofore gone, and make the journey as comfortable and convenient for ladies even, as it will be safe and instructive for all."[3] Using the scenery and attractions of Europe as his touchstone, Bowles not only familiarized Americans with the West but also imagined a Grand Tour across America.[4] He prophesied that in connecting East and West and making the West more easily accessible, travelers would flock to the scenic landscapes and the thriving cities and towns to see the expanding Republic in the making. People would travel cross-continent not simply to reach a desired destination but for the sheer pleasure of seeing the nation united and flourishing. In celebrating the wonders of the natural landscape, the diversity of peoples, and the abounding resources, Bowles thus transformed an arduous journey into a sightseeing pleasure trip.

In 1868 Bowles once again joined speaker Colfax and his party on a western excursion. He spent the summer "among the great folds of Mountains and elevated Parks that distinguished Colorado," which resulted in three more travel narratives, *Our New West* (1869), *The Switzerland of America* (1869), and *The Pacific Railroad—Open* (1869).[5] These narratives more fully defined this new type of travel. They enumerated the various "distinctive points of interest" of the West—"the boundless Plains; the snow-capped Mountains; the majestic Columbia; our Mediterranean of the North-west, Puget's Sound; the magic City, San Francisco; the wonderful Geysers; the Mammoth Trees; and the peerless Yosemite,"—and provided instructions for those who wished to see the vast extent of America for themselves. As Speaker Colfax articulated in a publicized letter to Bowles, "If our people, who go to Europe for pleasure, travel and observation, knew a tithe of the enjoyment we experienced in our travel under our own flag, far more of them would turn their faces toward the setting sun; and after exploring that Switzerland of America, the Rocky Mountains, with their remarkable Parks and Passes, go onward to that realm which fronts upon the Pacific, whose history is so romantic, and whose destiny is so sure; and which that great highway of Nations, the Pacific Railroad, will, this Spring, bring so near to all of us on the Atlantic slope."[6]

The extension of the railroad paved the way for what Bowles deemed the "Across the Continent Traveler." The ride from the Missouri River, which marked the edge of eastern settlement, to Denver was now only "a railroad ride of twenty-four hours." The "then long-drawn, tedious endurance of six days and nights running the gauntlet of hostile Indians," which Bowles withstood in the summer of 1865, "was now accomplished . . . safe in a swiftly-moving train, and in a car that was an elegant drawing-room by day and a luxurious bedroom at night." In describing the new Pacific railroad, Bowles gave readers a sense of what they might expect on the train ride west from Omaha to the coast. Detailing the first day's ride across the Plains to Cheyenne, he commented, "We yawn over the unchanging landscape and the unvarying model of the stations, and lounge and read by day, and go to bed early at night." However, as the track began to ascend into the mountains, Bowles noted, "the senses all dilate with what is spread before and around him [*sic*]." Bowles went on to describe the "desert of mountains," "the descent into Salt Lake Valley," the "Great Interior Basin," and the "road over the Sierras" into California. He concluded, "[The railroad] puts the great sections of the Nation into sympathy and unity; it marries the Atlantic and the Pacific; it destroys disunion in the quarter where it was ever most threatening; it brings into harmony the heretofore jarring discords of a Continent of separated peoples; it determines the future of America, as the first nation of the world, in commerce, in government, in intellectual and moral supremacy."[7] In Bowles's mind, the transcontinental railroad objectified the emerging nation-state, and traveling cross-continent inspired a new national consciousness.

Bowles, however, did more than just describe the wonders of the Pacific railroad and what travelers might see from the train window. He also counseled his readers on how to see the attractions beyond the train window. Recounting a trip into the mountains from Denver, he explained, "This independent camping habit is almost the rule for all pleasure parties into the mountains. . . . The taverns are not now frequent or good; the climate favors the outdoor life in the summer season; and with provisions in abundance, as blankets, a coffee-pot, a frying pan, and a sack of flour and a side of bacon, either in a wagon, or packed on an extra horse, if you are journeying in the saddle, even pleasure-travelers find it much the more comfortable and decidedly the more independent mode." He even went so far as to list the contents of his pack "as a model for the reader who shall follow our experiences." Similarly, after describing the scenic attractions of Yosemite, Bowles recommended June as the best month for an excursion to the valley. Offering a few final words of travel advice, Bowles concluded *Our New West* with a chronological outline of his "two months' journey," including information on the most suitable months to travel.[8]

In listing the various attractions of the West, in detailing the train ride, in providing travel advice, these four books describe the purview of the "across the Continent traveler."[9] This new type of tourism was more than just a pleasure trip, it was a voyage of discovery. It offered the chance to see and know America, to celebrate a united nation, to be an American. Bowles best expressed this sense of national understanding in his short guide to the Pacific railroad: "Whatever we go out to see, whatever pleasures we enjoy, whatever disappointments [we] suffer, this at least, will be our gain,—a new conception of the magnitude, the variety and the wealth, in nature and resource, in realization and in promise, of the American Republic,—a new idea of what it is to be an American Citizen." According to Bowles, "He is past appeal and beyond inspiration who is not broadened, deepened, greatened, every way, by such experience of the extent, capacity, and opportunity of this nation, and who does not henceforth perform his duties as its citizen with increased fidelity and a more sacred awe of his trust."[10] In promoting this Grand Tour across America, Bowles not only marked the transformation of resort vacationing to transcontinental tourism but also defined tourism as a patriotic journey linked to the discovery of the nation.

INVENTING A NATIONAL TOURISM

The word "tour," coming from the Latin *tornus,* which comes from the Greek word for "a tool for describing a circle," denotes a circular journey—a movement away from home, traveling from site to site at one's leisure and then returning home."[11] Although historians disagree about the origins and extent of tourism, the evolution of the words "tour," "tourist," and "tourism" make clear that this mode of travel has a long history, stretching back at least three centuries in Anglo-American culture.[12] The verb "tour," which entered the English language in the mid-seventeenth century, was followed by the noun "tourist," indicating "one who travels for pleasure or culture, visiting a number of places for their objects of interest, scenery, or the like."[13] This linguistic addition suggests that this type of traveler had become commonplace by the late eighteenth century as European literati celebrated scenic landscapes and advocated the Grand Tour of Europe to refine young gentlemen.[14] The emergence of the word "tourism" during the early nineteenth century, meaning an established "theory and practice of touring," reflected the cultural institutionalization of traveling from place to place in pursuit of culture and pleasure.[15] As the historical trajectory of the language reveals, just as social, economic, and technological developments were transforming the nature of work, expanding commercial markets, and decreasing geographical distance, tourism emerged as an elite pastime dependent on disposable income and increased leisure and a canon of scenic and cultural attractions made accessible by an expanding transportation network.

Europeans began to tour the United States almost immediately after the formation of the new Republic. Expanding on the tradition of the European Grand Tour, genteel British and European travelers came to the United States to survey the people and their institutions. Curious about the fledgling

Republic or concerned about the more portentous questions of politics and civilization, these travelers moved through the major cities along the eastern seaboard mingling with statesmen and civic leaders and visiting the various institutions and landmarks in an effort to understand the culture. Travel accounts such as Alexis de Tocqueville's *Democracy in America* or Harriet Martineau's *Society in America* have moved far beyond the realm of tourism or travel to become classic surveys of the American scene.[16] Similarly, a few genteel Americans began to follow in the footsteps of their British and European counterparts. Timothy Dwight, president of Yale College, journeyed through the New England countryside between the mid-1790s and 1815, producing a four-volume commentary on his travels.[17] Naturalist William Bartram journeyed through the South in the 1790s cataloguing the distinctive flora and fauna in his *Travels Through North and South Carolina, Georgia, East and West Florida* (1792). However, the majority of Americans with the means to travel were more interested in traveling abroad than in confronting their own country's poor roads and inadequate lodgings. As the exceptional travelogues reveal, domestic tourism in the United States remained a rare elite activity with no established economic infrastructure until the early nineteenth century.[18]

The confluence of a number of intellectual, technological, and economic crosscurrents transformed this situation during the early decades of the nineteenth century. In the 1790s, European intellectuals codified the experience of nature into three distinct categories: the sublime, the beautiful, and the picturesque. Reverend William Gilpin, an English author, published a number of books describing a series of tours through Scotland and England that helped popularize a tradition of "picturesque tours." Gilpin urged travelers to view the natural landscape pictorially, as a series of scenes that might elicit a variety of emotional and aesthetic responses. Romantic poets such as William Wordsworth, Samuel Coleridge, Lord Byron, and Percy Bysshe Shelley helped generate a cult of scenery through their renderings of the Lake District in northwestern England and the Swiss Alps. Responding to this flourish of romanticism, wealthy European and American travelers on the Grand Tour became increasingly interested in sublime and picturesque scenery.[19]

These ideas quickly spread to the United States, transforming the symbolic value of American landscape. Under the growing influence of romanticism, artists and literati produced a flow of images and essays extolling the wonders of the American landscape. Beginning in the 1820s, American artists of the Hudson River School, such as Thomas Cole and Ashur Durand, painted dramatic views of the Hudson River Valley and the White Mountains, while American writers such as James Fenimore Cooper, William Cullen Bryant, and Washington Irving memorialized northeastern scenery through poetry and fiction. These intellectuals turned to the dramatic landscapes of the Northeast to justify and legitimize the new Republic, arguing that dramatic natural scenery compensated for America's lack of history and provided the basis for a new civilization. In celebrating the wonders of Niagara Falls, the expansive views of the Catskills, and the magnificence of the White Mountains, artists and intellectuals sought to create a new nationalist creed, while transforming the mountains, the valleys, and the backwoods of the new nation into scenic attractions.[20]

Simultaneously, a series of technological developments began to make these scenic landscapes more accessible. Following Robert Fulton's success in 1807, steamboats began to ply the Hudson River on a regular schedule, offering fast, reliable, and, most important, comfortable transportation. In 1825 the Erie Canal opened, providing a slow but relaxing alternative to the grueling carriage ride across the landscape of upstate New York. By the 1830s railroads were beginning to extend their tracks into the hinterlands, expanding the network of commercial trade. But they also facilitated quick, easy travel, allowing travelers to take advantage of their convenience to reach previously remote destinations. As technological wonders that shrunk the distance between nature and culture, steamships, canal boats, and railroads were integral to the emergence of tourism in the United States.[21]

These technological innovations reflected the larger commercial and industrial development sweeping across the northeastern United States during the early nineteenth century. The increasing importance of industrial manufacturing, innovations in mass production, and improvements in commercial farming, combined with this growing transportation network, helped spur the expansion of the capitalist market. A widening array of ready-made goods, changing notions of work and leisure, an expanding middle class, and increasing levels of expendable capital revealed a consumer-oriented society in the making. The advent of tourism depended on these broad structural

Cover of *Summer Excursion Routes*, a promotional guide (Pennsylvania Railroad, 1894). (Division of Technology, National Museum of American History, Smithsonian Institution)

changes. Although tourists sought out scenic natural vistas and consumed intangible goods, tourism rested on the technological and the ideological infrastructure of this nascent urban-industrial consumer culture. The creation and marketing of unique attractions, the development of adequate modes of transportation, and the growth of a leisure ethic are what made tourism possible in the United States.

Not surprisingly, the earliest pleasure excursions and tourist businesses that developed in the United States were centered in the Northeast, the area of most rapid economic and technological development in the early nineteenth century. Between the 1830s and 1850s a canon of American attractions—including Niagara Falls, the White Mountains, the Adirondacks, Saratoga Springs, and the Catskills—became well established. "The fashionable tour" took tourists up the Hudson River to the Catskill Mountains or West Point. After stopping at Albany, tourists had the option to layover at the fashionable resort towns of Saratoga or Ballston Springs. Once rested, they returned to Albany and traveled to Niagara Falls via the Erie Canal or by stagecoach. By the 1850s rail lines had begun to extend into the White Mountains, providing access to a number of fashionable resort hotels. Although the scenic attractions, resorts, and watering places of New England and New York State predominated in the decades before the Civil War, a few other tourist destinations connected with American exceptionalism, industriousness, or achievement also attracted visitors.[22]

The tourist industry, however, was primarily regional in scope in the decades before the Civil War, despite patriotic allusions that linked scenic wonders with national greatness. This regional tourism might best be characterized as a combination of resort vacationing and cultural or literary pilgrimage in which travelers sought fashionable society, sublime scenery, and American achievement. Middle- and upper-class urbanites, anxious and able to escape city heat and humidity for a few weeks or even months, traveled to popular mountain villages, hot springs, lakes, rivers, and beaches seeking not only respite from summer heat and the workaday world but also fashionable company and natural verdure. Others traveled to battlefields, industrial sites, and literary shrines seeking patriotic or educational uplift. Although genteel nineteenth-century tourists linked the various "sacred places" celebrated through the tourist experience with an ideal of American identity, this expression of cultural nationalism had little connection with a political or geo-graphical ideal of the nation-state.[23]

It took the broad structural changes that occurred in the wake of the Civil War to pave the way for a shift from regional tourism into the national tour-ism that Samuel Bowles envisioned. The Civil War set in motion a process of centralization and consolidation that resulted in the formation of the modern nation-state and the emergence of a new kind of nationalism in the United States. The infrastructure of the nation-state—a strong and active national government, an established geographical territory, a national trans-portation and communication network, and a national market—was set in place. The triumph of the Union and the turn to westward expansion in-spired a new national consciousness and provided a more immediate famil-iarity with the geography and territory of the nation. As the railroad spread across the country, connecting specialized local and regional economies with distant markets, as advances in printing and communication technologies inundated people with new information and images, as brand-name goods and mail order catalogs created a shared material culture, the idea of Amer-ica as a united nation took on new meaning. In the political sphere, subjuga-tion of "renegade" Indian populations, suppression of radical workers, and regulation of monopolies and trusts served to reinforce this new sense of national purpose. Through this process of "incorporation" Americans came to terms with a more urban-industrial, corporate, and national culture.[24] Revolutionary changes in production and distribution transformed not only patterns and interactions of daily life but also concepts of distance, space, and time. Consumption became the norm and knowledge of distant places became commonplace.[25]

As the infrastructure of the nation-state was set in place, a mythic ideal of the West became the basis for a new national consciousness. In constructing the transcontinental railroads, in defeating the Indians, in settling the fron-tier, the ideal of America as a nation transcended the politics of states' rights. The meaning of America, as the title of Horace Greely's new magazine, the *Nation*, revealed, moved beyond the ideal of Union reuniting North and South. *These* United States became *the* United States. The ideal of the West as a vast area of free land combined with the promise of westward expansion and Manifest Destiny became central to the political concept of nation-ness that emerged during the Gilded Age. As Frederick Jackson Turner articulated so eloquently in his frontier thesis, the West embodied the process of becoming American—of moving into the wilderness, abandoning European traditions, and developing new behaviors and institutions that defined the American character. The West as celebrated in literature, art, political rhetoric, and pulp fiction had come to represent the "true" America.[26]

The stage was set for a more national tourism to take hold in the United States. Rising numbers of middle- and upper-class Americans now had the time, money, means, and desire to travel for pleasure. The transcontinental railroads outfitted with new Pullman Palace car service provided fast, easy access to distant locations. Railroad passenger agents and tourist advocates were producing a flood of information and images capitalizing on the popular ideal of the mythic West. American tourists simply needed to be encouraged to transfer their allegiances from the fashionable northeastern and European tourist destinations to the emerging opportunities of transcontinental travel.

The process of popularizing this new national tourism, however, was a slow one. Although as early as 1868 national boosters began to promote the possibilities of tourism in the United States and the transcontinental railroads quickly began to advertise and advocate pleasure travel along their lines, the tourist infrastructure outside of the Northeast was slow to develop.[27] In addition, an extended cross-continent pleasure trip was expensive. In the 1870s and 1880s, passenger fare for a round-trip transcontinental ticket cost at least three hundred dollars, and that did not include a sleeping berth.[28] Middle- and upper-class Americans still looked to Europe and established eastern attractions for fashionable and fulfilling tourist opportunities. It would take a sustained effort on the part of tourist promoters, guidebook writers, and railroads to turn the tide.

Western booster and publisher George A. Crofutt was one of the first to describe the possibilities of transcontinental tourism. Hoping to capitalize on the completion of the Union Pacific Railroad, Crofutt published the *Great Trans-Continental Railroad Guide* in the fall of 1869. Boasting "a full and authentic description of over five hundred cities, towns, villages, stations, government forts and camps, mountains, lakes, rivers, sulpher, soda and hot springs, scenery, watering places, [and] summer resorts," Crofutt's guidebook provided general information for a new breed of "transcontinental" travelers.[29]

This was not simply a description of the newly accessible western landscape. Rather, as suggested in the title, the guide promised to enumerate "what is worth seeing—where to see it—where to go—how to go—and whom to stop with while passing over the Union Pacific Railroad, Central Pacific Railroad of Cal.; their branches and connections by Stage and Water, from the Atlantic to the Pacific Ocean."[30] Unlike earlier first-person travel accounts, Crofutt provided train schedules, information on fares, and advice to travelers as well as a brief description of the region traversed. After a concise discussion of the various routes from the East Coast, the guide then provided an overview of the changing physical geography of the Union Pacific line, followed by short descriptions of each station along the line. As Crofutt explained in the preface to the 1870 volume, "We offer you no rehash of the unreliable newspaper and hearsay accounts; neither shall we present you a mass of old stereotyped time tables, but we do propose to take you step by step, station by station over the whole line—give you the full and authentic facts and figures, condensed and boiled down to the smallest possible space."[31]

Revised yearly between 1869 and 1876 and then reissued as *Crofutt's Overland Tourist* between 1878 and 1884, Crofutt's guide set the standard for transcontinental tourist guides. Concise, portable, and inexpensive, Crofutt's guide was sold at railroad stations and newsstands, providing quick and easily accessible information for business or pleasure travelers.[32] By 1878 Crofutt claimed to have sold more than three hundred thousand copies.[33] Competing guides such as *Appleton's Hand-Book of American Travel: Western Tour, Rand McNally's Western Railway Guide: The Traveler's Hand Book to all Western Railway and Steamboat Lines,* and *The Pacific Tourist: Williams' Illustrated Transcontinental Guide of Travel, from the Atlantic to the Pacific Ocean* began to appear in the 1870s. Like Crofutt's guide, these pocket travel guides sought to capture the expanding transcontinental tourist market by providing a convenient source of information for business and pleasure travelers.[34] As a whole, this new genre of guidebook taught Americans how to make a transcontinental tour.

In detailing the various stops along the line, in providing information about schedules and fairs, in touting the improvements in transcontinental travel and the comforts of Pullman Palace cars, and in codifying the geography of the newly accessible West, Crofutt and others who followed his lead

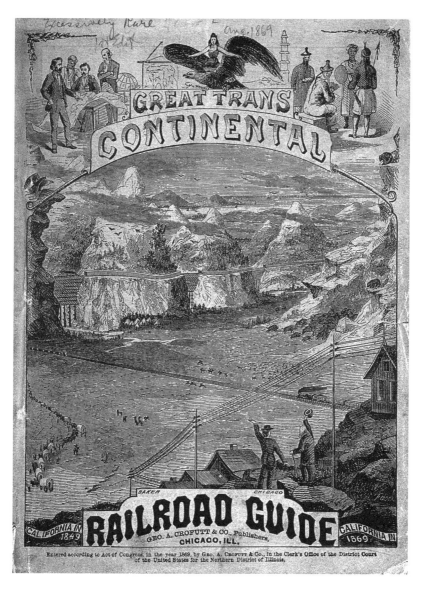

Cover of George A. Crofutt's *Great Trans-Continental Railroad Guide* (1869). (Reproduced by permission of the Huntington Library, San Marino, California)

celebrated the potential of the American West. "We [have] contented our-selves," Crofutt boasted, "in annually calling attention to the vast extent of rich mineral, agricultural and grazing country opened up—a vast country which had heretofore been considered worthless. We have pointed out, step by step, the most important features, productions, and advantages of each section traversed by the road; stated that the East and West were now con-nected by a short and quick route, . . . and finally, that its importance to the miner, agriculturalist, stock-raiser, the Government, and the world at large, few, if any, could estimate."[35] In this way, guidebooks not only legitimized the possibilities of transcontinental travel but also redefined the tourist expe-rience.[36] Transcontinental travel came to be understood as an extension of Manifest Destiny. "All has changed," Crofutt wrote in his 1869 guide. "The foam-crested waves of the pacific bear on their bosoms a mighty and steadily increasing commerce. A rich, powerful and populous section, comprising three States, has risen where but a few years since the Jesuit missions among the savages were the only marks of civilization. And all over the once un-known waste, amid the cozy valley and on the broad plains, are the scattered homes of the hardy and brave pioneer husbandman." American progress was transforming the nation: "The bleak mountains, once the home of the savage and wild beast, the deep gulches and gloomy canyons, are alive with the sounds of labor, the ring of pick, shovel and drill, the clatter of stamps and booming of blasts, which tell of the presence of the miner and the future streams of wealth which will flow into our national coffers; for as the individ-ual becomes enriched, so does his country partake of his fortune."[37]

The technological wonder of the railroad evinced national greatness, and the view from the train window, according to guidebook writers, revealed the bounty of the American nation. As one guidebook writer noted, "There is no journey which can be taken on the continent of North America that presents so much of interest to the tourists. . . . What a field for investigation, invest-ment or pleasure! These are the lands of gold, of silver, of coal, of agriculture, of all fruits known to the temperate and subtropical zones. These are the lands of new endeavors, of fresh impulses, and for these reasons are of special interest to tourists, business men, and seekers after health and pleasure."[38] Guidebooks celebrated the transcontinental railroad as a manifestation of the opportunities of an expanding republican empire. In touting westward progress and expansion, in promoting settlement and investment, and in encouraging business and pleasure travel, early guidebook writers not only championed the new nation but also implicitly linked transcontinental travel with the process of westward expansion. In doing so, they laid the groundwork for the emergence of a national tourism as opposed to more established conventions of regional and international tourism. Yet through the 1870s, transcontinental guidebooks focused predominantly on business and investment opportunities rather than pleasure travel. It would take the expansion of the railroad network, combined with the development of packaged tours, to instigate a shift from the fashions of eastern resort vacations and the European Grand Tour toward transcontinental travel.

In 1883, after a decade of financial uncertainty and insolvency, three new transcontinental lines were completed across the western United States: the Northern Pacific Railroad provided a northern route stretching from Minneapolis to Portland, Oregon; the Atchison, Topeka, and Santa Fe traversed the central region of the West from Kansas City, Missouri, to Los Angeles; and the Southern Pacific Railroad offered a southern route from New Orleans to Los Angeles. At the end of the following decade, the Great Northern Railway completed tracks to Seattle to become the fifth major transcontinental line.[39] As a result of intense competition for passenger service, railroad companies began to issue guides and pamphlets to promote the scenic attractions along their lines. In 1883 the Northern Pacific Railroad inaugurated its *Wonderland* guidebook series celebrating the dramatic landscapes of Yellowstone National Park and other scenic attractions along it route. The Santa Fe paired up with the Fred Harvey Company in the 1870s, beginning a long partnership devoted to promoting and packaging the Southwest. Similarly, the Denver and Rio Grande Railroad, the Santa Fe's close competitor, promoted itself as the "scenic line of America" with its "Around the Circle" tours. In 1898 the Southern Pacific Railroad launched a major publicity campaign through its publication of *Sunset* magazine, extolling the wonders of California.[40] Through these promotional efforts, the passenger departments of the major western railroads helped reimagine the West, transforming it from a desert wasteland to a tourist wonderland, rivaling, if not surpassing, the most famous tourist destinations in Europe.

As the expansion of the railroad network throughout the West provided increased opportunities for travel, tourist companies began to offer packaged tours across continent. Hoping to capitalize on the American centennial celebration, the British touring firm Thomas Cook, renowned for its Grand Tours of Europe, conducted its first annual excursion to California in 1876.[41] Cook's success spurred others to follow suit. During the 1880s, Cook's American competitor, the Raymond and Whitcomb Company, established a series of transcontinental excursions linked to the new resort hotels being built in California and Colorado.

Emmons Raymond and Irwin A. Whitcomb, the firm's founders, both had New England railroad connections. Originally the Boston-based firm concentrated its tours in the White Mountains, but it quickly expanded to include all the major resorts and scenic attractions throughout the Northeast. Raymond and Whitcomb excursions were known for their comfort, convenience, and exclusivity. Not only did Raymond parties travel as a group in private cars, assuring tourists first-class service and company, but they also stayed at the most fashionable hotels, including those owned and managed by the firm, such as the Crawford House in the White Mountains.[42] As one Raymond and Whitcomb tour brochure noted, "We can speak with pride of the select character of our traveling parties, and to persons who have accompanied us we confidently refer all who desire information as to the practical working of our system."[43] The tours were guided and arranged by "experienced conductors, thoroughly conversant with every detail of traveling and the wants of tourists, as well as with the routes passed over and the points of interest visited." In fact, if they desired, Raymond tourists could travel without cash. As one Raymond brochure explained, "Every needed expense is covered by the excursion ticket; a book of coupons, each of which covers some incidental part of the trip in the way of travel, hotel board, etc., being furnished each passenger."[44]

In 1883 Walter Raymond traveled to California to scout out new opportunities for the family business and find a promising site for a new resort hotel. He chose a choice parcel of land in Pasadena, in the heart of the rich citrus groves of the San Gabriel Valley at the foot of the Sierra Madre. Three years later, in 1886, the Raymond Hotel opened to great fanfare. A palatial Italian Renaissance structure encircled by a wide verandah that offered magnificent views of the valley and the mountains, the hotel surpassed even the most fash-

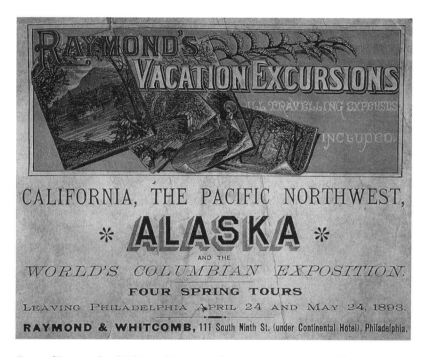

Cover of Raymond and Whitcomb's *Raymond's Vacation Excursions to California, the Pacific Northwest, Alaska, and the World's Columbian Exposition* (1893). (Reproduced by permission of the Huntington Library, San Marino, California)

ionable of the eastern resort hotels.[45] Although earlier Raymond and Whitcomb tours to California centered on a five-month "sojourn" at Southern Pacific's "famous winter health and pleasure resort of the Pacific coast, the elegant Hotel Del Monte" in Monterey, the Raymond quickly became the focal point of the firm's transcontinental tours.[46] For the 1887–88 season, Raymond and Whitcomb offered twelve winter tours, each of five months duration, which included extended stays at the Raymond as well as the Del Monte, the Palace Hotel in San Francisco, and "other famous Pacific Coast Resorts."[47] By the 1890s Raymond and Whitcomb's transcontinental tours were well established. In addition to its winter tours of California, the company also offered shorter spring and summer tours, which included stops in Colorado, New Mexico, California, Oregon, Washington, the Puget Sound country, British Columbia, Alaska, Idaho, Montana, and Yellowstone National Park.[48] On these shorter excursions, tourists not only stopped at the grand western resort hotels, such as the Antlers, the Raymond, and the Del Monte, but also visited an array of attractions, including Manitou Springs, the Garden of the Gods, Santa Fe, and the Yosemite Valley.

Despite its success in capitalizing on the new opportunities of transcontinental travel, in some ways the Raymond and Whitcomb Company still clung to the conventions of northeastern resort vacationing. Raymond tourists experienced the novelty of traveling cross-continent in the luxury of Pullman Palace cars, stopping to see various scenic and technological wonders of the western landscape, but Raymond excursions focused more on the social life of resort hotels than the experience of sightseeing. Raymond and Whitcomb "vacation excursions" might best be understood as transitional in that they situated the experience of transcontinental tourism made possible by the expansion of the railroad network within the framework of the more established experience of northeastern resort vacationing. As the firm expanded the possibilities for transcontinental travel, however, it began to highlight the opportunity of seeing the nation and the experience of sightseeing in general. As one brochure boasted, "No excursion ever planned has equaled this one in its comprehensiveness of American wonders. There are many American Travelers to whom the highways and by-ways of Europe and the East are familiar, but to whom the marvelously fine scenery of their own country is a closed book. Within the past decade great progress has been made in rendering even the inner recesses of our vast domain accessible to the tourist, and united to this fact is the equally important one that our special excursion trains carry to the most distant points of comforts and luxuries previously unknown in traveling this country or any other."[49] Similarly, although most Raymond tourists reveled in the social activities of Raymond excursions, some celebrated the experience of seeing the attractions of the West and traversing the nation. Stephen Merritt, a minister from New York City who traveled to California on a Raymond excursion in 1892, rejoiced in his diary on reaching California: "All hail! across the Continent from Ocean to Ocean, in and out,—up and down,—desert and solitude,—cultivated fields, crowded cities—amid the enterprise of bustling busy men, and this amid God's mountains and plains; with Indians, and Mexicans, and Chinese, and colored people. . . . All sorts, all sizes, all complexions and kinds." Assessing the value of his transcontinental tour, he concluded, "All hail! Vive

L'America, the land of the free, and the home of the brave! When this journey is over, we will know the land we fondly call our own, and more of more value than $10,000.00 in money will be the pleasure and profit we had received through this wonderful Raymond & Whitcomb trip."[50]

Despite the emphasis on fashionable hotels and exclusive society, packaged tours such as those offered by Raymond and Whitcomb helped to facilitate a more national tourism. In coordinating train schedules and sleeping cars, in arranging first-class accommodations, in organizing sightseeing excursions and popularizing a canon of western attractions, touring agents like Raymond and Whitcomb transformed the transcontinental journey into a pleasurable experience, and in the process aided the shift from vacationing to sightseeing. Yet the western tourist infrastructure remained relatively undeveloped through the turn of the century. A 1905 editorial in *Harper's Monthly* lamented that it was "rather difficult to travel in our own West." Going to Europe involved very little planning, the article explained. "One gets aboard a steamer and has a week in which to make the next plan, and if he makes no plan he can go ashore at Liverpool or Southhampton and do the next thing." But the West offered little to the average tourist unless he was an avid hunter or had some business prospect to occupy his time and attention. The editorial advised that travel to the West needed to be made "easier and less expensive, and more certainly entertaining."[51]

The *Harper's* criticism was well taken, for the tourist infrastructure in the West was still largely undeveloped. Only recently had the transcontinental railroads and their tourist bureaus begun to cater to wealthy travelers; most of their business lay in the transportation of freight. Although celebration of dramatic western scenery by scientific surveyors, artists, photographers, sportsmen, publicizers, and adventurous travelers had become commonplace by the early 1870s, access to these scenic wonders remained difficult.[52] The early western tourist experience was confined to scenic views from railroad tourist cars and resort life at exclusive luxury hotels. Tourists interested in a more intimate encounter with scenery had to suffer long, uncomfortable carriage rides.[53] Many preferred the comfort and cosmopolitan atmosphere of luxury hotels and plush Pullman Palace cars to the wild and barren landscapes of the West.[54]

Not until the 1890s did construction of scenic railroad lines, shortlines, and branches begin to make western scenery and attractions more accessible.[55] Northern Pacific completed spur tracks to the southern entrance of Yellowstone in 1883, and only then did hotel and road construction begin to make the park reachable by tourists. Not until 1903 did the spurline extend to the park boundary, five miles from Mammoth Hot Springs. Similarly, a spur line was not completed to the rim of the Grand Canyon until 1901, and construction of El Tovar Hotel took four more years.[56] Even with these developments, travel to the West remained expensive.[57] European tours and established eastern resorts remained more accessible and less demanding than western touring options. However, as transcontinental tourism became popular among white elites and increasingly visible as railroad passenger departments and travel agencies infused the national media with brochures, images, and advertisements, a group of western boosters hoped to open the West to tourism on a grand scale, thus instituting a more national tourism.

SEE AMERICA FIRST

Commemorating the opening of the See America First Conference on the morning of 25 January 1906, Governor John C. Cutler of Utah praised the 125 delegates representing boosters, businessmen, and politicians from across the West for the unselfish task they were about to undertake: "You will carry forward a work that has at its very base the inculcation of patriotism, the love of native land."[58] This was a historic moment in the forging of a united nation, according to Cutler. "The movement that you strive for in this conference," he declared, "will make better citizens of the tens of thousands of Americans who are now living in ignorance of their own land, will through the agencies of school, pulpit and press bring to the young men and maidens of the land a vision of the regions they know nothing of which are yet under the dominion of the flag we all revere." They were there, Governor Cutler proclaimed, "to preach the gospel of a better-known America." During their three days in Salt Lake City these men were showered with words of welcome and praise, they were toasted and cheered, and they were inundated with the charge to "go forth and . . . preach the doctrine of 'See America First.'"[59]

The See America First Conference marked the public introduction of a western booster campaign initiated in Salt Lake City by Fisher Sanford Harris, secretary of the Salt Lake City Commercial Club.[60] "See Europe if you will, but See America First" became the rallying cry for Harris's scheme, the central argument being that Americans had spent more than $150 million touring Europe during the 1904–5 touring season and that not only could this money be well spent in America but also tourism would help to educate ignorant easterners about the wonders and possibilities of the West.[61] Harris imagined the formation of a "tourist trust" organized to promote tourism throughout the intermountain West. The general idea was that this voluntary group, comprised of western businessmen, civic leaders, representatives from railroad publicity departments, and city and state politicians, "would pool their resources" in an effort to advertise the tourist attractions and develop the tourist infrastructure throughout the West, thus stimulating settlement, investment, and "the discovery of America by Americans."[62]

Delegates at the See America First Conference sought to put this plan into practice. Americans, conference leaders argued, must learn of "the actual financial loss they suffer each year" and realize that "scenery is a valuable asset." To keep Americans at home, they insisted "suggestive reproductions of American scenery" should be disseminated throughout America and Europe so that the public can appreciate "the volume of Niagara, the height of Mount McKinley, the depth and vastness of the Grand Canyon." Infrastructure was also crucial. "There must ensue in the West an era of hotel building, before travelers will give this country the attention it demands," they declared. "Caravansaries, rest rooms and resorts of all kinds must be placed adjacent to natural attractions." This had to be done carefully, however, in order "not [to] divest any primeval paradise of its God-given grandeur, nor belittle the infinite by the proximity of the finite." Building on this idea of scenery as an asset, conference delegates laid the groundwork for the formation of the See America First League, whose central role would be to promote the West by articulating "a grand, comprehensive scheme of publicity, involving in its beneficent results the welfare and development of a great industrial empire and calling into its service the best artistic and literary skill of the world, for the accomplishment of its far reaching purpose."[63]

Riding on the fervor generated by the conference, Fisher Harris, the newly appointed executive secretary of the See America First League, launched

As secretary of the Salt Lake City Commercial Club and executive secretary of the See America First League, Fisher Sanford Harris (1865–1909) sought to promote tourism in the intermountain West. (Special Collections, J. Willard Marriott Library, University of Utah)

Emblem of the See America First League (c. 1906). (Fisher Sanford Harris Papers, Special Collections, William R. Perkins Library, Duke University)

what amounted to a missionary crusade to convert the skeptics and save the ignorant.[64] He left Salt Lake on 11 February 1906, on a six-week lecture tour that took him first to Portland, Oregon, and then to Victoria, Vancouver, Tacoma, Seattle, Spokane, St. Paul, Minneapolis, Duluth, Des Moines, Chicago, St. Louis, Kansas City, New York, Washington, D.C., Harrisburg, Denver, and Colorado Springs.[65] His stops, except those in New York and Washington, D.C., were in cities that had sent delegates to the conference. Everywhere he was welcomed enthusiastically. He stirred the audiences of commercial clubs and chambers of commerce and received warm greetings from groups such as the Quoin Club, representing newspaper editors in New

York, and the Gridiron Club, consisting of reporters and editors in Washington, D.C. Even President Theodore Roosevelt spoke with him about the league, stating that he was "heartily in favor of it and would be glad to serve in any way he possibly could."[66]

Despite Fisher Harris's grand ideals, the See America First League was short-lived. Although the major purpose of Harris's lecture tour was to secure funds to establish the league on a stable foundation, it is unclear if he actually succeeded in his fund-raising efforts. Not long after his return he began entertaining the notion of using a magazine format to deliver the league's gospel.[67] The Southern Pacific's Sunset magazine and other railroad and chamber of commerce publications and urban weeklies had already demonstrated the success of such an approach.[68] Yet even this promotional plan was constrained by lack of financial support. Because he did not have the backing for his own publication, Harris appropriated Salt Lake City's booster magazine to further the cause of See America First. From December 1908 until Harris's death in November 1909, the Western Monthly: A Magazine Devoted to the Art, Literature, Progress, and Development of the Inter-Mountain West functioned as the "Official Organ of the See America First League." The magazine instructed readers on the scenic and commercial possibilities, not in all America, but within the intermountain West, and especially in Utah and Salt Lake City.[69] Harris reprinted a few of his articles to promote the cause.[70] Nevertheless, his grand patriotic vision resulted in little more than regional booster fanfare. Lack of funds, the financial panic of 1907, and the onslaught of what appears to have been tuberculosis limited the scope of the magazine and sapped Harris's energy and enthusiasm.[71]

Although Harris's attempt to institutionalize the See America First idea ultimately failed, others embraced the slogan after his death. Tourist advocates and western boosters revived See America First in an effort to encourage domestic tourism.[72] In 1911 M. L. H. Odea attempted to develop a national publicity organization, which he called the See America First Association, whose goal was to promote "the exploitation of natural scenery, the increase of geographical knowledge and the appreciation of the Western hemisphere."[73] Odea proposed the creation of a "systematized agency, a comprehensive, centralized bureau, under the auspices and advisement of trained and eminent men versed in statesmanship, commerce, transportation, education and business," which would be responsible for promoting "widespread and general interest and knowledge among the peoples of the American nations as to the scenic, industrial, recreative, social and similar advantages and characteristics of the western hemisphere." The objectives of the association, according to Odea, moved beyond the promotion of tourism in America to include the cultivation of patriotism, the development of "a more permanent peace among these neighboring nations . . . to inspire a more homogeneous race," and the appreciation of the arts in America.[74]

During the winter of 1911, publisher and booster A. L. Sommers of Tacoma, Washington, announced that in the interest of "promoting tourist travel in the United States," he was going to begin publication of a magazine entitled *See America First*.[75] In the first issue, published in March 1912, Sommers explained, "SEE AMERICA FIRST fills a want, being devoted to a patriotic endeavor of stimulating interest in America as a land for the traveler." The mission of this new magazine, according to Sommers, was to be educational in scope: "To make more enthusiastic Americans, to show the East what the Great West is and the West what the East has, . . . to tell the story of America in a dignified, truthful and entertaining manner and to so enthuse the people of this country that they will want to See America First, that is the mission of this modest endeavor."[76] The first issue included articles on President Taft's automobile tour of Mount Rainier, the proposed San Diego Fair of 1915, Seattle's scenic boulevards, and Point Defiance Park in Tacoma. The issue also included brief notes on the See America First movement, National Parks, Pacific Coast carnivals, festivals, and conventions, and various hotels and resorts. Based on the tradition of local booster magazines, *See America First* extolled not only the scenic attractions of the West but also the development and culture of western cities. Although the magazine made an effort to contain booster articles celebrating a variety of scenic areas throughout the West and occasionally some in the East, the Pacific Northwest received the most coverage. Businesses of the Pacific Northwest also provided the advertisements to support this new periodical venture, which suggests that the magazine's circulation was limited to the commercial organizations of the Pacific Northwest and a few other western cities.

Later the following year, the Trans-Mississippi Commercial Congress, an organization of western business interests, attempted to institute a national See America First Day. In a series of speeches at their annual conference, delegates insisted that Americans be educated about the wonders of their own country. As one speaker exclaimed, "America has been appropriately and truly described as 'God's Own Country.' No other country in the whole world exhibits such a wonderful combination of all that is possible in Creation. American scenery is not only most unique, but it cannot be compared, much less excelled, by any other nation on the globe's surface." He argued that Americans needed to be persuaded to See America First through "an aggressive and systematic campaign of broadcast publicity and advertising whereby the wonderful and unrivaled attractions of America are doggedly flaunted before their eyes and persistently dinned into their ears and minds." The result, he argued, would be "money in the pockets of hotel men, merchants, newspapers, magazines, railroads, banks, trolley lines, pleasure resorts, and manufacturers of motor cars," as well as "continually better wagon roads, better service to the traveling public, larger consumption of home products, more business for real estate men, bankers and professional men, more profit to the farmer, more American homes, more loyalty to the Stars and Stripes—and, greatest of all, more fervent and intense patriotism without the artificial stimulus of war."[77] In other words, See America First promised both commercial progress and increased patriotism.

Proposals for organizing and establishing this movement on a permanent basis ranged from complex publicity schemes to demands for the development of tourist facilities. Commercial Congress delegates suggested that an illustrated national souvenir book, compiled and paid for by various commercial institutions and transportation interests, be "published and liberally circulated." Similarly, they argued that more tourist resorts should be built to accommodate wealthy vacationers accustomed to extravagant European resorts. Overall the speakers reiterated the same general idea, that in order for See America First to succeed, "every Commercial Club, every business organization, every railroad company, and every state" needed "to work together, and work in harmony, for the purpose of letting the people of the East know exactly what the resources of the West are."[78]

Even Charles Lummis, ardent promoter of the Southwest, claimed "See America First" (both the slogan and the idea) as his own. In his August 1912 editorial column, "In the Lions Den," published in *West Coast Magazine*,

Lummis wrote, "More than twenty years ago the Lion originated the 'See America First' Crusade. Doubtless better men had thought so before, but the Lion was first to formulate the gospel and 'tell why,' and to do it on a large scale of publicity."[79] Lummis appropriated See America First to characterize his long-established promotion of the Southwest and southern California, and to link the See America First idea with southwestern tourist attractions such as the Grand Canyon, the Petrified Forest, Canyon de Chelly, the Mojave Desert, the California Missions, and the Big Trees of California.[80] In 1892 Lummis had walked from Ohio to southern California, subsequently becoming famous by describing his adventure in his book *Some Strange Corners of Our Country*. According to Lummis, this book, in which he encouraged Americans to see the Southwest, had instigated the See America First idea.[81] Although Lummis encouraged Americans to see the Southwest, he in fact borrowed the See America First slogan and linked it to his earlier work and his continued promotion of southern California and the Southwest in order to capitalize on the revived See America First idea.

Many of these See America First campaigns faded after their initial burst of booster fanfare. In July 1914, however, the outbreak of war stranded 150,000 Americans in Europe, effectively closing the Continent to American tourists.[82] In 1915 promoters for the Panama-Pacific International Exposition seized the See America First idea to promote the exposition.[83] The Panama-Pacific International Exposition succeeded in some ways where earlier campaigns had failed because of widespread corporate support combined with the rise of reactionary patriotism sparked by the European war.

Opening in the wake of the closing of European borders, the exposition provided American tourist industries and organizations with a podium from which to proclaim the possibilities of touring in America. After Congress recognized San Francisco as the official site for the 1915 fair, Charles C. Moore, president of the Panama-Pacific International Exposition, extolled the significance of San Francisco as a site in relation to the rest of the nation. In the tradition of the See America First idea, he wrote, "I know men who have never been west of Buffalo, New York, yet who go frequently to Europe, perhaps once a year. Such men would become better citizens of this country were they to see the West." He went on to explain, "In the choice of a western city as the exposition site the educational advantage of a trip across the continent was one of the impellingly favorable factors, and it is undeniable that the lure of the West will be the magnet that will draw tens of thousands to whom the Exposition will be merely incidental, an exciting cause for greater experience." According to Moore, Yellowstone, the Grand Canyon, Yosemite, Alaska, and even a voyage through the newly opened Panama Canal would "be some of the great educational features by which those who visit the Exposition will have the opportunity to learn of their own country under the most enjoyable conditions and at a minimum of cost."[84]

The use of the See America First slogan and idea by exposition promoters and exhibitors suggests that the "true" America could be seen in western scenery, where the promise of nature, representing both divine sanction of an American empire and the wealth of natural resources supporting the progress of that empire, offered an inspiring alternative to the decaying civilization of the Old World. The major transcontinental railroads all contributed elaborate displays to the exposition, glorifying the scenic wonders along their lines. In addition, a number of railroads, including the Union Pacific and the Santa Fe, set up concessions in the commercial section of the fair, marketing a re-created touring experience for fair-goers. The Union Pacific went so far as to reconstruct "the most noted objects in [Yellowstone] park," including Eagle Nest Rock, the Hot Spring Terraces, the Great Falls of the Yellowstone, the Old Faithful Geyser, and, finally, the "crowning feature," a reproduction of the Old Faithful Inn.[85] Similarly, the Santa Fe constructed a model of the Grand Canyon for fair-goers to explore. The model reproduced to scale "a trip of 200 hundred miles in length through a gorge thirteen miles across from rim to rim, 8000 feet deep . . . omitting no essential feature from the panorama." In addition to the replica of the El Tovar Hotel situated at the entrance to the concession, there was also a model village of Pueblo Indians, depicting the "Life of a Vanishing Race."[86]

In popularizing See America First, the Panama-Pacific Exposition helped to establish both a canon of American attractions that should be seen and the context in which they were to be understood. Guidebooks, in combination with the scenic reproductions such as those of the Grand Canyon and Yellowstone, as well as displays of lantern slides, moving pictures, photographs, and paintings, celebrated emerging tourist sites across the West. To See America First as directed by Panama-Pacific officials and exhibitors was

The Union Pacific Railroad re-created noted features of Yellowstone National Park along with a reproduction of the Old Faithful Inn at the Panama-Pacific International Exhibition in an effort to promote the possibilities of tourism along its lines. Postcard, *Union Pacific System, Yellowstone National Park* (1915). (Victor A. Blenkle Postcard Collection, Archives Center, National Museum of American History, Smithsonian Institution)

to see those natural landscapes of the West that had been deemed sublime, scenic, or extraordinary. These landscapes reinforced the central ideology of the exposition, which celebrated the United States as an increasingly powerful, imperial nation. In commemorating the completion of the Panama Canal, the exposition sought to position the United States in a larger narrative of progress that essentially built on the "westward the course of empire" ideal. As one historian has explained, the fair "sought to preserve people's faith in the idea of progress—with all its interlaced connotations of technological advance, material growth, racism, and imperialism—and to reshape that faith with a particular reference to the challenges posed by domestic and international turmoil."[87] The western tourist attractions celebrated at the fair were meant to provide physical proof of this emerging American empire.

The Panama-Pacific International Exposition marked a turning point for this new national tourism. The location, the theme, and the attractions of the fair all drew attention to the triumph of the United States as a modern urban-industrial nation-state. Beneath this overt celebration of Manifest Destiny lay the stark contrast of the European war, revealing the seeming failure of Old World civilization. The exposition implicitly and explicitly championed American nationalism. Simultaneously, visitors were encouraged to see the wonders of the nation firsthand, both through the fair's exhibitions and in the journey to and from the fair via the transcontinental railroads and the Panama Canal. In this way, the fair served to enhance the popularity of the See America First idea while solidifying the culmination of decades of work to develop and promote the tourist infrastructure throughout the West. Just as earlier world's fairs had showcased the latest technological developments, the Panama-Pacific Exposition celebrated the triumph of American transportation and tourist industries. Tourist advocates could actually substantiate their claim that American tourist attractions rivaled those of Europe. A national tourist infrastructure was firmly established. If one had to pick a moment at which touring the United States became feasible and fashionable, this was it.

As the meaning and messages of the fair suggest, the story of See America First was not simply about the development of tourism in the West, it was also about the negotiation of national identity. Just as southerners and midwesterners were engaged in inventing a shared public history in the aftermath of the Civil War in an effort to come to terms with the emerging urban-industrial nation-state, so westerners sought to fuse their history and identity with that of the modern nation-state. In the South, upper- and middle-class whites championed the ideal of the Lost Cause not simply to celebrate the Confederacy but to reintegrate themselves into the Union while reinforcing the norms of acceptable behavior in the face of increased commercialism and industrialization.[88] Similarly, white, middle-class midwesterners mythologized the legacy of free labor with its ideals of individual ownership, self-discipline, and community in the face of rapid changes brought on by industrialization in an effort to legitimize and reaffirm their values, aspirations, and their position in society. In the process they defined a myth of America that imposed those attributes on the rest of the nation and constructed a history, best evinced by Frederick Jackson Turner's frontier thesis, which glorified those values and aspirations.[89] These white, middle-class westerners also sought to link their history and their region with a larger ideal of the nation. See America First offered one way to express these concerns in the commercial sphere. In their attempts to instigate a national See America First movement, western boosters articulated a series of shifting ideas connected with the emergence of America as a modern nation-state and the place of the West within that nation-state.

See America First, as articulated by these western interests, expressed a sense of western identity and nationalism grounded in the intersection between the West as region and the West as myth, which had taken shape around the turn of the century.[90] Boosters and businessmen who conceived of the movement embraced a double consciousness. As westerners, they hoped that See America First would give the West equal status with the Northeast. As Americans, they believed that the ideal West, with its sublime scenery, abundant resources, and virtuous citizens, embodied the "true" America. In defining and developing the See America First idea to promote tourism in the United States, these westerners not only revealed their commercial interests but also their ambivalence toward the political and economic control of the northeastern industrial core.[91] See America First expressed both a fascination with and an anxiety toward the forces of industrialization, incorporation, and urbanization that were transforming the United States into a complex, modern nation-state.

On the one hand, See America First expressed the desires of western boosters interested in promoting scenery for the sake of increasing investment and settlement in the West. In this commercial guise, See America First rhetoric criticized easterners for their fascination with Europe and argued that the West had just as much to offer as the Old World, if not more. In this context, the slogan manifested a western regionalism in which businessmen and civic leaders sought to reframe the colonial relationship between the West and the northeastern industrial core by representing the West, with its potential for commercial development, as an equal partner in the framework of the nation. For example, Fisher Harris, the most prolific spokesperson for the See America First idea, scolded easterners for their "careless ignorance of the marvelous beauty and wealth" of the West, arguing that many easterners "simply do not know—they are not educated about our throbbing West. They do not realize that some day out of this great West will come a Shakespeare, a Byron and the nation's greatest statesmen."[92] He concluded that "the people of the East seem to be growing effete," manifested by their obsession with everything European.[93] In this context, the East and Europe were conflated to symbolize elitism, wealth, culture, big business, and Old World provincialism. The West represented democracy, freedom, nature, and economic opportunity. In attracting eastern attention, western businessmen and boosters hoped to unite East and West in a commercial partnership that would strengthen the nation. Thus the gospel of See America First was meant to dispel established myths and fallacies about the West and in the process rectify the unequal economic relationship between the two regions.

On the other hand, See America First, as promoted by these western boosters, went beyond commercial and regional concerns to deeper anxieties about the transformations taking place in American culture. Over and over boosters returned to the eternal value of western scenery. Mines and farms become "worn out and factories are no longer profitable," Fisher Harris wrote, "but the river running to the sea, the waterfall turning the old mill wheel, the cool, inviting canyon, the awe inspiring mountain, the laughing lake, the gorgeous sunset, remain forever."[94] Western scenery embodied the promise and potential of the nation, according to See America First advocates. "The golden West," Harris explained, "offers a treasure house filled to overflowing with the rarest gems of towering snow-capped mountains; noble rivers, bearing in their broad bosoms the commerce of a nation; blue lakes smiling in the face of unclouded skies, gorgeous sunsets, whose ravishing beauty fills the soul with reverential awe, while over all and around all there is an atmosphere so pure that simply breathing it brings life to the lifeless, hope to the hopeless, and happiness to the miserable." Harris celebrated "the health renewing, soul-uplifting qualities of outdoor life" available in the West, asserting that the region offered a place where overworked Americans could reinvigorate themselves and revive their sense of patriotism. By encouraging easterners to know the West, western boosters implicitly associated the East with corruption and the West with virtue. In this framework, western nature represented the antithesis of the industrial and overly civilized East, providing a therapeutic retreat from the demands of modern living. "The number of jaded, overworked men and women of the crowded cities who feel in their hearts the irresistible 'call of the wild,' is greatly increasing," Harris wrote. "To such as these the fields and streams, the mountains, lakes and canyons of the West lie fallow for the working out of their physical and mental salvation."[95] In other words, even though the frontier seemed to be dwindling and commerce seemed to be transforming the character of American society, the promise of western nature as both sanctuary and free land remained in those scattered sublime landscapes.[96] Tourism promised to preserve those landscapes while opening up all land not designated as "scenic" to development. In touring the West, Americans could see that promise, in effect consume that promise, and yet the West could reap the benefits of progress without suffering the ill effects that had corrupted the East. Tourism thus became an act of virtuous consumption capable of preserving the Republic. The See America First idea, according to western boosters, allowed the West and America to have the best of both worlds: the virtues of nature combined with the benefits of commerce.

As the ideals and anxieties expressed by these western boosters reveal, Bowles's vision of a national tourism had yet to become a reality. In many ways the tourist opportunities outlined by George Crofutt and the Raymond and Whitcomb Company and promoted by Fisher Harris and other See America First advocates defined western tourism in national terms. Yet this early form of transcontinental tourism simply offered another form of regional tourism attempting to capitalize on the emerging infrastructure of the nation-state. Just as regional business interests worked to tap into the national market through novel business associations such as pools, trusts, and monopolies, and southern and western farmers sought to compete with national corporations through alliances and cooperatives, similarly, western boosters hoped that by organizing, pooling their resources, and forming some sort of publicity cooperative, they might transcend their regional constraints and access a national market. However, like their political counterparts, the Populists, they were unable to compete with the emerging corporate order. Western boosters simply did not have the organization, the infrastructure, or the capital to shape a national tourist market. It would take the power and resources of the transcontinental railroads—the nation's preeminent national corporations—to transform western landscapes into brand-name tourist attractions capable of sustaining a national tourism.

2

CORPORATE DOMINION

I am in hearty sympathy with your "See America First" movement and with the economic and patriotic ideas that have inspired it. Intimate knowledge of our own country is a first step toward intelligent citizenship. It broadens the mind and informs the judgment. The promoters of the movement will more and more be confronted with national problems, economic rather than political and can be handled successfully only by those whose detailed information is of equal scope. My best wishes for the success of your convention.

—James J. Hill, president of Great Northern Railway, 1906

*O*N 25 MAY 1910, THE Great Northern Railway completed construction of a twenty-by-fifteen-foot billboard in front of its general offices in St. Paul. The large colored painting portrayed a scene of Lake McDonald and the surrounding Rocky Mountains in the newly created Glacier National Park. The slogan "See America First" was inscribed across the top. The *St. Paul Pioneer Press Dispatch* noted that two hundred of these billboards depicting twenty different scenes in the park were being erected "along the trunk lines near Chicago, Detroit, Cleveland, Philadelphia, New York, Boston and Buffalo" in order to boost Glacier National Park and the See America First movement.[1] These billboards were just one component of what *Printer's Ink* described as an "extensive campaign of newspaper, magazine and outdoor advertising." Herbert J. Smith reported that the Great Northern was launching a multimedia advertising cam-

Glacier National Park emblem (Great Northern Railway, c. 1910). (Great Northern Railway Company Records, Minnesota Historical Society)

paign "to attract tourists to the new Glacier National Park in northern Montana." All new Great Northern advertisements displayed the See America First emblem along with photographic images of scenes throughout the park. The campaign was "an effort to take full advantage of the opportunities" presented by the "natural attraction" of the Park.[2] As Louis W. Hill, president of the Great Northern, explained, "There is a variety of beauty in Glacier National Park ... which is not surpassed anywhere in the world. Americans spend millions of dollars in Europe each year to see sights which are already equaled in this country. They need to be educated to realize this, and Glacier National Park should go far to help the 'See America First' movement."[3]

Marshaling its resources to develop and disseminate this extensive advertising campaign, the Great Northern Railway appropriated what had been a motto for local and regional interests and publicized it on a national scale. Although western boosters had sought to promote the development of a truly national tourism under the rubric of See America First, limited resources and focus diminished their ability to move beyond the confines of regional markets. It would take the organizational skill and financial power of national corporations such as the Great Northern to create and sustain what might best be called brand-name tourist attractions that would capture the attention of a national clientele.[4] The major transcontinental railroads, the nation's preeminent corporations, used their vast systems of influence, distribution, and finance, to construct, market, and sell tourist attractions to a national market.[5] In building lavish resort hotels, in promoting natural wonders, and in advocating for the creation of national parks, transcontinental railway companies such as the Southern Pacific, the Northern Pacific, the Atchison, Topeka and Santa Fe, and, most notably, the Great Northern linked tourism with their mission of nation building and the national mythology of Manifest Destiny and in the process instituted a national tourism that depended on the technological, economic, and social infrastructure of the modern nation-state.

Railroads had long been associated with the development of the tourist trade. As rail lines extended into the White Mountains during the mid-1840s, creating commercial links between port cities and rural hinterlands, tourists began to take advantage of their fast and reliable transportation. The Atlantic and Saint Lawrence Railway, which brought tourists into the White Mountains, built the Alpine House on the eastern side of Mount Washington to encourage and profit from the increasing tourist trade.[6] By the 1850s railroads such as the Baltimore and Ohio, which called itself the "picturesque line of America," made natural scenery more accessible by promoting scenic tours along their lines and encouraging passengers to enjoy the view from the train window.[7]

The transcontinental railroad corporations of the late nineteenth century quickly adopted this practice to boost their lines and encourage western settlement and tourist traffic. Not only did railroad publicists produce a wealth of imagery and information encouraging tourists to see the West, but they also built lavish resort hotels to meet the desires of upper-class tourists.[8] During the mid-1870s, as the Southern Pacific Railroad was working to complete its transcontinental line, the company, under the aegis of the Pacific Improvement Company, bought seven thousand acres on the Monterey Peninsula for the construction of a posh resort hotel. The "Queen of American Watering Places," otherwise know as the Hotel Del Monte, opened for business in June

Engraving of the Hotel Del Monte. From Raymond and Whitcomb's *Raymond's Vacation Excursions Grand Trip to Colorado, California and the Pacific Northwest* (1884). (Reproduced by permission of the Huntington Library, San Marino, California)

1880. Designed by Southern Pacific architect Arthur Brown, the eclectic Victorian-style hotel boasted lavishly appointed guest rooms equipped with running water and telephones, an extensive garden with an evergreen maze, and an array of bathhouses and bathing pools.[9] Inspired by the best of European resorts, the Southern Pacific brought Old World elegance and caché to the West Coast in an effort to attract a national and even international clientele.[10]

YELLOWSTONE AND THE GRAND CANYON: BRAND-NAME TOURIST ATTRACTIONS, OTHERWORLDLY LANDSCAPES

The Northern Pacific Railroad took the development of the tourist infrastructure one step further by moving beyond European imitation to create a uniquely American tourist resort. In 1870 as the Northern Pacific railroad was extending its tracks farther west through southern Montana, Jay Cooke, financier and promoter for the railroad, became interested in a then-little-known region in northern Wyoming known as the Yellowstone. Hoping to capitalize on the geothermal wonders, Cooke hired Nathaniel Pitt Langford to publicize the region. In September 1870, Langford accompanied the Washburn Expedition to explore the Yellowstone area. Myth has it that the idea for a national park resulted from an enthused campfire debate about how to develop the wondrous landscape the party had been exploring. In actuality, Jay Cooke and other Northern Pacific supporters concocted the idea in an effort to promote the railroad.[11]

On his return to the East, Langford began to actively publicize the region and the railroad, lecturing extensively in major cites along the eastern seaboard and publishing a two-part series in *Scribner's Magazine* entitled "The Wonders of the Yellowstone." Celebrating the connection between the railroad and Yellowstone, he wrote, "By means of the Northern Pacific Railroad ... the traveler will be able to make the trip to Montana from the Atlantic seaboard in three days, and thousands of tourists will be attracted to both Montana and Wyoming in order to behold with their own eyes the wonders here described."[12]

Inspired by Langford's enthusiastic descriptions and the potential indirect support of the Northern Pacific, Ferdinand V. Hayden, head of the United States Geological and Geographical Survey of the Territories, petitioned Congress for funding to survey the region. In the summer of 1871 Hayden led a forty-man scientific team to document the Yellowstone area. Although Congress supplied forty thousand dollars to finance the expedition, the Northern Pacific still played a role in the enterprise. Jay Cooke provided a letter of recommendation to Hayden for the noted landscape artist Thomas Moran and gave Moran five hundred dollars to help defray the cost of the trip.[13] On his return, Hayden prepared to report his findings to Congress and at the urging of Northern Pacific officials included in his report a recommendation that Yellowstone be set aside as a public park, in the same manner as Yosemite had been, "for the benefit and enjoyment of the people."[14] Although Northern Pacific lobbyists reportedly stayed out of the debate, copies of Nathaniel Langford's *Scribner's* series were placed on the desks of every legislator, and William Henry Jackson's photographs and Thomas Moran's watercolors from the Hayden Expedition were displayed in the Capitol. On 1 March 1872, President Ulysses S. Grant signed the Yellowstone Park Act into law, nominally creating the nation's first national park and providing the Northern Pacific with a quintessentially American tourist attraction.[15]

The financial collapse of Jay Cooke's banking house in 1873 and the ensuing panic and depression curtailed any efforts on the part of the Northern Pacific to develop the Yellowstone region. However, a motley collection of independent hotels and bathhouses were established around Mammoth Hot Springs, Lower Geyser Basin, and Pleasant Valley during the 1870s and early 1880s. Only after it had completed its tracks across the continent and recovered from its financial instability did the Northern Pacific actively begin to shape the Yellowstone region for tourists.

Between 1883 and 1915, the Northern Pacific in collaboration and competition with a number of interests worked to consciously develop a brand-name tourist attraction for the railroad. In 1883 Northern Pacific completed a spur from its main line to Cinnabar, Montana, seven miles from the northern boundary of the park, providing access to Mammoth Hot Springs. Simultaneously, a group of investors backed by Northern Pacific filed with the Department of the Interior for monopoly privileges in the park. On approval of a ten-year lease to control a number of key sites throughout the park, the Yellowstone Park Improvement Company was formed and construction immediately commenced on a hotel at Mammoth Hot Springs, given the apt name National Hotel, and tent camps were established at Norris Geyser Basin and Upper Geyser Basin. The overall plan for park development also called for hotel facilities at Yellowstone Lake and the Grand Canyon of the Yellowstone. This initial burst of development quickly disintegrated into financial collapse and disarray as park advocates charged the Yellowstone Park Improvement Company with orchestrating a "park grab," decrying the monopolistic development of the park for personal gain. By 1884 Congress had voided the Department of Interior lease and the Yellowstone Park Improvement Company had filed for bankruptcy, turning its management over to a group of court-appointed trustees.[16]

Two years later, again under the auspices of the Northern Pacific Railroad, a group of investors stepped in to take charge of reviving development of the park. Charles Gibson, a noted hotel man from St. Louis, and Frederick Billings, former president of the Northern Pacific, purchased the bankrupt company with the help of Northern Pacific assets and commenced to negotiate new leases with the Department of the Interior. Calling themselves the Yellowstone Park Association, they worked to reorganize and centralize the development of Yellowstone. They took up where their predecessor had left off and began construction on facilities at both the Grand Canyon and Yellowstone Lake, working to tighten their control of the tourist trade by buying out competitors and pushing out squatters.

Between 1901 and 1916, under the leadership of Harry W. Child, a Montana banking and mining magnate, the Yellowstone Park Association, later renamed the Yellowstone Park Hotel Company, consciously reshaped the tourist infrastructure at Yellowstone to create a uniquely American tourist resort. Harry Child entered the Yellowstone concessionaire business in 1891 as a partner in the Yellowstone Park Transportation Company, which held the exclusive contract to transport Northern Pacific passengers through the park. In 1901 the Yellowstone Park Association was purchased by Child and his partners with a loan from Northern Pacific. Child was elected president of the company and quickly gained controlling shares. In 1909, attempting to avoid prosecution as a monopoly, Northern Pacific sold the company to Child on favorable terms, and it became the Yellowstone Park Hotel Company. Although the railroad publicly disassociated itself with park concessions, it continued to provide financial backing for development as well as promotional support. During this period Child emerged as a controlling force in shaping the tourist infrastructure of the park.[17]

Under his leadership, the built and natural environment of the park was designed, shaped, and standardized into a packaged tourist experience. From the trademark yellow "tally-ho" stage coaches that met passengers at the Gardiner station to the distinctive design of the Old Faithful Inn, Child worked to create a desirable and recognizable tourist product. He not only consolidated his hold on park transportation but also oversaw the construction of an array of new facilities, including a new entrance arch along with a series of hotels, lunchroom facilities, and tent camps. With the assistance of architect Robert Reamer, the support of the Department of Interior, and the silent and steady financial backing of the Northern Pacific, the landscape of Yellowstone was completely scripted for the benefit of the tourist and the railroad.

A Yellowstone tour promised deluxe service on the Northern Pacific's "Yellowstone Park Line," sublime scenery, and geothermal wonders accented with distinctive luxury hotels and a carriage escort. In 1902 Harry Child engaged architect Robert C. Reamer to create what would quickly become a

Yellowstone icon, the Old Faithful Inn. Child first came across Reamer's work in San Diego, where he spent his winters. Liking his style, he recommended Reamer to the Northern Pacific to design the new Gardiner Station for the extended park spur line. Simultaneously, Reamer began to work on the design for a new hotel in the park at Upper Geyser Basin. Constructed in 1903–4, the Old Faithful Inn manifested a new architectural style fitting for this uniquely American resort.[18]

Drawing from an amalgam of architectural precedents, including the Prairie and Shingle styles as well as late nineteenth-century examples of rustic architecture, the Old Faithful Inn was constructed of materials native to the park: rough-hewn lodgepole pine, basalt stone, and iron hardware hand-forged from Yellowstone ore.[19] As an organic extension of the natural setting situated on the edge of the Upper Geyser Basin, the front facade boasted a commanding gable roof, punctuated with dormers and topped with a viewing balcony, accentuated by an overhanging port cochere, which was supported on massive pillars of stacked logs. Inside, the seven-story lobby added to these dramatic natural effects. As one Northern Pacific guidebook noted, "As each day's contingent of tourists arrives it is the common experience for them to advance a few steps into this vast space and then halt and gaze about them in wonder and amazement."[20] Gigantic lodgepole pine columns supported a series of ascending balconies detailed with balustrades and railings of twisted limbs, and an eighty-five-foot lava-stone chimney, encircled by eight fireplaces, ascended through the log rafters. One observer described it as a "skeleton of some enormous mammal seen from within."[21] The log walls and stone chimney gave the effect of a frontier cabin. But this primitive detailing was softened by oriental rugs and modern conveniences. As one tourist commented, "With all this rusticity, comfort, convenience, and even elegance are everywhere."[22] In blending rustic detailing with civilized refinement, Reamer and the Yellowstone Park Association had succeeded in creating a grand luxury hotel in the American wilderness.[23]

The Old Faithful Inn became an archetype for national park architecture and an emblem for the park. Northern Pacific brochures touted it as "nearly as great an attraction as is Old Faithful Geyser itself." Like the exotic geothermal wonders of the park, Northern Pacific described the Old Faithful Inn as a distinct architectural attraction: a "unique structure [that] challenges the

Old Faithful Inn, Yellowstone Park.

Northern Pacific Railway distributed images of the Old Faithful Inn far and wide in an effort to establish Yellowstone National Park as a brand-name tourist attraction. Postcard of the Old Faithful Inn, Yellowstone National Park. (Lake County [Illinois] Museum, Curt Teich Postcard Archives)

admiration and delights the eye of every tourist that journeys to Wonderland."[24] Reamer also designed a number of other structures in the park, including the Roosevelt Arch (1902), the remodeled Lake Hotel (1903), and the Canyon Hotel (1911).[25] Although not all of these structures drew on the unique architectural vocabulary established at the Old Faithful Inn, Reamer's work played a significant role in scripting the park as a distinctly American tourist attraction.

Between 1901 and 1916, corporate interests reinforced by state support transformed the Yellowstone landscape into a premiere American wilderness resort. During this time, the Northern Pacific financed and promoted the construction and management of top-of-the-line hotels and tourist facilities while the Army Corps of Engineers completed construction of the "Grand Loop Road of the Park." The 150-mile figure-eight loop provided a "general circuit or belt line connecting all the important centers of interest": Mammoth Hot Springs, Norris Geyser Basin, Upper Geyser Basin, the

Grand Canyon of Yellowstone, and Yellowstone Lake.[26] Capitalizing on these improvements, Northern Pacific began to offer a five-and-a-half-day package tour through the park that provided tourists with a complete Yellowstone Park experience under the guidance of Northern Pacific and its subsidiaries. The tour included transportation throughout the park on Yellowstone Park Transportation Company carriages and accommodations at the Mammoth Hotel, the Fountain Hotel, the Old Faithful Inn, and the Lake Hotel, all maintained by the Yellowstone Park Association. The tour presented a regimented view of a select series of attractions in the park: the bubbling hot springs at Mammoth, the various geyser basins, Yellowstone Lake, and the Grand Canyon of the Yellowstone.[27] Rooms, transportation, meals, and guides were all included for an extra $40 added to the price of a Northern Pacific ticket.[28] Although other companies competed for business in Yellowstone, most notably subsidiaries of the Union Pacific system, which accessed the west entrance of the park, and the Burlington line, which provided entrée from Cody, Wyoming, most of the visitors to Yellowstone came via the Northern Pacific and took advantage of the package tours.

The Northern Pacific further defined the Yellowstone Park experience through a massive advertising campaign. Initiated under the direction of passenger agent Charles S. Fee during the early 1880s, the Northern Pacific created an imaginary geography of the park that centered around the image of the park as "Wonderland." Not only did Fee encourage and support the work of promotional photographer F. Jay Haynes, but he also oversaw the publication of a series of "Wonderland" pamphlets and guides celebrating the novel landscapes along the Northern Pacific line.[29] Although all of the region traversed by the line fell under the designation of "Wonderland," by the turn of the century Yellowstone had become "the gem of Wonderland."[30]

Fee was not the first to characterize the region in these terms. Nathaniel P. Langford had touted the "wonders" of Yellowstone in his first descriptive article for *Scribner's Monthly* in 1871.[31] A few months later, A. Bart Henderson, a Montana prospector, described the area as the "New Wonderland" in an article for the *New York Times*.[32] In 1871 Harry J. Norton published one of the first guidebooks to the park, entitled *Wonder-Land Illustrated*, which comprised a series of letters written to the *Virginia City Montanian* recounting a trip over the "Grand Rounds." Norton described the area as an "enchanted

land, surround on every side with mystery and marvel."[33] In 1878 another
independent tourist published an account of his travels through the park entitled *Rambles in Wonderland: or The Yellowstone*.[34] By this time the Wonderland sobriquet had gained widespread popularity. Only in the early 1880s did
the Northern Pacific appropriate the term to describe the region of the
northwestern United States traversed by its line. In the early 1880s, John
Hyde wrote a series of pamphlets for the railroad that built on the wonderland imagery, including "Alice's Adventures in the New Wonderland,"
which brought Lewis Carroll's famous Alice to Yellowstone to describe the
region.[35]

Through its *Wonderland* guidebook series, Northern Pacific capitalized on
this image of Yellowstone as an exotic landscape. Olin D. Wheeler, author of
the series, characterized Yellowstone as a "strange, almost uncanny, concen-
tration of so many weird and unusual manifestations of Nature."[36] He described Mammoth Hot Springs in cosmic terms as "a spot where the gigantic
forces of nature have fought a great fight, where a supreme struggle for mastery occurred between water, fire, and ice, and where each, in its turn victor, at
last gave over the conflict, and erosion, the commonest force of all, perhaps,
occupies the battlefield as final master."[37] But Yellowstone was not simply a
realm of "strange and weird" landscapes.[38] Yellowstone Lake provided vistas
of picturesque beauty, while the Grand Canyon of the Yellowstone offered a
sublime spectacle of nature "oriental in its richness and almost barbaric in its
novelty and variety."[39] Metaphors linking Yellowstone's geothermal wonders
and natural spectacles to Greek, Christian, and pagan mythology reinforced
this landscape of otherness. Even the nomenclature given to Yellowstone attractions—Giants Thumb, Cleopatra, Jupiter Terrace, Devil's Frying Pan,
and Fairy Falls—added to this imagery, drawing on the freakish associations
of the monumental and the miniature as well as the exotic and otherworldly.[40] Although Northern Pacific sought to link itself with the nation by
promoting and developing Yellowstone as a national park, and national images of soaring eagles, noble savages, and Lady Liberty graced the covers of
Wonderland guides, along with patriotic admonitions encouraging American
tourists "to show the world that we appreciate the Heritage God has given
us," the imaginary geography of Wonderland was not so much American as it
was otherworldly—"enchanted," "unusual," "unique."[41]

Northern Pacific's *Wonderland* guidebooks drew on established American imagery—the noble savage, soaring eagles, and lady liberty—to promote the Yellowstone tourist experience. Cover of Olin D. Wheeler's *Wonderland 1900* (1900). (Reproduced by permission of the Huntington Library, San Marino, California)

Adding to this otherworldly imagery, the Northern Pacific's production and promotion of Yellowstone as Wonderland was framed in terms of discovery and exploration. In the *Wonderland* guidebooks, Wheeler contextualized the description of Yellowstone with heroic tales of westward expansion and Manifest Destiny: the saga of the Lewis and Clark Expedition, Custer's Last Stand, the building of the railroad. In providing a comfortable view onto this exotic wilderness, in domesticating the sublime, in making this strange landscape accessible to tourists, the railroad positioned itself and the tourist experience as a part of the larger civilizing process of westward expansion. By defining Yellowstone as Wonderland, the experience of tourism as discovery and exploration remained a continual process and promise, rather than an accomplished fact or feat. As Wonderland, Yellowstone always remained just on the edge of civilization, waiting to be discovered and explored by the tourist. In this way, Wonderland was never fully incorporated into the nation, despite the fact that Yellowstone spectacles such as Mammoth Hot Springs, the Old Faithful Inn and geyser, Yellowstone canyon, and the buffalo and the bears became brand-name attractions for the Northern Pacific.

The Atchison, Topeka, and Santa Fe Railroad in partnership with the Fred Harvey Company sought to promote and package the Southwest in a similar manner. In the mid-1890s, the Santa Fe Railroad, under new ownership and management, commenced an extensive advertising campaign to publicize its passenger service across the southwestern United States and establish its reputation as a transcontinental line. Building on the example set by the Northern Pacific Railroad, the Santa Fe worked in collaboration with its corporate partner to develop and promote a then remote southwestern landscape, the Grand Canyon of the Colorado River.

The corporate partnership between the Fred Harvey Company and the Santa Fe Railroad was launched in 1876 when Fred Harvey, an English immigrant, opened a lunchroom at the Santa Fe station in Topeka, Kansas. Although the Harvey company began with a series of popular eating facilities, with Santa Fe support, the two companies built an empire that shaped and sold a romanticized southwestern tourist experience along the Santa Fe line. By the 1920s Santa Fe/Harvey operated over a dozen major hotels and had established its famous Indian Department for collecting and selling Native

American arts and crafts, in addition to the renown Harvey Houses. Through this symbiotic partnership, Santa Fe/Harvey built a systematized tourist infrastructure that relied on an extensive public relations enterprise to market and sell a standardized tourist product: the Southwest.[42]

The Santa Fe began to actively define and promote the southwestern tourist landscape in the early 1890s. The inaugural run of the California Limited in 1892, which offered direct service from Chicago to Los Angeles and on to San Diego, sparked a burst of promotional activity as the Santa Fe and its rival, the Southern Pacific, competed for passengers and prepared to promote themselves for the 1893 World's Columbian Exposition.[43] The Grand Canyon quickly emerged as an emblem of the southwestern tourist landscape. In an effort to popularize the site, the Santa Fe subsidized a summer excursion to the canyon for the then-famous landscape painter Thomas Moran and the equally noted landscape photographer William Henry Jackson. In return, Moran agreed to give the Santa Fe copyright and publishing privileges for one painting, and Jackson contracted with the railroad to produce a photographic album of the canyon.[44] Charles A. Higgins, the assistant general passenger agent for the Santa Fe, launched an extensive publicity campaign using the images of the canyon created by Moran and Jackson, among others, to illustrate a series of promotional brochures and pamphlets.[45] Yet through the turn of the century travel to the canyon remained difficult, as tourists were forced to endure an all-day stage ride from the main line at Flagstaff to the canyon rim as well as sparse accommodations along the way.[46]

In 1901 the Santa Fe completed a branch line from Williams, Arizona, to the south rim of the canyon and commenced to develop an elaborate tourist infrastructure. Building on its established success with the Fred Harvey Company in such places as the Alvarado Hotel in Albuquerque and the Montezuma Hotel in Las Vegas, New Mexico, the Santa Fe instructed Charles Whittlesley, chief architect for the Santa Fe, to design a grand hotel for the canyon.[47] Whittlesley, who had trained under Louis Sullivan and had gone on to design a number of structures referencing the region's Spanish and Indian heritage, designed a rambling rustic building that came to be known as the El Tovar. Like its counterpart in Yellowstone, the El Tovar was constructed of materials native to the area. However, the resulting building mixed rustic materials with more traditional design features to create an

The El Tovar Hotel, along with other tourist buildings constructed by the Santa Fe Railroad and the Fred Harvey Company, framed the Grand Canyon as an icon of the southwestern tourist landscape. Grand Canyon of Arizona Emblem (Atchison, Topeka, and Santa Fe Railroad, c. 1915). (Warshaw Collection of Business Americana, Archives Center, National Museum of American History, Smithsonian Institution)

eclectic effect. One promotional brochure noted, "The architect has combined in admirable proportions the Swiss Chalet and the Norway villa. . . . Not a Waldorf-Astoria—admirable as that type is for the city—but a big country clubhouse, where the traveler seeking high-class accommodations also finds freedom from ultra fashionable restrictions."[48] Situated on the edge of the canyon rim, the three-and-a-half-story structure featured a modified mansard roof with gabled window dormers, surrounded by a wooden balustrade and topped by a pointed Swiss tower. A large front porch constructed of peeled logs with arched stone supports led visitors into a lobby area designed to resemble a log cabin. Craftsman-style furniture, Navajo rugs, animal trophies, and southwestern pottery accented the self-consciously primitive style. Other public rooms, however, featured more traditional resort decor: decorated wallpaper, oriental carpets, and upholstered furniture. And guests could choose between colonial or Mission-style guest rooms.[49] Despite its eclectic design, the El Tovar quickly gained popularity for its unmatchable views of the canyon. "El Tovar commands a prospect without parallel in the world," touted one promotional brochure. "A perpendicular mile from rim to river ... and thirteen dizzy miles across to the opposite canyon wall. ... The roaring Colorado below looks like a silvery thread."[50] As one visitor described the view from his balcony, "The Sweep of our vision covers hundreds of square miles of the Canyon—an infinity of mountains, towers, domes, spires, strange temples and palaces, glowing with every conceivable color, all marvelously distinct. ... Words cannot give any adequate idea of the immensity of the Chasm."[51]

Santa Fe/Harvey did not stop with the hotel: between 1905, when the El Tovar opened, and 1916, when the National Park Service nominally assumed control of the tourist concessions, the partners created a complete tourist resort providing access to the canyon.[52] The Harvey Company contracted with Mary Colter, a young architect from St. Paul, Minnesota, who had designed the interior of the Indian Building at the Alvarado Hotel in Albuquerque, to design a similar structure for the Grand Canyon. The result was the Hopi House, completed in 1905. Modeled after traditional Hopi dwellings at Oraibi, Arizona, the three-story stone structure featured terraced walls with exterior stone stair cases accented with wooden ladders and clay chimney pots. Inside, smooth adobe walls and a ceiling structure constructed of rough-hewn log beams with smaller cross rafters composed of smaller logs, arrowweed, willows, and light brush accented the traditional design.[53] Santa Fe promotional material likened Hopi House to a miniature Indian pueblo.[54] There, Native American craftsmen marketed and displayed their wares. Although Colter modified the traditional Hopi dwelling to address its function as a commercial space, she intended Hopi House to be a re-creation and celebration of the distinct Native American culture of the Southwest. "Here are

Hopi men, women, and children—some decorating and burning exquisite pottery; others spinning yarn and weaving squaw dresses, scarfs, and blankets. Go inside and you see how these gentle folks live," exclaimed a Santa Fe brochure. The brochure went on to note the "tall, taciturn Navajos— smooth-faced, keen-eyed Bedouins—who live in adjacent 'hogans.'"[55]

Colter's work, enhanced by the Santa Fe/Harvey promotional apparatus, synthesized architecture with archeology and ethnography, and in the process she helped define the mystique of the tourist Southwest. Blending native materials with a sanitized and modernized manifestation of traditional Hopi architecture, Hopi House fused the dramatic canyon landscape with a romanticized ideal of southwestern Native American culture. Colter went on to design a number of additional structures at the canyon for the Harvey Company in a similar vein. Lookout Studio and Hermit's Rest, both completed in 1914, provided a viewing tower and a refreshment station for tourists, accenting the improvements to roads and trails. Both buildings were designed to blend with the canyon landscape. Constructed of stones taken from the canyon and detailed with rustic accouterments and references to Spanish and Native American traditions, these structures rounded out the Santa Fe/Harvey tourist infrastructure.[56] The balance between the rustic elegance of El Tovar, the staged authenticity of Hopi House, and the re-created ruins of Lookout Studio and Hermit's Rest helped frame the Grand Canyon as an icon of the southwestern tourist landscape.

Just as the Northern Pacific had transformed Yellowstone into a premiere American resort, so the Santa Fe and the Harvey Company also sought to promote, package, and sell the Grand Canyon as a brand-name tourist attraction. Santa Fe/Harvey not only constructed transportation facilities and tourist accommodations but also developed their own roads and trails. In 1912 the Santa Fe completed construction of Hermit Rim Road, a carriage road that ran along the south rim of the canyon west of Bright Angel Camp. A connecting trail, called the Hermit Trail, took tourists from the road down through Hermit Canyon to the river.[57] Capitalizing on these improvements, Santa Fe/Harvey offered a variety of tours in and around the canyon. In addition to the El Tovar, tourists could stay at the Bright Angel Camp, which was purchased and reopened by Santa Fe/Harvey in 1905, or the Grand View Hotel; or they could descend to the floor of the canyon and stay with the government Indian Agency in the Havasupais Indian Reservation for a night or two.[58] Santa Fe passengers were given stopover privileges at Williams, Arizona, where the Grand Canyon spur connected with the Santa Fe main line. Once they arrived at the canyon, tourists could take a series of carriage rides along the rim to Hopi Point, Yavapai Point, Maricopa Point, and Grand View. Or they were offered a series of horseback trips into the canyon ranging from a few hours up to three days. Although competing interests vied for control of access to the Canyon, Santa Fe/Harvey quickly monopolized the tourist trade.[59]

Promotional material published by Santa Fe and the Harvey Company touted this improved tourist landscape as a land of enchantment and the Grand Canyon as the "Titan of Chasms." Charles Higgins, assistant general passenger agent for the Santa Fe Railroad, described the canyon as an "unearthly spectacle." Like Yellowstone, the Santa Fe characterized the Grand Canyon as an otherworldly landscape: "An inferno, swathed in soft celestial fires; a whole chaotic underworld, just emptied of primeval floods and waiting for a new creative word; a boding terrible thing, unflinchingly real, yet spectral as a dream, eluding all sense of perspective or dimension, outstretching the faculty of measurement, overlapping the confines of definite comprehension."[60] The nomenclature assigned to the various attractions of the canyon—Bright Angel, Mystic Spring, Temple of Sett, Shinumo Altar—reinforced this otherworldly and exotic imagery. As one Harvey brochure noted, "The gigantic rock formations in the Grand Canyon, torn by the waters and worn by the weathers of the ages, in outline strongly suggest the temples of India and the modern explorers have given the more prominent ones Hindoo names, such as temples of Buddha and Brahma, Shiva and Zoraster."[61] Santa Fe/Harvey also depended on Native American references to frame the imaginary geography of the canyon.[62] "The Grand Canyon was known to the Pueblo Indians centuries before the white man reached America," a Harvey brochure explained. "Almost every tribe in the canyon region has its own legend of the origin of the great chasm. One of these tells of an ancient hero who made a knife thrust into the earth `through which all the water rushed out into the Sea of Sunset.'"[63] Once tourists had taken in the "stupendous panorama," they were encouraged to inspect the wares at Hopi House and enjoy the Indian performances.[64] As one promotional brochure

Promotional material distributed by the Santa Fe Railroad and the Fred Harvey Company depicted the Grand Canyon as an "unearthly spectacle." Cover of Charles Higgins's *Titan of Chasms: The Grand Canyon of the Arizona* (1906). (Reproduced by permission of the Huntington Library, San Marino, California)

detailed, "The Hopis are making 'piki,' twining the raven black hair of the 'manas' in big side whorls, smoking corn cob pipes, building sacred alters, mending moccasins—doing a hundred un-American things. They are the most primitive Indians in America, with ceremonies several centuries old."[65]

In privileging Native American culture, Santa Fe/Harvey emphasized the exotic and foreign character of the landscape, situating the Southwest and the spectacle of the Grand Canyon on the edge of civilization, where tourists could position themselves as adventurous explorers and amateur ethnographers. As scholars have argued, the Santa Fe and the Fred Harvey Company used their corporate resources to help create and disseminate a regional identity for the Southwest "based on an aesthetic appreciation" of primitive Indian cultures and spectacular desert landscapes.[66] Through this process, the Southwest became "America's Orient."[67] The Santa Fe/Harvey promotional apparatus encouraged tourists to think of their experience as a kind of modern-day "Columbian encounter" in which tourists were able to discover a "new world" in the spectacle of the Grand Canyon and come in contact with the exotic natives of this strange land, returning home with souvenirs and photographs to verify their discoveries.[68] Like the Northern Pacific in Yellowstone, the Santa Fe and the Fred Harvey Company packaged and promoted the Southwest and the Grand Canyon as brand-name tourist attractions, but like Yellowstone, the packaged allure rested in the promise of the foreign and the exotic rather than the national and the patriotic.

GLACIER NATIONAL PARK: GREAT NORTHERN'S AMERICAN ICON

The Great Northern Railway built on and combined the promotional strategies of the Northern Pacific and the Santa Fe to develop and publicize the dramatic mountain scenery of northwestern Montana that became Glacier National Park. Like its competitors had done with Yellowstone and the Grand Canyon, the railroad packaged and sold Glacier National Park as a brand-name tourist attraction. But unlike the Northern Pacific and the Santa Fe, the Great Northern also defined the park as a quintessentially American landscape. The Great Northern sought to create a distinctly national tourist attraction. Whereas the Northern Pacific and the Santa Fe touted the tourist experience in terms of the exotic and the foreign, the

Louis W. Hill, president of the Great Northern Railway from 1907 to 1912 and chairman of the board from 1912 to 1929, played an active role in shaping and defining the tourist landscape in Glacier National Park. Photograph of Louis W. Hill with the Blackfeet Indians of Glacier National Park (c. 1912). (Courtesy Louis W. Hill Papers, James J. Hill Library, St. Paul)

Great Northern used the See America First slogan to incorporate Glacier Park into a national geography. More than any other transcontinental railroad, Great Northern succeeded in linking the tourist experience with national identity and popularizing a national tourism.

In the March 1915 issue of *Sunset,* Rufus Steele recounted the story of Glacier Park's origin. The story focused on one man and his dream. That man was Louis Warren Hill, son of the famous empire builder, James J. Hill, and chairman of the board of the Great Northern Railway.[69] According to Steele, Hill was "no Wall Street railway president"; he was much more than that. "Louis Hill could make a living and a reputation as a musician, a landscape painter, a chauffeur on difficult roads, or as a hunter or wilderness guide." This unmatched captain of industry, Steele explained, was the man behind Glacier National Park. Steele's story told of how Hill had been exploring and enjoying the Rocky Mountain country along the edge of his road for many years. In a moment of epiphany during one of his mountain journeys "Louis W. Hill realized that he was a Christopher Columbus. He had discovered altitudinous America. With the realization came a vast ambition. It was that he might share his discovery with every American. He wanted to make it possible for every man, woman, and child, with or without a capable pair of legs, to stand in Gunsight Pass and saturate his soul."[70] It was Louis Hill's vision that gave shape to the east side of Glacier National Park.

Hill, who rose through the ranks of the Great Northern organization to the presidency in 1907, showed a much greater interest in passenger advertising than his father.[71] He knew that the success of Great Northern's public image rested on its ability to capture the romance of railroad travel. Coming to his position of leadership just as the Great Northern was settling into its status as a transcontinental line, he well understood the success of the Canadian Pacific Railroad's development of Rocky Mountain resorts like Banff and the Santa Fe's development of the Grand Canyon, as well as the successful affiliation that his closest competitor the Northern Pacific had established with Yellowstone National Park.[72] He recognized that Yellowstone represented not only a scenic curiosity but also a national symbol that enhanced the public image of the Northern Pacific and served to draw in passengers as well as investors and shippers.[73] Learning from his competitors, Hill began to express an interest in the possibilities of the Glacier district early on in his presidency.[74] By the summer of 1909, while the Glacier Park bill was being debated, Hill began to articulate his vision for the proposed park. After passage of the park bill by the house in mid-April 1910, Hill told the press that "a series of roads should be established throughout the park, with Swiss chalets scattered here and there, making a veritable American Alps." He explained that "the lodges would be located only far enough apart so that the man on foot even could make the trip and obtain sleeping accommodations," and that "hotel accommodations of a more prestigious type or tents for the most modest could also be furnished."[75]

Under Hill's direction, the Great Northern Railway began to actively develop the mountainous terrain located in northwestern Montana to accommodate increased tourist travel in the spring of 1910. Between 1910 and 1915, the railroad completely recast the east side of the park, guided by an idealized and multifaceted vision of wilderness, scenery, the West, and America. By 1915 Glacier had two rustic luxury hotels, nine chalet complexes, three tepee camps, and a series of roads and trails that stretched throughout the park connecting the hotels, the chalets, and the scenic vistas.[76] Not only did the physical arrangement of the accommodations compel tourists to walk or ride through the area, experiencing the mountain vistas, the glaciers, the dense forests, and the mountain streams firsthand, but also the atmosphere of these accommodations provided a context for understanding this experience in terms of America's past, present, and future. In its physical form Glacier National Park came to embody a wilderness experience that gave meaning to the company's new slogan, "See America First."

At Great Northern's Midvale Station, which was renamed East Glacier in 1912, the railroad purchased 160 acres of land from the Blackfeet Indian Reservation adjacent to the park and constructed a large hotel designed by Thomas D. McMahon and modeled on the Forestry Building at the Lewis and Clark Exposition.[77] Following the example set by the Old Faithful Inn and El Tovar, the Glacier Park Hotel served as the gateway to the park. "Here the east and the west meet, the American and the European, finding pleasure in the associations with bronzed and hardy mountaineers," explained one promotional brochure.[78] Situated directly opposite the newly named Glacier Park Station, the main facade featured a series of colonnades constructed of huge tree trunks, and a long verandah commanding a view of the Rocky Mountains ran along the west side. The "Forest Lobby," a three-story enclosed courtyard supported by "splendid fir-tree pillars four feet in thickness" brought "the outdoors indoors."[79] It was decorated with Blackfeet Indian rugs and blankets, oak furniture, tree-trunk lamp stands and lighted by Japanese lanterns. It also contained an open campfire set up on a bed of stones. Phone booths, a drug store, a cigar stand, a railroad ticket office, and a haberdasher were situated in the midst of this rustic decor.[80] Blackfeet Indians in full war dress, and rough-clad western guides brushed shoulders with newly arrived guests outfitted in the latest styles from Chicago and New York, even though Great Northern publicity material instructed guests to leave their city fashions behind, emphasizing that "there are no conventionalities in Glacier Park."[81] Waitresses dressed in Swiss costumes worked with a Japanese couple who served tea in the afternoons from a cart made of rough logs. By design and by chance, the hotel straddled boundaries of past and present, primitive and modern, East and West.

Hill was actively involved in the design, the decoration, and the layout of almost every component of the park, giving input on such issues as the style and siting of the hotels and chalets, the interior decoration of the forest lobby, the waitress costumes for Swiss chalet employees, and bulb selection for the decorative flower beds. He even went so far as to require that an agent be sent to Jackson Hole, Wyoming, to collect Elk horns and skulls "to be used in decorating the Glacier Park Hotel." They had to be freighted eighty miles by horse-drawn wagon before they reached the railroad, where they were shipped via freight to Glacier Park Station.[82] Hill's concern for the details reflected his desire to mold the park as a public expression of the first-class service of the Great Northern and as an expression of his personal ideal of American wilderness.

Hill was an outdoorsman. He not only hunted and fished but also dabbled in scenic photography, landscape painting, and gardening.[83] His hobbies reflected the larger interests of a society increasingly fascinated by the benefits of outdoor life and nature appreciation. Hill was one of many elites in the early twentieth century who came to define and value wilderness as an alluring counterforce to the powerful impact of decline and decay that seemed to be undermining modern society.[84] Many elites romanticized wilderness as a temporary refuge from overwhelming social, cultural, and political changes

Glacier National Park Hotel (1912). Photograph by Fred H. Kiser. (Great Northern Railway Company Records, Minnesota Historical Society)

that seemed increasingly beyond their control. Urbanization and increased immigration precipitated by the forces of industrialization and incorporation, underscored by what seemed to be pervasive societal corruption, caused many urban Americans to turn nostalgically to the wilderness represented in the disappearing frontier for a simpler more robust life. Increased enthusiasm for camping, hunting, fishing, all aspects of outdoor life, wilderness preservation, and nature study marked this shift. Hill's vision of the park grew out of these concerns. It was shaped by his ideal of wilderness as an escape from the overly civilized. He wanted the park to be a rustic refuge where elites like himself could regenerate themselves.

Although Hill described the park as "everybody's Park," distinct ideals about class were embedded in his vision of Glacier. The Americans he was addressing included those elites who commonly traveled to Europe. Hill developed the park as much for himself and his family as he did for the "American public." He built his own vacation chalet on St. Mary's Lake opposite the St. Mary's Chalet Camp, and his family spent at least part of every summer in the park. "Everybody" for Louis Hill signified those like himself, established, upper-class, white Americans. The personal manner in which he

Forest Lobby, at Night, Glacier Park Hotel (c. 1912). Photograph by Fred H. Kiser. (Great Northern Railway Company Records, Minnesota Historical Society)

promoted the park suggests that Hill conceived of Glacier's east side as an exclusive resort or private club open to those who were in a position to understand, appreciate, and benefit from the value of American scenery and wilderness.

Contrary to what might be assumed about the concerns of a railroad president, Hill was closely involved with the management of the park. He monitored tourists to the park, and his staff kept him abreast of "prominent visitors" scheduled to travel through Glacier each season.[85] The 1919 list, for example, included such notables as Arthur Meeker, the vice president of Armour and Company, R. M. Bissell, the president of the Hartford Fire Insurance Company, Mrs. Isaac Guggenheim, Theodore Roosevelt (he was listed as a prospect), and Mrs. George W. Vanderbilt, among others.[86] On the one hand, Hill wanted the Great Northern administration to be aware of who was coming to the park in order to make sure that the railroad was fully capitalizing on the tourist potential of the park. On the other hand, Hill's interest in knowing exactly who was coming to the park reflected his ideal of the park as a private resort of sorts where satisfied clients returned year after year and publicity spread by word of mouth, thus ensuring the "right" sort of clientele. Writing to the Department of the Interior near the end of the 1914 season to describe some of the most recent improvements, Hill observed, "The Glacier park is fortunate in being able to induce tourists to return each year. I have met several parties who were here last year and some the year before."[87]

It was not uncommon for Hill to provide personal itineraries and to check up on the service that prominent visitors received. When Dwight W. Morrow of J. P. Morgan and Company and his family traveled to the park in the 1919 season, Hill had a basket of mixed fruit placed in their private car and asked his staff in Glacier to try to have a fresh supply of milk shipped out for one of their children, who was recovering from an operation. Hill followed up by having one of his staff phone Morrow to make sure everything was "satisfactory."[88] Similarly, Hill sent a number of maps and brochures describing the park along with a day-by-day itinerary to Samuel Rea, president of the Pennsylvania Railroad, who planned to travel to Glacier during the 1916 season.[89] In effect Hill presented himself as the ultimate host of Glacier Park. In sending out promotional material, welcoming his passengers, and mapping out guided tours, Hill helped friends and business acquaintances define their park experience.

Hill also made sure that the Glacier staff upheld his standards. Staff guidelines and regulations encouraged employees to provide service "quickly, quietly, cheerfully and courteously and to let no guest depart feeling that everything and more was not done to make his visit . . . something to look back on with pleasure." The Glacier Park Hotel Company's booklet of service regulations and employee information provided a detailed description of the behavior expected of Glacier Park staff. "Unnecessary noise," "flashy or conspicuous clothing," "intoxicating liquors," and rudeness were prohibited. The booklet admonished, "Conversations with guests should be limited to business as far as courtesy will permit." Employees were expected to be polite, unobtrusive, inconspicuous, clean and punctual. They were expected to know and embody the Great Northern ideal of service. The booklet counseled, "Your attitude towards guests should be plain. You cannot, however, assume this attitude. It must not be an imitation." For example, in describing the acceptable attitude of Glacier Park telephone operators the booklet explained, "If you have cultivated the attributes of a true lady, your voice over the telephone will be all that our guests desire, you will be attentive to calls and under the most pressing circumstances you will find it easy to control your temper and to express your willingness to be helpful."[90] In requiring that staff be inconspicuous and restrained, the company instructed employees on how to behave as servants to an elite class and attempted to assure a tasteful atmosphere in the park. This ideal of service reinforced Hill's vision of the park as an exclusive resort by seeking to define service that would obfuscate all class difference that might become apparent between guests and staff.

In sending out information about the new park, in providing itineraries to friends and business acquaintances, and in making sure the Glacier staff was attentive to guests' needs, Louis Hill presented the park as an exclusive retreat for an elite American class who sought to transcend temporarily the social fluidity and disorder of modern urban-industrial life. To experience Glacier National Park according to Hill's vision was to encounter the best of America: the strenuous life, sublime wilderness, a healthy atmosphere, and an elite society balanced with all the comforts and conveniences of civilization. Glacier offered an atmosphere freed from commerce and free of class conflict. Here physical work like hiking and fishing brought immediate results, unlike the mind-numbing demands of bureaucratic management.

Here the machine was secondary to the scenery. Here the crass demands of the market were absent. Here the disruption of social unrest was subsumed by an established social hierarchy. Glacier National Park maintained the comforts and conveniences, along with the established social structure of eastern civility, while preserving the vigor, the immediacy, the authenticity of a simpler, everyday experience. In this ideal American wilderness white middle- and upper-class Americans maintained control of their status while reinvigorating themselves for the demands of modern industrial life.

The built and the natural environment in Glacier reinforced these culturally prescribed ideals. The image of wilderness represented in the rustic atmosphere of the Glacier Park Hotel rested on symbols of conquest—harvested forest, friendly Indians and their crafts, and the heads and skins of slain animals. These images suggested a timeless and harmonious past—an American frontier just civilized by Anglo-Americans, a simple, but strenuous life on the edge of wilderness. They marked an imagined past, which worked to provide security, authority, and legitimacy to those living in the present.[91] In effect, the rustic decor, which presented an ideal of the American frontier tamed by vigorous men, encouraged white upper-class tourists to identify with that triumph, to find power in recognizing themselves as the legitimate heirs of the white Anglo-Americans who had conquered the frontier.

Just as the Santa Fe highlighted the Hopi and Navajo at the Grand Canyon, so the Great Northern linked Glacier with the Blackfeet Indians, making them a central component of the frontier wilderness imagery. Not only were the cultural artifacts of the tribe appropriated to decorate the hotels and chalets, but the Indians and their culture were employed as a decorative presence throughout the park. Although the federal government in collusion with the railroad usurped the traditional territory of the Piegan, the Blood, and the Northern Blackfeet tribes (the three branches of the Blackfeet confederacy), forcing them onto an adjacent reservation, the Great Northern sanitized that history and adopted the Blackfeet as the official mascots of the park.[92] As one Great Northern brochure explained, "The Piegan or 'Blackfeet' Indians have made this region their gathering place for many years, and the Two Medicine country is rich in Piegan legend. To this day the Indians, whose reservation joins the park on the east, make many visits to the lakes where years ago, their ancestors held a double medicine ceremony. The Blackfoot is a friendly Indian, and the tribe has already endeared itself to hundreds of tourists who have visited Glacier National Park."[93] During the Glacier Park season a number of Indians from the reservation were paid to camp in a large tepee set up adjacent to the Glacier Park Hotel and perform a weekly powwow. The Great Northern employed another Indian to escort tourists from the Great Northern trains that stopped at the East Glacier Station up to the Glacier Park Hotel. J. A. Shoemaker noted in his 1913 report on Glacier that Big Top, one of the Blackfeet under the employ of the Great Northern, "made every No. 3 and No. 4 for sixty days and was able to take from twenty-five to seventy-five people over to see the Hotel each fifteen minute stop made by these trains. This feature was a means of sending at least 4000 boosters away from the Park this summer at a small cost."[94] The presence of "friendly" Blackfeet—nonthreatening but nonetheless "real" Indians, as represented by their authentic dress and ceremonies—became a central component of the Great Northern's constructed western wilderness.

Drawing on this established Indian theme, the Great Northern also set up two tepee camps for the 1914 season to promote walking tours of the park. Early in the season Louis Hill wrote to W. P. Kenney, vice president of the Great Northern, instructing him that the new Great Northern promotional booklets should call "attention to the fact that as an experiment we have established tepee village camps, one by the brook at the big hotel, where occupants may enjoy all the privileges of the hotel," and another at the Many Glacier Camp.[95] Each tepee contained four beds, which were rented for fifty cents a night. Promotional literature encouraged visitors who chose to eschew the hotels and chalets and tour the park on foot to follow "the dim and little-traveled trails of the Indian and ranger, into the wilderness, but always through a region of indescribable beauty, with new scenic surprises at every turn."[96] Thus Great Northern not only promised that tourists would have contact with authentic Indians but also allowed tourists to experience "real" Indian life firsthand.

This Indian imagery presented a double-sided message. The Blackfeet Indians with their animal-skin tepees, their colorful blankets, their feather and bead headdresses, and their primitive ceremonies represented an era and a lifestyle unscathed by the ravages of civilization. As one promotional pamphlet

The Great Northern used stereotypical images of the Blackfeet Indians to promote and define the tourist experience in Glacier National Park. Cover of *The Call of the Mountains* (1926). (Warshaw Collection of Business Americana, Archives Center, National Museum of American History, Smithsonian Institution)

explained, "[The Blackfeet] were one of the last tribes to come in contact with the white man and still retain most of their primitive customs and manner of living. Tourists are afforded an excellent opportunity to observe their rites and ceremonies. Their history and legends are perpetuated in the names of many of the mountains, lakes and glaciers of the Park."[97] Although the presence of the Blackfeet and their artifacts conveyed an ideal of wilderness and the primitive to elite white travelers searching for an alternative to modern society, their presence also reinforced a racial hierarchy. As objects on display, they implicitly became objects of conquest who had been subdued by a more advanced race. In consuming this Indian imagery, tourists implicitly became vicarious conquerors. Unlike the Santa Fe/Harvey's focus on Native Americans as foreign and exotic, the Great Northern encouraged tourists to embrace Indian culture as part and parcel of the American experience.

This primitive frontier imagery was tempered by the modern luxuries of the hotels and chalets. As one tourist noted, the Glacier Park Hotel had "everything that one would expect to find in a first-class city hotel."[98] A Great Northern brochure reiterated this point, describing the hotel as "combining in its rustic interior all the creature comforts and luxuries of the effete East."[99] Also, Glacier's image was further embellished by references to Europe and Asia, suggesting that the park offered not only wilderness but also sublime scenery and evidence of Manifest Destiny.

Even before the Great Northern began its building program, Glacier had been referred to as the "American Alps." Eight Swiss chalet complexes spaced along the mountain passes on lakes' edges and among the glacial valleys referred directly to design and development precedents well established in the Swiss Alps.[100] Designed by the Spokane, Washington, firm of Cutter and Malmgren, the chalet groups were constructed of materials native to the park. The log exteriors were covered by roofs "made of hand-made shakes surmounted by heavy logs and stones." The chalet designs were based on authentic Swiss models. The complexes which included a combination of dormitories, dining rooms and clubhouse chalets were situated between seven and twenty-five miles apart. As one promotional booklet explained, "The topography of the country and the conditions of the trails are such that men, women and children can make the journey between camps at any point in the park comfortably by horseback in one day."[101] Modeled on the hut

Many Glacier Hotel, Glacier National Park. Photograph by T. J. Hileman. (Great Northern Company Records, Minnesota Historical Society)

system in the Swiss Alps, the Great Northern encouraged tourists to walk or ride from one chalet camp to the next to fully enjoy the variety of wonders in the park, which was described as the "Switzerland of America."[102]

A second hotel, the Many Glacier, designed by the same architects who had done the Glacier, drew on the imagery of both the Glacier Park Hotel and the Swiss chalets. Designated as a hub for touring the interior of the park, promotional materials stated that it was "built to fit the heart of the park." The foundation of native stone was surmounted by a four-story gabled exterior of clapboards stained a dark brown, accented with yellow wooden trim and carved balconies with Swiss detailing. The plan was composed of five units: the lobby, the dormitory, a bridge, the dining hall, and the kitchen. "In place of being laid out along a formal ground plan," one promotional booklet explained, the five units were meant to "conform to the irregular outline of McDermott Lake's shoreline."[103] Like the Glacier Park Hotel, the interior of the Many Glacier contained a forest lobby. Although only half the size of the original, it had the same tree-trunk columns rising four stories to the ceiling and supporting a series of balconies opening on to each floor. The lobby also contained a large open campfire, rustic wooden furniture, buffalo heads, bear skins, Indian rugs and blankets, and an Indian frieze. The Many Glacier also combined the same rustic atmosphere with the modern conveniences of a city hotel. It housed a tailor shop, a barber shop, and a hospital, along with modern kitchen and laundry facilities. Like the other park facilities constructed by the Great Northern, the style and decor of the Many Glacier Hotel consciously drew on the same diverse array of references ranging from primitive to modern, rustic to civilized, Old World to New World, national to international to present the park as the essence of all the traditions that were united by American progress. As the final touch of Great Northern's development plan, the hotel completed the tourist infrastructure for the east side of the park.[104]

Just as Charles Whittlesley, architect for the Santa Fe, had used Swiss alpine details in his design of El Tovar, so the Great Northern chose to blatantly link the tourists experience in Glacier with established wilderness resorts in the Swiss Alps. American wilderness had long been understood in the context of European precedent. Since the eighteenth century nationalistic Americans, anxious about the status of the New World in relation to Old World civilization and tradition, looked to the American landscape with its abundant natural resources and its magnificent scenery to compensate for America's lack of an ancient past.[105] The vast wilderness of the American continent became pristine nature, uncorrupted by the hands of man and reflective of God's immanence. Scenic and sublime wilderness in America offered a natural legacy representative of American exceptionalism and even superiority over Europe that moved beyond human accomplishment and into God's realm. Writers, artists, cultural critics, and the like inscribed their own nationalistic desires and values onto the American landscape, implying that sublime scenery and natural richness evinced God's blessings bestowed on the New World. The cultural significance of American wilderness gained meaning from this implicit comparison to Europe. An idealized European civilization became the touchstone for America's natural legacy. To celebrate American wilderness was in some ways to declare that America was superior to the Old World.

The Great Northern was not simply trying to recreate Switzerland in America by using the Swiss motif in the park. Instead, the Swiss references served to locate the park in the context of European tourism. The company knew that it would be difficult to compete with the popularity of European tourism: the museums, the scenery, the remnants of antiquity, and its association with refinement and culture. The Great Northern counted on the Swiss motif to assure potential tourists that Glacier offered not only suitable tourist accommodations but also magnificent natural landscapes. In combination with wilderness imagery, the Swiss references suggested that American scenery represented the best of both worlds because it remained untainted by the effects of civilization. Domesticated American wilderness improved upon European precedents.

Japanese references further added to the eclectic mosaic presented in the park. The Japanese lanterns, the couple serving tea, and the cherry blossoms decorating the hotel dining areas embellished the oriental theme already exploited in the Great Northern's first-class transcontinental train, the Oriental Limited. The company prided itself on linking the United States and Asia through trade. The Great Northern Steamship Company, which connected Great Northern trains to Great Northern steamers, sailed to the Philippines, Japan, and China. In making these references to Asia, the Great Northern touted its role in both physically and economically linking the United States to Asian markets. The Oriental Limited was promoted as the physical symbol of this link.[106] The Japanese accents in the rustic decor of the Glacier Park Hotel added to this imagery, positioning the park, Great Northern, and by extension America in a global framework and suggesting that the strenuous life of the American frontier and domination of world trade were two sides of the same success story—Manifest Destiny. These eclectic references brought together to define the Glacier Park landscape embodied the vision of an American nation that borrowed from and built on an eclectic mix of cultures to create an ideal republican empire.

According to the Great Northern Railway, to See America First was to experience Teddy Roosevelt's robust western frontier: the home of the Black-

The Great Northern not only named its crack transcontinental train the Oriental Limited but also used oriental imagery in its advertising material and as design accents throughout the Glacier Park Hotel to highlight its connection with Asian trade. Cover of *The Oriental Limited*. (Warshaw Collection of Business Americana, Archives Center, National Museum of American History, Smithsonian Institution)

feet Indians conquered and befriended by brave westerners, the sight of unequaled sublime scenery, the physical promise of Manifest Destiny. It was to be refashioned as a modern-day explorer or an aristocratic sportsman and test strength and will against the wilderness. Simultaneously, the fast transcontinental train, the luxury hotels, and the European-style accouterments reminded tourists that they were never far from modern conveniences and civilized taste and style.

In addition to this massive building campaign, the Great Northern also initiated an extensive publicity campaign to package Glacier National Park as a brand-name tourist attraction. Borrowing the promotional strategies employed by the Northern Pacific and the Santa Fe, Great Northern brought artists and writers to the park and distributed brochures, souvenirs books, postcards, and publicity stories across the United States. Great Northern, however, took the promotional strategies of its competitors one step further by developing an extensive public relations campaign that centered on the See American First slogan. The railroad not only adopted the slogan as part of its logo and motto, but through a variety of promotional techniques, the company attempted to manufacture a national See America First movement. Great Northern hoped to capitalize on the fact that the general appeal of See America First would capture the public imagination and signify the tourist experience in Glacier National Park, connecting the general patriotic ideal with Great Northern Passenger service. In promoting the broader idea of See America First, the Great Northern sought to popularize a national tourism in addition to linking itself with a brand-name tourist destination.

Great Northern used the national press to publicize both Glacier National Park and the See America First idea. The Publicity Department distributed vast amounts of information via press releases and planted stories, and it encouraged those news papers and magazines that had advertising contracts with the Great Northern to editorialize in favor of See America First.[107] In the summer of 1911, H. A. Noble sent Louis Hill and W. P. Kenney a list of Sunday papers and periodicals containing "splendid publicity articles in reference to Glacier National Park and the Blackfeet Indian Reservation." He observed, "This form of publicity is along the lines of which I spoke to you regarding furnishing illustrated feature stories to Sunday papers and illustrated magazines. . . . After the story is once prepared it is merely a matter of clerical help to get it out and distributed to the proper papers." He concluded, "This is a form of publicity which I should like to expand in our field of operation as I think the amount of stuff we can get is almost unlimited."[108] The Great Northern rewarded those papers and magazines that published articles on the park by purchasing advertising space from them. Hill instructed Kenney to "always have an ad in these high-class papers when they give Glacier Park a write-up, that is the best time to use them. Later when there is no story, there is no advertising value. Wish you would see that it is so arranged hereafter."[109] Hoke Smith, formerly a reporter with the *Minneapolis Journal,* was hired by the Great Northern in 1910 to act as a one-man public relations department for the Great Northern and the park, planting as many promotional stories in as many newspapers as possible throughout the country.[110] One gimmick he used to work up "free publicity" for the park was to write to local newspapers and ask for information about the park, so that they would print detailed descriptions of the park and available tours and accommodations. His job was to keep the park before the public eye, and he and Louis Hill constantly exchanged ideas about various promotional stories and tactics.[111] In stories such as "America's New Wonderland—Glacier National Park," Smith touted the beautiful mountain scenery and the new tourist accommodations being constructed in the park, while in others he reported "newsworthy" information about people and events associated with the Great Northern and Glacier National Park.[112]

The Blackfeet Indians became one of the most popular sources for Great Northern publicity material. Smith used them both figuratively and literally to generate publicity for Glacier. Many of his articles featured stories about the park Indians, and in the spring of 1913 he organized an eastern tour for a group of Blackfeet as a publicity event. A number of Blackfeet were taken to New York City to participate in the Great Northern exhibit at the second annual Travel and Vacation Show. For twelve days the Indians camped in tepees on the roof of the McAlpin Hotel, apparently because, as Chief Three Bears was quoted as saying, "my people want air. . . . Hot room no good. Want plenty of outdoors."[113] At the Travel Show the Indians performed "war dances and other ceremonial exhibitions every half hour."[114] Shoemaker noted, "Many thousands, who attended the Travel and Vacation

Show, apparently came for the express purpose of seeing the Indians of Glacier National Park. As there was continued congestion around the Great Northern booth, which became so great in the last days of the show that we found it necessary to remove the Indians to a mezzanine floor in the building where they could be seen and heard, but would not be smothered by the crowd."[115] During their stay the Indians visited the Bronx Zoo, Fort Wadsworth, Governors Island, the aquarium, the subway, the Brooklyn Bridge, the ocean at Long Beach, Long Island, St. Patrick's Cathedral, and the Information Bureau of the *Brooklyn Eagle* newspaper. The press capitalized on their sightseeing excursions to publicize a kind of tourism in reverse in which awestruck Indians who had never before seen a large city wondered at the "mighty street canyons" and prayed to Manitou "that he would not permit the buildings to fall down on a poor Indian's head."[116]

Louis Hill and his Publicity Department also courted writers, just as his competitors did, hoping that small favors would result in Glacier Park stories. Hill encouraged writers to come to the park, enticing them with free passes over the Great Northern lines, providing suggestions for touring the park, and sending photographs for illustrations of their articles.[117] Hill and the Great Northern also developed close relations with some writers, utilizing their work to help construct a public image of the Great Northern in relation to the park. In March 1912 Robert D. Heinl, the Washington correspondent for *Leslie's,* published "The Man Who Is Building a Great National Park." The cover for that week featured an eagle soaring among snow-capped mountain peaks with the caption "See America First." Heinl painted a picture of Louis Hill as a selfless idealist who was generously donating his time and money to singlehandedly make Glacier National Park the most beautiful, accessible, and comfortable of the National Parks. Through Heinl's word's Hill became not only the ideal benefactor, presenting the nation with a national park, but also an ideal American. Heinl wrote, "Mr. Hill is an everlasting worker. His health is splendid, He is of sturdy physique. He believes in plenty of fresh air and never fears the cold or rain. His home life is ideal." In addition Heinl noted that Hill could sketch and paint. He was an avid photographer, "a well-trained music listener, and much interested in landscape gardening." Heinl concluded by noting that Hill was the author of "the magic slogan, 'See America First.'"[118] Heinl's composite of Hill served to advertise the new park and the accommodations being constructed by the Great Northern and to reinforce the public image of Louis Hill, masking his commercial motives for developing the park. In return Heinl was well rewarded; he was treated as a close friend of the Hill family. Louis Hill and his wife sent Heinl and his new wife a generous wedding present, and Hill gave him a free trip through the park with specific instructions to the park management to take good care of him.[119]

Similarly, the Great Northern courted Mary Roberts Rinehart, a popular writer famed for her short stories, comedies, and mystery thrillers. In 1915 Rinehart traveled through Glacier with noted western outdoorsman and dude rancher Howard Eaton. Rinehart and forty-one other "adventurers" trekked three hundred miles across the park from the Glacier Park Hotel up along the spine of the continental divide through mountain passes and glacial valleys to Lake McDonald on the west side of the park. She published her account of the Eaton expedition in a series of articles for *Collier's* magazine in April 1916.[120] Within a year it was published by Houghton Mifflin in book form.[121] Rinehart humbly remembered, "I wrote a small book on the trip through Glacier Park, with the unexpected result of advertising both Howard and the Park to a surprising degree. The little book became a guide book, and long before spring Howard's party for the following summer had grown to a hundred and fifty."[122] Louis Hill was immensely pleased with her work. He wrote, "I read your article the other evening and was very much interested. . . . I think the memory you have for details is marvelous and do not see how you can carry it all away with you. There is no question in our minds but that you have written the best article on the park, it is so readable and wakens and carries interest so easily."[123] In an effort to repay her for her unsolicited services and to encourage her to continue writing about and advertising the park, Hill went on to invite her and her family back to Glacier the following summer. Excerpts from her See America First series were incorporated soon after into the Glacier Park publicity material, and Rinehart published a number of additional stories and another book about her further travels in Glacier.[124] In return Hill continued to invite her and her family to visit the park at the railroad's expense.[125]

Throughout the teens and twenties the Great Northern continued to follow this policy of courting and supporting writers who wished to publicize

Popular periodicals such as *Leslie's* helped publicize and popularize Great Northern's See America First campaign. Cover of *Leslie's Illustrated Weekly*, 7 March 1912. (Courtesy of Enoch Pratt Free Library, Baltimore, Maryland)

Mary Roberts Rinehart camping in Glacier National Park. Rinehart's books, articles, and short stories published in such popular magazines as the *Saturday Evening Post* amounted to free publicity for the Great Northern, and Louis Hill rewarded Rinehart by subsidizing summer trips to Glacier for Rinehart and her family. From Mary Roberts Rinehart, *Through Glacier Park: Seeing America First with Howard Eaton* (1916). (Courtesy of the Library of Congress)

the park through their prose. M. E. Holtz and Katherine Bemis, who wrote *Glacier National Park, Its Trails and Treasures,* James Willard Schultz, who wrote *Blackfeet Indian Tales,* Grace Flandrau, who produced the "Seven Sunsets" booklet for the Great Northern, and Agnes Laut, who wrote a number of articles about the park, were all encouraged and supported by the Great Northern.[126]

The Great Northern, like the Santa Fe, also hired and lured visual artists to Glacier in an effort to publicize the park. Early on the chalets at Belton were used as summer studios for painters and photographers invited to the park by the Great Northern.[127] The Great Northern Publicity Department sent out "pictorial mailing cards [and] photogravure reproductions of scenes in the park" to all members of the American Federation of Arts to entice artists to Glacier.[128] In the summer of 1914 the company invited the painter

John Fery, famed for his painting of the El Tovar at the Grand Canyon, to come work in the park. Hill had arranged for Fery to set up a special tent at the various camps in Glacier where he could sketch and paint. The resulting paintings were then to "be left at the several camps" to "be disposed of" later. Advertising agent W. R. Mills wrote to the manager of the Glacier Park Hotel company to prepare for Mr. Fery's stay: "Mr. Hill asks that you make arrangements to provide Mr. Fery with the necessary transportation facilities, make arrangements so that he can procure provisions and such accommodations that he may require at the various camps, move his tent from place to place for him as he may require. We will supply Mr. Fery with such canvases, paints, stretchers, etc as is needed during his time in the Park."[129] Fery's paintings were later used to illustrate many Glacier Park brochures.

Following the example set by the Northern Pacific and the Santa Fe, Louis Hill sought to help transform the Glacier landscape into scenery by publicizing visual representations of the park. Just after the establishment of Glacier National Park, Hill invited artist Louis Akin, also famous for his Grand Canyon paintings, to spend the summer of 1910 in Glacier. Akin produced a number of sketches and a large painting of Iceberg Lake. Hill made every effort to bring the painting public attention. That fall Hill tried to have the painting included in the Corcoran competition for exhibition. He wrote to the chief clerk of the Department of the Interior, "The picture is wonderful in every way and I know will interest you . . . and others interested in Glacier National Park. . . . It is one of the finest mountain scenery pictures I have ever seen. I am writing you, and suggest, if possible, that you might interest some of the Corcoran people, or in some way see that the committee gives him [Akin] a chance to exhibit his picture as it will do the Glacier National Park a lot of good to have it in the show if they accept it."[130] Hill also suggested that the painting be "hung in one of the committee rooms when Congress is in session and give them an idea of what the scenery is out there."[131] Although his lobbying efforts were unsuccessful because the Corcoran competition had already closed, his motives were clear: he hoped that Akin's visual representation of Glacier wilderness would capture the imaginations of influential Washingtonians and inspire Congress to appropriate sufficient funds for the development of the park.

Early in 1909 Hill also enlisted the service of scenic photographer Fred H.

Kiser to help publicize the Glacier area through his hand-colored photographs. Kiser, who had been the official photographer at the Louis and Clark Exposition in 1905, had an established commercial photography studio in Portland, Oregon, and was renowned in the area for his ability to capture dramatic images of rugged mountain scenery and for his true-to-life hand-colored photographs.[132] Hill first became interested in Kiser's work after seeing some of his colored photographs of Lake Chelan, Washington.[133] He purchased a number of these photographs to use for Great Northern promotional material and postcards and put the originals on display at the St. Paul Auditorium.[134] After some discussion between Hill and Kiser about copyright privileges, Kiser admitted, "For the past three or four years, I have studied the grandeur of the scenery along your lines with the idea that someday I might be able to get you interested in making a set of 'Kiser' photographs for advertising purposes. If at any time you feel that you could give me the assistance needed to take up the work, let me know when I shall take the pleasure in submitting a proposition."[135] Hill responded to Kiser in February saying that he hoped they could make "a mutually advantageous arrangement."[136]

By the early spring of 1909 Kiser had signed a contract with Great Northern and was working with Hill to prepare an itinerary for photographing the scenery along the railroad's main line. In April Hill sent a priority list for Kiser to passenger agent A. L. Craig: "I would suggest as first in importance the Lake McDonald District, and St. Mary's and Flathead Lake. After that the Cascades, Wenatchee, Chelan and the upper Columbia."[137] Sites in the proposed park were first on his list, and Hill kept in close contact with Kiser's movements throughout the summer to make sure that he photographed the most spectacular views throughout the area. In late August Hill wrote to Kiser inquiring about his progress: "Have you taken any pictures of the St. Mary's Country. Would like to have a complete set of photographs of that country, as it is probably the best on the line and important to have high class photos in order to bring pressure to bear to get Glacier Park Bill through the next season."[138] Hill hoped that Kiser's colored photographs of the spectacular scenery in the area could stimulate support for the park bill that was then under consideration.

Great Northern employed Kiser to photograph the scenery in Glacier and along the Great Northern lines for four seasons, from 1909 to 1913.[139]

Kiser also established a photographic concession in Glacier Park, "selling and renting Kodaks, selling Kodak supplies, carrying on the work of developing and printing for the public at several hotels in the Park, as well as, sell[ing] all kinds of photo reproductions, photo novelties and post cards."[140] Kiser was noted as one of "the best mountain photographers in the country."[141] Great Northern displayed his enlargements in cities throughout the East in order to promote the park after its establishment in 1910 and used his photographs to illustrate both park advertisements and tourist brochures. By focusing on dramatic mountain peaks and picturesque views, Kiser's photographs reinforced the ideal of wilderness as pristine landscape untouched by the evils of modern civilization that the Great Northern sought to promote. Through the dissemination of his work, the landscape of Glacier was transformed into scenery.

Great Northern's relationship with popular periodicals and newspapers, journalists and writers, visual artists and photographers defined the See America First campaign devised to promote Glacier National Park. Great Northern actively produced advertising and publicity material by employing publicity men, writers, artists, and photographers to reproduce and disseminate visual and verbal images of Glacier, and indirectly promoted the park by boosting a general version of the See America First idea. Just after Great Northern's unveiling of the See America First campaign, H. A. Noble sent Louis Hill a number of editorials devoted to the subject. He observed, "In view of the fact that the attached [See America First/Great Northern] advertisement appeared in various sections of the country the last week of May and early in June, I am inclined to think that all of them were inspired by our efforts. The remarkable part of it is, that we have no contracts with any of these papers."[142] Hill responded, "It is certainly a remarkable circumstance that this matter should be taken up through so many sources at the same time. Evidently we struck a good line."[143] In appropriating See America First as their motto and logo, the Great Northern stumbled on a phrase that had the potential for widespread appeal because it transcended the specific commercial objectives surrounding the marketing of Great Northern passenger service. "See America First" worked to mask the act of promotion and consumption involved in tourism. The motto helped transform touring into a ritual of patriotism with widespread popular appeal. The campaign comprised a multifaceted promotional strategy that involved reshaping Glacier into an idealized image of American wilderness and then disseminating both the visual and verbal images of the park throughout the national print media network. The Great Northern inundated the press with their advertisements and promotional illustrations and articles. As one Glacier tourist remarked, "The park is so largely advertised it seems as though I saw it in everything."[144]

In the summer of 1911 Great Northern organized a ten-day tour of the new park for a number of journalists.[145] Representing papers from Chicago, Minneapolis, St. Paul, and Seattle, and including an artist, a travelogue lecturer, Great Northern passenger agent Howard Noble, and William Burns of the U.S. Forest Service, the group began their tour on 12 August 1911 at the Glacier Park Hotel on Lake McDonald. W. O. Chapman of the *Chicago Evening Post*, who kept a daily log of the expedition that was later published by the Great Northern as a promotional brochure, characterized that first day in terms of opposites, juxtaposing the overly civilized with the primitive:

> On this day and at this place assembled a corps of hothouse plants, city workers, persons who live under roofs, labor in skyscrapers, eat off a table and sleep in beds, and whose daily journeys are made by automobiles, suburban trains or street cars. They organized an exploring party to tread paths trod before only by Indians, trappers, the early woodsmen and by velvet-pawed beasts of prey. . . . This is the first stopping place in Glacier National Park. . . . This is the last evidence of civilization the explorers are to see until they emerge from the park a week or ten days hence.[146]

The group traveled from Avalanche Basin, where they fished and explored Sperry Glacier, over Gunsight Pass to Gunsight Camp, then to Red Eagle Lake and St. Mary's River, where they fished and camped, and then back to the railroad at Midvale. They experienced not only the delights and hardships of packing across the mountains and valleys of the park on horseback, but also explored the living glaciers in the park, fished, camped in the open, and viewed the pristine mountain scenery. This tour became the basis for the first series of promotional articles, some of which were made into booklets and distributed by Great Northern as part of its See America First campaign.[147] In addition, it set the tone for ensuing Great Northern promotional strategies and material. The company continued to sponsor tours of the park for journalists.[148] Like this first sponsored tour, subsequent tours generated widespread newspaper publicity for the park and Great Northern development projects.[149]

Great Northern publicity material drew on an ideal of American wilderness to promote the park. All the published accounts resulting from the 1911 journalist tour centered on the juxtaposition between civilization and wilderness. Journalist Clarence L. Speed of the *Chicago Record Herald* began his eulogy of the park with a short characterization of his own experience:

> An August sun blazed down on a parching continent. . . . Dwellers in the great cities mopped their streaming brows as they bent over their desks in field offices. . . . On the edge of a rim of rock sat two men from the city, escaped from the bondage for a few short weeks. . . . Three thousand feet below lay a little lake, blue-green in the high light. Its surface, which, mirrorlike in a calm, reflected every rocky peak on the opposite side of the valley, was broken here and there, by ripples made by the leaping trout. . . . As far as the eye could reach—and the range of vision extended for miles and miles—there was not a human habitation, not a curl of smoke betraying the presence of man. . . . And yet these travelers, but forty-eight hours before, had been dodging street cars, and starting at the honk of an automobile horn.[150]

For him, the cool, quiet solitude of the park was escape from the "bondage" of the city. The peaceful silence of the mountains had meaning because of the absence of city traffic and city toil. A. C. Brokaw of the *Minneapolis Tribune* expanded on this theme, describing the park as "God's country not yet despoiled by the devastating hand of civilization."[151] Similarly, Tom Dillon of the *Seattle Post Intelligencer* quoted a "bone-weary" Glacier Park packer as saying, "Here is where God sat when he made America." Dillon went on to explain, "Glacier Park has no sideshow for garrulous trippers; it has no Coney Island attractions; it has no geysers. . . . Those who have roamed the world with open eyes say earnestly that there is no spot where Nature has so condensed her wonders and run riot with such utter abandon; where she has carved and hewn with such unrestrained fancy and scattered her jewels with so reckless a hand."[152]

This juxtaposition between civilization and wilderness rested on gendered distinctions between the urban tenderfoot and the rugged mountain guide. In his "Diary of an Amateur Explorer in Glacier National Park," W. O.

Cover of *Glacier National Park: Where Fighting Trout Leap High*, a promotional guide (Great Northern Railway, 1912). (Warshaw Collection of Business Americana, Archives Center, National Museum of American History, Smithsonian Institution)

Chapman satirized the wilderness experience in the park by playing on the term, "amateur explorer." The city journalists were likened to "hot house plants" who agreed to tour the park only after "they had abundant assurance . . . that the Indian and the beast of prey would be kept at a safe distance."[153] Their city-soft muscles quickly grew tired after a day in the saddle. They were "soft-footed children," but, as Chapman explained, "Why try to commune with nature in its virgin state if the communing is to be done on tinted and perfumed paper, or by telephone?"[154] Although the metaphors Chapman chose to describe the journalists were not overtly gendered, their connotations suggest that modern city living had feminized these men, and that their experience in the park, close to nature without the comforts of city living, reinvigorated them and purged them of their overly civilized affectations. Tom Dillon similarly described the Lewis's Glacier Hotel at Belton Station, where the party began as the meeting place of civilization and wilderness: "It is the outpost of the white shirt, the stiff hat and the hobble-gown. They are seen here fraternizing with the blue flannel, the sombrero and the divided skirt."[155] Here, Dillon used fussy and restrictive city fashion to evoke the overly civilized, while practical rustic clothing symbolized those accustomed to the wilderness. The images created by these two wardrobes again suggest that city and wilderness carried with them specific gendered connotations. The Great Northern imagined their audience as overworked men, stifled by the routines of modern business life. Park publicity material suggested that the physical rewards of camping, hiking, and fishing promised sanctuary from the tedium and emptiness of middle-class work, which was measured by time and salary and produced only the intangible rewards of profit. Great Northern constructed a masculine world of leisure in opposition to the masculine world of the market. As Speed observed, "The man who feels the call of the wild in his veins, will be able to get back to the primitive in Glacier National Park."[156]

These characterizations of the park locate it within a cultural context of antimodernism, nostalgia for the frontier, and millennial American thought, all of which reflected a growing feeling of ambiguity and ambivalence toward the transformation of the United States into a complex, modern nation-state. In 1898 John Muir wrote, "Thousands of nerve-shaken, overly civilized people are beginning to find out that going to the mountains is going home, and that mountain parks and reservations are useful not only as fountains of timber and irrigating rivers, but as fountains of life."[157] This concern for the "overly civilized," for overwork and nervousness, drudgery and bondage, marked an increasing anxiety about "modern" life during the late nineteenth and early twentieth century. "By the late nineteenth century," one historian has explained, "the feeling of overcivilization signified more than just a provincial revival of republican moralism. It was a sign of broader transatlantic dissatisfaction with modern culture in all its dimensions: its ethic of self-control and autonomous achievement, its cult of science and technical rationality, its worship of material progress." Modern life seemed increasingly empty, sterile, "unreal." As a result, many disillusioned Americans "sought 'authentic' alternatives to the apparent unreality of modern existence."[158] As these newspapermen were shown, Glacier National Park, with its "towering snow capped peaks," its "dashing mountain streams," its "little hard fleshed trout," and its "smells of the forest, moist and fragrant,"[159] offered real experience, a temporary escape from the modern routine and a chance for regenerative play.

The association of the park with an ideal of the West further elucidated the growing concern during the early twentieth century for the future of modern American society.[160] In part this anxiety was characterized and understood in gendered and racially defined terms, and is perhaps best represented in the personal mythology of Teddy Roosevelt and his national project. Roosevelt's turn west after the deaths of his wife and his mother and his rejection of the eastern establishment for the realities and hardships of cattle ranching on the Dakota frontier provided the raw material for his view of American history as proof of the superiority of the Anglo Saxon race and its reliance on strenuous manhood.[161] The frontier experience for Roosevelt became a "means for generating the lost vigor of his class, and reversing the course of its political and biological degeneracy."[162] Scholars have argued that Roosevelt's myth of the hunter "was a rationale for class rule by a new aristocracy," but beyond this it was also a rationale for patriarchy.[163] In an address given before the Hamilton Club composed of conservative and wealthy Chicagoans, Roosevelt outlined his ideal of the virtuous citizenship in the terms he had used to characterize his western experience. Hard work, perseverance, and virility defined his ideal of the "strenuous life." In conclusion, he admonished his audience, "Let us then boldly face the life of strife, resolute to do our duty well and manfully; resolute to uphold righteousness by deed and by word; resolute to be both honest and brave, to serve high ideals, yet to use practical methods. . . . It is only through strife, through hard and dangerous endeavor, that we shall ultimately win the goal of true national greatness."[164] In his experience, the West came to stand for the potential of American society because it embodied the principles of self-reliance, rugged individualism, and vigorous manhood. As one western historian has observed, "The Roosevelt generation's sense of instability led to a general search for stabilizing forces in a fluctuating age." Roosevelt and many of his followers turned to the West as an embodiment of the "true America." In celebrating the West, they chose to emphasize the images that masked the threats of an increasingly urban-industrial society. Wilderness, uncivilized landscapes, and open spaces were imbued with the qualities of manliness, independence, and egalitarianism, in contrast with the East, which was seen as "industrial, urban, elitist, ethnically heterogeneous, and racially mixed," all those things that threatened the American mission.[165] The representation of Glacier Park as untouched wilderness—barren mountains and forests "populated by bear and mountain lion," as "deep and dark and 'wild' as in the days when Lewis and Clark first blazed a trail through the vastness of the West"—tapped into these culturally selected meanings.[166]

In 1921 Emily Bayne Bosson of New York wrote to Hill while visiting the park. In her letter, she recalled an earlier year, sitting around a fire at a friend's while Hill talked about the park, and she admitted that his "vivid description" had inspired her and her husband to travel to Glacier. She wrote in thanks, "This is just a little note of warm congratulation of the vision you have had for the West; every stand taken against super civilized modern life, is a right stand for the American people, if they are going to continue their energetic leadership of straight forward accomplishment in this present day world." She concluded, "See America First is a great slogan and it is splendid that you have opened up such a country for us to glory in. It is so uniquely America. Our spoiled East would gain immeasurably by getting some big free spirit of the West, that can only be acquired on the trails and tracks in places like Glacier."[167] Unlike Northern Pacific's Yellowstone or Santa Fe's Grand Canyon, Glacier, according to Louis Hill's vision, was not a wonderland or a foreign landscape to be discovered by tourists; rather, it represented the coming together of all the forces that defined the essence of America. It signified the culmination of an array of American myths about the nation's frontier past, Manifest Destiny, the republican tradition, and white elite status. Glacier, as shaped and promoted by the Great Northern, played out the ideal of the West as the embodiment of the true America.

In promoting and packaging Yellowstone, the Grand Canyon, and Glacier as brand-name tourist attractions, the Northern Pacific, the Santa Fe, and the Great Northern worked to boost their public images as nation builders while forging a national clientele. Just as other corporations adopted brand-name packaging and national advertising strategies to take advantage of the emerging national market, the transcontinental railroad corporations sought to construct and link themselves with iconographic landscapes that would capture the nation's attention and lure passengers to their lines. In building on the promotional strategies developed by the Northern Pacific and the Santa Fe, the Great Northern took these strategies one step further by linking their brand-name attractions with the broader idea of See America First. In this way, Great Northern succeeded at promoting and popularizing a national tourism where earlier western boosters had failed.

In fact, Great Northern's promotional campaign succeeded beyond the railroad's imagination. In April 1912 Louis Hill wrote to the solicitor for the Great Northern, inquiring whether "See America First" could be copyrighted. Although Hill was elated by the popularity of the slogan, he also wanted to make sure that the Great Northern could assure continued control over the use of the slogan. As a corporate motto and logo, it was essential that "See America First" primarily signify touring in Glacier National Park on the Great Northern Railway. Although the company sanctioned any general publicity generated around the See America First idea, Hill understood that excessive use of the slogan by outside interests might diffuse and abstract the meaning. The Great Northern solicitor did not respond to Hill's inquiry with encouraging news. According to copyright law, "See America First" could be registered as a trade name or trademark "in connection with some specific picture or symbol." However, "the phrase standing alone could not be registered as a trade name, nor could its long continued use in connection with any other picture or symbol." According to the terms of copyright law, the phrase itself was too general to be exclusively controlled by one individual or company. Anyone could use the slogan to promote his or her own interests. The solicitor concluded, "As I understand it, this company has perhaps used the phrase more than any other and began its use first, so that I do not think it possible for it to be deprived of the use thereof hereafter by any action which other companies may take."[168] Although Great Northern could never be prevented from using the slogan, it had to count on its own promotional and publicity resources to disseminate and control its meaning.

The popularity of the phrase, however, quickly surpassed the Great Northern's control. During the nineteen teens and twenties, a variety of interests promoted the idea of a national tourism using the See America First slogan. In the process, a canon of national attractions began to emerge sanctioned by the state. Under the leadership of the National Park Service, the United States government, in partnership with private corporations, began to define and promote a national tourism as a ritual of American citizenship. In the process, the national parks were transformed into a system of national assets, and tourism became integrally linked to national identity.

3

THE NATIONAL PARKS AS
NATIONAL ASSETS

Our national park system has come definitely to mean to the people
what . . . our flag means, namely the majesty and pride of the nation. It
is something extraordinary, inspiring, greater in quality and variety
than the similar possessions of any other nation—and it is tangible,
visible to all the world. Finally, it is idealistic in high degree, the con-
crete visible expression of a quality of mind and spirit which Americans
believe that they possess in higher degree than other people.
—Robert Sterling Yard, 1923

*I*N HIS REPORT TO the secretary of the Department of Interior in 1915,
Mark Daniels, the general superintendent and landscape engineer of the
national parks, noted, "We, as a people, have been accused of lacking in that
love of country which our neighbors in Europe are so plentifully blessed."
Advocating the development of a tourist infrastructure in the parks and the
creation of a centralized national park bureau, Daniels continued, "To love a
thing one must know it. . . . Ours is a great country, stretching from sea to
sea, and a knowledge of all its glories is given to but few. What more noble
purpose could our national parks serve than to become the instrument by
which the people shall be lured into the far corners of their land that they
may learn to love it?" Daniels believed that one of the central functions the
parks served was to stimulate patriotism. "For one who will encompass the
circuit of our parks," he explained, "passing over the great mesas of Colorado,

crossing the painted desert, threading the sparkling Sierra Nevada, and viewing the glaciers and snow-capped peaks of the great Northwest will surely return with a burning determination to love and work for, and if necessary to fight for and die for the glorious land which is his."[1] Daniels was not alone in linking the development of tourism in the national parks to a national consciousness.

Between 1910 and 1929 the nascent Park Service transformed the national parks from a collection of independent scenic wonders managed by various private railroad corporations into a system of nationalized tourist attractions overseen by an official, independent government bureau. As the larger political culture debated traditional notions of liberalism, the power of the federal government, the process of reform, and the issue of nationalism, park administrators participated by negotiating between private corporations and the federal government in an effort to define and promote the parks as a unified national system. For the first time the state became actively involved in the promotion of national tourism. Building on the broad structural changes that transformed America into a modern, urban-industrial nation-state—the construction of a national transportation network, the solidification of a national market, the development of a national print media, and the emergence of an economy of leisure—a small branch of the federal bureaucracy tentatively embraced tourism as a means of evoking a popular national consciousness that could "rally the citizenry in a collective ritual of nation building and national unification" and thus reinforce the emerging nation-state.[2] Tourism embodied a unique and symbolically powerful double-edged sword: it represented a form of consumption that depended on and supported the growing infrastructure of the nation state, and it offered a means of generating patriotism, thus reinforcing the democratic ideal of the nation. In mediating between the market and the nation, it became a kind of virtuous consumption. In effect, the Park Service, in defining and promoting the parks as national tourist attractions, tried to reconcile the democratic ideal of the nation with an organic ideal of the nation in an attempt to come to terms with the emerging nation-state.

PROMOTING THE PARKS

After a twenty-year hiatus following the establishment of Yellowstone National Park in 1872, the decades flanking the turn of the century witnessed a flurry of national park legislation with the creation of ten new national parks.[3] During this period the national park idea was transformed from an implicit ideal embodied by Yellowstone into a reality manifested by a system of national parks and monuments. However, no concomitant system emerged to define and manage the parks. Officially, three separate bureaus within the federal government oversaw the parks: the Department of the Interior, the Department of War, and the Department of Agriculture. Within the private sphere a variety of organizations vied for control over the images and meaning of the parks. Preservation groups such as the American Civic Association and the Sierra Club worked to define an ideal of nature preservation embodied by the parks. At the same time, various transcontinental railroads adopted public relations strategies that allied themselves with individual parks. Consequently, the national character of the parks was a contested ideal. The parks were "wonderlands," nature preserves, scenic assets, but there was no one voice that defined their national character. As various constituencies contended over the use and the meaning of the new parks, park advocates ranging from railroad interests to nature lovers began to seek some means of unifying park support and organizing park management.

In 1910 Allen Chamberlain, a prominent member of the American Civic Association and an enthusiastic outdoorsman, explained in an article published in *Outlook* magazine that despite the rapid establishment of national parks and monuments, the people of America knew relatively little about them. "During a recent trip which included several of the National forests, parks, and monuments," Chamberlain noted that "even those individuals whose tastes and inclinations lead them to take the greatest interest in such affairs have but an indefinite idea as to the actual location and extent of our National parks, to say nothing about the details as the statutory provisions which relate to them." Chamberlain conceded that the parks were becoming increasingly popular and people were growing increasingly interested in visiting them. But, he explained, "there are instances where the transportation facilities and the living accommodations now afforded are not calculated to make them attractive vacation resorts." "In short," he argued, "the Nation has in these parks a natural resource of enormous value to its people, but it is not being developed and utilized as it might be. . . . There is considerable danger, moreover, that unless the public is permitted to learn more about these properties selfish interests are likely to steal an important part of our birth-right." Thus Chamberlain urged that the parks be "fully protected against every encroachment." He concluded by suggesting that "a comprehensive codification and amendment of the National parks statutes" should be developed by Congress to assure the protection and management of the parks.[4]

Chamberlain was not alone in his concern for the parks and in his criticism of park management. Secretary of Interior Richard A. Ballinger had drafted a bill for the establishment of a bureau to oversee the parks at the request of the American Civic Association in 1910. His replacement, Walter L. Fisher, devoted a session to the issue at the First Annual National Parks Conference in 1911 held in Yellowstone National Park and also raised the issue in his annual report of 1911.[5] Embracing Fisher's recommendation, President Taft, in his annual message to congress in 1911, reiterated the need for a bureau of national parks.[6] Many others agreed. Yet opposition abounded. Foes of big government, Forest Service supporters, and various other private interests all held a variety of opposing attitudes toward the establishment of a national park bureau. Park advocates quickly ascertained that a widespread campaign to promote and popularize the parks was essential to the establishment of such a bureau. As one newspaper editorialized, "It is time steps were taken to secure wider publicity for the parks over which the government has assumed control. The public is only indifferently acquainted with the charms of many of these places of interest. . . . Heretofore it has been the government's policy to rest content with assuming control of the lands and posting rules and regulations regarding the conduct of visitors. What is needed, however, is a national campaign of education, such as Secretary Fisher has decided upon."[7] An extensive lobbying campaign ensued to generate the necessary popular support for the passage of such legislation.

Responding to the call for increased publicity of the parks, the administrators in the Department of Interior drew on meager funds to initiate a small publicity campaign. Clement Ucker, chief clerk of the Miscellaneous Section of the department, recounted that when he was appointed to the department he began "cast[ing] about for a method of bringing the parks before the people." A "conservative method of magazine, newspaper, and periodical articles under the supervision of Mr. L. F. Schmeckebier, Clerk in Charge of Publications" resulted. Following the failure in 1911 of the first national park bureau bill, the department in December of that year put together a small exhibition of photographs garnered from various railroad collections that was to be made available to libraries and other institutions.[8] The first set of photographs generated such high demand that a second set of photographs was compiled in 1912. In addition a catalog "containing short descriptions quoted from well known writers" was printed in connection with the exhibit. These traveling photo exhibits were displayed by libraries and various other institutions and used as the Department of Interior's official exhibit for various trade shows and expositions, such as the Travel and Vacation Exhibition held at New York's Grand Central Palace in March 1913.[9]

Ucker and Schmeckebier also encouraged the cooperation of railroad companies and movie industries in helping to popularize the parks. Building on the dissemination of photographic images, Ucker encouraged the Kinemacolor Moving Picture Company to make scenic films of the parks. Early in 1912 the secretary of the interior sent out a letter to the superintendents of a number of the major parks requesting that they submit an itinerary detailing the most scenic attractions and the most suitable time for "taking Kinemacolor moving pictures."[10] The company had arranged with the Department of the Interior to secure moving pictures of the Grand Canyon, Yellowstone, Yosemite, Glacier, Mount Rainier, and Crater Lake in order to create what they believed was the first series of scenic views in the principal national parks. Drawing on the growing popularity of the See America First idea, it was called the See America First series.[11] In addition to securing support from the Department of Interior in the form of permission for filming and detailed itineraries, Kinemacolor received financial assistance from business interests connected with the parks, including the Great Northern Railroad, associated with Glacier, the Holmes Transportation Company, associated with Yellowstone, and Will G. Steel, president of the Crater Lake Company. Owing to the lack of government funding for publicity, the department was forced to rely on this cooperative association established between the department and businesses connected with the parks in an effort to secure outside funding. Ucker explained the situation in connection with the Kinemacolor association: "I am strongly of the opinion that the Kinemacolor moving picture offers the best fields for national park publicity. It is for this reason that the Department called the attention of the Kinemacolor Company to the opportunities in the parks and communicated with the roads and concessionaires with a view to obtaining cooperation. This office has no funds that are available for use in connection with this work, its powers in the premises being limited to bringing the matter to the attention of the persons interested."[12]

Although the photographic exhibition and Kinemacolor's See America First film series represented the most extensive examples of the Department of the Interior's public relations work to promote the parks, Schmeckebier also tried to capitalize on other sources for park publicity. Drawing from the photographic collection he had compiled, Schmeckebier wrote an illustrated overview of the national parks and monuments for the June 1912 issue of *National Geographic* magazine. The article briefly highlighted the scenic wonders of the twelve existing national parks and the twenty-eight existing national monuments. While providing brief historical and descriptive overviews of the principal parks and monuments with a synopsis of touring possibilities, the article was lavishly illustrated with over forty photographs gathered not only from the U.S. Geological Survey but also from various businesses and park enthusiasts, including Great Northern and the Southern Pacific Railway, among others.[13] Building on this material, Schmeckebier delivered a slide lecture at the 1912 Trans-Mississippi Commercial Congress.

In addition, the department used its scant funds to develop in-house publications overviewing the parks. Schmeckebier compiled a series of small pamphlets detailing the rules and regulations and the scientific interests embodied in the parks. Seven pamphlets, "giving general information regarding the means of seeing the various parks," were issued in 1912. The department issued a series of pamphlets that detailed the geological history of the national parks, including *The Geological History of the Yellowstone National Park*, by Arnold Hague, *The Geological History of Crater Lake Oregon*, by J. S. Diller, *Some Lakes of Glacier National Park*, by M. J. Elrod, *Sketch of Yosemite National Park and an Account of the Origin of Yosemite and Hetch Hetchy Valleys*, by F. E. Mathes, and *Geysers*, by Walter Harvey Weed. These supplemented two earlier pamphlets on the archaeology of Mesa Verde National Park by J. W. Fewkes that had been issued by the Bureau of Ethnology in 1909 and 1911.[14]

Lack of funding and fragmented park management greatly restricted early park publicity efforts on the part of Department of Interior officials. Long waits for information and insubstantial pamphlets filled with rules and regulations and dry scientific information hampered tourists who were simply interested in traveling to the parks and finding out what there was to see. One park supporter provided a satirical assessment of the value of this early park publicity. "The average American," he explained, "who fain would journey to his native land to imbibe its splendor and revel in its wonders and who in his enthusiasm applied to this Government for information—inspirational information—has experienced the sensation of having his heated imagination plunged precipitately into a tank of freezing water, U.S. Inspected and Passed." According to this critic, the average tourist who applied to the Department of Interior for information regarding the parks would "after so long a time . . . receive two or three booklets printed on the cheapest paper. They gave him a digest of the geology of Glacier National, say, and told him just how long he would be imprisoned if he visited the park and violated any of the hundred and one regulations and rules promulgated by the Government for its management." When the disgruntled tourist then persevered and asked for information describing the parks, "in the course of a week he would get an acknowledgment of the receipt of his letter by the Interior Department, which department would regretfully inform him that owing to lack of funds it had no illustrated booklets on the National Parks available for free distribution," and the tourist would be directed to write the superintendent of printed documents for a fifteen-cent pamphlet. The resulting pamphlets, if their supply was not exhausted, would be "fearfully" written scientific descriptions of the geological features in the parks illustrated by photographs.[15] Although exaggerated, this satirical description of early park publicity was not far from the truth.

Scant funds for publicity and lack of a centralized bureau to manage the parks resulted in a diffuse ideal of the national park system. The parks were touted individually for their varied scenic, scientific, and historic attractions. Even Schmeckebier's attempt to provide a unified overview of the parks in his *National Geographic* article "Our National Parks" resulted only in a survey of the parks and monuments tied together with a brief chronological history of their creation. The article celebrated the geysers of Yellowstone, the glaciers of Mount Rainier and Glacier Park, the water falls, cliffs, and valleys of Yosemite, the big trees of General Grant and Sequoia, and the cliff dwellings of Mesa Verde. But the only thing that linked the parks was the political act of their creation—the fact that these "tracts of public land" had "been withdrawn from settlement and private exploitation and dedicated by act of Congress as national parks for the benefit and enjoyment of the people."[16] There was no attempt to link them as a national system of tourist attractions. Just as the promotion of a national tourism remained dispersed and fragmented as various private interests worked to capitalize on the growing tourist market, so the national character of the parks as a system remained vague and ill defined as park supporters and administrators struggled to unify and define the system.

The growing popularity of the See America First idea combined with the campaign to establish a separate parks bureau paved the way for a redefinition of the parks and a new phase of park publicity supported by Woodrow Wilson's incoming Cabinet. Franklin Knight Lane came to the office of the secretary of interior in March 1913 with a reform agenda. At the time of his appointment the department was an unwieldy collection of seemingly unrelated bureaus and federal institutions linked mostly by the fact that they were all in the same department. Lane hoped to organize and streamline the bureau, while encouraging increased access to resources through what he considered benign government regulation. "The major challenge Lane faced in his new position," according to his biographer, "transcended the stewardship of this wide array of disconnected administrative units that made up the Interior Department. In the spring of 1913, the department ... was in the midst of a debate about the degree and type of control the federal government should exercise over the nation's natural resources." The management of the national parks represented one component of that debate. In the summer of 1913 Lane and Adolph C. Miller, his assistant secretary, took an inspection tour of the national parks, and Lane began to develop a schematic policy for the management of the parks.[17]

The outbreak of World War I in August 1914 marked a pivotal moment for the promotion and status of the national parks. The war effectively evicted American tourists from European resorts and attractions. Simultaneously, it intensified the discourse of patriotism and loyalty in the United States.[18] Tourist promoters who had begun at the turn of the century to champion the See America First idea seized the moment to promote a national tourism. The railroads, which for many years had been the sole proponents of domestic tourism in the United States, expanded their promotional campaigns.[19] Good Roads advocates and organizations of automobile enthusiasts such as the Lincoln Highway Association celebrated the expanding opportunities for touring via automobile.[20] Promoters and exhibitors at the Panama-Pacific International Exposition scheduled to open in San Francisco early in 1915 publicized a grand tour of western America with the exposition as the grand finale.[21] In this context, touring in the United States took on the patriotic and commercial connotations of "Buy American."[22] Amid this fervor, the parks were transformed into America's preeminent tourist attractions, and touring the parks was presented as a ritual of citizenship. Park administrators worked to define a national tourism centered around the established system of national parks and monuments, and in doing so they participated in the larger process of nation building by defining and promoting an ideal of America as "nature's nation."[23] In other words, they worked to inscribe the nation into "the *nature* of things."[24]

The European war and the impending opening of the Panama-Pacific International Exposition in San Francisco inspired Lane to launch a "parks preparedness" campaign to develop and publicize the national parks, especially Yosemite, so that they might be ready for the crowds that would arrive in San Francisco for the exposition.[25] Expressing the core of his reform philosophy of "greater development and greater democracy," Lane envisioned "the national parks as a great economic asset which had theretofore been entirely overlooked by the Federal Government" and as national "playgrounds for the people."[26] He turned to a former University of California classmate and Chicago borax millionaire Stephen Tyng Mather to launch this new publicity and development campaign.[27] In his previous careers with the *New York Sun* and the Pacific Coast Borax Company, Mather had gained broad experience in the practice of public relations. Lane had specifically hired Mather because of his reputation as a "genius of publicity."[28] In January 1915 Mather was sworn in as assistant secretary of the interior. Lane charged him with the task of establishing "a business administration" to manage the fourteen existing national parks and the eighteen existing national monuments.[29] Mather began by organizing an extensive publicity campaign for the parks building on the See America First idea.

The Third Annual National Parks Conference held at the University of

California in Berkeley during the Panama-Pacific International Exposition initiated this publicity campaign. In his introductory speech, Mather articulated his ideas about the necessity for park publicity. "The parks," he said, "must be, of course, much better known that [sic] they are to-day if they are going to be the true playgrounds of the people that we want them to be. There is much that can be done in making them better known. There are many ways in which they can be brought home to the great mass of eastern people." Those at the conference agreed that "the policy of the present Administration to exploit the move to 'see America first' is a step in the right direction, and should be commended by the American public to the extent that they will make it their duty as well as their pleasure to assist in this patriotic movement."[30]

Mather hired Robert Sterling Yard "to work up a nationwide publicity campaign" to "get the people behind the parks."[31] Yard, an authority on publishing who had worked with Mather on the *New York Sun* and later edited the *Century Magazine* and the Sunday edition of the *New York Herald,* was hired as the publicity chief.[32] Although Yard was a self-admitted "tenderfoot" when it came to western wilderness, he proceeded to organize a park publicity bureau.[33] He began gathering information about travel to foreign countries and the promotion of tourists sights and then set out to tour the parks, gathering "information about our own scenic resources." On his return he established a national parks news service and began writing articles for magazines, issuing press bulletins, collecting and distributing photographs and statistics, and "encourag[ing] the preparation of publicity material by everybody in and out of government who had talents to be exploited."[34] In addition, he reissued the early national park bulletins and prepared a series of automobile maps for the parks. In effect, Yard pieced together a full-scale advertising and public relations campaign by consolidating and revamping existing government materials on the parks, by drawing on the resources of western railroads, and by generating free publicity through the dissemination of official information.

Yard's research and travels in 1915 culminated in two important publications: *The National Parks Portfolio,* an expensive picture book published in 1916, and a less-expensive pamphlet, *Glimpses of Our National Parks.*[35] The portfolio was composed of a series of pamphlets describing Yellowstone, Yosemite, Sequoia, Mount Rainier, Crater Lake, Mesa Verde, Glacier, and Rocky Mountain, the most prominent national parks, in addition to one on the Grand Canyon National Monument. Each park description was illustrated by a number of dramatic photographs, interspersed with brief tables providing an overview of all the parks and bound together in an expensive cloth folder.[36] The book came out in the midst of the congressional debate over the national park service bill, and every member of congress received a copy. In total, 275,000 copies were distributed by the U.S. government free of charge to a select list of recipients considered potential park supporters. *Glimpses of Our National Parks* was a short, illustrated booklet providing general information about the existing national parks to tourists.[37]

Both *The National Parks Portfolio* and *Glimpses of Our National Parks* were meant to educate Americans about the "wonders" of their own country, to instill a scenic patriotism that would unite the touring public in support of the national parks. In his preface to the portfolio, Mather drew on an established See America First argument. "This Nation is richer in natural scenery of the first order than any other nation," he wrote, "but it does not know it. . . . In its national parks it has neglected, because it has quite overlooked, an economic asset of incalculable value." He went on to explain, "The main object of this portfolio, therefore is to present to the people of this country a panorama of our principle national parks." Mather noted that this was the first "representative presentation of American scenery of grandeur" to be published, and he dedicated it to the American people. "It is my great hope," he concluded, "that it will serve to turn the busy eyes of the Nation upon its national parks long enough to bring some realization of what these pleasure gardens ought to mean, of what so easily they may be made to mean, to this people."[38]

The National Parks Portfolio functioned as a catalogue of the parks, displaying, codifying, and enumerating the dramatic natural landscapes that the government had set aside as "playgrounds for the people." The colorful descriptions of the eight major western parks and the Grand Canyon combined with over two hundred photographs of mountain views, lakes and waterfalls, glaciers, wild animals, and rustic hotels stated that the national parks embodied a physical experience that promised "thrills . . . never before experienced," "fairyland and the awe of infinity," "romantic Indian legend," along with health and peacefulness. Each section detailed the spectacles of one park, providing information on scenic character, the geological formations, wildlife, the Indians if applicable, and park accommodations. The purpose of the portfolio was to establish the parks as national assets, making them valuable national property rather than simply land set aside by the government and thus declared "unusable." It accomplished this by presenting the parks as ceremonial landscapes, icons of the nation.[39] Written descriptions celebrated the "sublimity" of the park landscapes, suggesting that they had the ability to inspire and uplift. The many photographs captured scenic views from their most alluring perspective, transforming the natural landscape into pristine iconographic images. In a number of the photographs solitary viewers or groups of sightseers were pictured surveying the landscape, in effect worshipping the natural icons that embodied the nation. In each section the text reasserted that the parks not only promised an "unrivaled" experience but also were valuable for their natural formations, which allowed for the firsthand study of nature. As Secretary Lane wrote, they were "the public laboratories of nature study for the Nation." As landscapes administered by the government, they embodied the democratic imperative of the nation. At the end of each descriptive section readers were reminded that the national parks belonged to them.[40] It was clear, however, that the imagined tourists, as evidenced by the photographs depicting well-dressed and elaborately outfitted sightseers, were white upper- and middle-class Americans who could afford to travel by train or automobile and spend a week or more vacationing in the parks. In promoting the national parks, the portfolio gave official government sanction to the preservation of scenery. The justification for preservation was based not so much on the aesthetic or intrinsic value of nature, but on the educational and the national value of scenic landscapes.[41]

Like *The National Parks Portfolio*, *Glimpses of Our National Parks* sought to establish the value of national parks as national assets. "The national parks, unlike the national forests, are not properties in a commercial sense, but natural preserves for the rest, recreation, and education of the people. They remain under nature's own chosen conditions. They alone maintain 'the forest primeval,'" wrote Yard. In separating the parks from the realm of commerce, *Glimpses of Our National Parks* defined their value in other terms, most notably through their potential to educate. Yard encouraged tourists to explore the national parks: to go "hunting . . . with a camera in Yellowstone," to study the formation of glaciers in Mount Rainier, to ponder the development of prehistoric civilizations in Mesa Verde, or to consider Major John Wesley Powell's

A number of illustrations in the *National Parks Portfolio* depicted white, middle-class tourists surveying dramatic natural scenery, which reinforced the idea that park landscapes represented national icons that deserved a certain level of reverence. From *National Parks Portfolio* (1916). (Courtesy of the Library of Congress)

"perilous passage" in the Grand Canyon. The dramatic land formations, the ancient Indian ruins, the giant trees, and the volcanic and glacial phenomena all revealed nature in its "pristine" form, untouched by man. In stating that the value of the parks rested on their "extraordinary scenic beauty," and "remarkable phenomenon," Yard set up an implicit opposition between nature as represented in the parks, and the ordinary built and natural environment. His celebration of the educational value of dramatic landscapes of the parks and his promotion of nature study raised the national parks to a level above the crass concerns of commercialism and the cheap amusements of common tourist attractions. "Every person living in the United States," Yard wrote, "ought to know about these eight national parks and ought to visit them when possible, for, considered together, they contain more features of conspicuous grandeur than are readily accessible in all the rest of the world."[42] Building on a long-established national mythology that identified America as "nature's nation," Yard essentially argued that the natural landscapes embodied in the national parks evinced America's greatness.

Mather supplemented and further spread Yard's publicity work through a series of highly publicized park tours, speaking to chambers of commerce, wilderness groups, automobile associations, and other interested organizations about developing the parks and making them more accessible to the American people.[43] He met with railroad representatives to negotiate reduced rates, suggesting that they issue "park tour tickets which [would] enable tourists to buy tickets at the starting point for a definite tour of national parks, all accommodations paid for and arranged in advance." In addition, he asked the roads to include information about the parks in their tourist brochures.[44] Mather also cultivated valuable working relationships with both Gilbert Grosvenor, editor of the *National Geographic* magazine, and George Horace Lorimer, editor of the *Saturday Evening Post*.[45] These connections assured a constant flow of park publicity.

The passage of the park service bill on 25 August 1916 and the first appropriation of funds to actually run the Park Service on 17 April 1917 marked the triumph of Mather's initial publicity campaign. The aim of establishing a unified park system had been accomplished. In 1918 the administrative policy for the newly established National Park Service was outlined in an official letter from the secretary of the interior to Mather. In defining the criteria for the creation of new national parks, the letter stated that the Park Service should seek out "scenery of supreme and distinctive quality or some natural feature so extraordinary or unique as to be of national interest or importance." These guidelines both set the criteria for the establishment of new parks and defined the value of preestablished parks. The national park system, according to the 1918 annual report of the secretary of the interior, "constituted one of America's greatest national assets."[46] This celebration of the dramatic natural scenery of the West, the remains of ancient civilizations, and pristine wilderness—the landscapes embraced by the parks—moved beyond the rhetoric of economic nationalism to express an ideal of nationhood. By focusing on wilderness, scenery, and ruins, park publicity glorified not the commercial and industrial developments that were catapulting the United States to world power and solidifying the nation-state, but the natural landscapes and ancient ruins that were symbolic of America's origins. The essence of American identity, according to the narrative of nationalism constructed by the Park Service, rested primarily in western wilderness, landscapes once inhabited by more primitive civilizations, then left untouched by man, yet still symbolizing the bounty of American nature. In this way the American landscape was infused with an ancient past and a divine promise. These "unique" landscapes embodied the "untouched" wilderness of the North American continent that had helped to forge a distinct nation.[47]

The growing wave of reactionary patriotism sweeping the nation with the outbreak of World War I brought added value to the national character of the parks. With Europe closed to American tourists, the economic argument associated with See America First lost its intensity and its edge. The interest in the Pacific expositions and the dramatic increase in park visitors proved that American tourist attractions could hold the interest of American tourists. Touring America became a fashionable patriotic pastime. As various groups struggled to define the character of the nation, those interested in promoting the parks began to argue that the parks were valuable not simply because of the commercial possibilities of tourism but also because they had patriotic value. As the *Chicago Tribune* editorialized:

> There is a higher and stronger reason for our effort to encourage better acquaintance with and greater use of the resources of natural beauty on this continent. It is a measure of Americanism. The nation needs a tonic knowledge of the physical

thing called America, a love of the body of Columbia, an inspiring sense of the nobility and splendor, the epic sweep and the intimate beauty of the land to whom our forebearers gave their devotion and we ourselves claim home.... An acquaintance with the mere physical quality of the country west of the Alleghenies would notably assist a deeper understanding of the American Spirit. The east should go west as the west goes east. There would be less colonialism there if that could be brought about.[48]

Yard developed and expanded on this idea in his various park publications and in the process began to define the parks in terms of an organic definition of nationalism. In other words, he presented the parks as representative of a distinctly American homeland. Now the parks were more than just economic assets, they were also natural laboratories and quintessentially American landscapes. Mark Daniels elaborated on this idea, explaining that there are three great functions of the national parks: "1. The stimulation of National Patriotism; 2. The furthering of knowledge and health; 3. The retention of tourist travel within the United States."[49] The connection between national parks and national consciousness had come to define their central value.

Clearly, this publicity campaign had laid the symbolic ground work for the transformation of the parks into a system of national assets. Despite this flurry of publicity, the nascent Park Service still faced the issue of laying claim to the parks as national landscapes controlled by the federal government. Specifically, this meant separating individual parks from the independent railroad corporations that had developed them, popularizing the parks as public landscapes, and making them more accessible. And this task meant constructing an official image of the parks as a system of national landscapes, linking the experience of touring the parks with a national consciousness and lifting the experience of touring the parks above the crass commercialism associated with tourism to a more virtuous or patriotic level. The mobilization effort for World War I and the eventual entry of the United States into the war provided the impetus for this transformation.

NATIONALIZING THE PARKS

In the spring of 1917, as the United States launched extensive war mobilization efforts, rumors abounded that the parks would be closed to tourist travel and excursions trips on the railroads would be prohibited. The resulting confusion caused a number of railroads to delay the announcement of excursion rates for the 1917 season. Concern over a pending bill for war taxes that called for the taxation of transportation tickets only added to the confusion. To counteract these rumors Secretary Lane made a public statement to the effect that despite the mobilization efforts, the parks would remain open to visitors and that "persistent rumors . . . have absolutely no foundation in fact. All of the parks are to be opened at the usual time." The press release went on to note that the secretary firmly believed that "it is even more important now than in times of peace that the health and vitality of the Nation's citizenship be conserved, that rest and recreation must materially assist in this conservation of human tissue and energy."[50]

The railroads cooperated with the Park Service and one another by promoting a number of park to park tours during the 1917 season. The Chicago and Northwestern line got together with the Union Pacific and established a tourist bureau headed by Howard Hays to promote a tour to Yellowstone and Rocky Mountain National Parks known as the "two parks in two weeks tour," and the Chicago Burlington and Quincy promoted a three-park trip to Glacier, Yellowstone, and Rocky Mountain National Parks.[51] In the meantime, Horace M. Albright worked behind the scenes as acting director of the Park Service to encourage travel to the parks while preventing the encroachment of commercial interests due to the war effort. His efforts paid off. Travel to the parks in 1917 almost reached the half-million mark, exceeding the two previous banner years by more than a hundred thousand visitors.[52]

In December 1917 President Wilson placed the railroads under the control of the United States Railroad Administration, where they remained until 1920. The Railroad Administration nationalized the railroads in an effort to speed and streamline the transportation of supplies and men to the war front, and all unnecessary expenditures on the part of the railroads were forbidden. Secretary Lane conferred in January 1918 with the head of the Railroad Administration concerning wartime travel, and it was agreed that the national parks would remain open and that visitors to the national parks would be accommodated on regular trains.[53] The administration nominally restricted railroad travel and limited luxury train service, but it continued to allow for and promote travel to the parks.

In April 1918 Mather proposed the creation of a western tourist bureau, the purpose being to make up for the decrease in individual railroad publicity efforts resulting from the demands of the war. The plan was to reorganize the existing Northwestern–Union Pacific Tourist Bureau headed by Howard Hays "by adding a few men connected with the principal western roads who have specialized in the promotion of national park travel." Representatives from these railroads would remain on the payroll of their respective roads but would serve on a cooperative committee to promote the parks which would be overseen by the Railroad Administration.[54] The proposed associated roads included the Chicago, Burlington and Quincy, the Northern Pacific, the Great Northern, the Santa Fe, and those other rail lines with a vested interest in the national parks. Edward Chambers, spokesman for the Railroad Administration, suggested the "United States Railroad Administration, Western Lines Bureau of Service, National Parks and Monuments" as an appropriate title, the idea being that this committee would act as "the point of contact between the Railroad Administration . . . and the Bureau of National Parks of the Interior Department, the concessionaires, and others interested in the promotion of this travel . . . and that they will act for all roads in conducting correspondence with the public and arranging for western tours."[55] In other words, the proposed tourist bureau would replicate the relationship between the government and railroads embodied in the organization of the Railroad Administration. The Western Roads Bureau of Service was formally established as part of the Railroad Administration on 7 June 1918.[56] In essence, the bureau was to represent all railroads associated with the national parks. More specifically, as Howard Hays, director of the new bureau, explained, "the Bureau shall take over from general passenger departments of railroads the correspondence relative to National Parks."[57]

Previously, transcontinental railroad lines had adopted extensive public relations strategies that allied them with individual parks. Many of these independent lines had spent as much as $100,000 on advertising budgets for booklets and printed matter, newspaper and magazine advertisements, as well as billboards and lectures. Because the Railroad Administration forbade the expenditure of unnecessary funds for promotional materials during the war, railroads cut their advertising budgets and curtailed their extensive promotional campaigns. It was intended that the Bureau of service would not only make up for this dramatic loss in advertising but also streamline the promotion of western attractions. This cooperative publicity effort served to effectively nationalize the national parks, presenting them as a set of attractions rather than as separate sights accessible only by separate roads. As Hays explained, "We see no reason why National Parks, as government properties, supported by national taxation, should not receive complete representation in every part of the United States. . . . Let us lift the principal National Parks and Monuments onto a higher level so that ticket agents throughout the United States will be converted to, and prepared for the great National Park idea which we must drive home to the American people when competition with European resorts is re-established."[58] By overseeing lectures, slide presentations, films, and photographs, by circulating pamphlets and booklets, by distributing newspaper and magazine advertising, by deploying bureau clerks nationwide to answer questions and supply information, and by regulating tourist tariffs, the Bureau of Service presented itself as the official tourist bureau of the nation.[59]

During its first summer under existence, the bureau walked a fine line between serving the war effort and promoting the parks. It hoped to quell rumors about the closing of the parks during the war while also understating park publicity in consideration of the wartime emergency. It used its official status to provide the appropriate character for its wartime promotional efforts. As the director explained in his first report, "[U.S. Railroad] Administration rulings against the encouragement of travel have compelled the Bureau to proceed cautiously."[60] However, even before the November armistice was reached, Howard Hays had already been considering the activities of the bureau after the war.[61] In the fall of 1918, Hays proposed that a series of booklets advertising the national parks be put together to overview available tourist possibilities. He requested the services of Robert Sterling Yard, chief of the Educational Division of the National Park Service, to assist in preparing the material.[62] By February 1919 the Railroad Administration had approved the publication of eighteen booklets promoting the principal national parks and monuments along with various other prominent tourist destinations.[63]

In the spring of 1919, the Railroad Administration dropped all barriers to a full-scale parks publicity campaign, announcing the removal of all restrictions on railroad travel. A circular letter sent out to railroad ticket agents

In 1918, despite travel restrictions brought about by American entry into World War I, the Western Lines Bureau of Service under the aegis of the U.S. Railroad Administration acted as a national tourist bureau responsible for advertising and promoting the national parks. Advertisement, U.S. Railroad Administration Summer Excursions to the National Parks, National Monuments and Principal Resort Regions (1918). (Records of the National Park Service, National Archives, College Park, Maryland)

Cover of the U.S. Railroad Administration's *Mt. Rainier National Park, Washington.* U.S. *Railroad Administration* promotional guide (1919). (Courtesy of the Library of Congress)

explained, "One year ago, under the pressure of war necessities, the public was requested to refrain from all unnecessary travel, and, under the stress of war conditions, the public was necessarily subjected to a great deal of inconvenience when it did have to travel. Now the war necessity is passed and it is the settled policy of the Railroad Administration to do everything reasonably within its power to facilitate passenger travel and to make it more attractive."[64] In addition to issuing the national parks booklets, the bureau also planned to spend almost half a million dollars on a national newspaper and magazine advertising campaign to promote the parks.[65] During the first six months of 1919, the bureau distributed approximately 1.7 million booklets and descriptive folders to railroads, ticket offices, tourist agencies, and travel bureaus.[66] This extensive campaign amounted to the first full-scale nationalized tourist campaign in the United States.

In some ways the national crisis brought on by American involvement in the war and the demands of mobilization served to solidify the nationalization of the national parks. The federally controlled promotional activities of the Bureau of Service fulfilled the long-established demand for a national tourist bureau. For a very brief period in 1919, the ideals, demands, and desires of those who had long called for the government to promote an American tourist industry were actualized. Thus the Bureau of Service as it existed under government control might best be seen as the culmination of the See America First publicity campaign begun by Lane and Mather in the early days of 1915. Although the bureau did not remain as a permanent government-sponsored organization, it helped shift the parks from separate and independent attractions into a system of national assets. In transferring the burden of publicity from independent railroad corporations to the Park Service and then on to the Bureau of Service, the parks became truly "national" parks, meaning they were no longer simply separate and unique scenic wonders connected with the nation through ideals of monumentalism that linked the nation with dramatic examples of sublime scenery.[67] Rather, through the official sanction of the Department of the Interior beginning in 1915, the creation of a special park bureau in 1916, and the nationalization of the publicity effort by the Bureau of Service between 1918 and 1919, the parks were defined as more than just scenic wonders. They became quintessentially American landscapes that objectified the American character and embodied the essence of the nation, and in the tradition of democracy, they belonged to the people, ever available for their benefit and pleasure.

After the war, the Park Service expanded on this connection between the parks and the nation. Despite the fact that after the war the Park Service's publicity efforts were restricted due to funding cutbacks, the service returned to collaborating with various organizations, individuals, and corporations interested in promoting the parks in an effort to compete effectively with the resurgence of European touring possibilities.[68] Building on previous publicity that had touted the parks as playgrounds of the people and linked seeing the parks with patriotic duty, the Park Service worked with park enthusiasts to capitalize on the rising postwar fervor for Americanization. In an article overviewing the various resources scattered throughout the United States that showcased dramatic photographs of the National Parks, Franklin K. Lane championed the cause of Americanization. "I find in dealing with this problem of making the foreign-born understand what Americanization is," he explained, "is that the first great difficulty is to make the American-born realize fully and be conscious of America in all its various senses and moods and spirits. And one of the things that I should like to conduct, if I were free to do so and had the means, would be a real geography class." What followed in the article was an attempt to do just that, and the national parks played a prominent role in his overview of the wonders and benefits of America. He concluded, "To know America is to love it. . . . Out of its wealth in things of the earth and its greater wealth in things of the spirit it is making a new society, different from any that is or that has been."[69] Building on this fervor, Park Service administrators helped to forward the ideal that seeing the parks was akin to assisting in the postwar reconstruction effort. The parks were promoted as natural sanctuaries where war-weary soldiers could recuperate. "We know," Mather asserted, "that recreation, or rather, re-creation, will be needed more than ever [after the war]; that our men coming back from the front will want to have a place where they can go for recuperation."[70]

A number of individuals and organizations interested in the promotion of domestic travel worked in conjunction with the Park Service to link the parks with the larger campaign for Americanization. In 1920 the Far Western Traveler's Association, an organization of traveling salesmen, took up the national park cause and initiated a publicity program in association with the Park Service. In his address before the annual banquet, John B. Patton, president of the organization, asserted that "every Far Western Traveler will become a salesman for the Parks." He explained that the association had "determined to take a vigorous part in the carrying out the government's reconstruction program. The association believes that Americanization is the most important plank in the reconstruction platform and that seeing America first is one of the most important courses of instruction through which Americanization will be attained." Not only would the annual banquet be devoted to celebrating park landscapes, but also a yearbook with articles by Mather, Yard, and other park enthusiasts illustrated with "color and halftone reproductions portraying the chief points of scenic interests" and edited and compiled by Sewell Haggard, formerly associated with *McClure's* and *Cosmopolitan*, was to be distributed at the banquet.[71] Park Service administrators willingly assisted in the compilation of the booklet.[72]

At the annual banquet in 1920, members of the association agreed on a program to promote the See America First idea and the national parks. It was decided that the organization would sponsor a trip for twenty Boy Scouts to the national parks.[73] As president Patton explained, "We want them to see America because it will help them to grow up better Americans.[74] Building on the touted educational value of the parks, the organization believed that seeing the parks would inculcate a sense of patriotic duty in city-bound boys, and they encouraged other organizations to join with them in forwarding the cause of Americanization in connection with promoting the parks: "If we can set on fire the spirit of romance that burns in the heart of each youth of this city and other cities with the inspiration that comes from mountains and the great drama of the pioneers who built the West, we can lay a foundation for the future of our nation that will make it eternal."[75] Parks administrators reinforced this ideal, as the overview of the national parks in the annual yearbook exclaimed, "Scenic assets of the highest importance, they will continue to play an ever-increasing part in the upbuilding of American manhood and womanhood and, through them, of national efficiency and contentment."[76]

During the 1920s, park enthusiasts worked in conjunction with the Park Service to develop the tourist infrastructure and expand on the idea of the parks as part of a unified system. Projects such as the national park-to-park

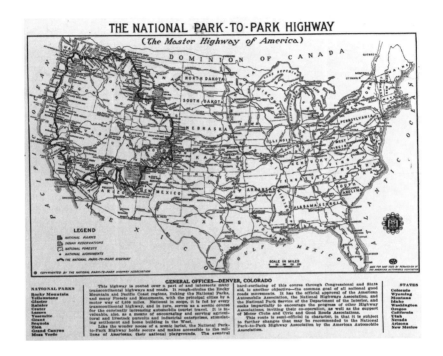

Map of the National Park-to-Park Highway from *Proceedings of the First Annual Convention of the National Park to Park Highway Association* (1920). (Albert Bacon Fall Collection; reproduced by permission of the Huntington Library, San Marino, California)

highway were promoted in an effort to actualize the ideals promoted in earlier Park Service publicity. Before the war, park administrators had focused primarily on publicizing the parks, but also on organizing park management, defining a concessionaire policy, and standardizing the relationship between park superintendents, the Washington office, and the various park concessionaires.[77] Once the management policy of the parks was settled, the Park Service could move from general publicity about the parks and the various sites to see and begin to promote a specific tourist program that encouraged a process of seeing the parks. The park-to-park highway was central to facilitating a national tourist experience. The Park Service encouraged tourists to see more than one park, presenting the parks as a canon of American tourist attractions. The park-to-park tour became the equivalent of the modern-day Grand Tour in America.

The freedom of automobile touring, made possible by publicly owned and accessible roads, provided the necessary infrastructure to promote and develop park-to-park touring, and the park-to-park highway championed by the Park Service provided the means of promoting this type of touring. As early as 1916, at a meeting of western commercial club members in Yellowstone, Mather suggested the development of an automobile highway connecting all the parks. In the aftermath of the meeting Gus Holmes of Cody, Wyoming, organized the Yellowstone Highway Association in an effort to develop a road between Yellowstone and Glacier National Parks, which was then extended to include Yosemite, the Grand Canyon, Mesa Verde, and Rocky Mountain National Park as well as a number of noted scenic attractions in between.[78]

The absence of a federal highway policy and funding system hindered development of a national park-to-park highway, and the war effort curtailed private fund-raising efforts. After the war, with the return of railroads to private control, the effort to promote a park-to-park highway was revived. Automobile touring seemed to be the wave of the future, and it promised to facilitate a touring program that furthered the newly emerging nationalized image of the parks. In the spring of 1919, Secretary Lane announced a proposed plan to develop "an automobile line from Denver, Colorado to and through Rocky Mountain, Yellowstone, and Glacier National Parks." A fleet of touring cars managed by H. W. Child and Row Emory, who held the transportation concessions in Yellowstone and Glacier, respectively, was to run between the three parks facilitating the process of interpark travel and forwarding the process of postwar reconstruction. As the secretary's press release explained, "It is Secretary Lane's belief that the Federal Government ought to actively encourage travel to American health and recreation resorts. . . . He believes that the National Park Service, which is in more than one sense the travel bureau of the Federal Government, ought to perform the same service for the American public that the Swiss, French, and other foreign government travel bureaus accomplish for European resorts."[79] In an effort to publicize this new touring service, the Park Service dedicated the so-called Geysers to Glaciers Motor Trail by escorting a select group of the *Brooklyn Daily Eagle* touring party on an inaugural run from Yellowstone to Glacier.[80] The publicity surrounding this official opening rekindled local interest in the development of a park-to-park highway, and in 1920 the old Yellowstone Highway Association reformed as the National Park-to-Park Highway Association. Adopting the slogan "You Sing 'America'—Why Not See It?" the association envisioned a master circular highway, also known as the master scenic highway of America, connecting all the western parks, centered on Salt Lake City, where a series of highways radiating like spokes would connect the opposite points of the circle.[81]

Extending from his support of automobile touring and his focus on park-to-park touring, Mather had begun by the mid-1920s to articulate and promote an ideal of the park touring experience that connected the possibilities of automobile touring with an ideal of national consciousness. Touring the national parks helped "break down sectional prejudice through the bringing together of tourists from all sections of the country," Mather explained at a conference promoting the development of state parks. He went on to note, "In the national parks there is one thing that the motorists are doing, and that is making them a great melting pot for the American people. . . . This will go far in developing a love and pride in our own country and a realization of what a wonderful place it is. There is no way to bring it home to them in a better way than by going from park to park, through the medium of an automobile, and camping out in the open. . . . It is just by trips of that kind that people learn what America is."[82]

THE PARKS AS NATIONAL ASSETS

As the parks became more popular and their scenic attractions became more accessible, Park Service administrators increasingly underscored the educational value of the parks. After the war, the Park Service had worked to promote the educational use of the parks. A nature guide service had been set up in Yosemite and Glacier by 1922. In 1923 Arno B. Cammerer, acting director of the Park Service, sent out letters to 134 universities and colleges throughout the United States in an effort to have them initiate some form of summer travel in the parks, calling on each school to form a "National Parks Travel Committee."[83] In a reformulation of national park policy in 1925, Secretary of Interior Hubert M. Work restated the three broad principles that Mather and Lane had laid out in 1918. In general, Work adhered to the principles of preservation, use, and national interest, but he reformulated the second principle, which originally stated that the parks had been "set apart for the use, observation, health and pleasure of the people," substituting "education" for "observation."[84] Work's restatement of the Park Service's mission reflected the growing interest in the educational value of the parks that began to emerge after World War I. Thus by 1925 the tourist program envisioned by the Park Service involved more than just seeing the parks and enjoying dramatic scenery; it meant learning about history, geology, botany, archeology and biology—in essence, learning about the character and spirit of the nation.

After the war, Mather and Yard launched a nonprofit organization to publicize and defend the national parks. With an initial gift of five thousand dollars and list of potential park supporters, Mather charged Yard with the task of creating a private lobbying organization along the lines of the National Forestry Association to provide a venue for park support and publicity that existed both beyond the confines of private interest and beyond the restrictions of the federal government.[85] The National Parks Association combined defense of the preservation idea represented by the parks with a commitment to publicizing the values of the parks. In its inaugural invitation to join the association promised:

1. To fearlessly defend the National Parks and Monuments against assaults of private interests and aggressive commercialism.

2. To study the National Parks and Monuments, their history, folk lore, and wild life, to interpret their scenic features and circulate popular information concerning them.

3. To encourage the literature of travel, wild life and the meaning of scenery.

4. To work for the extension of the National Parks System to represent the full range of American scenic examples, yet confined to such significance that they shall make the name National Park an *American trade-mark in the competition for world's travel . . .*

5. To bring together the best minds of the nation into the service of these objectives, and to enlist the co-operation of schools, universities, societies and institutions in using the National Parks to the best popular advantage.[86]

As executive director of the National Parks Association, Yard began to focus increased attention on this issue of education.[87] He called the parks "museums of native America" or "national museums." In summarizing park concerns for the association in 1923, Cammerer noted, "Particular attention is given to the development of the educational side of Park work,—the establishment of museums and nature guide service, which is going forward in leaps and bounds. The interest shown by universities in what the Parks have to offer in this regard is most gratifying, and a few more years will see this detail of service to the public developed to a high standard."[88] Cammerer explained in one promotional essay overviewing the parks, "To the observant visitor . . . soon comes the realization that aside from the recreational values, the national parks are from an educational standpoint,—biologic, historic, geologic, and botanic,—really outdoor classrooms of the country; that in fact, the future may see in them no less great educational centers of learning than a means to health and pleasure." He concluded, "It is, therefore, obviously not an exaggeration to say that the National Parks are truly Nature's outdoor classrooms, and that whatever their enormous value at this time as the great national play and recreation grounds, as Civilization crowds westwardly and the great open spaces are taken up bit by bit, the parks in their refreshing natural state, will constitute the Nation's great exhibition spaces where still the native flora, the wild life with its geologic and historic setting, are found untouched as in the days when this country was young."[89] Whether revealing the workings of volcanic action, glaciation, or erosion, harboring native flora and fauna, or simply providing an escape from urban scurry and work-a-day routines, the parks offered an array of benefits to American tourists. The newly defined educational value assigned the parks the same role as the a national museum or public school system—to inculcate patriotism and teach the values and meanings of citizenship.

This emphasis on education not only underscored the importance of the parks to Americanization programs but also reflected increasingly pervasive theories of progressive education that stressed learning through experience. The combination resulted in a theory of nationalism that grounded citizenship not simply in the ideal of a democratic political contract, but also in the relationship to territory or homeland. Building on the romantic notion of organic nationalism, the nation became a unique geographical entity. The feeling of American-ness was integrally connected to the nation's physical territory. Natural wonders and dramatic scenery came to symbolize not just the promise of tourist revenues and congressional appropriations but, more important, an ideal of homeland. Specifically, the American nation became an extension of wilderness as represented by the dramatic natural landscapes of the national parks.

During the 1920s the Park Service in cooperation with a number of outside businesses and organizations, most prominently the National Parks Association, continued to publicize the parks widely, establishing them as the nation's preeminent tourist attractions. In the process, the notion of the national parks as national assets was embellished and the ideal of the nation connected with the parks further solidified. Building on the educational value of the parks, promotional material defined the parks as the nation's natural laboratories and the nation's museum or alternatively "the museums of native America."[90] In a promotional speech to the Travel Club of America, Mather explained, "The National Parks are national museums. Their purpose is to preserve forever, in their original untouched condition, certain few, widely-separated examples of the American Wilderness of the pioneer and the frontiersman, of the works and process of Nature unblemished by man's hand; of our native wild animals living natural lives in the natural homes of their ancestors. We can pass on to posterity no other pleasure-giving and profit giving quality, combined with unique usefulness to history and science as the Museums of Native America."[91] The parks thus became more than just the "playgrounds of the people"; they became the equivalent of a recreational public school system. Through the act of tourism Americans could not only learn about the history and historical geology of their country and become familiar with the native flora and fauna of the nation but also imbibe the spirit or essence of America and rekindle their sense of patriotism.

Anthropologist Richard Handler has argued that the museum is "the temple of authenticity" for a nation or a culture, in that it allows people to come in contact with "authentic pieces of culture," thus enabling them to "appropriate their authenticity, incorporating that magical proof of existence into what we call our personal experience." He explains that authenticity is a cultural construct that is key to "the modern Western world."[92] Related to the emergence of individualism, the concept of authenticity allows the modern individual to define him or herself in opposition to the rest of the world. Handler goes on to note that this notion of authenticity is also applicable to individual cultures defining themselves as unique entities. He argues that in a society anxious about the "unreality" of modern life, this fascination with authenticity reflects an "anxiety over the credibility of existence."[93] This, in turn, can be linked to nationalist anxieties of the nation-state struggling for recognition. From this perspective, Handler argues, "the existence of a national collectivity depends upon the 'possession' of an authentic culture."[94] In other words, a shared national consciousness depends upon the collection, preservation, and display of this culture. Thus the metaphor of the parks as national museums or public classrooms served to sanctify an ideal of the nation.

In 1922 and 1923 a barrage of material promoting and defining the parks expanded on the image of the parks as a unified system of national landscapes. Increasingly during the twenties, as the parks suffered a series of attacks against their protected status, the Park Service began to emphasize the notion of controlled development in the context of wilderness preservation. Emphasizing education allowed the service to lift tourism to the level of highbrow culture. In this way tourism in the parks could be disassociated from commercialism and consumption and the parks could maintain their status as sacred national landscapes. During the 1920s a number of events coalesced to bring about a shift in Park Service promotional techniques. The attempts to allow some commercial use of the parks during the war instigated a barrage of attacks on the protective status of the parks. Water power and irrigation interests, specifically the Federal Water Power Act, which gave the power to lease public waters, including those in the national parks, for power generation, and the Fall River Basin bill, which proposed the damming of Yellowstone basin for irrigation purposes, threatened the integrity of national parks conservation. Additionally, the increasing popularity of parks as tourist attractions, resulting not only from extensive park advertising but also from increased automobile use, was threatening to transform the parks into amusement parks. "So rapid is the increase of travel to the parks," noted Robert Sterling Yard, "that it is none to early to anticipate the time when their popularity shall threaten their primary purpose. . . . While we are fighting for the protection of the national parks system from its enemies, we may also have to protect it from its friends."[95]

Responding to these commercializing threats, the Park Service and park advocates worked to redefine the value of the parks as above and beyond commercial interest. Park Superintendent Roger Toll explained that the parks were established "to set aside for the enjoyment of this and future generations, certain areas that are typical of our finest scenery. They are to be held free from commercial exploitation. The standing forests will prove more valuable than the lumber they would produce, the graceful waterfall will prove more precious than the power it would yield, the unscarred beauty of the mountain is worth more than the mineral wealth that may be buried in its heart." To preserve these representative natural landscapes while making them publicly accessible, Toll recommended a multitiered plan for park development. He argued that some parts of each park should remain accessible by automobile, whereas in other parts of each park horse trails and hiking trails should encourage a more intimate experience of nature. "The development of a park will, therefore, not be uniform throughout. Some portions will be fully developed, others partly developed, and still others will be left in their natural, wild condition," Toll stated. "The parks should be popular, but never commonplace. They should accommodate crowds if necessary, but without over-crowding. Animals should be protected in their natural surroundings rather than caged in a zoo. Outdoor recreation should supplant cheap amusements. Museums and nature study should be offered to stimulate interest along educational and beneficial lines rather than to accentuate sight seeing of an unintelligent order."[96] In this way the parks could be maintained as sacred national landscapes. They existed as sublime nature—God's creations—removed from the base concerns of commerce, and as such they were meant to remind Americans of their roots and to rekindle virtuous citizenship.

Other park supporters reiterated these themes throughout the 1920s. As executive secretary of the National Parks Association, Robert Sterling Yard became a vociferous advocate for the national value of the parks. In an attempt to fend off the commercial encroachment, Yard went so far as to argue that the parks had become "the shining badge of the nation's glory, sharing somewhat even of the sacredness of the flag. . . . They have become a part of the general popular conception of the greatness of America."[97] Their national greatness, according to Yard, rested in the fact that they existed beyond the concerns of commerce and industry. That "they embodied in actual reality, and in splendor, the American-born ideal of nature conservation, creating and protecting by law a mighty system of national museums of the primitive American wilderness, was an inspiring offset to the sordid commercialism and much advertised political rottenness of the times." As "national museums" the parks preserved not just wilderness and wildlife but "the geologic sequence of America's making."[98] As such, the parks benefited the "national mind" in a variety of ways, education being the most prominent. But Yard also argued that the parks promoted democracy:

> Nowhere else do people from all the states mingle in quite the same spirit as they do in their national parks. One sits at dinner, say, between a Missouri farmer and an Idaho miner, and at supper between a New York artist and an Oregon shopkeeper. One stages it with people from Florida, Minnesota and Utah, climbs mountains with a chance crowd from Vermont, Louisiana and Texas, and sits around the evening camp fire with a California grape grower, a locomotive engineer from Massachusetts, and a banker from Michigan. Here the social distances so insisted on at home just don't exist. Perhaps for the first time one realizes the common America—and loves it. . . . It is the enforced democracy and the sense of common ownership in these parks that works this magic. They have rediscovered to us the American people. Elsewhere travelers divide among resorts and hotels according to their ability to pay, and maintain their home attitudes. In the national parks all are just Americans.[99]

Highlighting a cross-section of the expanding American middle class from around the country, clearly, Yard's understanding of democracy focused more on geography than race or class. According to Yard, "Politicians, merchants, statesmen, legislators, artists of every variety, bankers, judges, millionaires and the merely fashionable," as well as "business and professional men and their families, teachers, lawyers, brokers, manufacturers of everything on earth, writers, publishers, advertising men—the well-to-do of all sorts and degrees. These constitute the great body of national park visitors."[100] Implying a nostalgia for a republican nation of free laborers, Yard's enumeration of park tourists celebrated a geographically diverse group of productive citizens ranging from farmers and miners to bankers and businessmen. The rising numbers of unskilled laborers were left unsung, as were other minority groups. What Yard didn't mention was that the Park Service consciously discouraged African

Americans from visiting the parks. As stated at the 1922 parks conference, "One of the objections to colored people is that if they come in large groups they will be conspicuous, and will not only be objected to by other visitors, but will cause trouble among the hotel and camp help, and it will be impossible to serve them. Individual cases can be handled, although even this is awkward, but organized parties could not be taken care of. . . . While we cannot openly discriminate against them, they should be told that the parks have no facilities for taking care of them."[101] Thus the ideals of democracy, the nation, and the citizen defined by park advocates and the Park Service were embodied by a newly emerging dominant class that was becoming a predominantly white, middle- and upper-class constituency in the twentieth century.

John Wesley Hill, park supporter and chancellor of Lincoln Memorial University, perhaps best expressed the ideal of the parks as national assets that had emerged after the war in his speech marking the annual opening of Yellowstone in 1923. Hill began by linking the creation of Yellowstone with the civilizing of the wilderness by the pioneer and forging of a unified nation by the railroads, noting that "the railroads came, and here we are in this wonderland of today, breathing its pure atmosphere, and exulting in our national estate because the railroads pioneered the way, because men of brain and faith and courage laughed at deserts and mountains and hardship and poverty." Hill went on to note that now people come by railroad and automobile from all sections of the country to mingle together in the national parks, "forming a higher, broader type of citizenship." But for Hill, the parks offered more than just the opportunity to view nature's wonders and overcome provincialism. In places like Yellowstone, according to Hill, "the soul of man hearing the voice of God in a wilderness of burning bushes, steps into the Presence Chamber of the Infinite and bows before the granite alter of God's vast Gothic cathedral."[102] According to Hill, the national parks embodied a combination of knowledge, democracy, and the sublime, and in so doing, they objectified the spirit of the nation and instilled a sense of national pride. "What is it that inspires love of the flag, that tunes the ear of America to sing, 'My country 'tis of thee?'" Hill asked.

> Is it superficial area, industrial efficiency, irrigation statistics or trade output? Is it our marvels of mining shown in the hideous ore dumps of the sordid mining camp? Is it the grim power house in which is harnessed the power of Niagara? Is

it the blackened waste that follows the devastation of much of our forest wealth? Is it the smoking factory of the grimy mill town, the malodorous wharves along navigable rivers? Is it the mutilating bill boards plastered with spread eagle advertisements that disfigure the broken landscapes along our line of travel? Is it even the lofty Metropolitan sky scraper that shuts out the sun and throws its dismal shadow over all below?

Hill argued it was none of these things. Rather, he said, "our devotion to the flag is inspired by love of country. Patriotism is the religion of the soil . . . [and] National Parks are our richest patrimony. They constitute a heritage which must be preserved inviolate by the American people."[103] Hill asserted that commercialism posed the biggest threat to the national park system and as such to the ideal of the nation. He likened those who would invade the parks for commercial ends to "money changers" in the temple. "The subjugation and utilization of the forces and products of nature by man is the foundation of successful economic existence and development, but is nature untouched unnecessary or undesired in our complicated scheme of living?" Hill asked. "Are not reserved places of rare natural beauty as important in daily life as those utilized areas that supply our physical needs?" Hill argued that the march of progress continued. "Gradually," he said, "the open spaces are being settled. . . . Are we to relinquish even one square mile of the choicest exhibits of our great national recreation areas without considering their inestimable value to the countless generations yet to come?"[104] For the sake of the future of the nation, Hill declared, the people needed to rise up and demand that the parks remain unscathed by commercial development.

This eloquent celebration of the national parks and dramatic plea for preservation revealed the value of the parks as sacred national landscapes. As sanctuaries of nature—the last vestiges of "virgin" land—that existed beyond the corrupting forces of corporate capitalism, the parks manifested an ideal of the nation grounded in a nostalgic republican tradition that linked pristine nature or free land with an ideal of civic virtue.[105] Ironically, in a capitalist society wedded to an ideology of progress reliant on private property and extensive natural resources, preserved nature, existing beyond the reach of commerce and industry, came to embody the ideal of the nation. And tourism, defined as a patriotic act, became a ritual of citizenship that transformed consumption into civic duty. These ironies reveal the fraught process of nation building.

Through a multistaged process—beginning with a publicity campaign that redefined the parks in national terms, moving through a process of nationalization where the state officially sanctioned the parks as national tourist attractions, and culminating in a crusade for preservation which transformed the parks into sacred national landscapes—the parks were infused with national value. They came to represent the essence of the nation, and the act of touring allowed the individual to experience and possess these sacred national landscapes, actualizing his or her membership in the nation. In effect, the cultural production of the parks as national assets sought to officially confirm the nation as a God-given entity embodied in the unique natural landscapes scattered across the continental United States. Defined as "primeval" wilderness, these landscapes suggested that it was not democracy or progress alone that begot the nation. The nation was not a product of the forces of history. Rather, it was preordained, innate, divine. By thus "inscribing the nation into the nature of things," the process of incorporation, subjugation, and exclusion that marked the transformation of the United States into a modern nation-state could be disregarded.[106] This totalizing process could mask the social, political, and cultural conflict with a universal ideal of a cohesive nation. Just at the moment when the mechanisms of incorporation—the emergence of a national market, the completion of a national media and transportation network, and the development of a strong national state—bound American society more closely together, solidifying the infrastructure of the modern nation-state, state officials became actively involved in the production of a shared national consciousness that depended upon and ignored those very forces of incorporation. Tourism as consumption depended upon the commercial and technological infrastructure that underlay the nation-state. Tourism as civic duty promised to revive the sentiment of patriotism that rested on an ideal of America as "nature's nation." In this way, the symbolism of the parks as national tourist attractions, defining an organic ideal of the nation, mediated the tensions between the national myth that celebrated democracy, individualism, and liberty and the nation-state that depended on incorporation, hierarchy, and hegemony.

The Park Service's promotion of the national parks as a system of sacred national assets solidified the emergence of a national tourism in the United States. Although a national touring bureau was never established, the Park

Service worked in cooperation with private corporations to define and popularize domestic travel. By the 1920s the parks had come to embody the central canon of American tourist attractions. Yet the growing presence of the automobile promised to redefine the tourist experience. The automobile dramatically expanded the possibilities of tourism in the United States while refocusing the emphasis of the tourist experience from seeing sacred sites to following the footsteps of history.

4

A NATION ON WHEELS

A Motorist's Creed: I believe that travel, familiarity with the sights and
scenes of other parts of the country, first hand knowledge of how my
fellow-men live, is of inestimable value to me and will do more to make
me patriotic and public spirited than daily intimacy with the
Declaration of Independence.

—*American Motorist*, 1917

*I*N THE SPRING OF 1915, Newton A. Fuessle wrote a series of three articles for *Travel Magazine* describing the possibilities of automobile
touring along one of the nation's early transcontinental highways, the
Lincoln Highway.¹ Using the chaos of the European war as a backdrop,
Fuessle noted that Americans were finally beginning to discover the wonders of their own country. "The tremendous significance which the whirl
of sinister developments in Europe's theater of war has given to the 'See
America First' movement, has clothed the project of the Lincoln Highway Association with singular importance," he explained. Automobile
touring promised to bring tourists to the heart of America—"its life and
manners, history and traditions, hopes and dreams and ambitions, its
multitude of interests, its tangle of industries, its wealth of resources,
power, color and endless beauties." The Lincoln Highway not only re-

SEVEN MILE STRETCH ON LINCOLN HIGHWAY, BETWEEN STOYESTOWN AND BEDFORD, PA

Postcard, *Seven Mile Stretch on Lincoln Highway, Between Stoyestown and Bedford, Pa.* (Lake County [Illinois] Museum, Curt Teich Postcard Archives)

vealed America's rich past but also displayed its promising future. It objectified America as a nation:

> Teaching patriotism, sewing up the remaining ragged edges of sectionalism, revealing and interpreting America to its people, giving swifter feet to commerce, gathering up the country's loose ends of desultory and disjointed good roads ardor and binding them into one highly organized, proficient unit of dynamic, result-getting force, electric with zeal, it is quickening American neighborliness, democracy, progress and civilization.

In his survey of the highway, Fuessle described in detail its route and the unique sights and experiences tourists could anticipate, arguing that only through this firsthand experience of automobile touring, made possible by the Lincoln Highway, could the tourist come to truly understand America. "One may whirl across the continent a score of times as a railway passenger and never sense the slightest fraction of the feeling of nearness to the States and cities traversed," he wrote. In contrast, "the Highway affords an incomparable inspirational course in Americanism."[2]

Fuessle perhaps most eloquently articulated the ideal of national tourism defined by the Lincoln Highway Association and other proponents of automobile touring and good roads. The automobile allowed the individual to exercise complete control over the touring experience, thus gaining a more intimate interaction with the people and places across America, and the emerging road network vastly increased the number of potential tourist attractions. In effect the automobile completely transformed the tourist experience and the rhetoric of nationalism associated with tourism. In contrast to viewing the landscape cinematically as it flashed by the train window, the automobile, according to good roads advocates and automobile enthusiasts, brought the tourist into the landscape. Transcontinental automobile touring allowed tourists to move beyond the passive act of viewing the landscape to actually experience both history and nature. This allowed for a complete reconceptualization of the tourist experience. From the perspective of the automobile, tourists could not only admire the scenic views and vistas, as they had from the train window, but also stop and explore. They could vicariously experience the people and places of America. Thus, as automobile touring became increasingly more popular after World War I, prescriptive literature publicizing the landscapes of tourism began to promote historic sites, places associated with historic events, and the local color of particular places, in addition to the scenic attractions typically associated with railroad tourism. Touring came to be understood as a much more intimate, personal, and authentic experience. Prescriptive material promoting automobile touring underscored this notion of authenticity, focusing on firsthand experience. Proponents for organizations such as the National Old Trails Association, the Lincoln Highway Association, and the National Highways Association argued that an extensive network of good roads served to both physically bind America into a united nation and promote a shared national identity by manifesting a cross-section of the "real" America for the tourist to experience firsthand. Promoters and advocates represented automobile touring as a quintessentially American experience—a democratic journey of self-fulfillment in which tourists could come face to face with the nation's past and present. Automobile enthusiasts and good roads advocates, in reconstructing and repackaging the tourist landscape for automobile tourism, essentially placed American culture on display encouraging tourists to view the landscape firsthand, to witness the "real" American culture, and to relive the historic events of America's past. In so doing, they worked to legitimate and authenticate an ideal of a united nation, further defining tourism as a ritual of citizenship.

THE RISE OF AUTO TOURING

In 1893 two bicycle mechanics, Charles E. Duryea and J. Frank Duryea of Springfield, Massachusetts, succeeded in building a motorized carriage powered by a one-cylinder gasoline engine. Although European engineers and mechanics had already developed a gasoline-powered automobile, the Duryea brothers brought the automobile age to America.[3] By 1900, 4,192 automobiles had been manufactured in the United States, selling for approximately one thousand dollars each, and automobiling had emerged as a novel sport for the well-to-do.[4] Those fortunate enough to afford the latest European or American motor car tested their machines along scenic boulevards and parkways, on perilous and unpredictable country roads, as well as in speed races, endurance tests, and long-distance reliability runs sponsored by automobile manufacturers. Many early automobiles had a long, low wheel base, copying established European design, and they required smooth, dry roads for optimal handling.[5] Wealthy automobile owners, concentrated in the Northeast, organized to improve road conditions and establish a system of public financing for road construction so that they might enjoy the new sport of motoring. As the automobile market expanded during the early decades of the twentieth century, those interested in motoring increasingly divided along the lines of speed versus distance. Automobile racing and automobile touring emerged as two distinct pastimes with their own social sets and supporting organizations. With the institutionalization of automobile racing as a competitive sport, amateur drivers increasingly took to the open road to test their machines and tour the surrounding countryside.[6]

Books and articles in various automobile journals encouraged automobile tourists to explore the northeastern countryside on the rapidly improving system of roads or to motor across the elaborate road network in Europe taking in the sites and scenery.[7] They offered tips on routes, equipment, and traveling expenses. At the same time, American automobile manufacturers

Automobile manufacturers sought to popularize automobile tourism as a new form of elite recreation during the early twentieth century. Cover of *Overland Motor Cars* (Toledo, Ohio: Willy's Overland Company, 1915). (Warshaw Collection of Business Americana, Archives Center, National Museum of American History, Smithsonian Institution)

and other enthusiasts defined and promoted the possibilities of automobile touring by sponsoring and participating in long-distance reliability runs. In 1897 Alexander Winton drove one of his cars from Cleveland to New York City in ten days, capturing popular attention for the potential of this novel mechanism. In 1901 Roy D. Chapin, president of the future Hudson Motor Car Company, took seven and a half days to drive a curved-dash "Merry Oldsmobile" from Detroit to the New York City Automobile Show.[8] Soon after, enthusiasts and manufacturers began attempting transcontinental runs to prove that automobiles could hold up under rough conditions and long distances. The first successful coast-to-coast run was made in 1903. Horatio Nelson Jackson, a doctor from Vermont, with Sewall K. Crocker acting as chauffeur, were credited as being the first to successfully complete a transcontinental trek between San Francisco and New York City via automobile. It took them two months and three days.[9]

Each year thereafter other automobile enthusiasts, alone or in caravans, completed transcontinental runs, adding record times, increased automobile reliability, and pathfinding adventures to the list of automobile accomplishments. In 1908 the American Automobile Association noted that Fred Trinkle had made the seventeenth transcontinental trip but, perhaps more significant, that the Jacob M. Murdoch family had traveled from Los Angeles to New York in a month. In 1909 the first woman succeeded in making a transcontinental run. Alice Huyler Ramsey and three other women traveled from New York to San Francisco in a Maxwell touring car provided by the Maxwell-Briscoe Company. Also, in 1910 A. L. Westgard and three other drivers motored cross continent to lay out a southern transcontinental route for the Touring Club of America.[10] Many of these early transcontinentalists were eagerly supported by automobile manufacturers anxious to publicly demonstrate the possibilities of their product. In addition to widespread press coverage, transcontinentalists presented stories, photographs, and testimonials of their adventures, which manufacturers published in advertisements and pamphlets to promote automobile touring, thus capturing the imagination of the American public.

Charles Glidden capitalized on the fascination for long-distance reliability runs by pioneering guided automobile tours. In 1904 he organized a tour that ran from New York City to the St. Louis World's Fair. In the following years he ran tours through New England and the eastern seaboard states. His 1911 tour, guided by A. L. Westgard, ran from New York City to Jacksonville, Florida. Glidden institutionalized the long-distance reliability run. His tours essentially extended the opportunity to participate in a reliability run to any automobile owner who might wish to participate by organizing his tours in conjunction with the American Automobile Association (AAA). Not only did Glidden tours require that owners drive their own automobiles, but the AAA also provided trophies for those who exhibited the best performance and driving skill.[11] By 1910 it had been well established that the automobile could hold up under rough conditions and over long distances.

The year 1911 marked a turning point for those interested in transcontinental automobile runs and long-distance tours. As part of the Premier tour, twenty-six men, ten women, and four children motored from Atlantic City to Los Angeles. Twelve cars, mostly driven by their owners and accompanied by a truck carrying baggage, made the transcontinental trip in a month and a half. As an article in *Motor Age* noted, "There was no trouble of any magnitude encountered, no illness en route and the physical condition of the members of the party was better at the end than at the beginning. The object of the tour was to prove the feasibility of a transcontinental route for amateur car owners—and incidentally obtain publicity for Premier cars."[12]

Similarly, in 1912 the Raymond and Whitcomb Company in cooperation with the American Automobile Association sponsored an automobile tour from New York City to Los Angeles which they called the "Raymond-Whitcomb Trail to Sunset." Eighteen people, including six professional drivers, a pilot and his wife, a press representative, and a tour manager, made the trip. The agency charged tour participants $875 each to be "personally conducted tourists, traveling for pleasure, in a train of automobiles, running on schedule time from New York to California."[13] After traversing the improved roads of the East, the tour followed part of the Trail to Sunset mapped by A. L. Westgard for the American Automobile Association.[14] Westgard traveled the route twice prior to the October second departure, according to the AAA, and made special arrangements for gas and oil along certain remote sections of the route. *American Motorist* informed its readers that these precautions would "insure safety and reduce inconveniences to a minimum." They assured their readers, "The route for the 'Trail to Sunset' has been carefully and deliberately chosen from a strictly touring standpoint, offering the most varied scenery and numerous points of historic interest." A map highlighted significant scenic wonders that tour participants would encounter along the way, such as "Lake, River & Mountain Scenery" in New York, "Grape Vineyards" along Lake Erie, "Splendid Farms" on the River to River Road in Iowa, "Ranch and Farm Country," "Mexicans, Adobe Houses," "Pueblo Indians, Colored Cliffs," "Apache Indians," "Copper Mining," "Desert Valleys & Mountain Scenery," and "Orange Groves." In addition, a four-day side trip was planned to take tourists on a special train from Phoenix to the Grand Canyon.[15] Raymond and Whitcomb's Trail to Sunset marked the first long-distance tour that did not hinge on the performance of the automobile or promote a particular manufacturer. The tour was organized purely for the pleasure of those who wanted to participate. No longer simply a long-distance reliability run, the transcontinental automobile trip, and long-distance automobile tours in general, were being promoted as tourist events. Automobile touring quickly emerged as a novel alternative to the well established regime of railroad travel. Capitalizing on the image of adventure and independence used to characterize early transcontinental reliability runs, automobile tourists were described as modern-day pioneers, braving rough, unmarked roads and unpredictable machines to escape the confines of urban-industrial society and revitalize themselves on the open road.

GOOD ROADS: REIMAGINING THE TOURIST LANDSCAPE

In 1908 the Ford Motor Company first began to sell the Model T, pricing it at $850. Designed as the "car for the great multitude," it was sturdily built with a high wheel base for rough terrain and a two-speed transmission (forward and reverse) for ease of handling. By 1914 Ford had perfected a system of assembly-line production that allowed for the production of one car every hour and a half. That year the company sold 260,720 Model Ts at almost half the original price. Other automobile manufactures struggled to keep pace. Between 1914 and 1917 the production of automobiles in the United States soared from a little over half a million to almost two million.[16] No longer a novel luxury, the automobile was quickly becoming a popular consumer product.

Despite the increasing availability of the automobile during the interwar period, however, the necessary road infrastructure required a more complicated mix of public and political support, financing, and planning.[17] Building on the political and institutional infrastructure established by bicycle enthusiasts around the turn of the century, elite automobilists intensified the demand for improved road maintenance and construction and a federally supported highway program. As a result of their efforts, an elaborate network of paved and improved roads began to crisscross the Northeast during the first decade of the twentieth century.[18] As the popularity and the affordability of the automobile increased, the interest in good roads expanded to reflect the increasingly diverse needs of the growing number of automobile owners. Farmers, doctors, and salesmen, among others, joined the ranks of those interested in promoting good roads, and a diversified Good Roads movement emerged. Advocates argued that an expanded system of improved roads would increase revenues for farmers, merchants, and manufacturers. They provided for more efficient and comprehensive postal delivery. They improved the quality of rural life, and they promised to eradicate illiteracy and foster formal educational standards.[19] As one supporter explained, "Mothers must aid in creating good roads sentiment, so that their children will as future citizens be educated to the axiomatic truth that good roads are the milestone that backs the advancement of civilization."[20] According to the rhetoric of the Good Roads movement, in addition to expanding the possibilities for touring, an extensive system of improved roads ensured the forward march of progress.

During the early decades of the twentieth century, the Good Roads movement worked to extend a system of interconnected and improved roads throughout the country. Principally, supporters discussed the issue of federal aid for road construction, debated direct federal construction versus state and township construction, argued over farm-to-market roads versus interstate highways, and vied to establish and gain financial support for particular long-distance routes. The movement was composed of thousands of township, county, and state organizations devoted in part or exclusively to the cause. Granges, chambers of commerce, and county governments boosted good roads or organized road dragging in their local communities. Most states had a good roads federation or association that grew out of a state or local chamber of commerce or was created by boosters with other interests. From the state organizations came a variety of Good Roads congresses and conventions that brought together state highway officials and delegates, politicians, automobile dealers and manufacturers, representatives from highway associations, chambers of commerce, automobile clubs, good roads organizations, and journalists. These constituencies formed named trails associations in order to promote a particular section of road in their region. Towns or cities wanting to be on state or transcontinental routes invented named long-distance or transcontinental routes and tried to transform them into reality by organizing other local boosters into national or regional associations.

While the political debate over federal aid for road construction raged between the 1890s and the 1920s, the Good Roads movement was far from unified. Advocates ranged from rural grange members to upper- and middle-class northeastern automobile owners. Diverse constituencies embraced different ideas about the implications of good roads. For example, farmers and those with related interests, such as rural physicians and traveling salesmen, wanted to develop a system of roads that would facilitate the transportation of produce to markets and eradicate rural isolation. They argued for a system of improved local and county roads that would reinforce the bonds of regional communities. In contrast, elite automobile owners interested in automobiling as a leisure activity wanted to establish a system of long-distance roads that would increase the possibilities for automobile touring. They advocated the establishment of an extensive interstate highway system. More than just an expression of the conflict between states rights supporters and strong federal government supporters, the debate over federal aid reflected in part the conflict between rural constituencies and elite, urban automobile tourists. Farmers and others with related interests did not want to bear the tax burden for the construction of an interstate highway system that they believed benefited only wealthy, northeastern automobile tourists. Automobile tourists, on the other hand, believed that an extensive national highway system would address the needs of those interested in local transportation over improved roads, as well as those interested in long-distance travel.[21] While farmers and others used the rhetoric of commerce to justify their ideal of local good roads, automobile enthusiasts turned to the rhetoric of national tourism to support their desire for long-distance improved roads.

Building on the growing popular appeal of long-distance touring, one contingent of good roads advocates began to call for the establishment of continuous long-distance and transcontinental roads. In the early decades of the twentieth century, a number of local, regional, and national organizations emerged to boost particular roads. Perhaps the earliest proposed transcontinental road was known as the American Appian Way. In 1906 *Good Roads Magazine* announced that the route of this proposed transcontinental road would follow the old National Pike from Washington, D.C., to St. Louis and then "split into two great boulevards," one going up through Montana to Puget Sound and the other passing though Denver and Salt Lake City to San Francisco.[22] Although this transcontinental road, like many other proposed roads, never materialized, representing only the aspirations of enthusiastic good roads advocates and automobile tourists, the emergence of named road or trail organizations marked a significant trend in the Good Roads movement. Each organization, whether local, state, regional, or national, competed for the attention of motorists, state or national legislators, and the general public, seeking to gain funds for the actual construction of the road. By the 1920s at least 250 named trails or roads and about one hundred "trail organizations" had been established to promote particular roads.[23] Many of the routes overlapped, and many of the organizations were obscure. Additionally, some critics accused the myriad of named trail organizations of boosting paper routes and taking cash donations and membership fees in exchange for little or no real service. Building on the traditions of boosterism, many of these organizations linked their cause with an ideal of nationalism in order to generate funding and publicity.

Good roads advocates and automobile enthusiasts adopted and modified promotional strategies that had been developed by railroad corporations and embraced by touring advocates to help popularize auto touring. They appropriated the rhetoric of national tourism and redefined it to suit the auto touring experience. Unlike railroad corporations that developed and promoted brand-name attractions in the hopes of shaping a national clientele of tourists, good roads advocates built on the broader ideals of nationalism promoted by the National Park Service, defining touring as a process rather than a product. They characterized transcontinental roads as national highways that united the nation, providing access to the people, places, and history that embodied America. Organizations such as the National Old Trails Association, the Lincoln Highway Association, and the National Highways Association promoted transcontinental travel as a ritual citizenship and a patriotic duty, arguing that good roads would benefit the nation.

The National Old Trails Road, one of the earliest privately promoted transcontinental routes, sought to link an ideal of good roads and the possibilities of automobile touring with an ideal of the nation. In 1911 the Missouri chapter of the Daughters of the American Revolution (DAR) published a pamphlet entitled *The Old Trails Road: The National Highway as a Monument to the Pioneer Men and Women*. Developed by the Missouri Good Roads Committee of the DAR, the pamphlet outlined a proposed plan to construct a national highway along the "old trails," which "were stamped out by Nature's engineers—the buffalo, the elk and the deer, . . . [and] followed by the Indians and later by the pioneer who blazed and broadened them into wagon roads, over which traveled opportunity, civilization, religions and romance."[24] As outlined, the Old Trails Road did not follow a single transcontinental route but traversed a system of historic roads and trails that extended from Washington, D.C., to Kansas City and from there branched out to California and the Pacific Northwest. The proposed plan included more than ten thousand miles of improved road, following the National, or Cumberland, Road, associated with George Washington, General Braddock, and Thomas Jefferson; Boone's Lick Road, connected with Daniel Boone and his family; the Santa Fe Trail, associated with the pioneers who settled the West; Kearny's Road, over which Gen. Stephen W. Kearny and the Army of the West marched; and the Oregon Trail, followed by the pioneers traveling to the Pacific Northwest.[25]

The pamphlet explained that these trails manifested "the story of American expansion, the story of the old trails, the story of the pioneer." The pamphlet went on to note, however, that although history commemorated the deeds of the brave generals, explorers, and pioneers who traversed these trails, it had "failed to record the pioneer women who braved the unknown wilderness or desert, succored their children and inspired their men, dauntlessly; who held the forts built by the men, and made homes and planted the civilization of the frontier." With an interest in preserving and expanding public appreciation of the nation's heroic past the Good Roads Committee of the Missouri DAR issued a grand appeal: "Men and Women of today: With the blood of such heroic stuff coursing through your veins, build a national highway from ocean to ocean over these old trails, as an enduring and fitting monument to the men and women of yesterday, the heros of the nation whose dauntless struggles left us the richest heritage in the world's history!" They argued that the road would not only be "practical for modern use" but also "would conserve the welfare of the people living upon it." These advocates defined this transcontinental road in democratic, regenerative, and unifying terms. Invoking both history and progress in democratic terms, the Good Roads Committee defined automobile touring as an extension of America's heroic pioneer past, arguing that through the process of touring, tourists could become better Americans. Just as Frederick Jackson Turner had argued in his well-publicized frontier thesis that through the process of civilizing the wilderness Europeans shed their civilized manners, adopting a more individualistic and democratic life-style that defined American institutions and character, the DAR committee members suggested that in using the automobile to escape the confines of urban America, auto tourists could not only vicariously reenact the nation's pioneer history but also embrace the democracy and independence of the open road through the modern technology of the automobile, thus reaffirming their true American character. The pamphlet concluded, "With such a wagon road, dotted with historic shrines and taverns and sprinkled with traditions, Americans will tour this continent instead of Europe." To actualize this ideal of seeing America first over a national highway, the pamphlet ended with an announcement of a proposed "DAR automobile pilgrimage" over the completed Old Trails Road to the 1915 Panama-Pacific International Exposition.[26]

The idea for the National Old Trails Ocean-to-Ocean Highway, later known simply as the National Old Trails Road, emerged in an atmosphere charged with enthusiasm for good roads, excitement about the potential for automobile touring, and increasing patriotic interest in preserving and commemorating the nation's history.[27] As early as 1907 good roads advocates in Missouri had proposed the construction of a cross-state highway, initiating a debate that continued through 1911.[28] While this proposal became mired in conflict over potential routes, the Office of Public Roads published a map depicting a proposed system of seven interstate highways, including an ocean-to-ocean highway that extended from Cumberland, Maryland, crossing through Missouri to Tacoma, Washington, thus sparking widespread interest in transcontinental highways.[29] Also during this period, several state chapters of the DAR—in keeping with their mission "to perpetuate the memory of the spirit of the men and women who achieved American independence, by the acquisition and protection of historical spots and the erection of monuments"—had instigated a program to mark the original path of the Old Santa Fe Trail.[30] Following the lead of the Kansas DAR, the state DAR chapters of Colorado, New Mexico, and Missouri had, with the aid of state appropriations and local donations, erected a number of stone markers along the Old Santa Fe Trail, commemorating historic sites and events.[31] In 1911 these divergent interests converged, resulting in the formation of the National Old Trails Road Association.[32]

Although sources dispute who actually initiated the idea for the National Old Trails Road, the proposed road was one of the earliest, perhaps the first existing, of the named transcontinental roads.[33] On 19 December 1911, a group of good roads advocates met at the Kansas City Commercial Club and resolved to form the Transcontinental Highway Association to construct a national highway extending from Washington, D.C., along the Old Cumberland Road through Maryland, West Virginia, Pennsylvania, Ohio, Indiana, and Illinois to St. Louis, Missouri, and then west along Boone's Lick Road and the Santa Fe Trail to Santa Fe, New Mexico, passing on to California through New Mexico and Arizona along the Sunset route mapped by A. L. Westgard for the joint AAA and Raymond and Whitcomb Trail to Sunset tour.[34] In April 1912 the newly formed organization held its first annual convention in Kansas City, hosting delegates from Ohio, Illinois, Missouri, Kansas, Colorado, New Mexico, and Arizona.[35] Despite conflicts between the DAR chapters' proposed route and the routes supported by other named-trail organizations, the delegates of the first National Old Trails Road Convention succeeded in agreeing on a single route, adhering primarily to one of the historic routes supported by the DAR that ran from Washington, D.C., to Los Angeles and along the El Camino Real (the King's Highway) to San Francisco. In 1915 *Better Roads* reported, "The entire road from ocean to ocean is graded, more than one-third of it is permanently built, and fully two-thirds of the remainder is under contract."[36] However, the section known as the

Grand Canyon Route remained unimproved in early 1915.[37] Despite the fact that sections of the road remained unfinished, A. L. Westgard, the noted pathfinder for the AAA and automobile guide, recommended the National Old Trails Road as the best automobile route to the 1915 California expositions. He wrote, "At the present time [the National Old Trails Road] takes first place, looked at either from the standpoint of surface condition, scenery, historic interest or hotel accommodations."[38] Westgard even proposed to conduct a transcontinental automobile tour to be sponsored by the National Old Trails Association, the National Highways Association, and the Automobile Club of Southern California, following the Old Trails Road to the 1915 expositions at $780 per passenger.[39] By 1915 the National Old Trails Road had thus been established as one of the central named transcontinental highways.

Advocates for the National Old Trails Road drew on and added to the established rhetoric of national tourism to promote the road and gain funding. Speaking before the Committee on Agriculture in the House of Representatives in defense of a bill introduced by Representative William P. Borland of Missouri to secure federal funding for the road, Elizabeth B. Gentry, chairman of the Old Trails Road Committee of the Missouri DAR, stated, "The DAR's interest in this highway is to perpetuate the pioneer history and to conserve the ideals of the Nation by building a National highway over the trails of the pioneer." She explained to the committee, "There is a phrase, 'See America First,' ... [that] has sprouted in light of to-day's Nationalism. The Department of Commerce and Labor statistics show that $290,000,000 was left in Europe last year by American tourists. Switzerland is not an agricultural country, but is supported by its crop of tourists; that nation practically exists because Americans prefer the Alps to the Rockies." Yet she noted that America could boast the scenery of Wyoming, the Petrified Forest and the Painted Desert of Arizona, the Seven Cities of Cibola in New Mexico, and the Grand Canyon, suggesting that a scenic and historic transcontinental road stretching across America, providing access to these scenic and historic wonders, would not only facilitate but also encourage tourism in America, thus keeping American dollars at home, drawing in foreign money, and promoting patriotism. She went on to tell the committee, "To make the road truly National I suggest that it be typical of each State or section through

Cover of *National Old Trails Road*, a promotional guide (Los Angeles: Automobile Club of Southern California, 1910). (Reproduced by permission of the Huntington Library, San Marino, California)

which it passes; that State parks or preserves lie alongside where native animals, trees, shrubs and grasses may be seen; that historic houses be preserved
as State museums and objects of local history be therein collected; that the famous old taverns of coaching-days be restored, so that the traveler may enjoy
the hospitality typical of each section of the country." Underscoring the "educational, historic, and patriotic motives" embodied in the National Old Trails
Road, she "urge[d] that a distinctive scenic highway should be dedicated,
built, and maintained by the National Government."[40]

In evoking the See America First idea, advocates for the National Old
Trails Road alluded to the superiority of the sentiment of patriotism over
the desires of commerce to justify not only the location of the route but also
federal funding for construction. At the first annual convention of the
National Old Trails Association in 1911, the dispute over the actual route of
the proposed road centered on the issues of sentiment versus commerce.
Ralph Faxon, president of the New Santa Fe Trail Association, arguing that
the official route of the National Old Trail Road should follow the New
Santa Fe Trail rather than the historic Santa Fe Trail proposed by the DAR,
exclaimed, "I pause for a moment to pay my respects to these Daughters of
the American Revolution. . . . But, I say, stripping it of its sentiment, there
must be organization and practical construction. There must be practical
work and must be men's work along with it."[41] Faxon was interested in securing the increased business that would come with the construction of an
improved through-road for the aspiring commercial districts that lined the
New Santa Fe Trail, which ran through the western half of Kansas to the
Colorado state border. Although he juxtaposed male against female and
practicality against sentiment, he was clearly arguing in favor of the promises
of commerce over history or patriotism. However, Faxon's commercial perspective failed to sway the convention.

Mrs. Hunter M. Merriwether, state vice regent of the Kansas City DAR,
perhaps most eloquently rebutted Faxon's criticism. In her speech to the
convention she explained that the "one great advantage" the National Old
Trails Road had over a commercial highway like the New Santa Fe Trail
was that "all the States of the Union can unite in this one grand, patriotic
movement, free from personal interest, graft, commercial gain, civic rivalry,
or politics." From her perspective the route selected by the DAR and even-

tually accepted by the delegates of the convention represented a monument to the nation removed from the tainted desires of commerce. "Men of brain and brawn, fling away personalities in this Old Trail's [*sic*] Road building," she exclaimed. "Root from your hearts the miasma of commercialism, which, in its fever and fury, blinds your eyes to the upper and higher aim, that of uniting hearts and hands across this great country of ours, to build a National Monument that will ever be pointed out as the Old Trail's [*sic*] Road . . . over which marched the civilization, opportunity, religion, development, and progress of our grand America." She went on to say that tourists would rather see historic landmarks than "some modern, new, commercial road." Explaining that only sentiment could make the road a reality, she concluded, "There can be union in the Old Trail's [*sic*] Road, as its object is memorial, historical, National, and of commercial value as well to all the country."[42]

In linking the National Old Trails Road to the sentiments of nationhood, the DAR in cooperation with good roads advocates, state highway departments, and boosters throughout the states traversed by the route linked tourism and nationalism in an effort to bring together the growing enthusiasm for good roads, transcontinental automobile touring, and American history. They argued that transcontinental highways—especially the National Old Trails Road—transcended commercial interests and concerns, and reinforced national unity by commemorating a shared national history. Through this process they constructed the experience of automobile touring as a patriotic pastime, suggesting that motor touring across good roads allowed tourists to better understand the America of the past and the present. Other advocates for good roads and automobile touring reiterated these themes, thus working to create and present a selective history in the tourist landscape that reinforced an ideal of America as united nation.

American Motorist, the official publication of the American Automobile Association, also championed the connection between good roads, automobile touring, and nationalism. In 1913 the magazine published a number of articles and essays to promote the possibilities of transcontinental touring. They began their new campaign with a series of double-page illustrations depicting various famous natural landscapes throughout the West, captioned "One of the Many Reasons Why You Should See America First." Photographs of the government road on Mount Rainier, the Pike's Peak automobile road, and Gould Mountain in Glacier National Park were among the scenes displayed.[43]

In addition to promoting these scenic attractions of the West in connection with the See America First idea, *American Motorist* also began to actively promote transcontinental touring. In the May issue, W. D. Rishel provided an overview of transcontinental touring, predicting that the "transcontinental tour in an automobile will soon push baseball for first honors as the great National Pastime." He explained, "The year 1912 saw the movement start, 1913 will see the big advance guard, and by 1915, when the Panama Exposition opens, transcontinental touring will be a mania." Laying out the four main transcontinental routes and describing the unique experiences of automobile touring in the West, Rishel went on to argue that transcontinental touring contributed to the development of good roads in the West. Drawing on notions of the See America First idea articulated by western commercial interests, he argued that automobile touring served to convince not only the "country population" that there was "money in the tourist trade" but also western businessmen and boosters that touring revealed the bounty of the West to eastern investors. Both of these interest groups were beginning to support funding for the development of good roads, according to Rishel. He also contended that through automobile touring, in contrast to train travel, "one is brought face to face with past memories of conditions that are gone forever." The automobile, Rishel argued, provided the best means of seeing the scenery, meeting the people of the West, and, in the process, fully realizing "what difficulties confronted its pioneers, when they claimed this land as their own." Transcontinental automobile touring, according to Rishel, provided a firsthand view of America, allowing tourists to experience and authenticate the nation's past. He noted that "five thousand crossed the country in 1912, and enjoyed their experience," and he urged more automobile owners to take to the highways to see America. "Those 5,000 people are following the advice of the late Fisher Harris of Salt Lake, who coined the phrase which means more to the prosperity of this country than any set of laws that can be placed upon statute books by Congress," Rishel concluded. "It is 'See Europe if you will, but see America first'—and the automobile is the proper means of doing it."[44]

Just as the National Old Trails Road Association and *American Motorist* promoted the connection between good roads, automobile touring, and nationalism, so too did proponents for the Lincoln Highway, probably the most famous of the named transcontinental roads. Evoking the See American First slogan, advocates for the Lincoln Highway touted their transcontinental road as a fitting expression of the national ideal manifested by a coast-to-coast highway dedicated to the president who succeeded in preserving the union.

The idea of constructing an improved highway to commemorate Lincoln was first articulated by congressman James T. McCleary. In 1901 Congress created the Lincoln Memorial Commission and appropriated twenty-five thousand dollars for securing plans for the construction of a monument to the nation's sixteenth president, Abraham Lincoln. As a member of the commission, McCleary traveled to Europe in 1905 to study established precedents and determine the most suitable form for the new monument. Citing the lasting example of the Appian Way, constructed in commemoration of the famous Roman general Appius Claudius, Congressman McCleary concluded that of all the various monuments he surveyed in Europe—buildings, arches, bridges, shafts, statues—the ideal memorial to Lincoln would be a parkway linking Washington, D.C., and the Gettysburg battlefield and commemorating Lincoln's historic pilgrimage to pay homage to those who died in that historic Civil War battle.[45]

McCleary suggested that a "greensward forty or fifty feet wide [of] well-kept lawn looking like a beautiful green carpet of velvet" lined with "flower gardens and other decorative features" be flanked on each side by "a smooth roadway forty or fifty feet wide, constructed according to the highest engineering standards of 'good roads.'" One road was to serve "swift-moving vehicles like automobiles," and the other was to be used for "slow moving vehicles like carriages and wagons." To round out the design, he suggested that "a row or rows of stately trees, the rows broken at points where could be obtained fine views of mountain or valley or river," should border the parkway. He went on to propose that each state in the union be given the opportunity to "embellish" an "allotted portion" of the parkway "in accordance with its taste and means." He wrote, "So long as patriotism glows in the hearts of the American people, it will be for them a labor of love to add from time to time to this expression of national affection, keeping 'The Lincoln Way' at the forefront as the best and most attractive highway in the entire world." In an effort to bring this plan to fruition, McCleary helped establish the Lincoln Memorial Road Association of America in 1910 for the purpose of promoting and developing that roadway they hoped would become "the nucleus of a great Trans-Continental Highway to be built by the States through which it will pass."[46]

While McCleary and his supporters worked to garner support for a memorial road to Lincoln in opposition to another marble monument, in the fall of 1912, Carl Graham Fisher, an Indianapolis businessman who founded the Prest-O-Lite Company, which manufactured automobile headlights and helped promote the Indianapolis Speedway, was busy generating support for a proposed "Coast-to-Coast Rock Highway" to be built with funds donated by automobile manufacturers and related industries. Fisher's proposal quickly caught the attention of Henry B. Joy, president of the Packard Motor Company. He wrote to Fisher, stating, "I think your Good Roads Committee . . . ought to get up a protest to Congress on the expenditure of $1,700,000 in a monument in Washington to Abraham Lincoln." Joy supported the idea of a Lincoln Memorial Parkway, and he concluded his letter, "Let good roads be built in the name of Lincoln."[47] Soon after Joy joined ranks with Fisher and the two melded their interests, agreeing that Fisher's proposed Coast-to-Coast Rock Highway should be constructed as a memorial to President Lincoln, thus joining the interests of history and commerce.[48] In the summer of 1913, Henry Joy, Roy Chapin, president of the Hudson Motor Car Company, Emory W. Clark, president of the First National Bank of Detroit, Arthur Pardington, a good roads advocate from the days of the League of American Wheelmen, and Henry E. Bodman, legal counsel for Joy, met and formed the Lincoln Highway Association. They formally agreed that their stated aim was the establishment of "a continuous improved highway from the Atlantic to the Pacific, open to lawful traffic of all descriptions without toll charges; such highway to be known, in memory of Abraham Lincoln, as 'The Lincoln Highway.'"[49]

Between 1913 and 1915 the association worked feverishly to transform the Lincoln Highway from dream to reality. After much debate over the proposed route, the association determined the three central factors that would guide route selection: directness, accessibility to points of scenic and historic interest and central population centers, and the support of communities

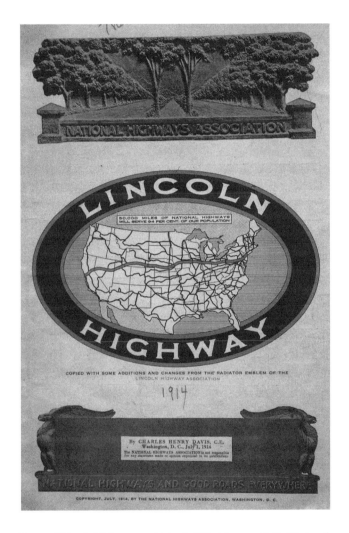

Cover of *Lincoln Highway,* a guidebook (Washington, D.C.: National Highways Association, 1912). (Courtesy of the Library of Congress)

along the way. In September 1913 Henry Joy publicly announced the official route.[50] From the starting point in Times Square, the road was to run from New York City to Philadelphia, on through Pennsylvania to Pittsburgh. It would then run through central Ohio, passing through Canton and Mansfield to Fort Wayne, Indiana, and north to Chicago. From Chicago, it would traverse northern Illinois and central Iowa to Omaha, Nebraska. Then it would run along the Platte River to Cheyenne, Wyoming, and west to Salt Lake City. After crossing central Nevada to Reno, the route would traverse California via Sacramento and Stockton and enter San Francisco through Oakland, where it would terminate at the Pacific Ocean in Lincoln Park. Clearly, issues of commerce had won out over the ideal of history and the sentiments of patriotism in the selection of the official route; the proposed road had little connection with Lincoln's life and travels. Rather, it connected many of the major urban centers across the northern half of the United States. However, the association still touted the Lincoln Highway in patriotic and historic terms. To advertise the proposed route the association sent out close to seventy-five thousand pieces of promotional literature.[51]

Like other good roads advocates interested in promoting automobile touring, the Lincoln Highway Association used the rhetoric of national tourism to generate support for the project. In a pamphlet entitled *Following the Path of Progress*, A. R. Pardington, vice president of the Lincoln Highway Association, detailed the progress made on the highway in its first year and encouraged automobile tourists to use the new highway to see the nation.[52] Pardington argued that the experience of automobile touring along the Lincoln Highway offered scenery, roads, and places of historic interest that equaled and surpassed the possibilities of touring in Europe. "From New York to San Francisco," he explained, "the tourist over the Lincoln Highway is treated to a moving, everchanging panorama of beauty and interest; he traces the footsteps of the pioneer and follows the path of the frontier as it moved ever westward." In this way tourists came in contact with "a cross section of America; her people, her thousand interests, her tradition, her history, her beauty, her resources, her magnitude, her power." West of Chicago tourists could experience the "memories of early days," such as the tragic adventure of the Donner Party, who perished trying to reach California, the fortitude of the Forty-Niners, the bravery of stage drivers and Indian fighters, and "the thrilling adventures of these hardy men who formed the vanguard of civilization in laying the Union Pacific." In the East tourists could drive over the same road "redcoats marched" and "men in powdered periwigs and three cornered hats . . . met to discuss the tax on tea or hatch plots against the crown."[53] Traveling by automobile along the Lincoln Highway, according to Pardington, brought tourists face to face with American history.

In a similar vein, *The Official Guide to the Lincoln Highway* argued that "See America First" had "become more than an appeal"; it had become "a necessity," given the estimated $120 million spent each year by Americans touring in Europe. The guide explained that for the man or woman who was willing to forego the excessive luxuries of the Pullman Palace car and enjoy "the great out-of-doors of America . . . whose yearning is for the open road, the far-flung horizons and the open air of heaven, who wants an outing, which will take him close to America's heart and soil and show him something of the trail his fathers trod and fought over, which will give him a new understanding of the beauties and magnitude of his country; to him the Lincoln Highway offers all these things."[54] The guide thus suggested that Seeing America First on the Lincoln Highway was about escaping the routines and restrictions associated with the overly civilized qualities of the Pullman Palace car and European travel. It was about directly experiencing the people, the places, and the history that made America unique.

Building on the imagery presented by earlier named trails organizations, Pardington and other Lincoln Highway advocates suggested that in escaping the restraints of urban industrial society, in vicariously reenacting a sanitized pioneer past, and in seeing America firsthand along the Lincoln Highway, automobile tourists became better Americans. Automobile tourism was defined as a ritual of citizenship that connected tourists with the diverse people and places that embodied the nation. In this way, the narrative of nationalism articulated to promote the highway and other early transcontinental roads posited a romantic or organic image of the nation in which nation-ness extended from an indigenous national culture and history rooted in a distinct national landscape.

During the nineteen teens and twenties, as named trail associations, good roads advocates, and automobile enthusiasts worked to promote the development of transcontinental roads for the benefit of long-distance automobile tourists, politicians and civic leaders debated the issue of federal aid for the construction of roads. Some argued that states and counties should be responsible for funding and constructing a network of local and regional "farm to market" roads. Others countered that the country needed a system of "National Highways" paid for and built by the federal government.[55] During the first six months of 1911 more than sixty bills "providing for some form of direct aid by the national government were introduced."[56] In 1912 the Congress passed the Post Office Appropriation Act, which provided funding for the improvement of post roads across the nation. The first Federal Aid Road Act was passed in 1916, providing funds to states for the construction and improvement of roads. The act was revised in 1919 and quickly replaced by the Federal Highway Act passed in 1921. The passage of the Federal Highway Act finally settled the debate between those who advocated for local and regional road networks and those who argued for a system of national highways.[57]

While this debate raged, a new organization emerged to unite those interested in national highways. In 1912, Charles Henry Davis, Senator Coleman DuPont, and C. H. Claudy, in collaboration with a number of other good roads advocates, met in Washington, D.C., to formally establish a national organization to promote the development of a national system of improved highways. They called the new organization the National Highways Association, describing it as

> a membership corporation which exists to favor, foster and further the development of NATIONAL HIGHWAYS and GOOD ROADS EVERYWHERE in the length and breadth of these United States of America, and to secure the benefits—social, moral, commercial, industrial, material, educational, and personal—in the progress and uplift of the American people which follow in the train of easy communication and transit between great centers of population and distribution and the great rural productive area of the Nation, and, [quoting John C. Calhoun], to "bind the states together in a common brotherhood, and thus perpetuate and preserve the Union."[58]

Davis and his supporters drew on the rhetoric of national tourism in an effort to articulate and popularize their cause.

Conceptualized as an umbrella organization to unify the Good Roads movement, the National Highways Association was the brainchild of Charles Henry Davis, an active Progressive Party member and a third-generation road builder and civil engineer from Massachusetts. Born in 1865, Davis received a degree in civil engineering from the Columbia University School of Mines in 1887 and worked for a number of electrical equipment manufacturers before setting out on his own as a private consultant. Involved in mining, engineering, railroad, and road construction activities, Davis served as president of the American Road Machine Company before retiring and launching the National Highways Association.[59]

When Davis conceived the idea for the National Highways Association in 1911 he envisioned an organization that could galvanize the Good Roads movement behind a system of national, federally funded highways. He began by initiating a letter-writing campaign in order to establish interest in the organization and then turned to the production of maps to illustrate his proposed system of national highways. The initial interest being established, the National Highways Association was formally incorporated, and it began to solicit members in an effort to unite good roads interests. Davis set up shop on his Cape Cod estate, hiring a number of draftsmen, public relations men, and stenographers, and began the principal task of publishing maps and pamphlets arguing for a system of national highways built by the national government and maintained by a National Highways Department.[60]

Davis's association quickly incorporated many of the major good roads organizations and its principal figures, including such associations as the National Old Trails Association, the Midland Trail Association, the National Automobile Association, and more than fifteen state good roads associations.[61] By 1913 the association had also secured A. L. Westgard, famous for his cross-continent pathfinding missions for the American Automobile Association and the Touring Club of America, as vice president, official pathfinder, and consultant for all map-making activities.[62] In addition to the Board of National Trustees, composed of Davis and Senator Coleman DuPont, the Board of National Councilors, the National Board of Directors, and a roster of national officers, the organization claimed a 94-member Council of Governors, a 123-member Council of Commissioners, 64 national advisors, and 54 divisions or departments. The Council of Governors consisted of governors and former governors of states. The Council of Commissioners consisted of members or ex-members of state highway commissions. The divisions or departments consisted principally of good roads organizations but also listed

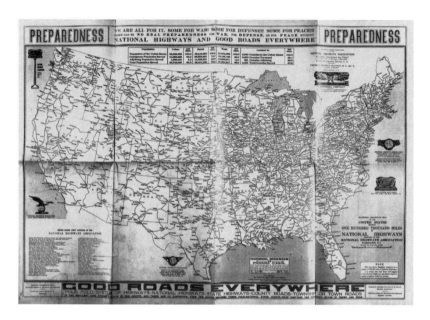

Map, *100,000 Miles of Road Proposed by the National Highways Association* (1915). (Division of Technology, National Museum of American History, Smithsonian Institution)

named roads organizations. By 1914, C. H. Claudy, director of publicity for the association, claimed in a promotional survey that the National Highways Association had not only succeeded in securing "a membership of many thousands throughout the Nation" but also had "issued more than 444 maps, pamphlets, bulletins, circulars, etc., of a total circulation of more that 5,306,113 copies." In addition the association had sent out more than 126,000 letters and collected and filed over 38,000 documents related to road conditions throughout the United States.[63]

The National Highways Association defined the problem of good roads principally in terms of the need to create a well-ordered system of highways throughout the country. To this end it promoted the idea of a "fourfold system of highways: national highways—state highways—county roads—township or town roads."[64] This hierarchy of roads reproduced the same structure as the highway system developed in the state of Massachusetts, with which Charles Henry Davis was undoubtedly familiar and which had reached a state of substantial completion by 1907.[65] In advocating this system, the National Highways Association argued for a network of federally con-structed national highways from which state, county, and township roads could extend. It argued that only by undertaking the project of building a national highway system would good roads in all parts of the country be assured.[66] Their publicity material explained, "The National Highways As-sociation ... favor[s] the construction of a system of trunk lines—about 50,000 miles in all—connecting the principal cities of the country, entirely at the expense of the government and under government control," adding that "the states should build certain secondary roads entirely at the state's expense and under state control; and that the counties should build a third class of roads entirely at the county's expense and under county control."[67] Building on the arguments used by the Good Roads movement, and particularly the transcontinental highway associations that argued that transcontinental or national roads would result in an improved system of secondary roads, the National Highways Association linked a conception of good roads to the ideal of an active federal government and a united and unified nation.

In promoting the aims of the National Highways Association, Charles Henry Davis incorporated the ideas of See America First and national tour-ism into his repertoire of good roads arguments to underscore the need for his proposed national highway system. On 1 August 1913, Davis addressed the North Carolina Good Roads Association, praising Joseph Hyde Pratt, state geologist, for his work in helping to develop the "Crest of the Blue Ridge Parkway," a scenic highway that was planned to extend across North Caro-lina from Marion, Virginia, to Cornelia, Georgia. He began his address with the exclamation, "See America first!" explaining that in 1912 more than one hundred thousand American tourists crossed the Atlantic to "do" Europe. He noted that most of these tourists would reveal, "if they tell you honestly, that it was the out-of-doors where the most enjoyment and recreation were found." According to Davis, tourists went to Europe because "Europe caters to tourists—especially American tourists. Everything is provided for their comfort." However, Davis remarked, "the State of North Carolina possesses scenery the equal of any in the world." The scenery was superb, the flora and fauna diverse, and the trout fishing excellent. He nevertheless argued that these facts would not be known without good roads. Europe had them, America did not. "Good roads abound in Europe," he declared. "Highways built primarily for scenic purposes are common in Switzerland, France, Germany, and most of the other countries of Europe. In America they are so limited as to be almost negligible." He went on to state that it would be necessary to follow the example set by the Appalachian Highway Company in its construction of the Blue Ridge Parkway and develop "Good Roads Everywhere" in order to correct the situation. Only through the development of good roads throughout the United States would American tourists be enticed to stay home and see America first. Davis concluded that a national system of improved roads would "mean more to this Nation than any other development since our Declaration of Independence."[68]

Davis used the See America First idea as an expression of commercial and scenic nationalism to connect the Good Roads movement and the aims of the National Highways Association with an ideal of America nationhood. He portrayed the lack of an improved highway network in the United States as a national disgrace, symbolic of both economic and military weakness. For Davis an integrated system of national highways would serve to physically, economically, politically, and spiritually unite America as a nation-state. A national highway system objectified the bonds of modern nationalism. Expressing that nationalism, Davis wrote, "May our beloved land be gridironed by National Highways."[69]

Arguing in favor of the "creation of a special National Highways Commission" to investigate the subject of good roads and how they might be constructed and financed, and to debate issues of National Highways versus federal aid, Davis further developed the relationship between his ideal for a federally funded system of national highways and national tourism. In an article outlining his ideas and how they might be practically implemented, Davis wrote, "'See America first' usually is intended to mean go west, instead of to Europe." He questioned, "should it mean that only, and why does it now only mean that?" Challenging the assumptions of many who adopted the See America First slogan to promote tourism in the United States, Davis argued, "There is no reason why 'seeing America first' should only mean going west. The East should not be passive and indifferent about it. The East should cater to the traffic which it can induce from the West just as much as the West now tries to cater for eastern traffic." He went on to note that the East could boast not only the Atlantic shore and a warm summer climate but also the wonders of "Niagara, the Adirondacks, [the] White Mountains, the lakes and woods of Maine, the shores of Cape Cod and Florida." He concluded that a system of National Highways approximately fifty thousand miles long "would let people of moderate means, from all parts of the United States, 'see America first.' But more than that, it would bring activity and prosperity to millions of other people yet unable to do the seeing, thus later giving many of them a chance to join the ranks."[70]

To reinforce his argument, Davis provided a statistical breakdown of the population in the United States by sections that he defined as the Northeast, the Southeast, the Southwest, the Northwest, and the Intermountain area. Comparing the area in square miles for each section with the percentage of improved road mileage, the overall population and the population per square mile, Davis demonstrated that it took twice as many miles of road to serve the number of people west of the Appalachians as it did those in the East. Therefore, he argued that until a system of national highways was constructed, linking the East and the West, the movement to See America First would be hindered. According to Davis, the eastern population, which had grown wealthy because of its extensive road infrastructure, would continue to prefer travel to Europe, because of the inadequacy of western roads and roadside accommodations. And the western population, although desirous of returning to its "ancestral home" in the East, could only travel east if made more prosperous by the improvement of their road infrastructure.[71]

As the most outspoken proponent for a federally funded, national system of highways, Charles Henry Davis and the National Highways Association perhaps most blatantly linked the development of good roads with an ideal of American nationalism. Arguing that a system of national highways promoted preparedness, prevented illiteracy, and stimulated prosperity, in addition to encouraging tourism in America, Davis and his associates championed an ideal of America united under the direction of an active federal government through commerce and progress. According to Davis a system of national highways would not only physically manifest a united nation but also, through tourism, these roads would serve to reinforce the bonds of nationhood. In promoting a system of national highways, Davis adopted and expanded the rhetoric of national tourism articulated by good roads advocates. Independent named trail organizations such as the National Old

Trails Association and the Lincoln Highway Association had predominantly encouraged eastern tourists to see the West as transcontinental railroad corporations had before them. Davis further developed and transformed this argument by embracing a more comprehensive and formal idea of the nation. Progressive in character, the object of the National Highways Association was to create an orderly network of highways that traversed the United States east to west and north to south, facilitating transportation throughout the nation. Thus Davis and his supporters encouraged automobile touring in the North and the South as well as the East and the West. They linked their plan for a system of national highways to an ideal of nationalism that extended from the power of the nation-state represented by an active federal government rather than section or state.

In the process of promoting both good roads and automobile tourism, these organizations—the National Old Trails Association, the Lincoln Highway Association, and the National Highways Association—helped reimagine the tourist landscape. Rather than focusing solely on the final destination as railroad corporations had before them, these organizations presented automobile touring as a process—an experience.[72] They encouraged auto tourists to see America firsthand on the expanding network of good roads. They argued that a system of national highways would bind the nation together and, through the experience of tourism, tourists could reaffirm their sense of American-ness by moving into the landscape and gaining intimate contact with American history and culture. In this way these organizations helped to further define touring as a ritual of citizenship.

SEEING AMERICA FIRST ON GOOD ROADS

By 1915 the European war and the California expositions had reinforced the growing popularity of touring in the United States. At the same time, the passage of the Federal Aid Road Act in 1916 reflected not only widespread acceptance of the Good Roads movement but also an acknowledgment of the need for federally funded roads. Although World War I prevented the immediate implementation of federal aid, the demands of mobilization underscored the need for a national road network and the continued improvement of existing roads.[73] The passage of the Federal Highway Act of 1921 addressed those needs by seeking to provide a connected system of interstate highways. As good roads advocates and legislators worked to develop an improved road system throughout the United States, automobiles became increasingly more affordable to the point that by the mid-1920s the cost of the Ford Model T had dropped to $290.[74] By 1920 there were approximately eight million cars registered in the United States; by 1930 the number had risen to almost twenty-three million.[75] During the twenties, improved roads, affordable automobiles, the development of roadside facilities, and increased prosperity laid the groundwork for the transformation of automobile touring from a novel sport for urban elites to a more popular pastime for native-born, white, upper- and middle-class Americans.[76] In the process, the possibilities manifested by the automobile and the developing road network, redefined the experience of touring in national terms. The federal government institutionalized the rhetoric of nationalism promoted by named trail associations and good road organizations by incorporating it into a newly rationalized system of numbered interstate highways, and auto touring advocates encouraged Americans to see America first by automobile.

In 1924 the American Association of State Highway Officials requested the secretary of agriculture, who had responsibility for the Bureau of Public Roads, to assist in the development of the new standardized system of marking the nation's roads. The first official meeting of the Joint Board on Interstate Highways, composed of representatives from the Bureau of Public Roads and various state highway officials appointed by the secretary of agriculture, was held in Washington, D.C., on 20 April 1925.[77] The two-day meeting resulted in a proposal for a national, numbered highway system with uniform signage throughout, embodied by a series of resolutions calling for a uniform system of route marking, the selection of transcontinental and state routes to be marked, and the replacement of the named trails organizations.[78] The Joint Board on Interstate Highways was formally established to implement this system. In addition to discussing the issues of standardized signage, the board distinguished between "reputable trails organizations" and those "individuals [which] have sought to capitalize the popular demand . . . collecting large sums of money from our citizens and giving practically no service in return."[79] The board recommended to states that the reputable trails organizations be permitted to continue marking routes until the new system was established, but added that no new road organizations should be allowed to form to develop state or federal highways. Each state highway department was requested to secure authority from its legislature for the marking and signing of roads. Furthermore, the states were to make recommendations on the designation of the interstate system for resolution in subsequent sessions. The board stated the principles to be followed for the development of these interstate roads, including the connection of important centers over reasonably direct routes, the dispersion of traffic over alternate routes to promote safety and ease of maintenance, and the selection of routes limited to 1 percent of the state's mileage each for roads of primary, secondary, and tertiary importance. In other words, the individual proposals by the states would be part of a comprehensive interstate system designed for efficient national travel.[80]

For the next two years the board pursued negotiations around the country with state highway departments to determine the choice of routes and to establish a uniform system of signage. The board resolved not to select or give official status to any existing named trail. The Lincoln Highway and the National Old Trails Road, as well as the other named roads, were to be replaced by a series of numbered roads, their official routes represented by several different numbers. In January 1927 the American Association of State Highway Officials approved the final location of a national highway system recommended by the Joint Board. The proposed system included "ten main transcontinental routes," which were to be designated by numbers that were multiples of ten. In addition, a number of major north and south routes were selected and numbered. A Department of Agriculture press release explained, "The route-numbering system which has been decided upon will be of great assistance to tourists in following through routes. All east and west routes bear even numbers while north and south routes have odd numbers. Frequently three digit numbers are used to indicate branches of through routes." The article added, "There will be no difficulty in following any selected route since a standard sign showing the route number has been adopted and also standard danger, caution and directional signs."[81] Reflecting the growing interest in efficiency, standardization, and order, this "planned system of arterial interstate highways, uniformly designated and marked by standardized direction, cautionary and informational signs," was developed by the Bureau of Public Roads in an attempt to eliminate the confused and inefficient private system created by the myriad of named trails and road organizations.[82]

The adoption of this standardized system sparked controversy among the many good roads advocates who had worked to promote and construct the named trails comprising the nation's first system of interstate highways. G. S. Hoag, secretary of the Lincoln Highway Association, explained that many tourists traveling by automobile learned a great deal about American history and geography by traveling over named trails and roads. An editorialist paraphrased Hoag's criticism of the plan: "There will always be a greater patriotic glow in the thought of having made a trip over a considerable portion of the Lincoln Highway, the Yellowstone Trail, the Dixie Highway or the Santa Fe Trail than could ever attach to the retrospection of a similar trek over U.S. Highway Number 11 or Number 60."[83] Another good roads supporter lamented, "There is no Columbia River highway on the official maps at Washington. It's merely 'No. 20.' . . . 'The Oregon Trail,' as a designation, is officially dead, and in its place is a couple of meaningless numerals. The Washington Bureaucrats have blotted out from the road maps and records the mighty meaning conveyed in those symbolic words, 'The Oregon Trail.'" He went on to liken those numbers to "figures in a cash register or on a bank ledger" that completely obliterated the history associated with many of the transcontinental roads that followed old pioneer trails. "One of the glories of a great highway system is the romance reflected in its nomenclature," he explained. "One of its lures, that will grow stronger and stronger with time, is its local name, which in a single word tells of an epoch and fires the imagination at the picture of a great historical background."[84] Essentially these good roads advocates deplored the loss of narrative associated with named roads. Roads such as the Lincoln Highway and the National Old Trails Road told a story about the nation—its past and its present—that these enthusiasts believed was central to the pleasure and experience of automobile touring. They feared that the bureaucratic system of numbered roads would subsume the narrative of history and progress objectified by the named roads.

In an effort to assuage these concerns and promote the new highway system, the Bureau of Public Roads attempted to associate the numbered interstate routes with American history and nationality, thus following the precedents set by proponents of named roads and trails. In the late twenties, after the new numbered highway system had been approved and adopted, the bureau prepared a series of press releases that detailed the routes followed by the major numbered roads and linked those roads with the sights and shrines of American history and progress. East-west interstate routes 30, 40, 80, 90, and 66, along with north-south routes 1, 41, and 99 were debuted as "Highway[s] of History" or "Paths of Pioneers."[85] Omitting all references to the named roads and trails that preceded them, these numbered roads were celebrated for their historical, scenic, and educational value. For example, the article promoting U.S. Route 1, which ran from Fort Kent, Maine, to Miami, Florida, boasted, "Stretching from end to end of the thirteen original colonies, . . . the connecting sections of the Atlantic Coast highway known as United States Route No. 1 have formed a highway of history for three hundred years." Detailing the location of the route, the article went on to link the road with George Washington and the Revolution.[86] Similarly, U.S. Route 99, which began at the Canadian line near Blaine, Washington, and ran to El Centro, California, on the Mexican border, was described as "the historic inland route of the Pacific Coast, traversing, in the Northwest, the land of the Indian, trapper and explorer of the 18th century, and, in California, the land of the Spanish padres and the 'Forty-niners.'"[87] Publicity for U.S. Route 40, which ran from Atlantic City to San Francisco, exclaimed,

> Westward in the path of empire, along routes traversed by the pioneers of America from the Atlantic to the Golden Gate, and including in the Ohio Valley, the longest stretch of practically straight road in the country, United States route 40 crosses 14 states, and offers to the transcontinental motor tourist a panorama of the mid section of the country that epitomizes the westward expansion of the Nation from colonial days to the present.[88]

The article went on to associate the road with Revolutionary and Civil War battles, the Old National Pike, Daniel Boone, the Mormons, the Gold Seekers, the Donner Party, and the planting of the U.S. flag in San Francisco in 1846. Like the named roads that preceded them, the numbered roads were linked to a narrative of national history.

The controversy over the shift from named to numbered roads and the attempt on the part of the Bureau of Public Roads to associate the major numbered roads with American history and progress manifests the ways in which the automobile in combination with the developing road infrastructure worked to transform the experience of touring. Seeing the country by automobile allowed individuals to both view the landscape and experience place firsthand. Prescriptive automobile touring literature shifted from the celebration of scenery and standardized destinations that characterized most railroad promotional literature and began to express an interest in history and local color. As one automobile enthusiast noted, automobile touring promoted a "love for the country." He explained, "There is no better way to impress upon the mind historical events than through object lesson. Automobile tours can be arranged to follow the roads of history, visiting places of historic as well as scenic interest, impressing indelibly upon the young mind through the landmarks associated with them, the earlier events in the history of the United States."[89] In the context of a society intrigued by the possibilities of learning through direct experience following the theories of Progressive educators, automobile touring seemed to embody a perfect opportunity for gaining "a liberal education."[90] In an article deciphering the many named and marked roads, Robert Bruce, a writer for *American Motorist*, remarked, "There is . . . a new and genuine interest in places, especially those of historic interest, which is rapidly dotting many important routes with tablets and other markers conveying information which a few years ago was beyond the reach of the tourist going through on schedule." He went on to explain that "when appropriately named, as most of them fortunately are, there is something in that fact to stir the imagination and help sustain the interest of the middle-distance or long-distance traveler."[91] Automobile enthusiasts and good roads advocates linked the experience of touring by automobile to a coherent narrative about America, its history, and its development. In traveling over named or numbered roads that followed the historic trails of westward expansion, in moving into the landscape, in having the opportunity to stop and explore historic sites, and literary shrines, and in coming into contact with the regionally diverse people of American society, tourists were encouraged to see and understand America as a coherent whole. According to the prescriptive literature, through automobile touring one gained an intimate and authentic understanding of the nation, thus reaffirming one's American-ness.

In May 1924 the editor of *American Motorist* announced, "With this number *American Motorist* presents the first issue of a series of state editions," with the intention that "eventually these state numbers will cover the United States."[92] In the ensuing years the magazine presented issues on Virginia, Florida, Pennsylvania, Ohio, Michigan, and Washington, D.C., as well as regional issues covering the South and the West, abandoning their initial plan to cover each state separately. In addition, during the later half of the twenties, the magazine also produced two national touring numbers describing automobile touring possibilities throughout the United States. In enumerating the possibilities for touring, these national touring numbers reflected the increasing interest in intimacy and authenticity that defined the experience of touring by automobile.

The 1926 national touring number presented by *American Motorist* included articles on the National Park-to-Park Highway, the Columbia River Highway in Oregon, the Redwood Highway running from San Francisco to Portland, Oregon, and the Lackawanna and Susquehanna Trails in Pennsylvania, as well as tours of Minnesota and Wisconsin, the Ozarks, New England, New York, Pennsylvania, New Jersey, Virginia, the Shenandoah Valley, North Carolina, the Eastern Shore of Virginia, and Kentucky. Focusing primarily on scenic highways, the articles celebrated the possibilities of escaping the "artificial life of the cities," getting into nature, and witnessing history.[93] In pointing out scenic vistas and historic shrines, the articles underscored the significance of firsthand experience—the notion that tourists were bearing witness not only to the places where important historic events occurred, but also to the distinct wonders of American nature. Celebrating the natural scenery of the Shenandoah Valley, one author noted that if you wanted to find nature, "if you want them all [the wonders of nature], if you want to sink deep into them as you sink deep into music, revel in them, then try that road which lies between Roanoke and the Shenandoah Valley."[94] From the road one did not just view nature, one was able to fully experience nature, and that rich experience would result in lasting memories. As one author, extolling the virtues of the big trees encountered along the Redwood Highway, remarked, "Imperishable memories dwell with you. Until you die you will retain in your mind's eye the picture of those giant trees, you will remember vividly the roar of the surf, the tang of the sea and pines, the colossal, brooding mountains."[95]

Automobile touring provided not only an intense experience within nature, it also allowed the tourist to relive the dramatic events of history. Describing the experience of traveling over the Columbia River Highway, one author noted, "One cannot refrain from wondering at the task that was before the venturesome pioneers of the late 1700 and early 1800 periods when Lewis and Clark and other pioneering heros first negotiated the stretch of the then virgin country that is now passed so swiftly and so easily."[96] Crossing the paths of famous pioneers allowed tourists to experience a vicarious and sanitized version of the adventures of westward expansion. Or, as Elon Jessup, a noted automobile writer, explained in describing a tour of the New England coast, "History has played its part along this rugged coast you are following. . . . It is sometimes a pleasing fancy to identify yourself with the first men to come this way. . . . In some respects, the Maine coast of that day couldn't have been very different from what it is at the present time."[97] In other words, automobile touring situated the tourist so that he or she might be able to identify with the events of history, in effect making history one's own story without suffering, controversy, or responsibility.[98]

The significance of this intimate and authentic encounter with the people and places of America reflected not only a fascination with self-fulfillment and "real" experience but also an interest in locating and defining the essence of American nationhood.[99] The Washington, D.C., number of *American Motorist* perhaps best expressed these issues. Drawing on the intimacy associated with automobile touring, the author promised, "A journey to the Nation's Capital will quicken [the tourist's] heart, stir his patriotism, and send him back home with memories which will delightfully people a thousand hours." He went on to note that in motoring through Washington, in visiting the "great buildings," the historic monuments, and the wonderful museums, "I discover that after all our political differences . . . are not even as important as the waves that disturb the surface of the ocean." He continued, "I learn that down below these petty surface conditions . . . there lies a mighty ocean of national greatness and governmental tranquillity that neither the winds of political controversy nor the swells of sectional unrest can disturb."[100] Seeing the sights of Washington offered him a vision of a united and unified America. As revealed by the prescriptive literature promoting the possibilities of automobile touring, his experience of touring in Washington was also true for automobile touring throughout the United States. In other words, automobile touring offered the tourist a privileged view of America that revealed the underlying substance of the nation. In providing tourists with an intimate and authentic encounter with the various people and places of America, in situating the tourist within the landscape so that he or she might gain a firsthand experience of place, the promise of automobile touring rested on a romantic theory of nationalism. That theory of nationalism linked the nation to land and soil, history and tradition, as well as the people and their customs. The development of a network of good roads to accommodate the automobile tourist provided a physical landscape, and a cultural context that positioned the individual so that he or she could see and appreciate America as a united nation. As one auto tourism advocate wrote, "This trip through the heart of America is coming to be known as the great American pilgrimage. No American can motor from New York to San Francisco without gaining a new conception of the lives of his fellow citizens, a knowledge of his country that will widen local horizons and stifle sectional prejudices, and achieve a pride in and an appreciation of his United States that can be gained in no other way."[101] Automobile tourism, in other words, might best be understood as a modern-day ritual of citizenship.

In expanding and reimagining the tourist landscape, good roads advocates and automobile enthusiasts redefined the experience and the ideal of national tourism. According to the prescriptive literature, automobile tourism provided a more intimate, personal, and authentic encounter with the "real" America along a network of good roads that offered access to a shared national history and culture. A national system of interstate highways supported by an active federal government promised to solidify the nation-state, and the technology of the automobile liberated the individual tourist from rigid railroad schedules and final destinations, as well as artificial, urban social constraints, thus redefining the promises and possibilities of liberal individualism. In this way, the cultural construction and representation of automobile tourism served to reinforce and legitimize the modern urban-industrial nation-state. It also helped to expand the popularity and allure of national tourism.

5

NARRATING THE NATION

> In this vast seven-foot [book]shelf panorama of our land a lasting mon-
> ument to the America we know has been created, one to which future
> generations may well turn as we now turn to the Doomsday book or
> the yellowed pages of "Niles's Register."
> —*Saturday Review of Literature*, 1941

*I*N OCTOBER 1941, HOWARD O. Hunter, commissioner of work
projects for the Roosevelt administration, announced that the second
week in November would be designated American Guide Week, acknowledging the publication of the Oklahoma state guide, the final volume of the WPA's American Guide series.[1] The series, begun in 1935
under the auspices of the Federal Writers' Project, a New Deal relief program, was touted as the first comprehensive set of guides to the United
States. "Through these guides," President Roosevelt noted in his endorsement of American Guide Week, "citizens and visitors to our country now have at their finger-tips for the first time in our history a series of
volumes that ably illustrate our national way of life, yet at the same time
portray the variants in local patterns of living and regional development."[2]
Displaying the slogan "Take Pride in Your Country," the sponsors of

American Guide Week, which included the Federal Writers' Project, the American Booksellers Association, the Office of Education in Washington, the American Library Association, and a committee of publishers of the various state guides, sought to encourage Americans "to refresh their knowledge of their country" by purchasing, reading, and using the WPA guides.[3] Building on and borrowing from the promotional strategies developed by western boosters, railroad corporations, the National Park Service, and automobile and good roads advocates, the celebration of American Guide Week linked tourism to the nation, further defining the tourist experience as a ritual of citizenship. As Roosevelt proclaimed in his letter of endorsement, "I am sure that this shelf of books about our people, the places they live in, the institutions they have developed, and the monuments of their history . . . will serve to deepen our understanding of ourselves as a people and hence promote national unity."[4] Seeing America, gaining firsthand experience of people and places across the nation, would reaffirm a sense of shared national history, culture, and identity.

Despite the promotional gloss of American Guide Week, the American Guide series was not the first set of guidebooks to survey the American scene. Rather, the WPA guides reflected the culmination of a century marked by increased interest in national tourism and a slew of promotional and prescriptive literature aimed at capturing the tourist market. Between the late nineteenth century, when tourism emerged as an elite popular pastime, and the early twentieth century, when tourism solidified into a popular leisure activity, writers and publishers sought to capitalize on the emerging tourist trade and encourage Americans to see and know their own country by codifying the sites and scenes of the nation into prescriptive tourist guides. As tourist advocates and civic boosters, railroad corporations and automobile interests, along with government agencies and independent organizations began to create and promote tourist attractions across the United States, expanding the possibilities of the tourist experience, written guides emerged to direct tourists. From early on prescriptive tourist literature took many forms, ranging from professionally written travelogues and scenic albums to railroad brochures and fact-filled tourist guides. Materials that sought to counsel tourists about various tourist destinations, transportation, accommodations, and other practical information ranged in form from personal travel accounts to

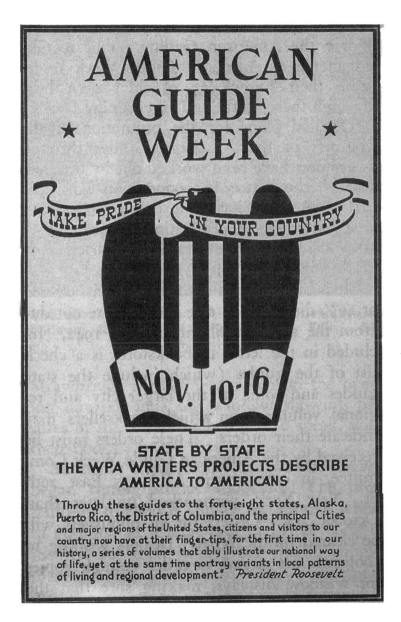

Poster, *American Guide Week, November 10–16, 1941.* (Reprinted with permission from the 11 October 1941 issue of *Publishers Weekly;* reproduced by permission of the Huntington Library, San Marino, California)

statistical compendiums of information. Evolving from earlier immigrant guides, statistical tourist guides provided information about transportation, accommodation, and attractions. Alternately, scenery albums, published to celebrate an ideal of scenic nationalism, codified scenic views and vistas for armchair travelers and cultural literati. Many early tourist guides were produced by railroads that had a vested interest in luring the tourist to their lines. However, independent writers and publishers quickly caught on to the value of the tourist guide and began to issue their own guides to various rail lines or tourist destinations. Of the more popular guides, George A. Crofutt's *Great Transcontinental Railroad Guide* (1869) focused primarily on the West made accessible by the recently completed transcontinental railroad. Moses King produced guides and view-books that oriented the traveler to the major cities in the Northeast. The *Baedeker Guide to the United States* was produced specifically to guide European travelers to the 1893 World's Columbian Exposition.[5] Whatever their form, these publications all functioned as authoritative textual guides, categorizing various sites and scenes and teaching the tourist how to get to, understand, and appreciate the tourist landscape. Few early guides attempted to provide a comprehensive overview of the tourist opportunities available throughout the country; rather, they focused on information relative to specific cities, sites, or regions. However, as the transportation network expanded and the possibilities of a national tourism began to solidify, writers and publishers attempted to codify tourist sites and scenes across America establishing a canon of American tourist attractions and encouraging tourists to see and know their own country.

D. APPLETON GUIDES AND THE DEPICTION OF NATURE'S NATION

New York publishing firm D. Appleton and Company, noted for its cyclopedias, dictionaries, and atlases, published a series of guides in the mid-nineteenth century that attempted to tap into the rising tourist market by providing a comprehensive overview of travel opportunities in America.[6] In 1846 the company published its first guide to the United States, *Appleton's Hand-Book Through the United States*, a guide for tourists and travelers providing an overview of principle cities, accommodations, routes, distances, and directions "through every part of the United States." Although the initial publication promised two parts covering the northern and eastern United States and Canada as well as the West and the South, it appears that only the first part was published. Billed as the "American Guide Book," the preface noted that "the writer has endeavored to confine himself to matter-of-fact descriptions of what ought to been seen, and is calculated to interest the tourist at each place." After providing a brief orientation to the traveler concerning issues of transportation, accommodation, currency, and "characteristics of the country," the guide presented a brief overview of the United States, detailing its geography, politics, industry, religion and education, history, and civil and social characteristics. A series of tours emanating from New York City, "the metropolis of the United States," then directed tourists to the principle cities and points of interests situated along major railroad and steamboat lines. Reflecting the tourist possibilities of the era, descriptions of New York and Boston as well as Saratoga Springs and Niagara Falls dominated the tour material.[7] Appleton's supplemented this initial guide four years later with a more comprehensive overview of travel opportunities. *Appleton's New and Complete United States Guide Book for Travelers: Embracing the Northern, Eastern, Southern and Western States, Canada, Nova Scotia, New Brunswick, etc.* detailed a series of tours extending from Boston, "the centre of a great railroad system," throughout New England, the mid-Atlantic states, the South, and the western states as far as Iowa.[8]

In 1857 *Appleton's Illustrated Hand-Book of American Travel* appeared, replacing these earlier tourist guides. Compiled as an annual publication, this guide promised to "guide our traveler truly and surely; to show him—hastily to be sure, as needs must be, yet intelligently—the past and the present, the physique and the morale, of the great country through which we have led him; its differing peoples and places, from the mountains to the prairies—from cities and palaces of the East to the wilderness and wigwams of the West." Unlike its predecessors, this guide provided a series of "skeleton tours" covering everything from a six-day tour from New York City to the Catskill Mountains to a "winter tour of six weeks" visiting the "invalid resorts" of the South. After outlining these various tours, the guide followed a geographical order beginning in the "extreme northeast" of Canada and extending state by state down the Atlantic coast to the Gulf of Mexico and then moving to the interior states and territories as far as Illinois and Minnesota and concluding with a section on California.[9] Each section included a geographical overview of the state along with established tourist routes followed by a list of the significant points of interest. The bulk of the volume focused on the states along the Atlantic seaboard with brief mention of the tourist opportunities in New Orleans and Cincinnati, as well as the Mississippi River and Mammoth Cave in Kentucky. In the following two decades this comprehensive guide was divided into three separate volumes covering northern, southern, and western tours, elaborating the tourist possibilities available to the traveler.[10] The northern and southern volumes simply reprinted an expanded version of earlier material, whereas the western volume acknowledged completion of the Union Pacific transcontinental line by outlining a series of transcontinental tours to the Pacific coast. However, like their predecessors, these guides were geared primarily to the foreign tourist, namely, those "accustomed to European habits."[11] As such, the guides deciphered American geography and customs for the uninitiated rather than celebrating national accomplishments for a domestic audience.

In 1855, following the lead of a number of other publishers, Appleton's supplemented its various tourist handbooks with a volume of engravings celebrating the scenery and achievements of the United States.[12] The preface touted "scenery as wild, romantic, and lovely as can be seen in any other part of the world." Covering both natural and manmade scenes ranging from the Cascade Bridge on the Erie Railroad to views along the Hudson River, to the White Mountains, to buildings in Philadelphia and Washington, D.C., to the Mississippi River and Mauch Chunk, the book was meant to illustrate representative scenes of American civilization. Although more of a picture album than a tourist guide, the volume supplemented Appleton's more informational guides, serving as a kind of survey for armchair travelers and suggesting a kind of national pilgrimage for those seeking out the essence of America. "If we wished to impress a stranger with what is most characteristic of this country in many ways, we would take him from the steamer upon his arrival in New York, whirl him along the Erie Railroad to Niagara, and return him by the Centrail Albany Road, and down the Hudson." The author proceeded to guide the reader on an imaginary tour of the various sites and scenes of the country pointing out the romantic vistas, the historic shrines, and the civic monuments that embodied America. Commenting on one of these scenes, he explained the nationalistic mission of the volume: the citizen, if "he be yet truly patriotic,—then, as he surveys this prodigious work, no less beautiful than strong, and considers that it is the symbol—as there are so many scattered all over from the country—of that country's genius and career[;] . . . he will say in his heart, and with an exulting pride, I, too, am an American!"[13] In many ways the album presented a series of vignettes and disconnected scenes, moving between New York and the mid-Atlantic states then up to the White Mountains and the Boston lighthouse and then west to the Mississippi and beyond. Despite the nationalistic undertones there was no overt attempt to define the nation except as a series of disconnected scenes and accomplishments, a collection of disparate attractions.

With the completion of the transcontinental rail line and the expanded possibilities of a truly national tourism, Appleton's issued a second, more comprehensive set of albums illustrating the American scene. Published between 1872 and 1874, the two volumes of *Picturesque America* edited by the romantic poet William Cullen Bryant and likened to a "gallery of landscapes" promised to "present full descriptions and elaborate pictorial delineations of the scenery characteristic of all the different parts of our country."[14] The album also claimed to be "a splendid pictorial cyclopedia of American life, scenery, and places": by "exhibit[ing] our people in their methods of living and travelling, and delineat[ing] the picturesque phases of commerce, as well as the sublime forms of our hills; it will show the often beautiful setting of our cities, and portray the active and brilliant panorama of our bays and rivers."[15] Thus *Picturesque America* marked the peak of Appleton's attempt to provide a survey of the American tourist landscape. With illustrations by some of America's most noted artists, including S. R. Gifford, Washington Whittredge, and Thomas Moran, *Picturesque America* embodied the surge of scenic nationalism that was sweeping through the United States in the mid-nineteenth century.[16] Anxious about the status of American culture, American artists and literati turned to the dramatic landscapes of the North American continent to justify and legitimize the new nation, arguing that dramatic natural scenery compensated for America's lack of history. Along with William Cullen Bryant, Washington Irving, James Fenimore Cooper, and Nathaniel Parker Willis argued for the superiority of American scenery based on the idea that the monumental landscapes of America reflected God's immanence bestowed on the New World and offered proof that America was destined to become a great civilization. Scenic and sublime wilderness offered a natural legacy representative of American exceptionalism and even superiority over Europe that moved beyond human accomplishments to the realm of God. Dramatic natural landscapes surpassed Old World scenery and compensated for the absence of ancient ruins, castles, cathedrals, and the grand art and architecture of European civilization. Indicative of the fervor of this cultural nationalism, one advertisement touted that the publishers offered the album "to the American public as not only the greatest and fullest exposition of our country that has yet been made, but as a monument of native art worthy of the genius and reputation of our people."[17]

Picturesque America also borrowed from and built upon the long-established tradition of picturesque tours. Since the eighteenth century European and American travelers had actively sought the panorama and the scenic vista.[18] Influenced by the writings of Englishman William Gilpin, wealthy European and American travelers on the Grand Tour of Europe became increasingly interested in sublime and picturesque scenery.[19] Nature came to be seen as a divine work of art that surpassed all human artistic creation. However, the interest in scenery soon moved beyond the confines of nature, and picturesque travel became a quest for scenic views of all sorts, including pastoral vistas, suburban scenes, cityscapes, and even technological wonders.[20] With the publication of *Picturesque America*, Appleton's sought to follow Gilpin's example and establish a series of picturesque tours throughout the United States.

In codifying the sights and scenes of America into distinct vignettes, *Picturesque America* not only established a canon of American tourist attractions but also taught tourists how to look at, understand, and appreciate the sacred sights of America. As Bryant explained in the preface, "It is the design of this publication . . . to present full descriptions and elaborate pictorial delineations of the scenery characteristic of all the different parts of our country." Ranging from the White Mountains to the rivers of Florida, from the coast of Maine to the valley of Yosemite, the two volumes of *Picturesque America* detailed a series of "superb panorama[s]" and "picturesque outlook[s]" across the nation. "On the two great oceans which border our league of States, and in the vast space between them," Bryant explained, "we find a

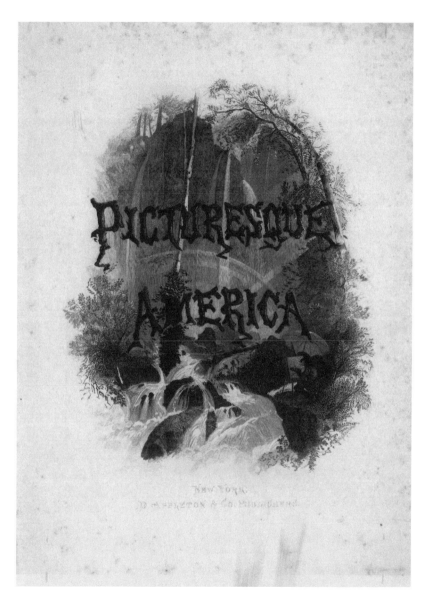

Title page of William Cullen Bryant's *Picturesque America* (1872–74). (Reproduced by permission of the Huntington Library, San Marino, California)

variety of scenery which no other single country can boast of." The volumes
elaborately described and illustrated a succession of mountain vistas and
river valleys, coastal scenes and lake shores, waterfalls and wooded glens,
desert canyons and forested gorges, as well as cityscapes and village scenes.
Presented as series of journeys "in search of the picturesque," each chapter
guided the reader to the best views, evoking the romantic lore of the region
through historic associations, literary allusions, and local tales and legend.[21]

As a compilation of disparate scenes, however, *Picturesque America* did not
provide a comprehensive overview of the nation. However, in teaching tourists how to look at, understand, and appreciate the sights and scenes of
America, the albums defined a tourist gaze that allowed tourists to understand the landscape in visual terms, reducing the nation to a series of framed
views, an assemblage of objectified landscapes. In seeing and collecting these
scenes, tourists gained a comprehensive view of the emerging nation.[22]
"People in search of the picturesque should understand the importance of
selecting suitable points of view. The beauty or impressiveness of a picture
sometimes greatly depends on this," one writer instructed. "It is often a matter of search to discover the point from which an object has its best expression. . . . The beauty of any object lies partly in the capacity of the spectator
to see it, and partly in his ability to put himself where the form and color impress the senses most effectively." The writer then went on to explain that in
order to gain the full effect of the views from Mount Desert Isle in Maine,
"no indifferent glance will suffice. Go to the edge of the cliffs and look down;
go below, where they lift in tall escarpments above you; sit in the shadows of
their massive presence; study the infinite variety of form, texture, and color,
and learn to read all the different phases of sentiment their scarred fronts
have to express. When all of this is done, be assured you will discover that
'sermons in stones' was not a mere fancy of the poet."[23] The prints throughout the volume illustrated a series of ideal views for each site. Often the artists included tourists surveying the scene in their depictions. In this way, the
albums taught readers or potential tourists how to frame the view, creating
a well-composed image in which anomalous surroundings could be edited
out.[24] As one writer described the view of Mount Shasta in northern California, "From the tower-house, the view of the great Shasta is very pleasing,
because one loses sight of the vulgar little mud-hills which . . . insist on

Engravings throughout *Picturesque America* taught tourists how to frame the view using the guidelines of the sublime, the beautiful, and the picturesque. Engraving titled *The Yellowstone*, from William Cullen Bryant's *Picturesque America* (1872–74). (Reproduced by permission of the Huntington Library, San Marino, California)

adorning the foreground, and one gets a noble idea of the glorious girdle of forest which clothes the base."[25]

From the tourist's perspective, landscapes became works of art, pictures, scenes to be consumed and admired for their color, composition, and mood. Describing Anvill Cliff in Virginia, one writer noted, "At sunset, the tops of the cliffs are illuminated with brilliant gold or bathed in vivid red, as the character of the evening may be, while all below is enveloped in cool, purplish shadow—a noble and exquisite scene, worthy in form and coloring of the best master in the land." The aim of viewing the landscape was "illusion," not reality. Descriptive overviews explained how to find and create this scenic aesthetic. "Get, if you can, upon a level with the water, and catch the color of the tips of the waves when they are raised up heavenward, and are between your eyes and the sky," one of the writers describing the coast of California suggested. "Then you will . . . cease to hear the thundering strokes of the waves upon the sea-walls of the rocks, and you will live only in color."[26] Framing sights and scenes through descriptions and drawings, the albums transformed the nation into a collection of scenic views, panoramas, and spectacles—an assemblage of "sacred places"—and tourists learned to seek out and appreciate the American landscape in visual terms.[27]

In reducing places across America to their visual and aesthetic qualities, tourists were given the power to comprehend them and ultimately possess them. Detailing a climb up Maryland heights, one writer counseled the reader to "pause on the ascent and look back. Fair and open lies the northern landscape, bounded by its semicircle of mountains. How the mind expands and feels a sense of delight and power as the eye takes in, at one sweep, the glorious scene!" Tourists were reduced to an all-encompassing "roving eye" in search of picturesque views.[28] The view extended from the tourist's gaze, positioning the tourist as spectator at the center, and allowing him or her to comprehend and consume the landscape through the act of viewing.[29]

By reducing America to a series of sights and scenes valuable for their artistic character, *Picturesque America* validated and envalued the landscape in nationalistic terms. The albums framed a series of landscapes as icons of the nation, sacred landscapes available for the tourist gaze.[30] And tourists were encouraged to seek out and consume those views in order to better know and appreciate the promise of American civilization. Despite the fact that the albums presented a series of disconnected views, in defining the tourist gaze and building upon the growing fervor of scenic nationalism, they linked the tourist experience with national consciousness. As authoritative texts, they helped to define tourism as a ritual of American citizenship and paved the way for more extensive guides that would attempt to provide a comprehensive survey of the nation and address the expanding opportunities available to the tourist.

THE SEE AMERICA FIRST SERIES

In 1914 the Page Company, a noted Boston publishing firm established at the turn of the century, launched the See America First series in an effort to capitalize on the growing interest in domestic tourism and the wave of scenic nationalism that had swept across the country in the onslaught of the European war.[31] The collection of travel guides included twenty-one volumes published between 1912 and 1931 covering a range of regions and states, including the West and New England, California, Texas, Arizona, Oregon, Florida, Colorado, Alaska, New York, New Mexico, Virginia, Utah, Maine, and Ohio, as well as British Columbia and Panama. Advertisements for the guides stated that the series was to include volumes that would cover "the whole of the North American Continent," although the series focused primarily on the United States.[32] As explained in the forward to one of the guides, "Ours is a great and beautiful Country with an interesting history! We ought to know more about it!"[33] Unlike the standard Baedeker-style guidebook, which simply listed attractions, hotels, restaurants, travel suggestions, and pertinent information on local customs, the See America First series promised to bring the tourist "into the very heart of the country."[34] The Page Company hoped to not only respond to the upsurge of patriotism generated by the European war but also inspire patriotism and a sense of national unity through their guides. "We are only life tenants of this land of ours," exclaimed one author in the series, "let us enjoy it *intelligently* while we may! The 'SEE AMERICA FIRST' series . . . will aid you to do this."[35] Progressive in scope, the series was the first to attempt a comprehensive overview of the tourist opportunities throughout North America.

The publication of *California, Romantic and Beautiful* by noted southwestern advocate George Wharton James officially launched the series.[36] The title-page advertisement suggested that the editors pulled together a number of titles previously published under the Page label, covering not only the scenic wonders of the American West and the historic shrines of colonial Virginia but also the history of Panama and the development of the Panama Canal to fill out the newly established series.[37] These early volumes presented no overriding structure or clearly articulated themes. Instead, this initial collection of titles was drawn together to capitalize on the wave of tourists, who, unable to go to Europe, would travel west to the two California expositions opening in 1915.[38] After the expositions, Page dropped the Panama titles from the series and reissued the two other books under new titles in the series. Although there was no overriding model for the series, James's volume on California set the standard and defined the company's objectives for their American travel guides.

Unlike the typical guidebook of the period, *California, Romantic and Beautiful* did not list the most notable sites throughout the state, or provide extensive suggestions for tours. Instead, James provided a broad overview of California's character, with a brief survey of touring possibilities. In the preface he exhorted,

> Go further! Seek more! Demand more. Get into the very heart of the country. Understand its genius, grasp its spirit, comprehend its universality and cosmopolitanism, survey its all embracing life, feel its freedom, revel in its indifference to precedent, absorb its individuality, bask in its sturdiness, turn your eye to its manifold facets, drink from its endless variety of life-giving streams, yield yourself to the abandon of its healthful naturalism,—in other words let the exuberant flood of spontaneous life flow through you, and thus you will speedily know the real California, the natural home of beauty, romance, and abundant life.[39]

James's travel guide was meant to convey the essence of California life, not simply codify the scenic and historic wonders of the state. He surveyed a wide array of topics, including history, topography, geology, climate, flora, fauna, natural resources, land reclamation, education, and the arts. In describing the many adventures of California history, in detailing the reclamation of the desert valleys, in celebrating California authors and artists, James, in essence, worked to legitimize the place of California within American national culture.

Influenced by the popular theories of the Progressive era, James followed the trend of Progressive history, which sought to reveal the "special identity of America" by highlighting the ways in which California contributed to America's unique national character.[40] He utilized a social scientific approach and presented a rational overview of California, categorizing the state as a series of integrated component parts: scenery, history, geology, ecology, ethnography, and culture.[41] Together these parts revealed the evolution of California's development. From the Indians to the Spanish conquistadors and Franciscan priests, to Mexican rule, which was surmounted by the Anglo-America pathfinders, goldseekers, and pioneers, all the way to the present-day scientific farmers, James mapped the stages of California's development, using an evolutionary model to explain the origins and the course of California's progress.[42] Akin to the fact-finding missions of social science surveys, and perhaps extending from the reform work James did in Chicago, his broad presentation of California, covering not only the history and topography of the state but also such topics as art, education, and flora and fauna, reflected the Progressive era's interest in order, narrative, and codification.[43]

James's other guides for the series, *Arizona, The Wonderland* (1917), *New Mexico, The Land of the Delight Makers* (1920), *Utah, The Land of Blossoming Valleys* (1922), and *The Lake of the Sky, Lake Tahoe* (1928), followed essentially the same format as his California guide. They all presented the same broad overview of their respective states and articulated an evolutionary view of history that favored Anglo-American settlement and the march of progress that followed.

Many of the other guides in the series adopted this same format. Nevin Otto Winter's *Texas the Marvelous* (1916) and *Florida the Land of Enchantment* (1918), Mae Lacy Baggs's *Colorado the Queen Jewel of the Rockies* (1918), Archie Bell's *Sunset Canada: British Columbia and Beyond* (1918), Agnes Rush Burr's *Alaska Our Beautiful Northland of Opportunity* (1919), Nathan H. Dole and Irwin Leslie Gordon's *Maine of the Sea and Pines* (1928), and Charles Edwin Hopkins's *Ohio the Beautiful and Historic* (1931) followed the example set by *California, Romantic and Beautiful*. Each of these volumes began with a survey of the state's attractions, followed by a history of exploration and settlement, an overview of present-day development, a discussion of the Native American inhabitants, a review of the natural resources and agricultural developments, and a discussion of the touring possibilities in the different regions of the state, including overviews of the flora and fauna, the arts, and education. Although these guides did not duplicate one another in structure, organization and format, they shared a similar approach that resembled James's initial model.

Yet not all the guides in the series followed that model. A number of the guides reverted to an earlier tradition of prescriptive travel writing that used the personal travelogue to guide tourists through various states and regions. Thomas Dowler Murphy's *Three Wonderlands of the American West* (1912) provided the model within the series for this type of touring narrative.[44] Murphy's book was unofficially the first volume of the See America First series, although when it was published in 1912, the Page Company had not yet launched the series.[45] Chronicling the tours Murphy took through Yellowstone National Park, Yosemite National Park, and the Grand Canyon of the Colorado River, *Three Wonderlands of the American West* taught tourists how to view and appreciate dramatic western landscapes in the tradition of Bryant's *Picturesque America*. The structure of the narrative followed the route of his tours describing how to get to the various attractions, the available accommodations, and the best method for seeing the scenery. Unlike James's *California, Romantic and Beautiful*, Murphy did not provide a broad progressive overview of the West. Instead he focused on the aesthetic experience of viewing nature. *Three Wonderlands of the American West* followed the example of Murphy's earlier travelogues, which grew out of a long-established tradition of travel writing and picturesque tours.[46] Murphy presented his tours of Yellowstone, Yosemite, and the Grand Canyon as models for the reader to follow, and he adopted the voice of the tour guide, explaining what was worth seeing and how to see it. He celebrated these dramatic western land formations because of the aesthetic value of their scenery. His narrative re-created the views and panoramas for the reader, detailing the colors and shapes of natural landscapes, likening these spectacles to paintings and transforming the landscape into artworks far superior to anything produced by the human hand. For Murphy these were nature's masterpieces.

Murphy's other guides for the See America First series, *On Sunset Highways, A Book of Motor Rambles in California* (1915), *Oregon the Picturesque* (1917), and *New England Highways and Byways from a Motor Car* (1924), followed the same format as *Three Wonderlands*. Catering primarily to the automobile tourist, Murphy's books presented touring as either an escape to nature and a quest for scenic views and panoramas or as a pilgrimage to historic shrines. Only one other author in the series followed his example. William Copeman Kitchin's guide, *A Wonderland of the East, Comprising the Lake and Mountain Region of New England and Eastern New York* (1920), described a series of automobile tours taken through "the mountains of Eastern New York, Vermont, New Hampshire, Maine, Massachusetts and Connecticut, with a side tour through the Finger Lakes district of Central New York."[47] Like Murphy, Kitchin's touring narrative focused on scenic views and historic shrines.

Together, George Wharton James and Thomas Dowler Murphy were responsible for almost half of the volumes in the See America First series. It is probable that their distinct styles reflected the desires of two different Page editors. In the absence of an overarching editorial model, the Page Company editors used the guides produced by both James and Murphy as standard bearers for the rest of the series titles. In bringing together these two disparate styles of travel writing, Page melded the established tradition of the personal travelogue with the newer social scientific survey in an effort to provide a comprehensive view of the American tourist landscape.

The twenty-one volumes of the Page Company's See America First series, however, did not reflect a systematic overview of the touring possibilities available in America. There was indecision about whether each guide should rely on the political boundaries of the state or the geographical boundaries of the region. Regional guides overlapped with state guides. In some cases the states and regions covered by the series, such as California, Colorado, Arizona, New England and Florida, were established resort areas with famous tourist attractions. In other cases, such as with the Texas, Alaska, and Ohio guides, their inclusion seemed to be an arbitrary decision. Although the series covered travel opportunities in the West fairly thoroughly, it overlooked many long-established eastern tourist attractions such as Niagara Falls, Mammoth Cave, and Virginia's natural bridge. A number of volumes planned for the series, including guides to Georgia, Louisiana, Nevada, the Great Lakes, and eastern and central Canada, were never completed. The vicissitudes of the publishing industry seem to have prevented the Page Company from rounding out this series it had promised would "include the whole of the North American Continent."[48]

Despite its inconsistencies, the Page Company attempted to provide a guide series that was national in scope. Although the states and regions included in the series were seemingly chosen at random and there was no strictly defined format for each guidebook, the series as a concept subsumed the diversity of American society under a common framework. Instead of each guide existing on its own, representing just one state or region, each guide became part of the larger narrative of the series. In creating the series, Page essentially defined "America" as a unified concept available to the reading and touring public. The guidebooks worked to define a set of shared traditions, an overarching history, a common development that could be named or labeled as "American," and in the process they located those characteristics in the landscape. Throughout the guidebooks, sites across the North American continent were marked, deciphered, and celebrated and in the process transformed into national heritage, providing the reader with a territorially and historically bounded image of America. In effect, individual volumes served to "museumize" America, surveying, codifying, and deliberately selecting and arranging facts, historical events, and anecdotes related to various places across North America to present a coherent narrative. The reader, whether reading one volume or the whole series, was placed in a position of power where he or she, through the process of reading, could order a diverse array of facts into an imaginary wholeness.[49] As a complete set, the guidebooks sought to forge a shared heritage by locating, deciphering, and sacralizing a national landscape ordered into states and regions that could then be recognized and shared by the touring public. Commemorating scenic views and natural wonders, Indian and Spanish ruins, historic sites and literary shrines, the guides worked to reconcile the inherent conflicts between nature, history, and technology, thus legitimizing the ideology of progress that underlay the Progressive era.

Building on the well-established tradition of scenic nationalism, the See America First series showcased natural landscapes throughout the country, presenting a complex ideal of nature as the essence of American national identity. Following a well-established tradition in travel literature, the guides glorified dramatic scenery and encouraged tourists to seek out scenic vistas and natural panoramas. Pristine nature as both sanctuary and source of the sublime was celebrated as an ideal tourist attraction. The majority of the guides published before 1920 focused on the western states and regions, commemorating the dramatic scenery in national parks and monuments as well as other established wilderness retreats. The California guides boasted the sublime scenes of Yosemite, the Sierras, Lake Tahoe, and the redwood forests along with the picturesque coastline. Arizona was noted for the Grand Canyon, the Petrified Forest, and the Painted Desert. Oregon had

Crater Lake, the Deschutes River Canyon, and the Dalles. *Sunset Canada* celebrated the Canadian Rockies and the scenic resorts around Lake Louise, Revelstoke, and Banff. The Colorado guide commended the American Rockies, including Rocky Mountain National Park and Pike's Peak. Alaska had Mount McKinley, the Malaspina Glacier, and the Yukon River. Of the early guides that did not focus on the western states, the Texas guide celebrated the prairie lands of the panhandle, and the Florida guide commended the Everglades. Later guides to western states and regions, including *New Mexico: The Land of the Delight Makers, Utah, the Land of Blossoming Valleys,* and *Seven Wonderlands of the American West,* added to the list of western attractions the lava fields and the cliffs of Ciboletta in New Mexico, Zion National Park and Bryce Canyon in Utah, and Glacier National Park in Montana. Following the promotional rhetoric of automobile enthusiasts and good roads advocates, after 1920, the series began to include more states east of the Mississippi River. New York was noted for the Catskills, the Adirondacks, Watkins Glen, Ausable Chasm, and Lake George. New England had Mount Katahdin, the Lafayette National Park on Mount Desert Isle (now Acadia National Park), and the White Mountains. And finally, Ohio landscapes were commended in general for their "pleasant richness" and "bucolic beauty."[50]

Drawing on an established American mythology surrounding the importance of nature in America, the series suggested that dramatic natural landscapes revealed the extent of geological time, providing an ancient tradition for a nation that seemed devoid of history. Thomas Dowler Murphy, for example, noted that scientists had dated Old Faithful geyser in Yellowstone National Park to an age of "tens if not hundreds of thousands of years" old. "Bearing this fact in mind," he explained,

> one will experience a strange sensation as he gazes on this weird, intermittent fountain, justly considered one of the gems of the wonderland. When Columbus discovered America this great white column at regular intervals was playing and glittering in the primal solitude . . . when Christ was on the earth its strange beauty fell on the eye of the infrequent savage, who gazed on it with a superstitious awe . . . before man himself trod the earth Old Faithful, robed in showers of diamonds and the glories of the rainbow, rose and fell with none to see and admire.[51]

But the allure of nature rested on more than just age. Sublime scenery also suggested divine presence, and the guides both implicitly and explicitly referred to natural scenery as God's creations. Thus George Wharton James described the Painted Desert:

> Imagine this a cast pallet-board, and that a superhuman artist with mighty arm has just squeezed out the color from his mammoth tubes. Here is a patch, ten, twenty, fifty miles in diameter of white; close by is an area equally large of black, and dotted, as artists are want to dot their painting boards; here and there and everywhere are patches of red, green, blue, yellow, madder, lake, orange, violet, pink and every color known to man. . . . It is as if this place was the place where divine thoughts were tested for man's benefit, and then the pallet-board was left for man to see, to wonder at and revere. Such, with profoundest reverence, are the feelings evoked in the presence of this most marvelous of colorful regions.[52]

Often the guides used sublime scenery to evoke the image of God as the master artist, revealing his power and his divine sanction through the landscape. In the mountains the tourist would come to understand that "over all broods the peace of God which passeth all understanding and assures the heart of man and woman that we are, indeed, the Sons and Daughters of God, and that His mountains are blessed gifts to us."[53] Thus sublime scenery not only compensated for America's lack of an ancient past but also revealed the blessings of God bestowed on the New World and provided divine justification for American exceptionalism. Simultaneously, the ideal of sublime scenery suggested an image of the Divine as the master clockmaker who set the works in motion and sat back to let time follow its own course. God's intentions were present in sublime scenery, but the Creator himself was absent, thus justifying man's exploitation of nature for his own ends.

The guides also represented nature as refuge and sanctuary, a counterbalance to the ills of modern society. As Thomas Dowler Murphy explained in his guide to the scenic West, "The man or woman who takes a vacation trip as rest and relaxation, is learning that these boons are hardly to be found in crowded cities and fashioned-hampered hotels. For real restfulness one must get near nature, out under the unsullied skies, among the mountains, with their painted crags, towering pines and leaping streams."[54] The See American First series suggested that the experience of touring was primarily an experience in nature. Camping, hiking, automobiling, fishing, riding horseback, climbing, enjoying the outdoors—these were the activities of the tourist. As George Wharton James exhorted his readers in his introduction to the New Mexico guide, "Come out in the open! Let us fill your lungs with the purest of sun-laden, balsam-charged air. Let us induce you to walk, to exercise, to ride, to golf, to motor, to row, to swim, to climb, and thus brush the cobwebs from the brains and muscles, strengthen the body, vivify and quicken the legs, and, better than all, free the spirit, and give new life, vim, ambition, activity to the will!" Touring—getting out into the landscape—offered an escape from workaday routines and congested cities. Yet nature represented more than a refuge from urban-industrial living; it was also a counterbalance to the corruptions of commerce, history, and progress. According to George Wharton James, touring promised to restore "vigor and strength to the hundreds of thousands who have lost them in their mad and pathetic chase for wealth, or a livelihood, in the crowded cities of the East and Middle West."[55]

Intertwined with this celebration of nature were ideals of the primitive as represented by Native Americans and the ruins of Native American cultures. "The Red Man of America appeals intensely to the imagination," wrote Mae Lacy Baggs in her guide to Colorado. "All that is wild, primitive within us is aroused when we reflect upon the care-free life which must have been his before the white man's coming." She went on to explain,

> That sentiment may have small appeal to the humanitarian who is probably saying this primitive man lacked civilization, knew not progress, nor education, nor the missionary zeal. But somehow, that great cataclysmal horror, the European war, while not weakening our moral force has drained our powers of nerve resistance, and we feel that if we could remove ourselves, say, just for a little while into the wild and free, we might get rest and restoration and our bearing. Not but we would back up all that civilization is trying to do, and has done. Not that we could live the life of the primitive for long, we who have profited by the wealth and accumulation of the ages.[56]

The memory of the noble savage and the continued existence of domesticated tourist Indians enhanced the ideal of nature as the antithesis of modern civilization by celebrating the Indians as quintessentially natural. Many of the guides in the series, especially guides to western states, described the various pueblos and cliff dwellings and recounted the Indian legends associated with particular land formations, instructing the tourist on the value of the nation's Indian heritage. The Hopis, Navahos, and Apaches of the Southwest, the Native Americans of Alaska, California, and the Pacific Northwest, and even the memory of the Seminoles of Florida became celebrated figures in the tourist landscape. Indians embodied the simplicity and self-sufficiency of preindustrial living. They preserved all that had seemingly been lost in modern industrial society: a tradition of hand-craftsmanship, a strong local culture, strong religious faith, strong family ties, a symbiotic relationship to nature, as well as vigorous health. Indian ceremonies such as the Hopi Snake Dance and the Navaho Fire Dance became tourist spectacles, and Indian crafts, including religious icons and idols, baskets, pottery, and blankets, were marketed as tourist collectibles—souvenirs of the primitive.[57]

The series' guides constructed a tourist spectacle of primitive Indian societies living in harmony with nature that served to augment an ideal of nature as a refuge from modern society. Although the guides did not encourage tourists to adopt the ways of the Indians, in viewing the Indians, tourists were instructed on the ameliorative effects of a life in harmony with nature. In consuming this spectacle, tourists vicariously experienced a life close to nature. In effect they purchased and thus participated in the primitive lifestyles embodied in romanticized tourist Indians, and that process reinvigorated and renewed them so that they might return to the ordinary—work, home, modern society—with a refreshed and purified outlook on life.[58]

Paradoxically, the See America First series also celebrated the power and abundance of nature as natural resource. National forests revealed a wealth of timber resources as well as the potential for grazing and the protection of watersheds. "Rugged mountains" promised "profitable ores."[59] Surging rivers manifested electrical power. Scenic views over the natural landscape evoked not only the sublime, but also they revealed America's vast supply of grazing land, timber, minerals, and water power. George Wharton James's eulogy to Mount Shasta in *California, Romantic and Beautiful* perhaps best characterized this seemingly contradictory celebration of nature. He described the mountain as an "altar," to which overworked city dwellers should be taken so that they might "lift up their hearts to the sun-lit sky, the serenity of the stars, to the pure blue atmosphere, to the majesty and strength, the nourishment and beauty it contains." Here they would not only witness the workings of the "master artist" and the spectacle of dazzling sunrises and sunsets, but also the power of the mountain streams that fed into "roaring" rivers. "I would urge them on," wrote James, "and they should see the water taken out and used to turn the water-driven dynamos that supply the light and power for towns and cities hundreds of miles away, thus adding to the comfort and power of man." In addition to the wonders of water-generated electricity, James also directed tourists to the power of mountain water harnessed for land reclamation. "They should see these waters poured forth into giant canals and smaller laterals, through the head-gates into distributing ditches where trees and vegetables, alfalfa and timothy by the thousands of acres, hundreds of thousands, eagerly drink of the nourishing stream and pour forth a compensating flood of train-loads of almonds, walnuts, peaches, nectarines, plums, prunes, oranges, lemons, and hay for the feeding of the sons of men and the financial enrichment of their producers."[60] Nature not only provided an aesthetic escape from the workaday routines of urban-industrial living but also embodied the power that fueled the advances of urban-industrial life. Although this double-sided celebration of nature seems contradictory, James saw no contradiction. In his mind, both of these images of nature rested on the power of God. All of James's guides included a chapter or at least a section on the resources of the national forests. Nature's beauty and nature's bounty revealed God's divine sanction of progress, while ameliorating the destructive and corrupting forces of commercial development.

Many of the other guides in the series followed this example, enumerating the natural resources of their respective regions amid their celebration of the scenic views. This paradoxical glorification of nature as both the antithesis of modern industrial society and as the source of modern industrial society reveals the particular concerns of the Progressive era. As the forces of industrial capitalism worked to transform American society from a rural agricultural nation to an urban-industrialized nation, nature became a contested site. Conservationists and preservationists argued over the role and the use of nature in an increasingly modern America.[61] Although on the surface the battle between conservationists and preservationists centered on the use and development of natural resources, the underlying concerns of this battle revolved around issues deeply ingrained in American political theory. According to traditional republican theory, an unlimited expanse of free land promised to balance the march of progress. Within this framework the development of American society could remain outside of the corrupting forces of time and history because the seemingly unlimited expanse of nature provided a permanent counterbalance to the forces of commerce. By the early decades of the twentieth century, however, it was clear that republicanism was threatened by the forces of industrialism; history, progress, and commerce had seemingly triumphed over nature. America's natural resources and the expanse of free land represented by the frontier were not unlimited. The frontier was closed, and the abundance of American nature was being rapidly developed. On a practical level, these concerns were played out as conservationists and preservationists disagreed over whether the abundance of nature could be sustained through scientific management or whether some natural landscapes needed to be set outside the realm of commerce. On a more theoretical level, antimodernists such as George Wharton James urged Americans to escape the routines of urban work and get back to nature. Within the prevalent framework of liberal individualism that characterized the expanding consumer society of the era, the balance between nature and progress or nature and civilization could only be preserved if the individual had contact with nature, even if only temporarily. The technology of tourism provided that opportunity. Both the railroad and the automobile promised to make nature accessible to the individual. Tourism allowed the individual to escape the routines of work and the demands of the city without rejecting the possibilities of modern society. It allowed individuals to reinvigorate and rejuvenate themselves by purchasing a nature experience. This possibility ensured an outlet from urban industrial life and promised to preserve a permanent balance between nature and civilization. Tourism, in uniting the technology and the mechanisms of commercial capitalism that accommodated the liberal individual, worked to ensure the continued development of a virtuous society within the framework of history and progress.

In this way nature—sublime and picturesque scenery, the primitive, and natural resources—represented a defining characteristic of America's distinct identity as a nation. Building on well-established cultural mythology, the guides depicted nature as central to the nation's heritage. Specifically, sites of sublime scenery such as Yosemite, Yellowstone, the Grand Canyon, and Crater Lake evoked an aesthetic experience that revealed God's divine sanction of the America nation in its physical presence and connected these dramatic natural landscapes with the development and preservation of a virtuous American society. Idealized images of Native Americans as embodiments of the primitive reinforced the ideal of nature as a refuge from modern industrial society. The guides also suggested that the power of nature as evinced through the wealth of natural resources underlay the onward march of progress and provided the source of American exceptionalism.

Although natural attractions dominated the guide series, historic sites and literary shrines added to the national narrative presented by the guides. In his guide to New Mexico, George Wharton James asked his readers, "Is it not self-evident that boys and girls will take more interest in events that have occurred on their own native soil,—the place of their present everyday habitation—and in the men who shaped these events, than they will in those of the far-away Homeric lands and days?" He went on to offer his own answer: "The sooner we can put into the hearts of our youth the thought that they are as capable of great deeds as any people in history the nobler their lives and the higher their aspirations will become."[62] James was specifically commending New Mexican history, but his desire to link the experience of touring with an understanding of the nation's history permeated all the guides in the series. The guides oriented the reader to the tourist landscape by presenting a narrative of American history. Battle sites, Indian and Spanish ruins, the paths of explorers and colonizers, and literary shrines were marked as tourist attractions. In delineating these sites, the guides mapped the history of America onto the landscape, commemorating certain landscapes because of their historic associations, others for their literary associations, highlighting some events while passing over others. Constructing sacred landscapes by connecting significant events, images, and people of the past with particular places, the guides identified a series of historic landmarks that objectified the evolution of American development, and through this process they constructed an idealized version of American history.

On one level the guides pointed out historic sites in an effort to reveal that America, like the Old World, had its own history and traditions. As George Wharton James exclaimed, "Talk about human interest in the ruins of

Europe attracting American travelers there! Surely there is enough of human interest in the ancient historical ruins of Arizona to give one his fill."[63] Readers and tourists were guided along the paths of explorers, colonizers, and pioneers. They were shown the ground made sacred by bloody battles and fearless heroes. They were directed to the homes and graves of famous writers and the settings that inspired famous pieces of American literature. These commemorative landscapes served to verify the fact that America had an ancient tradition, a living history, and an established literary culture. In describing the Hudson, Lake George, and Lake Champlain, William Copeman Kitchin noted that "the American has no need to go abroad in order to see places made memorable by deeds of epic valor or to visit fields where were fought battles decisive in the destinies of mankind."[64] Similarly, Nevin O. Winter described the old fort in St. Augustine, Florida, as "an imposing gray pile reminiscent of the days of feudalism." He noted, "It conjures up pictures of splendor and cruelty that one is apt to associate with the medieval castles of Europe."[65] In the same vein, Thomas Dowler Murphy likened the Spanish missions of California to the romantic and historic "charm of England's abbeys."[66] The cliff dwellings of Arizona, Colorado, and New Mexico, the Spanish missions of California, the battlefields of New York, New England, Ohio, and Texas, the literary shrines throughout Massachusetts and Connecticut, these sites commemorated and legitimated an American tradition. They were celebrated as representations of the passage of time; they envalued the effects of age. In this way, ruins, shrines, monuments, and markers authenticated an American antiquity and a historic tradition.[67] And in doing so, they served to justify the status of American civilization, measuring the nation's history and culture in relation to the Old World.

However, the act of marking these historic sites and literary shrines went beyond the desire to bolster the existence of an American tradition. The guides did not simply celebrate a generic ideal of history, they defined a very particular narrative of American history by deliberately selecting and presenting certain historical facts. In mapping and deciphering the landmarks of history, the series chronicled the process by which the boundaries of the nation were formed. The guides described the march of history as a series of conquests. First came the Spanish conquistadors confronting the native inhabitants throughout the Southwest and in California and Florida in their search for treasures. Then the Franciscan priests subdued the Indians through conversion. They were followed by French colonists and Jesuit priests, and then the English and their Puritan colonies. Finally, the Americans, united in their quest for freedom and democracy, broke free the bonds of empire and expanded across the continent, conquering the Indians and forging a free and democratic nation. Through this narrative the guides presented the stages of American development, inventing an American tradition that reinforced the Progressive era's ideal of progress and obscured the racial and ethnic conflict that marred the nation's past.

Many of the guides began by detailing the exploration and colonization of their respective states. The California, New Mexico, and Texas guides used the ruins of Spanish missions to illustrate stories of Spanish exploration and colonization. In chronicling his tour of the missions of southern California, Thomas Dowler Murphy revealed the imaginative power of these Spanish ruins. For him, "the crumbling vinecovered ruins" embodied "a glamour of romance and an historic significance." He wrote, "The memory of human sacrifice and devotion, and the wealth of historic incident . . . is not wanting in these … remnants of the pious zeal and tireless industry of the Spanish Padres to be found in so many delightful nooks of the Sunset State." Murphy explained that tourists would be welcomed at the missions by "brown robed priest[s]" and conducted throughout to see "the relics, paintings, vestments, old manuscripts, and books" as well as the graves of "old padres" and "the monster grapevine" that supplied the mission.[68] Nevin O. Winter counseled tourists, "The old missions erected by the religious order in some parts of our Southwest were the forerunners of the civilization that was to follow. To fully appreciate their significance one must allow his imagination to run back a century or two, and try to picture the conditions as they then existed."[69]

Although Indian attractions and the Indians themselves were particularly linked to nature, in an antithetical way Indian ruins also served to objectify the progress of history. Sites of Indian battles and the ruins of Indian civilizations marked the triumph of European settlers over the native inhabitants. For example, George Wharton James noted that the scenes around Roosevelt Lake in Arizona, an area he called "Apache-Land," "have echoed to the shock of firing of guns and field pieces. Cook, Lawton, Miles, King, and others have commanded troops here to follow Apaches to their death."

He went on to tell the reader/tourist, "Cochise, Mangas Colorado, Geronimo, and other Apache chiefs, have ridden wildly, madly, furiously, ahead or behind American troops over every mile of this region."[70] Descriptions of savage Indian battles and elegies of deserted Indian ruins did not incorporate Native Americans into the narrative of American history. Rather, they glorified the destruction of Native American culture and suggested that since the Indians no longer posed a threat to American society, their artifacts and ruins might be commemorated as representations of a distinctly American antiquity.

Overall the guides adopted an elegiac tone in describing ruins, implicitly underscoring the failure of both the Spanish and the Indians to establish a lasting civilization in the New World. The remains of these civilizations revealed the richness of the American past, but as ruins they also revealed that the march of progress had passed over them. These were places that evoked nostalgia, melancholy, and reverie. Quoting another historian, Thomas Murphy noted in one of his guides, "There is a pathetic dignity about the ruin [of the San Antonio Mission], an unexpressed claim for sympathy in the perfect solitude of the place that is almost overpowering. It stands out in the fields alone, deserted, forgotten."[71] In embodying the passage of time, they objectified the decline of empires and civilizations. Of the old Spanish fort in St. Augustine, Nevin O. Winter wrote, "The fortress has seen one band of intruders after another set foot on the shores here, and has witnessed all the changes through which these United States of America has passed. Its outlines have been tenderly softened by time and the elements . . . but the imagination restores all these things, and one is soon lost in reverie."[72] The description of these ruins evoked a mythical past while reaffirming the status of the present.

The guides also eulogized the ruins of English colonization. However, where the Spanish and Indian ruins were celebrated in an elegiac tone, the ruins and relics of English colonization were presented as vibrant and inspiring examples or remnants of American society. Frank and Cortelle Hutchins celebrated the "handful of ruins of vanished James Towne" during their trip by houseboat up the James River.[73] "As we walked along the curving road, we caught glimpses now and then of the venerable tower; and gradually it emerged as out of the shadows of the past, and we stood facing it," they wrote. "Silently we gazed at the ancient pile, the most impressive ruin of English colonization. A hollow shaft of brick, with two high arched openings, a crumbling top, and a hold on the heart of every American."[74] Similarly, the guides celebrated the relics and remains of the pilgrims. These English ruins objectified the "true" beginnings of American history. Recounting his tour of New England, Thomas Dowler Murphy wrote, "On Burial Hill . . . beneath a wilderness of weatherworn slate headstones, sleep many of the dignitaries whose names we had noted in our round of Pilgrim Hall. . . . Our underlying thought as we gaze on these storm beaten memorials is of the hardships endured and the sacrifices made by the men and women who laid the cornerstone of the American Republic."[75] Detailing his tour in eastern New York, William Copeman Kitchin wrote of Oriskany battlefield,

> Here before us lay the ravine where General Herkimer's advance division fell into the deadly ambuscade. Here, and along the slopes and on the summit of the hill rising from the ravine, the fierce battle had raged with appalling fury. To-day, the frenzied shouts, the wild war-whoops, the mingled roar and tumult, all the horror of blood and death of that red sixth of August, 1777, are separated from us by nearly a century and a half of silence. The scene now is one of profound pastoral repose. . . . But . . . we felt like putting the shoes off our feet, so holy seemed the ground on which we stood.[76]

Similarly, Thomas Dowler Murphy noted in his guide to New England the many small towns of New England that retained their colonial character, preserving the nation's past as a vital part of the present. Battle sites, graveyards, old houses, and pioneer trails underscored the triumph of Anglo-American settlers as they moved across the North American continent.

In detailing the series of conquests that served to unite the American nation, the guides presented a history that glorified the principles and courage of the revolutionary colonists and the rugged pioneers who settled the continent. In his guide to Lake Tahoe, George Wharton James informed the reader of the historic associations of the eastern rail route to Tahoe: "From the east the traveler comes over what is practically the long known and historic overland stage-road, over which so many thousands of gold-seekers and emigrants came in the days of California's gold excitement. Every mile has some story of pioneer bravery or heroism, of hair-breath escape from hostile Indians or fortuitous deliverance from storm or disaster." The rail route became not simply a means of transport through space but also a means of transport back through time. He encouraged tourists to use their own journey to remember the journeys of other pioneers. Indian and Spanish ruins exposed the failure of those earlier civilizations that had tried to subsist in the America wilderness. It was the trappers, the gold seekers, and the pioneers who had tamed the American wilderness and forged the bonds of the nation. The physical narrative of history depicted by the guides represented a cast of historical characters in hierarchical order: the Indians were nature's children, easily subdued by the European and Anglo-American explorers and settlers; the Spanish were greedy explorers, exploiting the land for their own self-interest; the Anglo-Americans were guided by the principles of freedom, and only they had the ability to triumph over the wilderness. The historic tourist attractions made manifest the story of how Anglo-Americans succeeded, where others failed, in molding a vast continent of wilderness into a powerful nation. Thus, the history recounted in the guides revealed the evolution of American development toward progress, while ignoring the more conflicted side of American history.

Literary shrines served to reinforce this presentation of American history by reaffirming the fact that not only had Anglo-American colonists founded their democracy and conquered and settled the free land of the West, thus forging a united American nation resting on the principles of individual freedom and equality, but through this process they had also produced a vibrant and living culture.[77] In addition to his celebration of the various places associated with Jonathan Edwards, Longfellow, Emerson, Thoreau, Hawthorne, William Cullen Bryant, Thomas Bailey Aldrich, Louisa May Allcott, Harriet Beecher Stow, and Catherine Sedgwick, Thomas Murphy devoted a whole chapter in his New England guide to the places associated with nineteenth-century poet John Greenleaf Whittier. Describing the "narrow strip of land between Newburyport and Haverhill," Massachusetts, as "Whittier-land," Murphy directed tourists to Whittier's birthplace, his childhood home, and his grave. Murphy and his companions "pause[d] reverently" at the desk where "Snow-Bound" was written and admired a display of "the poet's staid broadcloth dress coat and 'stovepipe' hat," which, Murphy noted, when "taken together with the very excellent portraits extant, enable one to form a very vivid picture of his [Whittier's] appearance on `state occasions.'"[78] In addition to celebrating the established literary culture of New England, the series noted the literary and artistic culture emerging in the West. The guides to California, Arizona, New Mexico, and Colorado included chapters detailing the literary and artistic accomplishments associated with their respective states. The pilgrimages to literary shrines portrayed in the series not only enumerated an established canon of American literature but also revealed the organic relationship between the nation and its literary and artistic expression. Culture became another example of the forward march of progress.

Strikingly absent from this story of conquest and culture was the sectional and racial strife that had resulted in the Civil War. Civil War battlefields and Civil War heroes were glaringly absent from the guides. Focusing primarily on the West and New England and skipping over the South, except for Florida and Texas, the series told the story of the golden age of the Revolution and westward expansion. This omission clearly reveals the objective of the series to construct a narrative of national unity. Rather than remind tourists of the sectional strife that existed between North and South, rather than accentuating existing conflicts by commemorating the battlefields of Gettysburg or Vicksburg, or the court house at Appomattox, rather than imply the racial impurity of America, the guides moved from colonial relics and ruins directly to the conquest of the Indians and the settlement of the West. The story they told exposed a view of American history that grew out of the post-Darwinist theories popular during the Progressive era.[79] The guides presented American history in a series of stages: Indian life in harmony with nature, Spanish exploration and colonization, English colonization and settlement, the founding of the American nation, Anglo-American conquest of the Indians, expansion westward, and present-day progress. This narrative served to delineate the origins of and the evolution toward the achievements of the Progressive era. Interestingly, these guides were written during a time of increasing black migration to northern cities, institutionalization of Jim Crow laws, and rising nativism and immigration restriction.[80] In other words, the guides recounted a history of American progress that glorified white, Anglo-Saxon America, thus allowing tourists to retreat into this idealized America, escaping the realities of racial and ethnic conflict and other growing tensions in American society.

In addition to natural and historic sites, the See America First series also celebrated technological landscapes in their roster of tourist sites. Describing his excursion to Roosevelt Dam, Thomas Dowler Murphy wrote, "As we came out upon a promontory, we got a full view of the mighty arc of stone that shuts the vast wall of water in the heart of the blue hill range before us." He noted, "Torrents were pouring from the spillways and a rainbow arched the clouds of mist and foam that rose at the base of the three-hundred foot fall. We paused in wonder and admiration to contemplate the scene—for once the works of man rival the phenomena of nature in beauty and grandeur."[81] This was sublime nature harnessed by man.

The guides commemorated dams, bridges, tunnels, roads, artificial lakes, and irrigation projects as examples of man's mastery over or improvement of nature. Roosevelt Dam was perhaps the most popular of these technological wonders. However, the guides also commemorated a number of engineering feats and artificial wonders. Mae Lacy Baggs celebrated Colorado's Gunnison Tunnel as "the most spectacular engineering feat in the history of man."[82] The guides also venerated reclamation and irrigation projects of California and the Southwest; mining activities in Arizona, Colorado, New Mexico, and Utah; artificial reservoirs constructed to supply New York City, San Francisco, and Los Angles; the Panama Canal and the Bourne Canal, which traversed Cape Cod; and even the mill towns of New England. Thomas Dowler Murphy wrote, "The great towns . . . Lawrence and Lowell are modern as compared with the places we had just visited. . . . These cities are the outgrowth of the restless enterprise and ambition of the New Englander, who, denied the advantage of broad acres and fertile soil, turned his ingenuity to the development of great manufacturing industries which should make their small and comparatively barren states among the wealthiest."[83] This reference to the cities of Lawrence and Lowell was unique; most modern American cities were glaringly absent from the guides.

This last group of tourist attractions might best be understood as the culmination of the natural and historical narrative presented by the series. These technological attractions revealed the pinnacle of development in the onward march of American history. They objectified progress, implying that they extended from the combined forces of American nature and American history. Embodying the technological sublime, they revealed the power and triumph of man over nature. Thus the narrative of the nation presented by the series extended from an ideal of progress as the nation's birthright and destiny. Man, with the assistance of industrialization and the blessings of God, could end scarcity and assure the good life and the gift of plenty. America's identity as a world power rested in this ideology of progress.[84]

Where once Americans looked solely to the presence of nature to legitimate an ancient tradition outside of the corrupting forces of history and to underscore American exceptionalism, by the 1880s and 1890s an interest in and concern for history intensified.[85] More than retrospection resulting from the trauma of the Civil War and the passage of the American centennial, this interest solidified around the anxiety generated by the emergence of an urban-industrialized society. With the symbolic closing of the American frontier, Americans were forced to reconcile their ideal of America with the forces of history, to justify American exceptionalism within history. The narrative of the nation presented by the See America First series attempted to reconcile the forces of nature, history, and progress. Using the evolutionary theories characteristic of the era to define the stages of American development, nature and history were united, culminating in the triumph of progress. As represented by the series, technology mediated the inherent conflicts between nature and civilization. First, the technologies of tourism—the railroad and the automobile—promised to give "every" individual access to pristine nature, thus ensuring that a permanent balance could be maintained between the advance of civilization and the virtues of nature. By transforming natural landscapes into scenery, an idealized image of nature was perpetually preserved, leaving all the land not designated as scenery free to be developed and expended for the progress of civilization. Second, the guides suggested that the course of American history revealed, through the stages of progress, the coming together of nature and history. No longer was civilization a threat, because technological advances allowed men to contain and improve on the power of nature. Through technology man now had the capability to preserve and extend the benefits of nature, guaranteeing the existence of a moral society within history. Reflecting the prevalence of American exceptionalism during the 1920s, the series expressed these concerns on a popular and commercial level, constructing a narrative of the nation that glorified technological progress as the element that assured that an ideal society could exist within history.

Despite it's inconsistencies, the See America First series represented an attempt to produce a comprehensive set of guides to America that reflected not only the expansion of tourist opportunities during the interwar period but also changing concepts of the nation. Whereas the albums of *Picturesque America* defined the nation in terms of highbrow culture by presenting a canon of picturesque views to be seen on a grand tour of America, the See America First series moved toward a more romantic conceptualization of the nation. The nation was more than a collection of dramatic landscapes, it was the product of a distinct geography and history. In its mission and scope, the series paved the way for what would come to be known as the "first indigenous guidebooks" of America, the WPA guides.[86]

THE WPA GUIDES

In September 1935 President Franklin Roosevelt formally approved a congressional appropriation of $6,288,000 for the employment of an estimated sixty-five hundred writers on relief to create the Federal Writers' Project. As part of the Works Progress Administration's white-collar relief program, the project proposed, among other things, to produce a set of comprehensive travel guides to the United States known as the American Guide series. Between September 1935 and February 1943, when the remnants of the program were shut down, approximately ten thousand writers across the country helped compile, write, and produce forty-eight state guides, three touring guides surveying regional highway routes, and a number of city guides and pamphlets focusing on local attractions.[87] The American Guide series is perhaps the most famous legacy of the New Deal relief effort. Comprehensive in scope, the state guides, along with guides to the District of Columbia, Puerto Rico, and Alaska, embody the most systematic attempt to document and codify the nation for the benefit of the touring public. Lewis Mumford claimed they were "the first attempt, on a comprehensive scale, to make the country itself worthily known to Americans." As such, Mumford argued that the American Guide series represented "the finest contribution to American patriotism that has been made in our generation."[88] Although politics, bureaucracy, and an uneven work force complicated and compromised the production of the American Guide series, as one of the more visible and successful New Deal projects, the guides officially sanctioned tourism as a ritual of citizenship, firmly linking tourism with a patriotic and nationalist agenda.

Historian Warren Susman has argued that the 1930s might best be characterized by a pervasive interest in culture: not the established notion of culture evinced by achievements in art and literature, but the more anthropological concept of culture denoted by a shared set beliefs and behaviors. "Americans," Susman notes, "began thinking in terms of patterns of behavior and belief, values and life-styles, symbols and meanings," and in the process they sought to define or discover a distinct "American Way of Life."[89] Other scholars have reiterated these themes, describing the era as "an adventure in national rediscovery" or noting the attempt to create "a literature of collective self-consciousness, a people's and a nation's biography, a story of physical and human geography."[90] In both its scope and design, the WPA American Guide series manifested this desire to document and define a unique and indigenous American culture. Although the guides are dominated by an excess of information that is difficult to condense into neat summaries, their attention to detail and diversity reflects a more populist narrative of the nation embedded in this new conceptualization of culture. In effect, the series sought to map out and celebrate an inherent American culture across the landscape and thus position America as a modern folk nation.

Once funding for the project had been secured, WPA administrators began to assemble a staff to administer the project. Jacob Baker, assistant director of Work Relief and Special Projects and responsible for organizing the white-collar relief programs, brought together a central core of East Coast intellectuals engaged with issues of social reform to define and direct the project. Baker first called on his friend Henry Garfield Alsberg to act as national director of the Federal Writers' Project. Alsberg, a New York intellectual who had worked as an editorial writer and a foreign correspondent, and then served in the foreign service in the U.S. embassy in Turkey, and had gone on to get involved in a variety of liberal causes, including relief work in Russia and independent theater in New York, was noted for the overriding sense of vision and mission that he brought to the project. Alsberg was assisted by George Cronyn, associate director in charge of administrative and editorial matters, and Reed Harris, assistant director in charge of administration for the project. Harris, a New York journalist, and Cronyn, a college professor, novelist, and magazine and encyclopedia editor, brought administrative and editorial skills to the project.[91] Katherine Kellock, who had worked as a social worker at Lillian Wald's Henry Street Settlement House and written for the *Dictionary of America Biography*, was appointed national tours editor and assisted this three-man administrative core.[92] Although a number of additional editorial assistants, secretaries, stenographers, and typists filled out the Washington office, this administrative core established the parameters of the guide project.[93]

While the Washington office defined and oversaw the production of the American Guide series, state offices were responsible for collecting, writing up, and editing local material for each state. Alsberg nominated directors for each state office, and they in turn hired the "nonmanual" workers from the relief rolls to serve as field workers responsible for collecting the primary data for the guides. Although a number of state directors gained their position through political maneuvering, noted writers, university professors, historians, journalists, and others also administered the guides from state offices. Field workers came from even more varied backgrounds. The project shepherded a number of notable writers, including John Cheever, Richard Wright, Saul Bellow, Ralph Ellison, and Conrad Aiken. Because of restrictions on hiring only those on relief, however, many Federal Writers' Project employees had only nominal professional writing experience. Teachers, lawyers, businessmen, and librarians, among many others, filled the ranks of state offices to conduct interviews and research and to write the preliminary copy for the guides. The combination of federalized bureaucracy, political infighting, and an unevenly qualified work force produced an unwieldy and unpredictable organizational structure that resulted in a constant struggle for control of the final project. The Washington office required that all state copy gain editorial approval from Washington. Manuscripts sent to Washington were subjected to a multitiered review process, passing from Alsberg and Cronyn to various editors, then on to a project director, and finally to a checker.[94] Despite attempts on the part of various state employees to present their own vision and express their own voices, the central office in Washington constantly worked to impose a standardized systematic template on the guide series.[95]

The initial plan for the series developed by the central office staff called for the publication of a five-volume guide covering the various regions of the United States. Early instructions for the project explained, "Regions have been based on careful study of topographic features, historical factors, and existing auto, rail and air routes."[96] Based on a modified version of the regions delineated by the American Automobile Association, the five geographic divisions included (1) New England, the Mid-Atlantic states, and the Lake States, (2) the South, (3) the northern states of the trans-Mississippi West, (4) the Southwest, and (5) the Pacific states, including Nevada and Utah.[97] The idea was that local field workers under the direction of state administers would collect material that would be culled and edited at the state level and then sent on to the federal office, where it would be systematically organized and reedited and compiled into regional volumes. An early template for the regional guides explained, "Each book will have to be planned to allow for the differences of accent within the region, that is to say the chief characteristics of a region will determine expansion or restriction of treatment of a given topic."[98] The planning staff in Washington wanted to capture the richness and diversity—what they called "local color"—that defined America. As one press report boasted, "Unlike the usual commercial guide book publishers, the Federal Writers' Projects [*sic*] have been able to follow a method which allows definite local color and feeling to penetrate into the guides. Material has actually been collected locally, on the spot, by Guide workers who are native to the location and can catch its real spirit. This local material has been assembled in state editorial offices and rearranged and rewritten somewhat, but there has been constant attention to the problem of catching and keeping the local color."[99] Through this method the five regional volumes promised to preserve this local diversity that defined American culture. The Washington staff believed that by gathering material at the local level, organizing that material by state, and then culling and editing it into regional volumes, they could best convey the essence of America as a nation.

Early on, however, the Washington staff began to debate the feasibility of the regional guides. Not only were there disagreements over the definition of regional boundaries, but there were also political concerns about maintaining state support for arbitrarily defined regions. As a compromise, they agreed to focus on the production of state guides and then use the state material to produce the regional volumes.[100] Once the project was underway and state workers began to collect, edit, and send in material to the central office, the production of the state guides took precedence until finally the original concept of the multivolume regional guide was abandoned.[101] The state guides became the core components of the American Guide series, depicting a federalized nation defined by its diversity and local color.

In an effort to closely control the production of the state guides the Washington office issued a series of eighteen manuals that instructed state offices on the proper procedures for collecting material, preparation of guide copy, textual organization and structure, style, arrangement of tours, guidelines for maps and illustrations, as well as such minutia as grammar, filing, and indexing. The initial manual and early supplements reflected indecision and ambivalence among the Washington staff concerning the purpose and audience for the guides. Henry Alsberg envisioned the guides as a literary compendium of American culture, whereas George Cronyn thought the guides ought to present an encyclopedia of the nation. Both men imagined that the final product would be a series of books serving armchair travelers and curious readers interested in a survey of American culture. Katherine Kellock, on the other hand, saw the guides specifically as tourist guides, believing that they should serve tourists first and foremost.[102] These competing visions became evident in the early manuals.

The first manual produced by the Washington staff in October 1935 adhered to the original vision of a five-volume regional guide to America and explained that the purpose of the guide was to provide "an inclusive picture of the scenic, historical, cultural, recreational, economic, aesthetic, and commercial and industrial resources of the country." The manual defined the intent to collect information into one easily accessible source, to provide "an understanding of the native and folk backgrounds of rural localities," and to produce "a convenient and compact series of reference books, for tours, sightseeing, and investigation of notable landmarks, objects of interest, fictional association, or other data of value to citizens throughout the country." Local field workers were provided with sample questionnaires and instructed to gather data through observation, interviews, and research, compiling all information gathered into weekly field reports. Finally, tours constituted "the final step in data assembling." As originally conceived, tours could be custom made to accommodate regional and local conditions. The only stipulation was that the tour "must move toward some point of the compass" rather than following a circular route.[103] Subsequent manual supplements presented a system of classification and an organizational structure that defined the parameters of the state guides. Beginning with a series of introductory essays covering such topics as geography, history, growth and development, racial elements, government, industry and commerce, educational facilities, and contemporary culture, the guides then addressed information related to touring possibilities, including transportation, accommodations, recreational facilities, points of interest, cities, towns and villages, maps and illustrations, and sectional descriptions of tours.[104] Despite these extensive instructions, the early manuals still left many decisions about textual organization, tours, and specific essay topics up to individual states. The resulting confusion forced the Washington office to rethink and revise their instructions.

Through the spring and summer of 1936, as attention shifted away from the regional guides to the production of the state guides, the Washington office distributed a new series of manuals to replace existing instructions and implement a more standardized state guide model. An introductory letter justified the new, more rigid template, explaining that the state guides needed to follow "a uniform pattern, so that when volumes are collected they will form a set and the person accustomed to using a Maine Guide will be able to find what he wants in a Utah Guide." According to the new manual, each state guide would follow a strict and standardized system of organization. A preliminary section of introductory essays outlining the physical character and history of the state and surveying a variety of topics detailing the social, cultural, and economic character of the state would be followed by sections on cities, towns, and villages and a list of points of interest, concluding with a series of tours criss-crossing the state. Although the manual noted that the number and length of introductory essays might differ for each state, the overriding organization of the table of contents provided a uniform model for state guides. The guides still embodied the varied interests of Washington editors combining discursive essays, city overviews, and tours; and these three distinct components of each state guide provided a survey of regional and local culture, an encyclopedic compendium of cities, villages and towns, along with a guide to tourist opportunities. However, tours now took precedence over all other material. The revised manual explained,

"Introductory essays should give only the picture as a whole or by regions. *The main section of a guide is devoted to tours.*"[105] With this new series of instructions, the guides embraced the more practical task of travel guides and the tours became central to their organization and content.

No longer just descriptions of sectional tours, the tours section of the guides took on a more regimented format. The new instructions stipulated that all tours had to run either north to south or east to west, beginning at one state border and ending at the opposite border. Side tours could then branch off from main tour routes to reach those points of interest not accessible via main highways. As Henry Alsberg explained to the director of the Connecticut project, "In planning the State guides, each of which is a unit in a 48-volume set, we have had to ask for uniformity in order that travelers going from State to State shall not have to learn a new guide system with each volume, and shall know exactly where to find the same kind of information in each volume."[106] The survey of information presented in the first two sections of the guide had to be relevant to the tours. For example, the instructions stated emphatically that "All Possible material should be tied to geographical locations and made part of tour-descriptions."[107] A complicated system of cross-referencing linked the introductory essays, the survey of cities and towns, and the list of points of interest with the various state tours. As the tours came to predominate, the purpose and intent of the series as defined by the Washington staff became more pointed and focused. "One of the most important contributions of the American Guide Series to the knowledge of America," according to the Washington staff, was "the detailed and explicit treatment of thousands of points of interest that heretofore have passed unnoticed. . . . We are trying to heighten the interest of Americans in their own historic relics and architectural features, and in the best examples of the Country's social and economic life by pointing out the physical evidence."[108] The American Guide series was intended as more than a survey of American culture; it was meant to encourage Americans to see and know the nation firsthand and to become better Americans in the process.

An early press release explained that "the characteristic feature" of the American Guide series would "be its peculiar value to Americans." Unlike the Baedeker guide, which served as a foil for the series, the Washington staff asserted that the American Guide series would be "designed to open up to Americans human and natural resources and monuments that have been largely overlooked" in the United States. Following standard guidebook format, the series would provide information about transportation, accommodations, and travel facilities; but beyond that, it also promised to present "a mass of systematically arranged material on folk lore [*sic*], history, art, architecture and archeology, education, social backgrounds, industry and geology."[109] In combing the nation community by community and state by state for scenic attractions, historic monuments, and literary shrines, in surveying the political, economic, social, and cultural development of each state, and in documenting the diverse natural settings and local cultures throughout the nation, the Washington office hoped to capture and codify the richness and variety of the American nation to enable Americans "to rediscover their own country."[110] Although Alsberg and the Washington staff justified the project along practical lines, arguing that it benefited white-collar workers in need of relief across the country while providing a much-needed "convenient and inexpensive" guide to the United States, they also believed the guides would benefit the country during a time of need by chronicling the distinctive features and the diverse cultures that defined America as a united nation.[111] Through both the process and the final product, project administrators hoped to create a shared public culture inscribed across the American landscape. "By producing books that are helping us to know our country," Harry Hopkins, head of the WPA, explained, "the Writers' Project helps us to become better acquainted with each other and, in that way, develops Americanism in the best sense of the word."[112]

The progressive motives and idealistic aspirations of Washington administrators to revitalize American culture shaped the image of the nation presented by the series. As documentary records and informative texts, the guides conveyed a neutral quality that seemed to reveal an objective view of the nation verified by the authority of publication and sanctioned by the national government. However, the Washington office embraced a specific reform agenda that rested on a politically motivated expression of cultural nationalism. As one historian has argued, "The national office running the Writers' Project was intent on mapping out America according to a regular grid and a progressive ideology, thus effecting cultural as well as economic recovery."[113] Influenced by the prevailing theories of regionalism, the culture of documentary expression, and the underlying principles of the New Deal, project administrators envisioned a harmonious and unified American nation comprised of diverse local communities rooted in distinct regional landscapes.[114] Beyond the familiar state monikers (e.g., Kentucky the Blue Grass State, Nebraska the Corn Husker State) and the often repeated state slogans (e.g., North Carolina, "A vale of humility between two mountains of conceit," or Kansas, "First in freedom, first in wheat"), the WPA guides expand into an excess of details that are difficult to condense into neat summaries or ordered categories.[115] Rather, the structure imposed on the guides more accurately conveys the underlying narrative of the nation embodied by the series. Both the organizational framework of the project and the editorial guidelines defined and controlled this national ideal. The central staff believed that by having resident or "native" field workers collect primary material they were guaranteed access to authentic, indigenous, local color. "Unlike the usual commercial guide book publishers, the Federal Writers' Projects have been able to follow a method which allows definite local color and feeling to penetrate the guide," a press release from the central office boasted. It went on to explain that "material has actually been collected locally, on the spot, by Guide workers who are native to the location and can catch its real spirit."[116] Guidebook manuals and editorial reviews also instructed field workers and state editors on how to find and capture local culture. In letter after letter the Washington staff explained, "There are various places where such material can be found—old biographies, memoirs, old-time newspapers, contemporary newspapers, books on folklore, family histories, unpublished manuscripts that have been deposited in libraries, and so on."[117]

The standard table of contents for each state guide reinforced this image of an indigenous nation. According to the directive of the guide manual, each state guide was to begin with a brief overview of practical information for the traveler, providing facts about transportation, climate, and a calendar of events. This introductory section was followed by a series of short essays surveying the development of the state, beginning with an overview of the contemporary scene and followed by essays on the natural setting, first Americans, history, and economic and social development. The guide manual explained that the opening essay on the contemporary scene should provide "a general picture of the mental 'climate,' or way of looking at life in the

Cover of the Federal Writers' Project's *Nebraska: A Guide to the Cornhusker State* (New York: Viking Press, 1939). From the collection of Peter W. Williams. (Reproduced by permission of the Nebraska State Historical Society)

State. This essay should try to reveal the forces that have produced the present culture . . . ; it should indicate current attitudes toward economic or social ideas; and trace the values that predominate in the state."[118] After presenting the indigenous culture of the state, subsequent essays explained the origins and development of that culture. The essay on the natural setting, which covered such topics as geography, topography, climate, geology, natural resources, and flora and fauna, came next, drawing from prevalent tenets of regionalism that correlated landscape and culture. The next three essays documented the growth of an indigenous state culture. The essay on first Americans verified an ancient tradition by covering Indian cultures and their archeological remains. The history essay traced the rise of a localized American culture by examining the progression from exploration to settlement, to colonial development, statehood, and form of government. As one supplementary manual explained, "The essayist should try to let his story develop in natural sequence, expanding as the actual history expanded itself. He should follow the spread of settlement, noting the founding of communities and the establishment of and change of government as it spread."[119] The final set of essays addressing social and economic development assessed the culmination of the historical trajectory by surveying industry, commerce, labor, transportation, agriculture, racial elements and folklore, education, religion, social life, and so on. Washington administrators encouraged state editors to capture "the epic of American commerce and industry, agriculture and education" in these essays as well as the racial and social character of the state.[120] Although seemingly arranged in chronological order, the sequence of the essays betrayed an underlying theory of cultural progression that linked culture to landscape and posited an evolutionary trajectory from colonization and settlement to the emergence of a native folk culture, culminating in the developments of modern capitalism. This progressive narrative not only reflected a vision of national development but also implied the promise of recovery as the nation continued to progress.

The Washington staff claimed that states had some flexibility in determining and organizing the essay section. The revised guide manual noted that "there need be no rigid pattern to fit all states" and that the "arrangement of essays topics will differ from State to State since the order of the narrative is dependent on the material."[121] However, the underlying conceptualization of the relation between landscape, culture, history, and economic development remained fixed. As George Cronyn explained to the director of the Washington state project, "Keep in mind that any State can be understood only when three factors have been fully considered: its climate and geography, its racial ingredients, and its history. To neglect any of these features is bound to result in an inadequate summary [of the state]."[122] Whether the flow of topics in individual state guides highlighted geology or topography, agriculture or industry, racial elements or immigration, the overriding structure of the essay section mandated by the Washington office expressed a theory of cultural development that linked each state as a distinct physical and political entity into a diverse yet cohesive whole, defining America in pluralistic terms as an indigenous nation.

The remaining sections of the guides covering city descriptions, points of interest, and tours inscribed this image of the nation onto the landscape. While the introductory essays provided the framework, the remaining two sections of each volume filled in the details. As the revised guide manual explained, "The introductory essays should not occupy a disproportionately large part of the book; it should always be kept in mind that the volumes are guidebooks devoted to the things that people want to go and see."[123] The tours were the principle focus of the guides, and only "as a matter of convenience" were city descriptions and points of interest divided into a separate section.[124] The Washington staff reasoned that "tours, even more than cities, carry the illustrations and enlarge on the story summarized in the essays." Specifically, they provided the details of "of Indian occupation, of exploration, of settlement, of the exploitation of natural resources, and of the rise of civilization in the States at the places where the events occurred."[125] As Henry Alsberg explained to the director of the Nevada project, "The rule is 'X marks the spot.' Travelers like to feel that they are standing on the very spot where somebody nearly died of thirst, where some traveler's cattle died, leaving him helpless."[126] By mapping local culture and historical development on the landscape, the tours served to authenticate the narrative of the nation presented in the essays. Articulating the underlying theory of the tours, the revised guide manual noted, "Roads have not developed by accident; the general course of all routes of importance has been worn by the movement of large numbers of people who wanted to go from one place to another. Many routes were developed by migrating hordes." Accordingly, tour routes following main highways provided "a thread on which a narrative can be built, with history, from the days of the Indian occupation of the country to the present, told in geographical rather than topical or chronological sequence."[127] The touring format naturalized the image of the nation represented by the guides, suggesting that a distinct and diverse American culture existed in situ waiting to be discovered by the tourist.

Beyond the regimented structure and format, the Washington office also imposed its national vision on the state guides by dictating research strategies and writing styles that underscored "human interest" and cultural diversity.[128] Over and over Washington counseled state editors to capture the "sights, sounds, and smells of the country," in contrast to dry, statistical material.[129] Commenting on Arkansas tour copy, Alsberg criticized that it failed "to give those bits of vivid detailed descriptions that make the reader feel that he is actually covering the route." He continued, "Try to remember to record the greens, yellows, browns, and reds in the landscape. When you describe an industrial plant try to make the reader see the people who work in it. If you describe a cotton gin, describe the people who bring in the cotton and the appearance of the wagons as they stand waiting at the door."[130] Or as Katherine Kellock explained to the director of the Vermont project, "I want to enter the houses, know what the people do on weekdays and holidays, how they manage to send their children to college."[131] Washington editors also instructed state employees to focus on the experiences of the common people and everyday life. Using a draft of the Iowa guide as an example, Alsberg commented to one state editor that "by the device of describing one town on county fair day, a farm at harvest time, a town during the annual church picnic, another town on the night of a watermelon raid, [the Iowa staff] has managed to make continuously interesting copy that in the end builds up a complete picture of how Iowa people live, work, love, hate and vote."[132] Following these guidelines state offices were directed to capture and convey the diverse cultures of the state, which would then be "worked into unity in Washington."[133]

In an effort to counteract the homogenizing influence of mass culture characteristic of travel advertising and booster literature, the central office directed state editors and field workers to focus on local color, folk culture, and "real" life. Building on the notion that America was a pluralistic nation the manual explained, "The Guides should point out what is unusual about a city, town or section, rather than what the city, town or section has in common with the majority of cities, towns or sections of the country."[134] The Washington staff encouraged state employees to seek out and highlight local difference. "How do people take their politics, do they have election day fights, have they a liking for strange electioneering tactics, do they unite in non-sectarian religious groups or do they support a dozen churches in small towns?" Alsberg questioned the director of the Nebraska state guide. "All these points paint a picture of the present day people and show wherein they differ from the people of other states." To tease out these local details he counseled, "In the towns that were settled by Germans, be sure to note whether there are still traces of foreign habits and ways of thinking and acting. In the Indian towns note whether the inhabitants are Americanized in dress and speech and, if not, what the differences are."[135] Whether a community had a unique immigrant presence, a distinct racial history, a noted industrial impact, a dominant agricultural character, or a singular historical background, the state guides would map and detail that distinct character across the landscape of the state.

Folklore and folk customs were of particular interest because they revealed the diverse traditions that underlay regional and local cultures. As one supplement to the guide manual noted, "The American Guide is being compiled primarily to introduce Americans to their own rich culture." The Washington office instructed field workers to "survey their towns and districts with fresh eyes." The guide manual counseled, "very often a worker fails to recognize that lore and customs he has known all his life are novel and interesting to people from other parts of America."[136] Celebrating a romantic ideal of the folk suggestive of the Brothers Grimm, the guide manual instructed field workers to document religious customs, unique celebrations, customs related to birth, death, courtship, and marriage, social customs such as quilting and community blessings, table and dress customs, and any other unique communal expressions of local distinction. Folk material included local legends, tall tales, ghost stories, jokes, and animal tales. Indian legends and "Negro lore" were of particular interest, and supplementary manuals instructed field workers on the fine points of interviewing former slaves and documenting landmarks associated with Indian lore.[137]

However, Alsberg and his staff were not simply interested in a sanitized celebration of localized folk cultures. Following in the tradition of documentary expression and New Deal politics, they wanted to depict "the real America."[138] As George Cronyn explained, "The American Guide is not designed merely to give the rosiest picture of all localities in the course of their development." Rather, Cronyn continued, "we are eager to give an authentic picture of the past and present, omitting no vital facts, even though at times they may seem rather grim and sordid."[139] Again and again the Washington office told state offices not to ignore or overlook important labor developments, minority groups, and less affluent classes. Alsberg scolded the director of the Illinois project for glossing over "certain distasteful phases" of Chicago's past, particularly material on the Haymarket riot, which he argued "had an important bearing on the realization of the 8-hour day" and thus deserved fuller treatment.[140] Similarly, Washington cautioned various state offices to avoid stereotypes when dealing with Indians and racial elements. The guide manual specifically instructed state offices not to "call every Indian victory a 'cruel massacre of whites,' and every white aggression 'a courageous and noble defense of homes.'"[141] This focus on the "real" reinforced the claim that the guides presented an accurate and authoritative, true-to-life survey of America, a document of the nation.

However, not all the state guides strictly followed the imposed guidelines of the Washington office. Vardis Fisher, director of the Idaho project, assumed almost sole control of the Idaho guide in an effort to insure that the Idaho volume would be published first in the series. Fisher blatantly resisted Washington directives, positioning himself as a rugged individual fighting against the conformity of Washington bureaucracy. Not only did he disregard the uniform tour organization by running Idaho tours south to north as opposed to the mandated north to south, but he also championed Idaho wilderness over all other cultural and economic developments despite Washington's desire to provide a more balanced and objective survey of the natural and urban amenities of the state.[142] Similarly, other state directors rebelled against Washington's editorial control. Historian Ray Allen Billington, who became the second director for the Massachusetts state guide, challenged Washington's conception of what constituted an acceptable history essay. He wrote in response to Washington's comments:

> We cannot agree with the point of view implicit in the editorial comment that history is a series of unrelated chronological and biographical facts. Did we share this view, we would have suggested the elimination of the history essay and we would have compiled information for the conventional tourist in a barren chronology. If the point of view is to be eliminated, there is no need for an essay in this or any other guide book. We do not conceive the purpose of the introductory essays to be, as your editors say, "comprehensive." On the contrary, we understand their function to be interpretive and designed to contain enough of the facts to render the book intelligible.[143]

Disagreements with Washington ranged far beyond the simple desire to control guide copy. A number of southern states actively thwarted attempts on the part of the Washington staff to provide a survey of African American contributions to American culture.[144] In response to criticism from Washington, the director of North Carolina project wrote, "I feel strongly that the guide should not so overemphasize the Negro that it will arouse hostile criticism."[145] The director of the Oklahoma project called the imposition of the essay on racial elements "an infringement from [sic] states' rights."[146] In Mississippi the project director skirted Washington corrections for the racial elements essay by pushing through a rushed draft that included a number of veiled and overt racial slurs.[147] Despite attempts on the part of the Washington office to shape the production of state guides according to a uniform model, individuals within each state struggled in one form or another to assert their own agendas and maintain control over the process and the product of cultural representation. As one historian has argued, "The WPA guidebooks were forged amid the collisions and negotiations among these varied interests."[148]

While state offices rebelled against Washington directives, political opponents constantly threatened the continuation of the project and questioned the objectivity and loyalty of the Washington staff. In 1938 Congressman Martin Dies directed the newly formed Committee to Investigate Un-American Activities to investigate charges of Communist activity and propaganda on the part of the Federal Writer's Project. A year later, a subcommittee of the House Committee on Appropriations questioned the funding needs of the project. In the fall of 1939, the Writers' Project was reorganized under state control with reduced funding. At that time less than half of the state guides had been published; the remaining guides were brought to publication during the next two years under drastically comprised circumstances. Red tape, political infighting, conflicts over sponsorship, and a circumscribed central staff marred the final completion of the state guides.[149]

Despite these external problems and internal idiosyncrasies, the American Guides series presented a cohesive and systematized survey of the nation. From the beginning, the Washington office had encouraged state directors to consider issues of continuity and narrative. They wanted each of the state guides to become part of a larger national narrative. Not only did the Washington office want each volume to "have a certain continuity, or *flow*, so that there [would] be a steady and logical progression from beginning to end" (emphasis original), but they also wanted each state volume to fit within the larger narrative constructed by the series.[150] The series was envisioned as "the complete, standard, authoritative work on the United States as a whole and every part of it."[151] In both scope and purpose, the series presented America as a cohesive whole, a united nation. The fifty-one guides conveyed the prevailing conception of America as a nation comprised of diverse communities.[152] In focusing on the common, the quotidian, the local, and the real, the Washington instructions consciously and unconsciously projected an image of a diverse yet personalized America. America became a nation of neighbors. From this perspective, the country was not a homogenized, rationalized, industrial behemoth on the verge of collapse. Rather it was a nation of individuals and common folk who dealt with the vicissitudes of everyday life in a myriad of ways, all of which conveyed a certain dignity and character unique to each situation. In this way ethnic, racial, and social division and conflict were transformed into pluralistic diversity. History became heritage.[153] The nation was revealed as a united and cohesive unit, an "imagined community" in which conflict was neutralized and naturalized across varied regional and local landscapes.[154]

The WPA guides represent the most comprehensive survey of the nation as well as the culmination of a growing popular interest in national tourism. While earlier guides to America fell short due to compromised vision or incomplete coverage, the American Guide series succeeded in recording and documenting the nation in extensive detail. Cultural anxiety and an undeveloped tourist tradition and infrastructure circumscribed Bryant's *Picturesque America,* and corporate interests and lack of popular acclaim limited the See America First series. In contrast, the WPA guides benefited from government sponsorship and the widespread popularity of tourism in the United States by the 1930s, combined with the sense of cultural uncertainty that marked the Depression years and the New Deal desire to instigate economic and cultural regeneration. In collecting and codifying American history and traditions, in celebrating economic and industrial development, in documenting everyday people and their work across the American landscape, the guides tapped into a rising tide of cultural nationalism that sought to revive American culture during a moment of crisis. The guides presented a stabilized physical image of the nation with a "united, harmoniously diverse citizenry" and reaffirmed America's position as a mature and viable civilization. In the process, they defined a new set of "guidelines to cultural citizenship in modern America."[155]

In building on an established prescriptive tradition that linked tourism with an ideal of the nation all of these guides helped to further define tourism as a ritual of citizenship. Although the explicit purpose of *Picturesque America,* the See America First series, and the WPA series was to promote and encourage national tourism in the United States, the overall intent of all three guide sets was to catalog and thus legitimize America as a united nation. In following the directive of the guides, in seeing America, in experiencing the nation firsthand, tourists could reaffirm their identity as Americans. In this way, all three guide sets presented a new ideal of the mobile citizen in which the rights of citizenship were defined not in traditional terms of political rights and social identities, but rather in terms of geographical mobility and commercial access.

The shifting images of the nation represented in the various guide sets reflect not only shifting conceptions of the nation but also a longstanding ambivalence about how to define the nation. *Picturesque America* looked to American scenery to define and legitimize the nation; the See America First series celebrated the triumvirate of nature, history, and technology as the basis for national unity and cohesiveness; the WPA guides positioned America as an indigenous folk nation. All three series reflected the prevailing anxieties and the pervasive theories of cultural nationalism that characterized their respective eras. However, the desire to define and codify the nation suggests an underlying need to unite and legitimize the modern nation-state and support the process of incorporation in order to sustain a constituency of national consumers and tourists. Just as ambivalence and contradictions were embedded in prescriptive narratives of the nation presented in the various guide sets, so tourists expressed that ambivalence in their experience of national tourism.

6

TOURIST ENCOUNTERS

> It would be very pleasant to write nothing but eulogies of people and places, but after all if a personal narrative were written like an advertisement, praising everything, there would be no point in praising anything, would there? . . . I think it best to let the story stand as it was written; taking nothing back that seems to me true, but acknowledging very humbly at the outset, that after all mine is only *one* out of a possible fifty million other American opinions.
>
> —Emily Post, 1917

*I*N 1919 SINCLAIR LEWIS published his fifth novel, *Free Air*, which recounts the possibilities and the perils of early automobile touring. Growing out of a transcontinental trip Lewis took in 1916 with his wife, Grace Hegger Lewis, the novel traces the physical and social distances traversed through the experience of automobile touring.[1] Claire Boltwood, a high-society Brooklyn Heights girl, and her father, an overworked business magnate, set off on a transcontinental automobile tour in the hopes that fresh air and the adventure of the open road will relieve Boltwood of his "nervous prostration" brought on from overwork.[2] Their first day on the road they meet up with a mechanic, Milt Daggett, from Schoenstrom, Minnesota, who abandons his garage and his midwestern roots and takes to the road in pursuit of Claire and the possibilities she represents. Traveling from Minneapolis to Seattle in a Gomez-Deperdussin roadster, Claire

Sinclair Lewis's autotouring novel *Free Air* was first published in serialized form in the *Saturday Evening Post* in the late spring of 1919. Illustration from Sinclair Lewis's "Free Air," *Saturday Evening Post*, 13 May 1919. (Courtesy of the College of Wooster)

descends from the exclusive, overly civilized world of Brooklyn Heights into the "real" America. For the Boltwoods this is a "voyage into democracy."[3] For Milt Daggett this is an opportunity to refashion himself, leaving behind his provincial and unsophisticated roots. He skitters and jounces behind the Boltwoods in his Teal Bug, always available to rescue them from the uncertainties of the road and automobile, and in the meantime he educates himself about the social graces of proper etiquette and rhetoric.

The novel hinges on the possibilities of the road—the tourist landscape. In motoring through small western towns and windswept prairies, over gleaming mountains, and along stretches of open road, Claire discovers not only the "real" people and places of America but also her own power and independence. Meanwhile, Milt Daggett escapes the confines of small-town, middle America and learns the ways of urbanity and sophistication. In the tourist landscape Claire and Milt are not defined or restricted by their respective social settings. Claire is no longer of Brooklyn Heights and Milt is no longer of Schoenstrom. They inhabit a "nonordinary" setting, in many ways liminal space, a place of re-creation and social fluidity where they are outside of the social as well as the physical confines of home and work.[4] In the tourist landscape Claire and Milt transcend the ordinary boundaries of social status and reinvent themselves so that they can be partners on an equal basis. In detailing the adventures of automobile touring, Lewis aptly describes the imaginative possibilities embedded in the tourist experience. He celebrates both Claire and Milt as individuals rather than as products of their social environments, underscoring the potential of American democracy, but at the same time he exposes the possibilities of touring. He reveals the tourist landscape—in this case the open road—as a place outside or beyond ordinary life and social conventions where the tourist can refashion him or herself and escape the restrictions of occupation, social class, and family background.

Free Air represents one of many narratives, both fictional and documentary, that detailed the experiences of American tourists. In the context of the extensive literature of tourism, these travel accounts reflected a middle ground between prescriptive material and unmediated individual response. Organized around themes of departure, discovery, and return, they presented the tourist experience in subjective terms. Although they embodied the tropes of advertising literature—adventure, escape, regeneration—they brought a personalized dimension to marketed messages and meanings. As narratives, they defined the cultural meaning of tourism.[5]

From its inception in the early nineteenth century, touring in the United States resulted in a literature of social and cultural commentary. Early transcontinental railroad tourists and pilgrims to natural, historic, and literary shrines set down their experiences, thoughts, and reactions in letters to home newspapers, essays in popular magazines, and travel books.[6] During the nineteenth century, however, the touring public remained relatively small. Consequently, early touring narratives focused less on the experience of touring and more on social commentary facilitated by the touring experience. Using the early tourist experience to frame their observations, Samuel

Bowles, Horace Greeley, and Mark Twain documented and commented on western culture and character. Similarly, in *The American Scene*, Henry James used his return to the United States as an opportunity to write a travel account that explored the transformation of American culture that had occurred in his absence. These acclaimed travel narratives, and many lesser known imitations, used the novelty of tourism to direct their attention outward to the world through which they traveled.[7]

As automobile ownership and use expanded during the early decades of the twentieth century, touring became increasingly popular among native-born, white, upper- and middle-class Americans. Unlike the railroad, where rigid schedules and standardized stops limited passengers to preplanned final destinations, the automobile provided a much more suitable means of transportation for the individual tourist.[8] The automobile, catering to the whims of the individual driver, fostered a personalized journey: traveling at one's leisure, individually customized tours, a unique experience. Tapping into the core desires and ideals of liberal individualism, the automobile shaped and defined the popular touring experience. As a result, the novelty and the expanded possibilities that came with automobile touring spawned a myriad of publications commenting on the popular touring experience in personalized detail. The early twentieth century witnessed the publication of a vast number of articles, touring journals, pamphlets, diaries, manuals, travel accounts, and novels. Some tourists kept touring logs and privately published chronicles of their tours. "Freelance writers with a keen eye for a potential fad wrote accounts of transcontinental journeys for newspapers and magazines, while more serious essayists probed the long-run implications for society as a whole," notes one scholar.[9] Despite their diversity in form, this eclectic literature shared the desire to celebrate the experience of touring, and in the process defined the popular touring experience in subjective terms.[10]

Just as Sinclair Lewis revealed the social fluidity and the possibilities of the tourist landscape, so other tourist literature and touring narratives commented on the ways in which tourists appropriated the marketed tourist experience as their own and experienced the tourist landscape. This vast and varied literature shows that tourists did not thoughtlessly consume the images of America promoted by prescriptive touring literature and objectified by tourist attractions. Many of the touring narratives published during the early twentieth century reveal that tourist responses ranged widely from trite notations to thoughtful meditations about their travels. In many of these narratives, individual journeys of self-realization are set in the context of prescriptive ideals about touring. Some upper- and middle-class tourists bought into the marketed tourist experience without question. Others, self-conscious about their status in an increasingly modern society fraught with working-class unrest, urban vice, ethnic and racial conflict, and overseas foes, revealed their ambivalence by celebrating an idealized and nostalgic image of America in which they, as spectators, remained in control of their own and the nation's destiny. Still others used the experience of tourism to reinvent themselves as independent individuals temporarily rejecting or stretching the social and cultural boundaries of early-twentieth-century American society. Overall these narratives shared a common theme: written by and for white, native-born, upper- and middle-class Americans, they all participated in and expanded the discourse of national and individual identity intrinsic to the widespread characterization of tourism as a ritual of citizenship.

DISCOVERING AMERICA

On the morning of the Boltwood's second day out on the road, after a particularly harrowing first day of touring in which the Gomez-Dep got stuck in the mud and had to be towed out, and an uncomfortable night at a run-down drummer's hotel in Gopher Prairie, Minnesota with, "poison-green walls" papered with insurance calendars, Claire stopped at a garage to take on gas. While waiting for the car she had a revelation: the people she had met at the hotel the night before were not rude as she had originally assumed. It was her own air of eastern exclusiveness that had made these people seem offensive and intrusive. In a moment of epiphany she exclaimed, "Why, they aren't rude. They care—about people they never saw before. That's why they ask questions! I never thought—I never thought! There's people in the world who want to know us without having looked us up in the Social Register!" This moment of realization introduced a central theme in the novel. While Claire stood there waiting for her car, she noticed a sign on the air-hose at the garage that read Free Air. "There's our motto for the pilgrimage," she declared. The narrator noted, "Thus Claire's second voyage into democracy."[11]

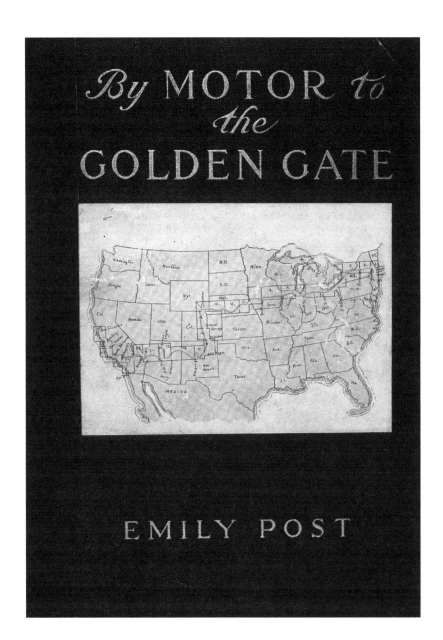

Social commentator Emily Post wrote a detailed account of her transcontinental motor tour taken in 1915. Cover of Emily Post's *By Motor to the Golden Gate* (1917). (Courtesy of the Library of Congress)

The Boltwood's transcontinental automobile tour was not simply a therapeutic journey. This was a voyage of discovery. Claire was moving into the real America. As the title, drawn from a pun on the gas station air pump, reveals, the Boltwood's tour was a journey away from the exclusive and sheltered environment of the East represented by Brooklyn Heights and into the open spaces of America, a place of democratic openness and infinite possibility. In developing this theme of discovery, Lewis suggests that in many ways the experience of tourism was integrally connected with the desire to see and know the real America. Touring offered a way to learn about America, and in seeing America to become an American. As Claire says later in the tour while sitting with Milt around a campfire at Yellowstone Park, "There is an America! I'm glad I've found it!"[12]

Many tourists revealed in their narratives that, like the Boltwoods, they took to the road to discover America. Their narratives suggest that the prescriptive literature promoting tourism as a ritual of citizenship was successful in shaping the ways in which tourists imagined and experienced their tours. Some narratives simply chronicled the events of touring day by day, noting the sights seen, the mileage covered, and the condition of hotels. They bespoke an uncritical acceptance of patriotic promotional literature that encouraged them to consume the sacred landscapes of America and thus become better citizens. In one of the earlier transcontinental touring narratives, Emily Post informed her readers that the "advertisements" prompted her to take a transcontinental automobile tour to the 1915 San Francisco expositions. Very early in the description of her tour she commented, "One thing that we have already found out; we are seeing our own country for the first time!"[13] Vernon McGill, in his *Diary of a Motor Journey from Chicago to Los Angeles,* chronicled the journey his family took in a Wyllis Knight motor car. Detailing the route between McPherson and Garden City, Kansas, McGill noted, "In 'seeing America first' along this route, one passes many points of historical interest. Today we passed the stamping ground of the famous scout, Kit Carson, and at another point a sign called our attention to a place where General Custer battled with the Indians."[14] Like that of McGill, some tourist narratives simply ticked off the popular attractions tourists visited. Others celebrated the experience of the road and the people encountered along the way. Beatrice Massey in her account of a transcontinental motor trip from New York City to San Francisco counseled readers that touring offered "the only way to get a firsthand knowledge of our country, its people, the scenery, and last, but not the least its roads—good, bad, and infinitely worse." Similarly, Mary Crehore Bedell, who took a circular tour around the United States with her husband, noted, "Generally speaking we found a desire among the American people for right living and right thinking, and we were often touched by the kindness shown to us by perfect strangers. There is no better way of discovering the fine traits of our fellow countrymen than by packing up a kit and going-a-gypsying."[15] In addition, Effie Price Gladding, in her tour from the Pacific to the Atlantic via the Lincoln Highway, celebrated the "intimate knowledge to which the motorist alone can attain." Summarizing the benefits of her tour, she wrote, "We have a new conception of our great country; her vastness, her varied scenery, her prosperity, her happiness, her boundless resources, her immense possibilities, her kindness and hopefulness. We are bound to her by a thousand new ties of acquaintance, of association, and of pride."[16] In a similar vein, Maria Letitia Stockett encouraged her readers, "By all means see America First and then see it again. Don't miss the rangers. See the National Parks—it will restore your faith in democratic government—almost—but I do not wish to exaggerate."[17] Nature writer Dallas Lore Sharp, recounting his transcontinental tour from Massachusetts to California, perhaps most eloquently explained that the purpose of crossing the country by motor was to see, feel, and understand America, "that so we might have faith and love for this broad land, its forms and terms and manners, its habitable soil, its cheerful sky, its many and mighty cities, its multi-tongued, multi-millioned, but not amorphous, people."[18] These narratives reveal that tourists stopped to admire natural scenery, historic sites, and technological wonders, just as the prescriptive literature instructed them to, and in doing so they sought to come in contact with the people and places that embodied the real America.[19]

As the divergent tourist literature prescribed, in seeing the sights of America history and the landscapes of the nation, tourists experienced first-hand the character and nuances of the nation, and their narratives overflow with references to the various America types and the distinct American places they surveyed. The sites they saw and the people they met, however, did not always correspond to the official images of America prescribed by the tourist literature. Through these narratives, individual tourists constructed

THE PACIFIC AT LAST!

Many tourists sought to document the milestones of their journeys. From Emily Post's *By Motor to the Golden Gate* (1917). (Courtesy of the Library of Congress)

their own images of America as they traveled through the tourist landscape. At times, those images were just as idealized as those presented in the prescriptive literature; at other times, tourists presented a seemingly more realistic view of the landscape they traversed. On the whole, however, tourist narratives appeared less concerned with constructing an image of national unity and more concerned with discovering a place in which they felt "at home." These narratives reveal a diverse series of underlying anxieties that suggest that individual tourists took to the tourist landscape, not only for pleasure but also to discover or invent an America in which they, as white, native-born, upper- and middle-class citizens, threatened by increased immigration, labor unrest, racial diversity, and a sense of powerlessness and "weightlessness" manifested in modern urban-industrial living, could regain some sense of identity, security, and control.[20]

Frederic F. Van de Water, a journalist and free-lance writer famous for his adventure stories, mysteries, travel writing, and essays, wrote in his introduction to a touring narrative describing his family's transcontinental tour that after "five weeks and two days, three originally smug New Yorkers underwent a slow and amazing transformation. . . . At the end of the ordeal they were no longer New Yorkers, but Americans, which, they learned, is something surprisingly and heartenly different."[21] Van de Water's narrative, *The Family Flivvers to Frisco,* tells the story of the Engineer, the Commodore, and the Supercargo—a husband and wife and their six-and-a-half-year-old son—who drove from the suburbs of New York City to San Francisco in a Ford touring car they called Issachar, autocamping all the way. Written primarily to direct others who might wish to make a transcontinental automobile tour, the book describes the experience of automobile camping: the necessary equipment and clothing, the life and social character of autocamps, and the pleasures and hazards of the road. Beyond its prescriptive tone, the narrative also chronicles what the family discovered out on the road. What they found was America. Writing about the benefits of the tour, Van de Water noted, "As for the engineer, much has come to him in the way of knowledge. . . . For the first time in thirty-five years, he has been able to visualize the American nation." He concluded, "To us 'America' no longer is an abstract noun, or a familiar map of patchwork, or a flag, or a great domed building in Washington. It is something clearer and dearer and, we think, higher. It is the road we traveled." Van de Water proclaimed, "You cannot comprehend America unless you go and see it. You cannot see it with the intimacy, the closeness that only a motor-camping trip affords without returning to your home . . . a broader more confident, immensely heartened person."[22]

Like Claire Boltwood, the Engineer, the Commodore, and the Supercargo left New York in a cynical and snobbish frame of mind, ignorant of an America outside of their exclusive milieu. They saw the bucolic farms of Iowa, the rolling prairie of Nebraska, the pungent sagebrush of Wyoming, the natural wonders of Yellowstone, the rolling hills of Oregon, and finally the bustling streets of San Francisco. They arrived in San Francisco "thin" and "tanned, brown as Indians," transformed into "native" Americans not only by the scenery and the historic sites and shrines they witnessed but also by the friendly, democratic Americans they encountered along the way. In autocamps across the continent they met the common people of America, touring, working, and tramping. Van de Water noted that days spent in camp revealed the community of makeshift automobile camps. He commented on "the warming friendliness of neighbors who rested." He continued, "By grace of the fact that they were all there, the campers regarded each other as acquaintances. They squatted together in the shade and debated many things. They compared equipment. They sought information regarding the roads ahead. The camp was filled with lazy, pleasant talk all day long."[23] Tourists shared in the community of the road seemingly free of the boundaries of social class and family background. For Van de Water the community of the autocamp represented an ideal democratic community, with an "unguardedly friendly, almost family-like air"; a community not unlike an idealized version of the nineteenth-century, rural, small towns that were being rapidly supplanted by large urban centers and a national commercial and technological network.[24] He reflected, "We had been taught as children that Americans were the best people in the world. Now, in our early middle age, we believe it, for we have seen them and lived among them, all the way across the continent."[25]

In witnessing the landscape of America firsthand, in communing with "real" Americans, Van de Water suggested that he and his family came to be better citizens. "Traveling, as we traveled, through the heart of the nation," he mused, "brought us a new definition of what constitutes nationality." He noted that the urban dweller who lived in an apartment rarely knew his neighbor: "In streets where one hurries, severely intent upon his own affairs, life is individualistic and egocentric." In this atmosphere one "never savors the full flavor of what citizenship in the republic means." Only by traveling in the "open land," he argued, could one begin to comprehend "the advantages of being an American." He concluded, "Gradually, it dawns upon him that citizenship by itself, that existence in these regions untouched by the blight of New York is the faint equivalent of membership in a brotherhood, the due guard and sign of which is a word of greeting and a smile."[26] The benefits of citizenship did not rest in political rights or private property but in the seemingly classless community of the open road and the freedom of geographic mobility. Beyond the details of autocamping lore, Van De Water's story suggests that touring really was about discovering America, but the America he discovered was clouded by a kind of imperialist nostalgia: a wistful desire for an older idealized America made accessible through the wonders of modern technology.[27]

The nation he described was a homogeneous America composed of courteous, generous, friendly people always willing to lend a helping hand in times of trouble. It was an America of open spaces, rural landscapes, and sublime scenery. Celebrating the tour, Van de Water wrote,

> We have seen America with an intimacy and a closeness of contact from which a traveler by train or even motorist who stops at hotels is forever barred. We have been temporary dwellers in thirty-odd towns, cities and villages in twelve states. We have sat about camp fires and talked informally and at length with citizens of forty commonwealths. We have seen the background of the nation's birth roll past us on either hand as Issachar rattled West. We know America and Americans as only those who go motor camping can learn to know them. We have discovered a people and a land whose existence the average New Yorker never even suspects. The scenery, the vast extent of America have awed and thrilled and lifted us up, but its people have stirred us the most—its dear, kind, friendly people.[28]

Van de Water suggested that, just as advocates of national tourism promised, touring stimulated patriotism by revealing through firsthand experience both the physical wonders of the nation and the democratic spirit of the America people. On the road he found real Americans: the "Swede from Minnesota and his broad-faced, wide-shouldered wife," a Florida couple promoting winter resorts, a traveling watchmaker, "a Dakota farmer and his family" traveling for "therapeutic value," along with road tramps, hikers, and plain old tourists like themselves. He wrote, "The people we met, the, to New Yorkers, strangely kind and friendly people of America—the real America—are among the most thrilling and warming memories of the journey."[29]

The America tourists celebrated extended from the community of other automobile tourists met along the road. Like Van de Water, many touring narratives noted that the community of the road was a democratic melting pot reflecting a wide geographical mix and a broad cross-section of middle-class tourists.[30] For many tourists, according to their narratives, the experience of automobile touring reaffirmed their faith in the democratic principles on which America was founded. On the road they encountered a regionally diverse cross-section of American society and a sense of brotherhood, community, family. Over and over touring narratives commemorated the democratic community of the road. Social difference and class conflict were neutralized into pluralistic distinction and geographic diversity. In essence these narratives idealized the America they discovered while touring, con-

Touring narratives celebrated the democratic community of auto camps, where tourists shared stories and information about the road ahead. Postcard, *Car Camping in Yellowstone National Park.* (Lake County [Illinois] Museum, Curt Teich Postcard Archives)

structing a mythological image of America that more accurately reflected their dissatisfaction with and their fears about the status of democracy in an urban-industrial America than it did the realities of America life.

In reality, the America of automobile camps, tourist attractions, and the open road comprised a relatively homogeneous community of native-born, upper- and middle-class, urban, white Americans. Although occasionally auto tourists met up with traveling salesmen, migrant workers, and tramps, automobile touring took time and money. During the late teens and the early twenties it was a pastime enjoyed by a select few who had the time and money to put aside commitments to home and work and take to the open road. Despite the fact that car ownership dramatically expanded during the early decades of the twentieth century as a result of assembly-line production and installment buying, only established middle-class professionals and white-collar workers who had secure salaries and paid vacation time had access to the democracy of the open road.[31] To say that this select community reflected the diversity and democracy of America ignored the immigrants crowding American cities; it ignored increased African American migration as well as labor unrest and city slums. In others words, it completely denied rising ethnic and racial diversity and the resulting conflicts and concerns that characterized the Progressive era, as well as the increasingly urban and corporate character of American society. The America these tourists saw and eulogized looked back nostalgically to a Jeffersonian ideal of an American society composed of independent yeoman landholders or farmers living in a pastoral setting. In taking to the road, automobile tourists moved into a middle landscape, away from the cities and into the rural, open landscapes of America.[32] This open space, the antithesis of bustling urban centers, combined with the homogeneous and seemingly classless community of the road transported tourists into an imaginary and nostalgic landscape of small-town, rural America. Through the power of the tourist gaze, automobile tourists imagined themselves and their fellow tourists as independent citizens enjoying the bounty of the American land and existing self-sufficiently with the help of their fellow "citizens." Just as tourist advocates and industries constructed and promoted an idealized image of America for tourists to consume, tourists themselves took to the road in search of an ideal America that might assuage their feelings of anonymity, powerlessness, and status anxiety. Although the images of America promoted by tourist advocates varied and did not always match the ideals celebrated by tourists, both promoters and participants took part in the discourse surrounding an ideal America that resulted from a growing uncertainty surrounding the social and cultural relations of urban-industrial life.

Many of the touring narratives expressed this anxiety about the status of American society by looking for and finding an America of democratic, rural, small-town communities primarily associated with an idealized West and the open road. The West became the antithesis of the northeastern industrial core. Tourists associated it with democracy, freedom, friendliness, and community. They saw only a land of farmers, ranchers, cowboys, and friendly Indians—people who lived close to the land. Time and again touring narratives idealized the West as the "true" America in opposition to the overly civilized, urban East. As Letitia Stockett exclaimed in her chronicle of a cross-country tour, "To see the real America go west."[33] Similarly, Kathryn Hulme noted in her touring narrative, *How's the Road?* that after crossing the Mississippi River, "something within us that had been taut, suddenly loosened. We actually felt ourselves expanding in the genial sunshine and we seemed to take up more room in the seat."[34] Rather than depicting the realities of western society, this idealization implicitly revealed the anxiety felt by upper- and middle-class tourists about the shifting character of democracy—the anonymity, and the bureaucracy associated with modern, urban-industrial living. Implicit in the celebration of unfettered western vistas and rugged western individuals was a critique of overcrowded cities and workaday routine. In idealizing the West, tourists blatantly ignored not only the ethnic diversity of the West but also its increasingly urban and industrial character.[35]

Other narratives, however, expressed fears about the transformation of American society even more blatantly. In 1926 Clara Walker Whiteside published *Touring New England on the Trail of the Yankee*, which described a motor tour through New England taken by Whiteside and her companion Ada C. Williamson. Whiteside and Williamson set off with no definite itinerary in search of the historic attractions—"a true record of pre-Revolutionary days"—located throughout New England. Traveling through New York, Connecticut, Rhode Island, Massachusetts, New Hampshire, and Maine, the pair took to the road in search of old houses and churches as well as "quaint old stories" about historic personas and events. Like other tourists, they went "to discover for [themselves] old landmarks and to uncover traditions as well as achievements." However, their tour was more than just a quest for the traditions of colonial New England. They sought out the Yankee in an effort to escape the foreign influence of the "Irish, the Italian, the Portuguese, and the Canadian French," as the well as the "Greeks," "Hungarians," "Poles," and other unnamed immigrant groups who, they believed, were diminishing or obscuring the customs, traditions, and beliefs, the culture, of the "pure" American—the New England Yankee. After stopping to ask directions to Westbrook, Connecticut, from a man cutting the lawn of a seventeenth-century house and realizing he did not understand English, Whiteside lamented, "The passing of the old-time Yankee strikes a sad note. We found him being replaced by alien life. The familiar austerity of the countryside is now enlivened by folk-dances; by unfamiliar and strange music." She commented that the villages of New England, which had witnessed the diminishing of their populations since the Civil War, were "now taking on a new life." She was not, however, impressed with this "alien life." "We wanted the real Yank with his raucous voice," she explained, "but we heard instead the guttural tones, harsh in their volubility, proclaiming a nationality remote and strange."[36]

After traveling through the towns and villages of New England, exploring colonial houses and listening to the tales of heroic and historic events, Whiteside noted that they had seen both the old and the new in their adventures, and that "in some places the contrast was depressing." She concluded, "Efficiency in some of the towns seemed to be the only goal, and the old stock, which should by reason of heredity have owned the land, were markedly absent, in many places. Foreigners were on the farms and along main streets doing business under the Elms and in pre-Revolutionary houses, and it soon will be necessary to learn their languages unless we are willing to wait a few years or so, and then they will have learned ours. They assimilate us much more quickly than we assimilate them." Nevertheless, their tour revealed that enclaves of "the best traditions" still remained in the forgotten corners of New England, preserved by historical and antiquarian societies, suggesting that there was still hope for preserving the "real" and "pure" America.[37] More explicit than most, Whiteside expressed her concerns about the transformation of American society from a society of small-town "island communities" to a commercialized, urban-industrial society that valued efficiency over tradition.[38] Her tour through New England served to reassure her that some aspect of America's "true" heritage still remained amidst the barrage of "alien life" infiltrating the nation.

Not all took to the road to escape or assuage their xenophobic anxieties about the changing character of American society. And not all tourists sought a pure, homogeneous, ideal America. In *Hoosier Holiday*, Theodore Dreiser expressed a completely different view.[39] Driving through Pennsylvania, Dreiser remarked that he had been reading "much magazine sociology of the kind that is labeled 'The Menace of Immigration,'" which argued that America was "being overrun by foreigners who were completely changing the American character, the American facial appearance, the American everything." Yet surveying the people he met and saw along the road, he saw "no change in American character here or anywhere." He noted, "In the cities there were thousands of foreigners but they were not unAmericanizing the cities." On the contrary, these foreigners were being swept in—Americanized—by the forces of popular, commercial culture. "Instead of throwing bombs or lower-ing our social level, all bogies of the sociologists, they would rather stand on our street corners, go to the nearest moving pictures, smoke cigarettes, wear high white collars and braided yellow vests and yearn over girls who know ex-actly how to handle them, or work to someday own an automobile and break the speed laws." He explained, "They really are not so bad as we seem to want them to be. They are simple, gauche, de jeune, 'the limit.' In other words, they are fast becoming American."[40] For Dreiser, the immigrants did not repre-sent an "alien life"; rather, they represented the essence of America and the power of commerce in shaping a homogeneous and, from Dreiser's perspec-tive, mediocre society.

Like other tourists, Dreiser took to the road to see America on his jour-ney back to his boyhood home in Indiana. Traveling with Franklin Booth, an artist friend, the two set off in Booth's automobile in the summer of 1915 to drive across Pennsylvania, New York, and Ohio to Booth's studio and home in Carmel, Indiana. Dreiser and Booth did not seek out established tourist attractions; their tour moved beyond the confines of the marketed tourist experience. Dreiser's narrative transcended the celebratory and pro-motional tone that characterized many of the published automobile touring narratives. In describing his journey, he presented a much more complex, complicated, even contradictory, view of America. The America he depicted had little resemblance to the mythologized nation marketed in prescriptive touring literature.

The sites Dreiser mentioned in his narrative marked places of personal in-terest, places he associated with significant events in America history—his own interpretation of American history, not the official version promoted by tourist industries. For example, driving through Patterson, New Jersey, Dreiser remembered and even commemorated the Patterson Strike, "in which all sorts of nameless brutalities had occurred, brutalities practiced by judges, manufacturers, and the police no less than by the eager workers them-selves." Similarly, in Wilkes-Barre, Pennsylvania, he recalled "the great an-thracite coal strike in 1902," which marked for him "the great days of capitalistic struggle for control in America." For Dreiser, the country he tra-versed reflected the progress of incorporation, not the triumphs of Anglo-American colonists and American pioneers. He remembered the conquests of the robber barons, "the great financiers," such as John D. Rockefeller, Andrew Carnegie, William H. Vanderbilt, and Jay Gould, "who plott[ed] and conniv[ed] the enslavement of the people and belabor[ed] each other for power." The cityscapes of Buffalo and Cleveland reminded him of the struggle for power and money that had transformed American society after the Civil War. "We have endured so much," he wrote. "That brood of giants that rose and wrought and fell between 1870 and 1910—children of the dragon's teeth, all of them—wrought shackles in the night and bound us hand and foot," Dreiser raged. "They have seized nearly all our national privileges, they have bedeviled the law and the courts and the national and state seats of legislation, they have laid a heavy hand upon our highways and all our means of communication, poisoned our food and suborned our colleges and newspapers." For Dreiser, touring offered a means to experience firsthand the effects of mass culture and to critique the excesses of capitalism. He was not interested in a sugar-coated view of a mythologized America. "Nothing is more interesting to me," he explained, "than the general spectacle of life itself in these thriving towns of our new land—though they are devoid of anything historic or in the main artistic (no memories even of any great import)."[41]

Like other tourists, Dreiser commemorated small-town America, but the image of the Midwest he portrayed reflected an ambiguous vision of American society. He had mixed feelings about the America he discovered on the road. On the one hand he saw America as a prosperous, productive, and idealistic young nation; on the other hand he characterized America in a Menckenesque tone as a nation of boobs, idiots, and philistines. Traveling through the small towns of the Midwest he noted that the most one could say about them was that "they were brisk and vivid and building something which in the future will no doubt seem very beautiful." However, he noted that despite the fact that America did not have the artistic or historic attraction of Europe, "it was actually better than Europe." He went on to explain, "Because of a certain indefinable something—either of hope or courage or youth or vigor or illusion, what you will; but the average American, or the average European transplanted to America, is a better or at least a more dynamic person than the average European at home." He had "grit, verve, humor, or a lackadaisical slapdash method which is at once efficient, self-sustaining, comforting." But the best thing about the American, according to Dreiser, was that he did "not appear to realize that he [was] not free or that he [was] in any way oppressed." Dreiser celebrated America for its youth, its vitality, its prosperity, its "optimism or buoyance of soul," as well as its ability to sustain "faith in ideals and the Republic."[42] He was awed by the ability of Americans to continue to dream of and hope for a better life, even when to him that life seemed virtually unattainable.

Dreiser nevertheless saw this dream as an illusion. "Dear, naive America!" he wrote. "When will it be different from a dreaming child?"[43] On the road he witnessed the sincerity and idealism that shaped the American quest for progress. In his eyes the people he saw while touring did not simply pursue commercial success for the sake of financial gain. They naïvely transformed the desire for progress into a religious quest. "Dear, crude, asinine, illusioned Americans! How I love them!" he exclaimed, ruminating about the morning he awoke in the typical country town of Factoryville, Pennsylvania:

> And the great fields from the Atlantic to the Pacific holding them all, and their dreams! How they rise, how they hurry, how they run under the sun! Here they are building a viaduct, there a great road, yonder plowing fields or sowing grains, their faces lit with eternal, futile hope of happiness. You can see them religiously tending store, religiously running a small-town country hotel, religiously mowing the grass, religiously driving shrewd bargains or thinking that much praying will carry them to heaven—the dear things![44]

In a condescending yet captivating tone, Dreiser celebrated what he saw as an earnest, uncritical belief in progress and the future. He commemorated America's faith in principles and ideals and possibilities. He saw this as the essence of the American character. And yet he saw this naïveté, this faith in illusion, this inability to see the social and economic and political realities that constrained the individual, as the source of a mediocre society.

The point at where the dream became illusion marked a point for Dreiser where the promise and optimism of small-town America became narrow-mindedness, self-righteousness, and provinciality. Passing through Oswego, New York, Dreiser remarked on the moderate and traditional character of the town, but instead of seeing ambition and vitality, he saw only the "conventional point of view." He mused, "Men are animals with dreams of something superior to animality, but the small-town soul—or the little soul anywhere—never gets this straight." Presenting a condescending critique of mainstream culture from his perspective as a cosmopolitan urban intellectual, he commented, "These are the places in which churches flourish. Here is where your theologically schooled numskull thrives, like the weed that he is. Here is where the ordinary family with a little tradition puts an inordinate value on tradition. . . . I never was in such a place for any period of time without feeling cabined, cribbed, confined, intellectually if not emotionally." Dreiser also saw the underside of American idealism. In some ways what Dreiser defined as the strongest quality of Americans, their ability to sustain the dream of a better future, also reflected their biggest weakness. Yet in the end, despite the limitations he perceived, Dreiser celebrated the possibilities embraced by Americans. Concluding his touring narrative, he wrote, "My native state and my country are as yet children, politically and socially—a child state and a child country. They have all the health, wealth, strength, enthusiasm for life that is necessary, but their problems are all before them. We are indeed a free people, in part, bound only by our illusions, but we are a heavily though sweetly illusioned people nevertheless. A little over a hundred years ago we began with great dreams, most wondrous dreams, really impossible ideals, and we are still dreaming them."[45] To dream still held the possibility to sustain the dreamer.

Despite his nostalgia for the ideal of small-town America, Dreiser's narrative perhaps best reveals the anxieties that tourists sought to assuage on the road. Where most tourists masked their anxieties beneath eulogies of sacred American landscapes, Dreiser's ambivalent depiction of small-town life expressed both his ideals and his fears about America. Like other tourists he feared the effects of incorporation on American society. He worried that the ideals of democracy, the notion that each individual had the power to shape his or her own life and future were being subsumed by the powerful forces of big business and commerce. Rather than actualizing the individual's dreams of what might best be understood in terms of Nietzsche's ideal of the superman, Dreiser saw small-town, middle-class Americans focusing their energies on a false dream of commercial success and acquisition, reinforced in his mind by provincial and meaningless traditions. Although he concluded on a note of optimism, his narrative suggests that he feared America might succumb to the forces of commerce and celebrity and lose faith in the ideal dream of the individual. The result, he believed, would be the triumph of triviality and paltriness extending from a fascination with meaningless commercial fads and empty traditions.

Although other tourists presented their visions of America in a more optimistic manner, disguising the uncertainties they had, they shared Dreiser's anxieties and implicitly revealed their concerns through the image of America they eulogized in their touring narratives. In celebrating the democracy and friendliness of the road, the community and freedom of the West, the authentic New England village, and the idealized small towns as the real America, tourists expressed their own desires to imagine an America devoid of the conflict and complications of modern urban-industrial society.

Like other commemorative events and activities, tourism was multivocal. It brought together "powerful symbolic expression—metaphors, signs, and rituals—that give meaning to competing interpretations of past and present reality."[46] The range of touring narratives suggest that the personal as much as the prescriptive shaped the tourist experience. Prescriptive touring literature explicitly and implicitly celebrated an ideal of national unity. Touring narratives, on the other hand, did not concern themselves so much with national unity as with finding some personal understanding of what America represented and where tourists as individuals fit within that America. Ordinary people embrace and appropriate images of official culture in a variety of ways. They both accept and appropriate official interpretations of reality, and they reinterpret them creating alternative renditions of reality. Through their touring narratives, tourists embraced the values of the official culture expressed by prescriptive literature in their search to discover America, and they simultaneously challenged the official ideal of national unity with their own concerns, ideals, and anxieties. Many touring narratives presented thoughtful meditations of self-discovery in which tourists measured their lives and their identities in both positive and negative ways. They used the landscape of tourism as a venue to consider their role, place, and purpose in American society and in the larger context of life. They also challenged the realities of their contemporary society by imagining a more nostalgic ideal of small-town America. Political concerns, social status, and gender identity influenced the ways in which individual tourists conceived and presented these journeys of self-exploration.

VOYAGES OF SELF-DISCOVERY

In *Free Air* Milt Daggett used the social fluidity of the open road and automobile camps to escape his small-town roots and refashion himself as a more cultured and urbane young man. He told Claire Boltwood on their first meeting that he had taken to the road "to get in on" the government railroad and Alaska. "I've never been out of Minnesota in my life," he explained, "but there's a couple of mountains and oceans and things I thought I'd like to see." Seeing the world and seeking out new possibilities embodied the potential of self-transformation. While on the road he observed the behavior of traveling salesmen, whom he called "pioneers in spats," so that he might learn the ways of the city, and he bought a book of rhetoric so that he might improve his speech. By the time he reached Seattle he had set his sights on going to school and becoming an engineer rather than settling for owning a small-town garage in which he was "owner, manager, wrecking crew, ignition expert, thoroughly competent bill-collector and all but one of the working force." In the process of his tour, he traversed social space to win the hand of Claire Boltwood. On the road, Milt became an individual unfettered by his social background, his small-town roots, his high school education, and his provincial manners. He could rely on his own skill and intelligence to solve the problems that confronted him. The appearance of Milt's old friend Bill McGolwey, the proprietor of the Old Home Lunch place in Schoenstrom, at his flat in Seattle revealed the extent of Milt's transformation. In recognizing that "Bill's face was dirty, his hair was linty, the bottom of his trousers frayed masses of mud," Milt wondered to himself, "Was this the fellow he had liked so well? These the ideas which a few months ago he had taken as natural and extremely amusing."[47] In essence, the freedom of the tourist experience allowed Milt to actualize the myth of the self-made man. Through Milt's transformation, Lewis presents the landscape of tourism as a special place—a place beyond the restrictions of work and home—where one was freed from the confines of occupation, social class, and family background, a place where one could actualize, if only temporarily, the American dream.

As sociologist Dean MacCannell has explained, tourist attractions are best understood as cultural productions. As staged representations of various aspects of life, tourist attractions conveyed a totality that was increasingly absent from urban-industrial life.[48] The tourist gaze transformed the built and the natural environment into scenery and spectacle.[49] Through the experience of touring, individuals became spectators, surveying a variety of scenes and sites that represented nature, work, history, art, other—the totality of modern life. Anthropologist Nelson Graburn has defined tourism as "a special form of play involving travel." Looking at the tourist experience as the antithesis of the experience of everyday work and routine, Graburn suggests that through the tourist journey the individual is transported to a "nonordinary state wherein marvelous things happen."[50] From this perspective tourism shared the characteristics of ritual and festival. Like the experience of going to the theater, an amusement park or the movies, the experience of tourism provided a setting in which individuals could refashion themselves.[51] As historian George Lipsitz has noted, "Theater attendance enabled individuals to play out fictive scenarios of changed identities, to escape from the surveillance and supervision of moral authorities and institutions." He argues that "the fantasy world of the theatrical stage encouraged audiences to pursue personal desires and passions at the expense of their socially prescribed responsibilities."[52] The experience of tourism offered similar possibilities. As spectators in a nonordinary environment tourists could transcend the social boundaries associated with everyday life. By going on vacation, "vacating" the workaday routines, tourists moved beyond both the physical and imaginary boundaries of home and work that shaped and defined their everyday identities. They entered a realm of fantasy, they communed with strangers, they witnessed the foreign. In this liminal environment, tourists as anonymous spectators surveyed the tourist spectacle from the outside, and yet only from their perspective did that spectacle have meaning.[53] As outsiders they were free to adopt any role. As strangers they experienced a kind of "privacy in public" where they could act spontaneously without fearing the judgments of their quotidian milieu of family, friends, co-workers, and acquaintances.[54]

Many tourists spoke of the possibilities embedded in the tourist landscape in their narratives. Dallas Lore Sharp and his wife Daphne took to the road in search of "a better country." Recounting their experience in his book *The Better Country*, Sharp detailed both his perceptions about America and his own transformation on the road. The Sharps had reached their middle fifties, their four boys had all gone off to college, and the house was empty.

After twenty years as a professor, Sharp explained that he had grown tired of "teaching the same thing to the same freshman." In allegorical terms, Sharp wrote, "Daphne and I found ourselves at the top of the long hill up which for so many years we had been climbing." If they followed the main road they descended to "Pension Place . . . Cemetery beyond. End of Road." Instead, they decided to turn off on "an old trail, unimproved, unposted, and utterly untraveled." Their goal was to motor cross-continent from their home in Hingham, Massachusetts, to meet two of their sons for Christmas in Los Angeles and then settle in Santa Barbara so that Sharp could finally write his "great book." So they "started on a second honeymoon and a new adventure in the world."[55] As a modern-day combination of *Pilgrim Progress* and pioneer legend, Sharp's narrative drew from a range of cultural texts to define and present his touring experience.

Scheduled to deliver a series of lectures at various stopping points between Hingham and Topeka, Kansas, and then slated to meet their sons' train in Los Angles, the Sharp's tour was hemmed in by a strict itinerary that left little time for exploring or wandering off the beaten track. However, that did not prevent Sharp from musing at each stopping point about whether they had reached the "better country." He celebrated the impressive busyness of Chicago, the beautiful farms of Iowa, the western character of Dodge City, the Old World character of Santa Fe, and, finally, the natural fecundity of Santa Barbara. In the end, however, they returned to their home in Hingham. Their journey allowed him to discover that "the better country" was not a place so much as a state of mind.

"The better country" signified an escape from the responsibilities of home and work. It embodied the meaning of Sharp's retirement in gendered terms. It stood for the potential of the golden years of their married life, when the obligations to children and success were past and only the possibilities of leisure, pleasure and self-realization remained. As Sharp explained, "We forgot . . . Hingham and the thing called 'duty,' as we lingered along the curves in the climbing road trying to satisfy the insatiable thirst of our souls." After Sharp had fulfilled his final lecture obligations in Topeka, he began to fully appreciate the open road. "To go. To arrive. To have no audience but Daphne. To sleep. To wake. To go on for another day, and still with Daphne, only myself and Daphne. We had never done the like before." It was in this landscape of tourism that Sharp discovered his freedom. Driving out of Dodge City, he began to understand just how constrained he had been by his responsibilities as a professor. "I had been collared and toed and timed, and trained to say what is conventionally true, and to behave mannerly at every sort of public table, and at home, as far as I was able," he mused. However, he went on to resolve, "I would break training now. ... I would never utter another epoch-making word to anybody, nor consult another time-table, nor own another alarm clock, nor care what day of the week it is, what hour of the day." From the perspective of the open road he began to escape from the restrictions that his ordinary life—fatherhood, academics, marriage—had imposed upon him. "I knew," he explained, "that at last I had actually left Hingham and was even now entering . . . that Better Country of whose reality I had been persuaded, and toward which, a stranger and a pilgrim, I had been always on the road."[56] It was on the road—through the experience of tourism itself—that Sharp achieved the state of mind embodied by his quest for "the better country."

This "better country" Sharp went in search of manifested all the possibilities of the tourist landscape. For the tourist the road was a place where one was no longer tied to the social conventions of society. The landscape of tourism provided a place where one could discard the social self and actualize the personal self. It represented both a public and a private space where the individual—the tourist—had the opportunity and the power to define what was meaningful and what was not. For some the tourist landscape embodied a place of self-fulfillment and self-expression removed from the strictures that defined acceptable social behavior in everyday society. Thus, recalling the exhilaration of shoveling his car out of a snowbank, Sharp wrote, "For this was shoveling! And it was play and poetry, the pure poetry of unconditioned existence. I had broken into a new freedom, and now the hampering drifts had freed me from motion onward, the last inhibition, to motion inward, outward—complete, self-expressing motion."[57] He had moved from the life of the mind to a more vigorous, unrestrained, physical experience. Although the framework of the market defined the landscape of tourism, individual tourists used this landscape to transcend the social boundaries of urban-industrial society. Ironically, in seeking to actualize the self in this liminal environment, tourists adopted the desires of the therapeutic, anonymous individual central to the consumer society they thought they were fleeing.

For many tourists this sense of freedom and authenticity was tied to the gendered experience of the strenuous life. Writer Hoffman Birney reveled in the adventure of touring the Southwest. His touring narrative is filled with tales of sleeping under the stars and exploring Indian ruins and desert landscapes, scavenging for Indian pottery and arrowheads and photographing the sights and scenes of the desert landscape. Writing of a pack trip to Rainbow Bridge, Birney challenged his readers, "If you have in you a love of the true solitudes, if you can find a thrill in penetrating lands that have not changed since the cliff-dwellers built their homes in the red walls of the Tsagi, if the silent, calm, beautiful, savage, treacherous desert means more to you than all the wildernesses of steel and brick that men call cities—then you will revel in that ride to Teas-ya-toh, [the Cottonwood Water, on the way to the Rainbow Bridge]!" The difficulties of a pack trip—managing the mules, negotiating dangerous trails, and camping outdoors—and the experience of viewing the "wonders" of a country where "nature has run riot," effected a profoundly moving personal experience, according to Birney. He could respond only that God had been very good to him for allowing him to witness these wonders. In conclusion he admonished his readers, "Go there; and if you do not come away a little better for the experience, a little more closely in tune with the Infinite, I'll pay for your trip!"[58]

The early decades of the twentieth century witnessed a great upsurge of interest in the strenuous life—a movement perhaps best represented by Theodore Roosevelt and his excessively masculine quest for health, athleticism, and action. Advocates of the strenuous life presented physical exercise of all sorts as a curative for the nervousness or neurasthenia that seemed to be overwhelming the middle classes of urban-industrialized America. Just as bicycling was seen as a reinvigorating exercise, so touring narratives suggest that automobile touring offered the necessary adventure and action for personal regeneration.[59] Birney's narrative revealed that touring offered more than just the challenge of physical adventure and intense experience. As a retreat into nature, it also held the promise of spiritual renewal.

The personal revelations brought on by the touring experience, however, were not always so positive and inspiring for individual tourists. Dreiser's tour became a voyage of self-discovery, as much about seeking out his own past and his home as about seeing America. In celebrating America's faith in the dream, Dreiser also nostalgically sought the dreams of his youth. His search for the qualities that defined the American character was intertwined with a more personal search for the roots or origins of his own identity. It is not surprising that during this period of transition in American society—as modernization, incorporation, urbanization, and industrialization redefined the relationship between the individual and community, as well as redefining notions of individuality and community—that Dreiser and other tourists' desire to discover America extended into a desire to define their particular place or identity within a changing America.

Dreiser traveled through time as well as space on his tour from New York City to his boyhood home in Indiana. Summing up the journey, he wrote, "We had crossed four states and traversed this fifth one from end to end nearly. I had seen every place in which I had ever lived up to sixteen years of age, and touched, helplessly, on every pleasant and unpleasant memory that I had known in that period. The land had yielded a strange crop of memories and of characteristics to be observed." Dreiser hoped that in physically returning to the scenes of his boyhood he could revive and relive the dreams of his youth; in essence he sought an idealized youth and a mythological home. But as he viewed the places and towns associated with his past he found them "dreary" and "disappointing." Buffalo, Cleveland, and Toledo reminded him of what he saw as failed dreams of attaining success as a newspaper writer. Chronicling his arrival at his old hometown of Warsaw, Indiana, he wrote, "I looked about me, and beginning to recognize familiar soil, such as a long stretch of white road ending in an old ice house, a railroad track out which I had walked, felt a sudden, overpowering, almost sickening depression at the lapse of time and all that had gone with it." One of his boyhood homes had become a tenement, another was engulfed by new, prefabricated houses. His old friends had moved away or died. His boyhood loves had grown old and married. Prominent citizens had failed and been forced to shut down their businesses or move. Marking this change, Dreiser recognized that one of the houses of a prominent lumber dealer of his day had now become an automobile showroom and another had become the location for the local Knights of Pythias organization. Commerce and time had taken their toll. Only a few older townspeople whose prime had long since past were left to tell him what had become of the people and places of his youth. In Terra Haute, where he had lived as a young boy while his father managed a mill, he found the same things. "Houses and landscapes and people go by and return no more," he ruminated. "The very land itself changes. All that is left of what you were, or of what was, in your own brain is a dwindling and spindling thing."[60]

In returning to the landscape of his youth, Dreiser found a reality he commonly referred to in his own fiction—a reality of constant striving and unfulfilled dreams.[61] He discovered that as an individual he was powerless to stop or turn back the hands of time. "Life moves so insensibly out from under you," he mused. "It slips away like a slow moving tide."[62] In some ways his journey of self-discovery paralleled his survey of America. He praised the vitality and the dreams embraced by Americans just as he sought his own youthful dreams in the landscapes of his past. However, just as he surmised that Americans were in some ways naïve, that the history of the period between 1870 and 1910 had transformed their dreams into illusions that ignored the confines and limitations embedded in American society, so he found that with the passage of time his own dreams had been dissipated. They too had become illusions he could not return to. Yet it seems that he did not maintain the same faith in himself as he maintained about America. While Dreiser preserved his faith in the ability of Americans to sustain their dreams, he saw himself as past his prime. He most clearly reveals this feeling when he describes his inability to act on his attraction to the two young ladies he meets while staying with Franklin Booth in Carmel, Indiana. Like Hurstwood in *Sister Carrie*, Dreiser presents himself as too old to actualize his desire. This missed opportunity essentially acts as the climax of the touring narrative; it embodies the youthfulness that he has lost.[63]

Dreiser's touring narrative reveals that the experience of tourism—the landscapes of tourism—opened up the possibility of reimagining or rediscovering the self in both positive and negative ways. The experience of tourism moved beyond the marketed experience prescribed by tourist industries and tourist advocates. As Dreiser explained it, driving through the landscape sent him to "dreamland . . . not into actual sleeping dreams, but into something that was neither sleeping nor waking."[64] In this space he was able to step back and judge his life.

As historian T. J. Jackson Lears has written, "Throughout the twentieth century, a recoil from overcivilized qualities of modern existence has sparked a wide variety of quests for more intense experience ranging from fascist fascination with death, to the cult of emotional spontaneity of avant garde artists to popular therapies stressing instinctual liberation."[65] In some ways the experience of tourism might best be understood in this context. Touring narratives celebrated the strenuous life out in the open, overcoming the hazards of poorly constructed and ill-marked roads, camping out, confronting nature. They also celebrated the quest for self-realization. In this way, touring embraced both risk and physical exertion, promising intense experience and self-fulfillment.[66] From this perspective, touring reflected the larger cultural concerns expressed by the therapeutic ethos: the desire for vigorous health, the desire for authentic experience, and the desire for self-fulfillment. Touring narratives suggest that as a voyage of self-discovery, tourism promised "temporary escape to a realm of intense experience far from the stiff unreality of bourgeois culture."[67] Many tourists used the language of the therapeutic ethos to define their tours. For men this language reflected an anxiety about their own powerlessness as individuals in a corporate, urban-industrial society. For women, this language suggested that the desire for self-fulfillment embodied specifically gendered meanings in a society still wed to the ideology of separate spheres.

In *Free Air* Claire Boltwood not only discovered the real America but also discovered power, independence, and adventure. As a member of the exclusive social world of Brooklyn Heights, Claire was accustomed to plush surroundings, servants, and high culture. She was "used to gracious leisure, attractive uselessness, [and] nut-center chocolates." She was an ingenue, she was helpless, she personified the ideal of a refined young woman. As the book's narrator explained, she knew very little about the life that existed beyond her social set of Brooklyn Heights and Manhattan, and she had had to do very little for herself throughout her life. The first day out after leaving Minneapolis, hopelessly stuck in thick Minnesota gumbo, Claire realized that her life would be different on the road. When her father finally told her to go get someone to help them out of the mud, she responded, "No. One of the good things about an adventure like this is that I must do things for myself. I've always had people do things for me." She continued, "Maids and nice teachers and you, old darling! I suppose it's made me soft." Instead of seeking help, she scavenged in the wet mud for brush to provide footing for the tires and she reveled in being wet and dirty. She became like a "pioneer woman," the narrator explained, "toiling" on the land. On that first day out Claire had her first experience of real physical work. Once out of the mud hole and back on the road, her hands became "sturdy," her eyes "tireless," and she was ready to "drive forever." The next morning she rolled out of bed, tired and stiff, but she soon realized that "she was stronger than she ever had been, that she was a woman, not a dependent girl."[68] Lewis uses the language of regeneration, self-realization, and self-fulfillment to detail Claire's transformation.

In setting out on a tour alone with her ill and helpless father, in negotiating muddy, rough roads, in checking radiator water and tire casings, Claire assumed an air of authority, responsibility, and independence that would have been symbolically unacceptable and unattainable in the social structure of Brooklyn Heights. In the tourist landscape she transcended the ideological boundaries of the upper- and middle-class cult of domesticity. As a tourist she escaped the confines of separate spheres. She not only ventured out into the landscape, a landscape of dangerous roads and potentially dangerous strangers, she also entered into predominantly masculine spaces, like the drummer's hotels and the town garages. Midway into her tour, talking low by a campfire in Yellowstone, she asked Milt Daggett, "Will I get all fussy and ribbon-tied again, when I go back [to Brooklyn Heights]?" His response revealed the gendered possibilities of the tourist experience. "No. You won't," he said, "You drive like a man."[69]

In experiencing the strenuous life, in searching for self-realization, touring took on added meaning for women measured against (judged by) the standards of the cult of domesticity. The landscape of tourism offered women a venue outside of the domestic sphere in which they could reimagine themselves as independent, self-sufficient, active members of society. As drivers, women challenged the restrictions placed on them by the ideal of the upper-middle-class woman who stayed at home, outside the public sphere, and cared for her family, letting her husband deal with the demands of making a living.[70] In the tourist landscape, upper- and middle-class women could embrace and adopt the persona of the New Woman.[71] Interestingly, a majority of the published touring narratives were written by women who set out on the road to find freedom and independence, and many of these narratives expressed a gendered understanding of the tourist landscape.

In 1928 Kathryn Hulme privately published *How's the Road?* which chronicled a tour from New York to San Francisco taken by the author and a woman friend, "Tuny," short for Petunia. Gliding smoothly and quickly across the paved roads in the East, the pair decided to take the northern route across the West after they crossed the Mississippi. They braved the gumbo of South Dakota and Wyoming, and went on to Yellowstone and through Montana to Glacier National Park. From Glacier they motored north to Canada to Banff and Lake Louise. The last leg of their journey brought them back into the United States through Idaho and on through Washington and Oregon to California. On reaching San Francisco they sold their car and returned to New York by train. Although their accomplishment was largely understated in the touring narrative, their tour allowed them to escape the confines of the domestic sphere and reimagine themselves as independent and self-sufficient young women in a society bounded by the ideology of separate spheres.

"Ashamed of [their] woman's heritage of fickle fancy," Hulme and her friend Tuny took to the road to see America because they were "hungry for the outdoors" and, as Tuny explained, "because we'd rather drive our own car than be driven by a ship."[72] In many respects their decision to make a transcontinental tour represented a declaration of independence. They named their roadster Reggie, in opposition to the men that "name their cars Sally or Lizzie," referring not only to the medieval tradition of knighthood, but also implying the feminine control of the masculine machine.[73] From the start they asserted their rights as women to enjoy the public sphere defined by the road and the automobile, despite the disapproving looks of "motherly" women who frowned on their queries about the location of hotels after dark. Versed in the basics of auto mechanics and the regimen of camping, Hulme and Tuny were more than self-sufficient and had few fears about traveling alone.

The pair tackled thick prairie gumbo, worn tires, mechanical problems, dirty hotels and lunch rooms, and collapsing tents in the drenching rain with the same skill and fortitude as their male counterparts. Despite the understated tone, it is clear from the narrative that the they understood their touring experience in gendered terms as a challenge to standard assumptions and expectations about the woman's place and role in American society. Hulme

HOW'S THE ROAD?

BY

KATHRYN HULME

*"Now the joys of the road are chiefly these:
A crimson touch on the hardwood trees;
A vagrant's morning wide and blue,
In early fall when the wind walks, too;
A shadowy highway cool and brown,
Alluring up and enticing down . . ."*

Bliss Carman

PRIVATELY PRINTED
SAN FRANCISCO, CALIFORNIA
1928

Title page of Kathryn Hulme's *How's the Road?* (San Francisco, 1928). (By permission of Brandt & Brandt Literary Agents, Inc.; reproduced by permission of the Huntington Library, San Marino, California) represented Tuny and herself as embodiments of the New Woman of the twenties—educated, single, economically independent, and socially equal to men.[74] On the road they became the companions of traveling salesmen, college boys, cowboys, and farmers. As tourists, they gained access to the male dominated public sphere—the drummer's hotels, the blacksmith shops, the town garages, and the great outdoors.

In the narrative, Hulme was careful to distinguish Tuny and herself from the stereotypical "girls" of the 1920s. Early on, she recorded her amazement at the "elaborate toilettes" of two young women in a communal bathroom at the autocamp in Pierre, South Dakota. "The place looked like the dressing room of a Follies girl," she commented. "Make-up paraphernalia was scattered all over the tables. . . . Lipsticks, rouge, eyelash beading outfit and powderpuffs of theatrical dimensions." Eavesdropping on their conversation, Hulme learned that the "girls" were preparing themselves for a visit from "the army" stationed at a nearby army base. She remarked that their "cheap little faces were rather effective with their layers of unreal pink and white, if one didn't look beyond the face. Below their chins were dingy tanned necks encircled by riotous silk scarves . . . [and] below the scarves were incongruous outfits of drab, uneventful khaki—loose shirts and shapely glove-fitting breeches, and their costumes ended up with silk stockings and sandal slippers." As "the girls" left, Tuny's only comment was "Hell's Bells," a subtle pun on the established social standards of feminine beauty and the realities of an American society that idealized restricted roles for women. In contrast, Hulme and Tuny wore "utterly disreputable" outfits of "dingy" tweed knickers, wash-streaked shirts with mud-blackened oxfords. And they paid little attention to make-up or hair "that had been smoothed down with a bacony hand, that had ridden bare through dust storms and hung over smoke and had sometimes been rudely jammed up against the black greasy housing of Reggie's underside during various tinkerings."[75]

Rejecting the standards of feminine beauty and behavior, Hulme and Tuny embraced the adventures of automobile touring and camping. They braved thick prairie mud where others feared to cross. They traversed the Big Horn Mountains in Montana despite warnings that "no one [had] made it so far this year." And they traveled through "practically uninhabited" country "tast[ing] a little of the exultation of the soul and the despair of the body that the early pioneers must have felt when they first looked upon that glorious barrier, [the Rockies] shimmering like white heat under its covering of eternal snow." Recording a triumph in South Dakota, Hulme wrote about an episode in which a road had been washed away and a group of automobile tourists were forced to take to the open prairie, "every man for himself and his car." Resorting to irony, Hulme noted that she and Tuny—two women—were the first who dared to cross the stream that would take them back to the road. "We hit the water. Reggie tore through it like a torpedo. Liquid mud flew as high as the windshield. . . . For a moment we were invisible in brown spray. Then we hit the opposite bank and roared up the incline shaking diluted gumbo from every quarter like a spaniel. A yell of acclaim from the other cars and they retraced their tracks to cross at Reggie's ford," she wrote.[76] Hulme used the language of adventure to subtly draw attention to their success and self-sufficiency as two lone females in a society which valued the action of "every man for himself."

Able to negotiate the adventures of difficult driving and treacherous roads, they were also "good mechanics, capable of making any repair of the car." Although few of the men they met on the road had faith in their skills, they could change tires, flush the crank case, and grease the grease cups as well as any garage mechanic. Hulme explained that they had to begin "tinkering [on their car] in lovely lonely spots" because they had "many experiences with the 'assisting' man camper who thinks that when a woman gets anything more complicated than an egg-beater in her hand, she is to be watched carefully." She explained that the farther west they traveled, the more men offered their services unnecessarily. "Finally," she wrote, "we couldn't do any work on the car at all unless we retreated to the desert where there was nothing more chivalrous than a stray deer to impede our progress."[77] Celebrating their ability to manage not only the intricacies of the machine but also their own work, Hulme used the masculine images of machinery and work to underscore the possibilities of the tourist experience for women.

The farther west they traveled the further they retreated from the bonds and boundaries of eastern society and associated gender restrictions. The wide open landscapes and small towns of the West reflected not only the absence of eastern cities and urbanity but also the seeming disappearance of the social restrictions of urban and suburban life. Hulme noted when they neared the Mississippi River that they were "anxious to get out of the shadow of cities to the broader spaces," where they could camp and enjoy the outdoors. "Between New York and Chicago we hadn't been off paved roads or graded gravel for more than a few miles at a stretch," she explained. "We were utterly weary of monotonous cement." Cement roads signified more than just boring driving for Hulme, they also objectified the restrictions and limitations of an urban-industrialized and eastern social structure that narrowly defined the woman's sphere and the acceptable activities for women within that sphere. When they finally crossed the Mississippi in La Crosse, Wisconsin, Hulme remarked, "Something within us that had been taut, suddenly loosened. We actually felt ourselves expanding in the genial sunshine and we seemed to take up more room in the seat." Hulme and her companion linked their new-felt freedom and independence to the West. In this land of cowboys, ranchers, and farmers the pair abandoned the refinements of "lady-like" behavior and enjoyed their experiences with an unaffected pleasure. Hulme recalled sharing meals with the cowboys at a small western inn: "In the shadow of their famished onslaughts upon the food, Tuny's and my voracity went unheeded. We wallowed through second and third 'helpings' and after meals we slept off the effects of our gorgings, like so many stuffed pythons." She went on to remark, "It was disgraceful, but it made us one of them. After the second meal they ceased referring to us as the 'two young ladies from the East' and called us 'the girls.'"[78] This new label was in no way connected to the two young women they had met in the bathroom in Pierre, South Dakota. Rather than reflecting their distinctly feminine characteristics, in Hulme's mind this label identified them as fellow westerners and fellow cowboys, freed from the restrictions of eastern and feminine refinement.

In abandoning feminine refinements and adopting the guise of self-sufficient tourists, Hulme and Tuny gained admission to places that had been predominantly associated with men.[79] They mixed with the traveling salesmen at drummer's hotels and followed their lead on difficult roads, negotiating chuckholes, rocks, and gumbo like professional travelers.[80] They camped on the open prairie alone and entertained two cowboys who stopped to greet them. When stopping in towns they haunted garages and blacksmith shops, purchasing supplies or overseeing repairs. The blacksmith in Choteau, Montana, invited the pair in to watch him work his forge.

"He found a rod, scanned it critically, seeming to see through its rusty stiff-ness, the curving bracket he could make of it," wrote Hulme. "Then he thrust it into the live coals of his forge. He pumped the bellows and a spurt of red sparks shot up the chimney. And while the rod heated, he led us around his shop, exhibiting specimens of his wrought-iron workmanship."[81] He even went so far as to show the pair his bulging biceps. The sexual under-tones of Hulme's description ironically reinforce the symbolic importance of their female presence in this masculine space. As tourists, Hulme and her companion were thus able to vicariously experience this traditionally mascu-line work. Sociologist Dean MacCannell has suggested that the tourist view of various aspects of work allowed tourists to comprehend the totality of work in a modern society in which the experience of work was completely fragmented and seemingly meaningless.[82] However, for upper- and middle-class women this comprehensive tourist view had added meaning. At least in the early twentieth century it legitimately admitted these women into the realm of masculine work from which they had been ideologically excluded, without the stigma attached to lower-class women laborers.

Many other women tourists wrote of their tours in a similar vein, cele-brating their sense of power, individuality, and independence. Emily Post, Winifred Hawkridge Dixon, and Letitia Stockett, to name only a few of the women tourists who published touring narratives during the teens and twenties, all commented in one way or another about the gendered experi-ence of being on the road.[83] An early transcontinental motorist, Post trav-eled from New York to San Francisco for the California expositions with her son and another female relative in the summer of 1915. Her son did all of the driving, the party stayed at the best hotels along the way, and Post com-mented primarily on the quality of accommodations, roads, and the sights to be seen. She recounted, however, that from the start people responded to the news of her trip with incredulity. In many ways, her narrative, which she had arranged to publish serially with Collier's, offered proof that a woman could comfortably make a transcontinental automobile tour. Winifred Dixon and her friend Toby toured throughout the Southwest admiring the Indian ruins, witnessing Indian ceremonies, and viewing the dramatic desert land formations. Although they frequently encountered skepticism about their ability, as two lone women, to brave the dangers and uncertainties of

THE CAR SAGGED DRUNKENLY ON ONE SIDE.

FORDING A RIVER NEAR SANTA FE.
Crossing fords, to our hubs, which yesterday were mere trickles and to-morrow would
be raging torrents.

ON THE WAY TO GALLUP.
Jack and all sank in the soft quicksand beneath the weight of the car.

Winifred Dixon documented the difficult driving conditions she and her traveling companion encountered while motoring through the West in 1919. From Winifred Dixon's *Westward Hoboes: Ups and Downs of Frontier Motoring* (1921). (Collection of the author) road and car, Dixon's narrative reveals that they succeeded at traversing the West from Texas to Montana on their own. The experience of managing steep mountain passes, muddy roads, and necessary car repairs gave them "courage to meet new contingencies" and to overcome all feelings of "helplessness."[84] Similarly, Letitia Stockett occasionally noted the disparaging comments made by skeptical men in her touring narrative that recounted the adventures of a transcontinental tour taken by three Wellesley girls. Like the others, her story revealed the gendered significance of the touring experience for women.

These narratives suggest that many of the upper- and middle-class women who took to the road found added meaning in the freedom and adventure of the touring experience. Women writers used the imagery of self-realization and renewal that characterized the therapeutic ethos to express the gendered possibilities of the tourist landscape.[85] Despite the fact that they sometimes worried about the dangers and uncertainties of the road or had to rely on the help of a passing man, women represented themselves in their narratives as independent, self-sufficient, and responsible, in contrast to the overly civilized, refined young ladies they left behind. Just as women took advantage of the opportunities presented by the theater, the amusement park, and the dance hall to escape the confines of patriarchal domination, so they used the experience of tourism to liberate themselves from the ideal of the refined, soft-spoken lady, who stayed at home, nurtured her family, and submitted to the will of her husband. In the tourist landscape upper- and middle-class white women were able to transcend the expectations—the limitations—of the domestic ideal, thus paving the way for the New Woman, who embraced an ideal of heterosexual interaction within the public sphere where men and women could come together as equals.

The diverse array of prescriptive material disseminated by industries to encourage Americans to tour America presented a complex assortment of images of the nation. Businesses and organizations such as the Salt Lake City Commercial Club, the Great Northern Railway Company, the National Park Service, the Lincoln Highway Association, the Daughters of the American Revolution, the National Highways Association, the Page Company, and the Federal Writers' Project, among others, promoted tourism as a ritual of citizenship, attempting to map and define a fixed ideal of the nation across the landscape. Although the resulting visions differed, reflecting the divergent concerns of the individuals and organizations who created them, they all shared in the desire to construct and promote official, marketable images of a unified and united American nation. In part, this desire reflected an attempt to transform a diverse American public into a unified group of tourists or consumers—to provide a coherent subject or object—America—for tourists to see, understand, and consume. However, the construction and promotion of America as a unified national entity on the part of tourist industries and advocates also reflected a pervasive apprehension about the emergence of a modern, urban-industrialized nation-state. The representation of tourism as a ritual of citizenship was part of a larger discourse that revolved around the changing meaning of America as the forces of industrialization, urbanization, incorporation, and immigration reshaped the political, the economic, the social and the cultural boundaries of American society.[86]

Touring narratives reveal that tourists also participated in this discourse. Many tourists took to the road to discover America, but the America they found did not always conform to the images presented by prescriptive touring literature. Many tourists followed the directive of prescriptive literature and frequented the sacred landscapes promoted by tourist industries and advocates, but the America they saw reflected the desires and interests of promoters and expressed the concerns and ideals of native-born, white, upper- and middle-class Americans anxious about their own status and identity in a modern, urban-industrial society. Through their touring narratives, tourists celebrated a nostalgic image of America that referred back to a nineteenth-century society of small towns, middle landscapes, and face-to-face interaction. In this idealized landscape, outside the confines of everyday life, tourists sought to define themselves as empowered individuals. As an adventure into the nonordinary, touring provided an opportunity for intense experience, spiritual renewal, and self-realization. This experience had different meanings for men and women. For both men and women, however, this quest for self-discovery was integrally connected to the larger discourse of citizenship and national identity. As historian John Higham has written, "We are well aware of the aggressive nationalism that sprang up after 1890. We do not so often notice analogous ferments in other spheres: a boon in sports and recreation; a revitalized interest in untamed nature; a quickening of popular music; an unsettling of the condition of women."[87] Anxieties about finding the "true" self implicitly expressed apprehensions about the bureaucracy, the anonymity, and the "weightlessness" of modern American life, as well as the place of the individual in American culture. They tapped into the messages and meanings of modern consumer culture. In seeking to actualize the true self in the tourist landscape, tourists revealed themselves as modern consumers and implicitly redefined the rights of citizenship in commercial terms.

7

TOURIST MEMENTOS

We are here in San Diego at last and it seems a long way from home. I can see so plainly in my mind the map of the United States as I looked at it at home and saw a little dot way down in the south west corner on the Pacific and such a big country between. And now I am really in that second little dot and the first one — Boston — is fully three thousand miles away. It seems so difficult to imagine it all.
—Amy Bridges, 1886

We had not in these two months added to our material possessions; we had merely by supreme effort come to know the most violent river as few can ever know it. While memory lasts, I have a priceless possession in the recollection of these glorious, thrilling, dangerous days on "rough water."
—Mildred Baker, 1944

*O*N 24 JUNE 1882, AT Niagara Falls, the final stop of a two-month Raymond and Whitcomb transcontinental excursion, Amy Bridges reflected on the extent of her tour in one of her final diary entries. "So our trip has taken us from the Atlantic to the Pacific, from Mexico to Canada, the length and breadth of the land," she wrote.[1] Bridges had traversed the nation, recording her observations and experiences along the way. In 1886 she participated in another transcontinental Raymond and Whitcomb excursion. Her diaries for both trips detail a canon of American tourist destinations distinguished by Raymond and Whitcomb tours: Chicago, Manitou Springs, the Garden of the Gods, Pike's Peak, Denver, Clear Creek Canyon, a gold mine in Black Hawk, Colorado, the Cave of the Winds, Las Vegas Hot Springs (New Mexico), Santa Fe, El Paso del Norte, Los Angeles, Sierra Madre Villa, the San Gabriel Mission, Yosemite, San Francisco, the Monterey Peninsula, Salt Lake City, and Niagara Falls. In careful and evocative prose, Bridge's diaries describe the plush accommodations and cosmopolitan atmosphere of the Raymond tour, as well as the sublime and the picturesque views she encountered along the way.

Almost fifty years later, in 1931, Mildred E. Baker, a private secretary in a Buffalo, New York, investment firm, traveled to the Southwest. In her scrapbook of the trip she recounted, "I had planned and dreamed of this trip . . . for many long moons, and to me at least, the culmination of those dreams was all that could be hoped for."[2] Between 1931 and 1942, Baker made eight trips to the West. She visited many of the central tourist destinations of the region: the Grand Canyon, Rainbow Bridge in Utah, Taos and Santa Fe, Carlsbad Caverns, the Grand Tetons, as well as the Canadian Rockies. To memorialize her journeys, she created elaborate leather-bound volumes for each trip with hand-colored, illuminated title pages and typescript narratives illustrated with captioned snapshots, cutouts from tourist brochures, postcards, and purchased photographs. She also included transcriptions of poems, newspaper clippings, and lists of the plants and birds she observed.

Both Amy Bridges and Mildred Baker sought to memorialize their tourist experiences by documenting their travels. Bridges kept detailed handwritten diaries sprinkled with pressed flowers recording her impressions and experiences on both of her journeys. Baker compiled elaborate scrapbooks combining snapshots, tourist materials, and typewritten journal entries. The differences in representation reflect the transformation of tourism from an elite pastime to a popular phenomenon. But the similarities in sentiment and theme reveal the integral yet ambivalent connection between tourism and consumption. Between 1880 and 1940 tourism emerged in tandem with an expanding consumer culture, offering a form of geographical amusement for an expanding contingent of white, middle-class Americans. Building on the infrastructure of the modern nation-state—the national transportation and communications network, and the expanding national market—tourist industries developed, marketed, and sold sacred sites and dramatic landscapes across America. And tourists, taking advantage of increased leisure time, excess capital, and geographical mobility, sought the tourist landscape to escape workaday routine and embrace a more uplifting ideal of American nature and culture. Both tourist industries and tourists defined and imagined the tourist experience in cultural rather than commercial terms. However, the production of tourist mementos suggests that the social, economic, and cultural practices of consumption underlay the tourist experience, and that ultimately tourism was part of the larger process of incorporation that was transforming America into a modern nation-state. The connections between tourism and the culture of consumption reveal that the relationship between tourism and nationalism was not simply a marketing ploy embraced by tourist industries and tourists alike to envalue the tourists experience. Rather, in defining the tourist experience as a ritual of citizenship linked to national identity, in glossing over the commercial underpinnings of the tourist experience, in connecting the tourist experience with social status and personal identity, tourist industries and tourists were involved in the complex and complicated process of defining an ideal of the nation and citizenship that responded to and reinforced the emerging corporate, urban-industrial nation-state.

Historians of consumer culture have shown that in the decades surrounding the turn of the century, business leaders, magazine publishers, advocates of the leisure industry, advertisers, social theorists and the like helped create what has been called a "culture of abundance."[3] The development of the corporation with its dramatically expanded capacity for production and distribution sparked a wide reaching transformation in the economic, social, cultural, and physical landscape as marketing and merchandising reoriented everyday life around the consumption of goods.[4] In the process, purchasable goods became more than objects of necessity or luxury, they were imbued with symbolic value that promised adventure, escape, leisure, drama, the "good life." The language of advertising and the landscape of the department store promised more than the mundane benefits of possession, they promised fulfillment of personal desire, fantasy, celebrity, status, escape. Or, in the terms of the therapeutic ethos, they promised intense experience, self-realization, and personal reinvigoration as a hedge against urban-industrial anonymity and routine. In other words, consumer products took on meanings that ranged far beyond their physical and utilitarian use; they embodied the dreams and desires of those who were captivated by their novelty and allure.[5] This emerging consumer consciousness was linked to an expanding culture of leisure in which a trip to the department store was akin to a stay at a fashionable resort or a night at the theater.[6] All of these experiences depended on the newly expanded commercial nexus of consumption, leisure, social fluidity, salaried work, the separation and segmentation of urban, suburban, rural, and natural landscape, and the expansion of the communication and transportation networks. The cultural practice of tourism was grounded in this framework.[7]

The development and experience of tourism was integrally connected to the emergence of a modern, corporate, urban-industrial nation-state and the concomitant development of a society centered around consumption and leisure. The expanding urban upper middle class that emerged with the rise of national corporations used their surplus salary and leisure time to venture out into an extended axis of respectability that included posh resorts and tourist destinations promoted in popular magazines and made accessible by an extensive transportation network and the increased availability of the automobile.[8] Born of modern consumer capitalism, tourism offered a paradoxical promise: a one-of-a-kind personal experience as a mass-produced phenomenon. Because tourism trafficked in the sale of experiences and spectacle rather than objects, it could promise a singular, personal, adventure for each individual. In this way tourism distanced itself from the process of commodification. Yet tourist attractions were ultimately constructed, marketed, and sold in the same manner as brand-name goods. As a consumer experience, tourism occupied a strange middle ground between consumption and leisure and mass media. Like consumption, it was dependent on interactive exchange. However, like leisure activities and mass media, it was centered on the creation and dissemination of spectacle and illusion. The tourist was simultaneously a consumer and a viewer. In crossing these boundaries, tourism manifested the unique possibilities and contradictions of the emerging consumer culture: the possibility of intense personal experience, an escape to liminal space where the self could be temporarily reimagined or refashioned, an opportunity for physical and mental reinvigoration, a glimpse of the "good life." Yet the experience of tourism offered no tangible product. In other words, the possibilities of tourism as consumer experience also defined its limitations. It offered the potential of a personalized, one-of-a-kind experience, but at the same time it offered no proof of purchase—no visible object of meaning in a world increasingly defined by commodities. It promised both the exchange of interactive consumption along with the wonders of spectacle, but the exchange was intangible. Theoretically, it had no discernible meaning in the context of consumer consciousness.

The production of souvenirs, postcards, scenery albums, and the creation of tourist mementos suggests that the tourist industry and tourists themselves were conscious of the dilemma of tourism as a consumer experience. Tourists understood that in order to make sense of the experience in the context of this emerging consumer consciousness they needed to somehow objectify their experience. Many tourists kept detailed diaries or created meticulous scrapbooks memorializing their journeys; others settled for ready-made souvenirs and postcards.[9] These personal mementos reveal more than just the various routes followed or the "sights" visited. They show the consciously constructed visual, verbal, and physical narrative of the actual and imaginative journey. Diaries, photo albums, and scrapbooks suggest that tourists made their journeys into stories, highlighting the sites and events that were most "memorable" and locating themselves in the tourist landscape. These compilations provide a view into the give and take between marketed tourist experiences and individual tourist fantasies and the connection between the two. The physicality of tourist mementos as well as the personalized recollections and representations they contained served to position tourists within the larger consumer culture. Mementos objectified the tourist experience, transforming experience into substance. In addition, the memories they represented expressed a complicated and complex response to the economic and social transformation taking place in American society.

TOURIST MEMENTOS

Travel diaries have a long and illustrious history. Famous travelers from Marco Polo to Frances Trollope chronicled their journeys in dairies and letters, documenting their itineraries and preserving their experiences and observations. An established tradition of travel writing both preceded and shaped the European Grand Tour.[10] Building on the literature of discovery and exploration, aristocratic ladies and gentlemen who set off on extended tours to refine their education and social standing mimicked early travel narratives by sketching the sights seen and keeping daily accounts of their tours. The rise of romanticism and the emergence of picturesque tours further encouraged the documentation of personal experiences and observations. Travel journals offered a record of the actual, the educational, and the imaginative journey. By

During the nineteenth century genteel tourists emulated their European predecessors, who sketched the sights and scenes they came across on picturesque tours. Watercolor sketch of the Napa hills from Andrew Charles Gunnison's Sketchbook (1887). (Western Manuscripts Collection; reproduced by permission of the Huntington Library, San Marino, California)

the mid-nineteenth century, as the tourist industry took shape in the United States and tourism emerged as an elite pastime, many tourists emulated their aristocratic predecessors by recording their tours in diaries and sketch books. Travel diaries both codified the tour as a singular experience and served to memorialize one's journey.

Taking advantage of technological innovation and attempting to capitalize on this desire to record and memorialize, tourists industries and associated businesses marketed commemorative brochures, picture albums, postcards, and souvenirs. Early in the nineteenth century railroads began to distribute illustrated brochures and albums to illustrate the scenic attractions along their routes and entice the emerging tourist trade. Enterprising manufacturers, by the late 1890s, developed a full-fledged "souvenir industry," selling commemorative spoons, china, glassware, handkerchiefs, as well as jewelry and knick-knacks. At the World's Columbian Exposition in Chicago innovative promoters sold the first American souvenir postcards. In the ensuing decades, postcards soon emerged as one of the most popular form of tourist souvenirs, allowing tourists to document and preserve a visual record of their journey and send personal messages to friends and relatives back home.[11]

In 1888 George Eastman invented the Kodak, the first hand-held amateur camera. Loaded with a one-hundred-exposure roll of film, one had only to point the camera, push the button, and send the camera with the exposed film off to the factory, where the film was removed, processed, and replaced with a new roll.[12] The Kodak not only revolutionized photography but also transformed the way in which tourists documented their travels. As one Kodak advertisement stated, "Bring your vacation home in a Kodak."[13] Or as a Kodak advertisement for the World's Columbian Exposition read, "What's Worth Seeing Is Worth Remembering."[14] Kodak advertising encouraged consumers to document their travels and their lives through photography. An advertisement for the Kodak No. 1 camera explained, "A collection of these pictures may be made to furnish a *pictorial history of life as it is lived* by the owner that will grow more valuable every day that passes."[15] Specifically, Kodak attempted to connect vacationing with "Kodaking," arguing that "a vacation without a Kodak is a vacation without memories," and "Vacation Days are Kodak Days."[16] Building on the established travel dairy and borrowing from marketed tourist brochures, photo albums, and postcards, tourists began to use the camera to document their tours in novel forms. In snapshot albums and scrapbooks, tourists represented their journeys through a combination of images and text, including snapshots, postcards, prescriptive images, and professional photographs combined with quotations, labels, and journal entries. Some tourists created elaborate collages, whereas others relied predominantly on snapshots or postcards to document their experiences. Visual images, both amateur and prescriptive, began to supplement and at times replace detailed written accounts of the tourist experience. This shift in the form of representation from the textual to the visual reflects the increasing commercialization and popularization of the tourist experience. As tourism shifted from an elite pastime to a more widespread, middle-class leisure activity during the early decades of the twentieth century, tourists embraced the aristocratic traditions of documenting their travels, but they used the technology and the prescriptive imagery of the emerging consumer culture to memorialize their travels. Tourists simulta-

Twentieth-century tourists created elaborate collages of prescriptive material, post-cards, snapshots, and personal notations in their scrapbooks to memorialize their tours. From Miriam A. Musgrave's scrapbook (1933). (Collection of the author)

neously connected themselves to and distanced themselves from consumer culture. They created singular objects—mementos—to embody tours that extended from commercialized corporate culture. In this way, tourists person-alized the marketed tourist experience. But mementos also helped tourists make sense of their experiences in a culture in which cultural meaning and identity increasing revolved around the circulation of goods.

TOURIST ENCOUNTERS

Diaries and scrapbooks reveal that both early elite tourists such as Amy Bridges and later middle-class tourists such as Mildred Baker overtly acknowledged the connection between tourism and consumer culture in a variety of ways. Tourists often remarked on the process of memorializing their journeys, linking their activities to collecting and consuming. The collection of ephemeral objects and the purchasing of souvenirs became a central component of the tourist experience. Amy Bridges recounted that she filled a small bottle with water from the Pacific Ocean at Cliff House in San Francisco to take home with her as a souvenir. She gathered ceremonial paper ornaments scattered behind the hearse of a Chinese funeral, picked up leaves and pine cones from an excursion to the big trees near Santa Cruz, collected seashells on the Mexican border, and saved the Sunday menus from the Raymond Hotel. In addition she noted that she and her companions signed autograph books and exchanged tintypes.[17] Other early tourists remarked about purchasing spoons and "specimens" or commented on taking snapshots. Stephen Merritt, who traveled on a Raymond and Whitcomb tour to the Pacific coast and Alaska in 1892, commented in his diary, "The black crows, that sail or lite and hop on the ice are the only living things that give color to the picture, while here and there are Kodaks, and photographic amateurs and masters to take the picture and treasure it for remembrance or for sale as a memento of the peculiar morning of the history of this place."[18] These early diaries suggest that tourists were consciously engaged in memorializing their experiences through physical and visual remembrances, that in a culture shaped by possessive individualism they felt the need to objectify and possess their experiences.

Later tourists did not so much remark on collecting or purchasing souvenirs; instead, they displayed them in their scrapbooks. Mildred Baker included grasses and flowers in the pages of her scrapbooks, alongside purchased photographs, cutouts from tourist brochures, postcards, and snapshots. Tourists also pasted ticket stubs, programs, maps, match covers, printed packaging, newspaper clippings, receipts and other ephemera into their scrapbooks to memorialize their travels.[19]

Tourists also commented on the things they bought or the various shopping excursions they took. Amy Bridges delighted in a shopping excursion in San Francisco. "I am very much pleased so far with San Francisco," she wrote. "The streets are broad and clean and the stores are handsome. One which we visited is called Diamond Palace, it is small but gorgeously fitted up." She went on to describe the elaborate interior: "The walls are all of large mirrors which reflect the cases of jewels until one is deceived of the size of the store. The ceiling is round and a border of pictures of eastern ladies in their magnificent costumes (where there are jewels in their costumes some sparking stone had been set and the effect is dazzling) surrounds the room. The ceiling is finely frescoed."[20] Her description of the curio stores in Chinatown were less flattering. Similarly, August Tripp noted a number of shopping excursions on his 1893 Raymond and Whitcomb tour to the West Coast, noting of his excursion to Los Angeles, "We first visited the shops and then rode about the City on cable and electric cars."[21] Comments like these suggest that shopping was a standard component of the tourist experience. Miriam Musgrave, who compiled a scrapbook of her auto trip the to Chicago World's Fair and the intermountain West in 1933, noted that she "shopped around the stores" in Denver, Colorado. "May Co. has a store here," she wrote. "I bought a turquoise Indian ring and pendant."[22] Mildred Baker also recorded various shopping excursions and purchases that she made during her travels. Describing the "Indian Detour" she took to Frijoles Canyon, she recounted in her narrative that they stopped at Ildenfonso Pueblo, "famous for its shiny black pottery, and here Florence bought me for my birthday a lovely bowl made by Marie."[23] Similarly, describing her experience at the Grand Canyon, she noted, "In going and coming on this trip we passed . . . [the] hogan of an old Indian woman who claims to be 107 years old. She still makes baskets. . . . The young women too are making baskets again and I bought a small tray made of willow and cat's claw made by Mecca Uquella." Later in the trip she commented that their party stopped at a Navajo trading post and bought rugs and jewelry. She included a snapshot of the trading post, labeled "where the wonderful silverwork can be purchased."[24] In effect tourism offered the opportunity for novel consumer experiences, and tourists elevated shopping to a kind of connoisseurship in which they positioned themselves as discriminating collectors and souvenirs and purchased mementos were elevated to objects of art. In this way tourist consumption was both equated with and distinguished from everyday shopping.

Beyond the overt consumption goods, however, tourists also frequently commented on their quest for scenic and panoramic views, suggesting that the tourist experience was primarily a visual one in which tourists voraciously

Snapshot from Ethel Richardson Allen's photograph album (1921–23). Photographic Collections. (Reproduced by permission of the Huntington Library, San Marino, California)

consumed the sights and scenes of the tourist landscape. As Amy Bridges described one of her daily excursions from Manitou Springs, Colorado, "It was the hardest climbing I ever did. The path was very narrow and deep, filled with small stones and loosened soils. We had to take care not to lose our footing. . . . In some places Lily and I crept on our hands and knees, in others clung to the roots and branches of trees and pulled ourselves up and in some places Prof Lond and Lutio dragged us up the steep rocks. It was very hard work and I could breath with difficulty, but when we reached the summit the view fully repaid all our efforts."[25] Describing his experience in Yellowstone Canyon, Stephen Merritt wrote, "We feasted our eyes on spires, and turrets, and battlements, till we shouted for joy." According to Merritt, the tourist was constantly barraged by visual spectacle: "Every look is enrapturing, every view is sublime, every turn opens a new and more entrancing vision."[26] Later tourists consumed views by collecting and displaying snapshots and postcards that depicted the sights and scenes they witnessed on their journeys. Facetiously commenting on this quest for views, one tourist went so far as to include a snapshot in her album that depicted a camera tripod framing a panoramic view labeled "the eternal triangle—?"[27] Diaries and scrapbooks reveal that tourists characterized and understood their experience as a accumulation of visual images to be surveyed, collected, and consumed. In conceptualizing the tourist experience in visual terms, tourists actively participated in the transformation of American nature and culture into a commodified landscape of scenic goods.

Tourists not only characterized tourism in terms of consumption but also connected the tourist experience with the larger process of incorporation and the rise of the modern nation-state. Although later tourists took the national infrastructure for granted, many early tourists commented on the vast extent of the national transportation network, explicitly linking the tourist perspective with a new understanding of the nation. As Amy Bridges wrote on reaching San Diego, "We are here in San Diego at last and it seems a long way from home. I can see so plainly in my mind the map of the United States as I looked at it at home and saw a little dot way down in the south west corner on the Pacific and such a big country in between. And now I am really in that second little dot and the first one—Boston—is fully three thousand miles away. It seems so difficult to imagine it all."[28] Augustus Tripp was more able to comprehend the extent of the nation and the transformation that had taken place in American society as he traversed the country. On Washington's birthday he wrote, "Our long ride suggests the thought that the 'Father of his Country' did not dream of so large a posterity as he has and will have, nor of so large a Country, nor of the vast improvements that have been made in it in a Century. His beginnings were small, at times unpromising and discouraging, but he had patience and persistence, and through these and his wisdom and integrity the Nation was born and established; and by the will and integrity of the people has been maintained and developed to the marvel of the world."[29] However, C. D. Irwin, who traveled across the United States to Hawaii in 1885, perhaps best detailed an image of the modern nation-state in contemplating the extent of the Union Pacific line. His long description deserves to be quoted in full. Arriving in Salt Lake City after his trip across the country, Irwin reflected on his journey:

There is something about the appearance of the long Union Pacific Train which awaits our arrival at Omaha, that indicates a long journey. In fact, it seems as if the Union Depot at Council Bluffs should be the arbitrary division between the "East" and "West." Its structure and arrangement impress upon the traveler this idea. It is an interesting sight to see the five express trains coming into the east side of the station, over five great railroads, at the same instant, and empty their live freight through the great arches to the western side of the depot, where they are all combined and loaded into one great train of twelve or more cars! Witnessing this scene, one cannot help thinking what vast improvements are constantly being made in railroading, and what marvels are daily accomplished, which we have come to regard as matters of course. Only a few years ago the Union and Central Pacific Ry's formed the only transcontinental line, and it seemed like undertaking an ocean voyage to start across the great plains, deserts and mountains to the Pacific Coast. Now see how the map is cut up with railroads, not only crossing the continent in various latitudes, but penetrating into every nook and corner of its wildest mountain ranges. And think of the comfort and elegance with which we ride through hundreds of miles of desolation! This was forcibly impressed upon me by our porter. As there was no room in the Ogden Sleeper we had a section in the Green River car. I wondered why a car should be run to the latter point—a huddle of houses in the midst of a desert. I asked the porter why that car should stop at Green River.

"Hit don't stop!" said he. "Dis year car runs plumb though to Poahtland, Oregon! Goes by de Oregon Short Line cross contry fom de U.P. at Green River."

"Do you go with it?"

"Yes, sah! Leave heah (Omaha) Wednesday night. Get to Portland Sunday. Eleven days round trip. Breaks porters all up!"

Well I should think it would. It's the longest run made by any car of which I know, altho this same porter told me he used to run from San Francisco to New Orleans—over 2000 miles—and return. Where else in the world can a man ride so far in the same car, using the same currency and language, and not be annoyed by any custom house officers?[30]

Early tourists marveled at the ease with which they traveled cross-country and the expanse of the national railroad network. They understood that their journeys extended along an expanding metropolitan corridor, paralleling the flow of goods and urban amenities from one coast to the other.[31] And they remarked on their newfound ability to imagine and comprehend the nation as a coherent whole, suggesting that the tourist experience gave form and substance to the abstract images of the nation represented by countless maps of the United States etched in their imaginations. In other words, early tourists perceived the integral connections between the extensive railroad network, the national market, and the nation.

The emergence of new modes of transportation gave later tourists a different perspective on the expanse of the nation. Mildred Baker and her friend traveled from Buffalo to Chicago by commercial airplane in 1935 to commence their journey to New Mexico. She noted that even though they were given newspapers and magazines to amuse themselves, they spent most of the flight mesmerized by the expanse of landscape visible from the window of the plane.[32] Although the national infrastructure had become so commonplace to later tourists that they no longer felt the need to acknowledge it, they too must have well understood the link between the tourist experience and the modern nation-state.

The recollections and representations contained in tourist mementos expressed more than a surface acceptance of and participation in the larger consumer culture; they also revealed a more complex relationship between tourism as a consumer experience and the rise of modern corporate culture. A journey into the tourist landscape offered a strategy for the expanding middle class to seek identity and distinction by appropriating and adapting the leisure activities of an older more genteel culture associated with the aristocratic tradition of the Grand Tour. The practice of keeping travel diaries extended this connection with the Grand Tour and upper-class refinement and sensibility. Through diaries and scrapbooks tourists delineated and defined the social meaning of the tourist landscape.

In using the metropolitan corridor to serve the tourist, early touring companies sought to separate the tourist experience from the public exchange and interaction of commercial culture that took place in railroad cars, hotels, and city streets. Early on tourist agencies such as Raymond and Whitcomb offered a sense of exclusivity and refinement, assuring elite tourists that they would circulate among people of their own social standing and milieu. As one tourist wrote, "The Raymond & Whitcomb Excursions are a decided success— there is no lack of anything in any way. Jay Gould, who is following us up, can have no more or better attention than we. This is the Perfection of Travel."

Raymond and Whitcomb tours guaranteed the exclusive social boundaries of the tourist experience at a time when the boundaries between the tourist landscape and the metropolitan corridor were blurred and the connection between the social space of tourism and social status was not firmly established. Participation in a Raymond tour assured tourists that they would be distinguished from migrants, drummers, homeseekers, and other utilitarian travelers. Raymond tours guaranteed polite social interactions and a shared sensibility and appreciation or approach toward the travel experience. As one Raymond tourist commented, "We are becoming a very happy family as we journey along and get better acquainted; everything is so pleasant." The Raymond and Whitcomb Company reserved a special group of Pullman Palace cars or state cars for their tourists; they contracted with designated hotels, such as the Del Monte in Monterey and the Palace Hotel in San Francisco, or they built or purchased their own hotels, such as the Raymond in Pasadena and the Antlers in Colorado; and they provided their tours with special guides to distinguish the Raymond tourists from all other travelers. As Stephen Merritt commented, "We take a guide to visit the Springs and Terraces and a very right thing it is to do. We walk, a company of kindred spirits under his directions."[33] In this way elite tourist agencies helped designate and patrol the social and spatial boundaries of tourism for their clientele. Raymond and Whitcomb tourists well understood these distinctions and commented on any transgressions in their diaries. As Amy Bridges commented on her train trip to San Francisco, "This was the first in which we had to mingle with other passengers and it did not seem pleasant to me. I'm afraid Pullman cars are making me feel Aristocratic."[34] Stephen Merritt lamented in a similar fashion when they departed the Raymond tour, "We are now out of the guardianship of our blessed protectors—the Raymond & Whitcomb and are learning to go on our own hook."[35]

In portraying the social scene at posh tourist resorts, in taking in the sights of cosmopolitan cities, and in glorifying sublimes scenes and picturesque views, Amy Bridges's diary, along with other early elite tourist diaries, associated the tourist experience with an air of cultural refinement and social exclusiveness that situated the tourist landscape as part of an extended terrain of highbrow culture and as part of the expanding milieu of the newly emerging upper middle class.[36] Bridges reveled in the elegance and social scene of resort hotels such as the Raymond in Pasadena. "So here we are at the Raymond and I wish I could describe its glories for it certainly has them. The hotel is one of the finest interiors I ever was in," she remarked. The diary entry went on to note the "large and airy, great halls and rotunda[, the] beautiful parlors, reading, writing and billiard rooms and a grand ballroom with piano, organ and stage, etc. for theatricals[,] all so very nice."[37] Similarly, Stephen Merritt described the Del Monte as "beyond description; so clean, sweet, lovely. Every appointment of the very best, not loud, not gingerbread, not attempting anything, but doing everything, the brightest spot on the globe, with its indescribable trees, flowers and plants; its lake, birds, and ocean."[38] For early tourists, hotels such as the Del Monte and the Raymond embodied elegant and exclusive social spaces that allowed for refined and respectable social interactions—reading, writing, painting, strolling, dancing, dining, and socializing—with people of similar means and status, all of which could take place in a controlled space outside of the increasingly commercialized metropolitan corridor. In this way elite tourists defined and understood the tourist landscape as a new kind of public space, extending the upper-middle-class spaces that proliferated in modern cities and suburbs.[39]

Early tourists highlighted the distinction between these refined social spaces of exclusive tours and crowded, commercialized, urban centers in their diaries. On reaching Chicago, Amy Bridges commented, "I do not like Chicago very well even if it does have such wide straight long streets. . . . . I never saw so many advertising signs of all sizes and descriptions in my life before. Every building was glittering with signs." She went on to note the "endless passing of crowds of people through the streets," concluding, "There seemed such a rush and excitement in the city that I do not like it."[40] Her assessment of Los Angeles, in juxtaposition to the elegance of the Raymond Hotel, was even more scathing. "I think Los Angeles is the dirtiest city I ever saw," she wrote in her diary. "The buildings are not very high and a great many seem to be only cheap little buildings which were first put up when the place began to grow." She found the commercial character of the city to be filthy and disagreeable. "Most of the stores are dirty little holes and even those which are very nice within would hardly lead you to suppose as from their outside. . . . I've seen the dirtiest stores and goods for sale I ever want to see. I don't see how anyone can buy them. The side-walks are mostly of wood and the planks broken and worn in many places and all covered with dirt in the most disagreeable way."[41] Comments like these suggest that in participating in exclusive tours, in socializing at resort hotels, and in surveying city scenes, early tourists used the tourist gaze to position themselves outside of or beyond the increasingly unruly and expanding commercial sphere, in a more refined atmosphere attuned to culture rather than commerce. In the process, of situating themselves in these new social spaces, they helped to associate the tourist experience and particular tourist attractions and accommodations with highbrow, upper-middle-class status and behavior.

In addition to separating themselves from the larger commercial culture through exclusive tours and posh resorts, elite tourists also adopted notions of the sublime, the beautiful, and the picturesque to elevate their tourist experiences from superficial and commercialized amusement to the level of highbrow culture.[42] This aesthetic classification of nature, first articulated in the late eighteenth and early nineteenth centuries, helped transform wilderness into scenery: the sublime scene embodied by dramatic natural landscapes—mountains, waterfalls, cliffs, and canyons—conveyed the power of God through its infinite, rugged, and overwhelming character and provoked a more expansive vision; the beautiful landscape with its gentle curves and inspiring vistas, along with the picturesque landscape, with its romantic ruins and pastoral character, evoked literary and artistic conventions, connecting the viewer to a long tradition of refined genteel culture. From the nineteenth century on tourist industries and advocates had relied on these ideas to define and legitimize nature appreciation and "picturesque tours."[43] Despite the fact that references to the sublime, the beautiful, and the picturesque had become commonplace in prescriptive tourist materials, tourists often appropriated these tropes to articulate their responses to the tourist landscape.[44] For example, recounting her initial view of the Rocky Mountains from the train, Amy Bridges described her appreciation of the scene in aesthetic and spiritual terms: "Before noon we saw the Rocky Mts," she wrote. "They were a beautiful sight. Most of them were covered with snow and the light and shade upon them made them wonderful. Beautiful Mountains! . . . These mountains in the west are so grand and fascinating. There is something new about them every time I look. They are never tiring though so immovable. There is something very restful in their grand, calm presence and eternal stillness. . . . 'The everlasting hills' is a wonderful simile of the ever-lasting faithfulness of God."[45] Stephen Merritt referenced the sublime more literally in describing his visit to Yosemite valley: "We descend deeper and deeper into the Valley, below the level of the sea," he exclaimed:

> Now all is lost and swallowed up in the sublimity of the scene that breaks from the floor of the vale. El Capitan; one bristling solid tower of rock without a break, or bush, the earth rises up majestically 3300 feet, the monarch of them all. It seemed like a portion of the rock of ages, as the foundation stone of this earthly temple; it speaks of the Almighty; it lifts up our hearts in praise to God our Heavenly Father who made them all. All around are the lovely falls, by their sweetness and gentle beauty, adding to His magnificence. The Bridle Vail [sic]; a thing ethereal, seemingly coming down from God out of heaven, laughing, shouting, leaping to be free to come down to earth. It grows with every look, you shut your wearied eyes, as they are to rest, and when you open them the rocks, the falls, the river, the surroundings are grander, loftier, more sublime than before. I experienced an ecstasy of joy, or exultation indescribable, a feeling I cannot express. Sacred Awe is the nearest I can come to it. . . . No pen can portray it, no pencil picture it, no photograph reproduce it; it is God's own handiwork, marvelous indeed.[46]

Later on in his journey Merritt wrote about his impressions of Alaskan scenery: "It must be seen to be appreciated; it can never be described, and once seen is to have it daguerreotyped on your soul forever."[47] These are just a few examples of how turn-of-the century tourists literally and metaphorically evoked the sublime to explain and envalue their encounters with dramatic natural landscapes. In expressing their inability to find the words to describe these natural wonders, in suggesting that these indescribable views had to be experienced firsthand to be fully appreciated, in discerning a spiritual presence in their encounters with dramatic natural scenery, tourists drew upon the well-worn, popularized tropes of the sublime to suggest that the tourist experience had pushed them to embrace a more expansive vision of the world. In appropriating the established tropes of the sublime, tourists linked themselves to genteel traditions of the European Grand Tour and, in the process, elevated tourism from the level of an everyday excursion or mundane observation to an aesthetic and spiritual experience.

Similarly elite tourists referenced the beautiful and picturesque in their descriptions to further define and envalue the tourist experience. Evoking an image of a middle landscape with the railroad nestled in a pastoral landscape, Amy Bridges detailed the view that unfolded before her through the train window: "We have been steaming though a beautiful green country where the railroad was bordered with flowers, intersected by pretty little rivers bordered by trees which inclined their green branches over their winding course. Low, hills, broad stretches of green fields with cattle feeding, beautiful woods almost southern in their luxuriant appearance, and funny little villages, we saw upon the banks of one river an encampment. . . . The country is not as level or as monotonous as I thought it would be."[48] A. A. Butler sought to categorize the beauty of the landscape in Cheyenne Canyon outside of Manitou Springs according to aesthetic standards. He wrote, "There is no spot that has not its own peculiar beauty. Now it is the beauty of lofty pine spruce, now the famous lofty beauty of towering cliff and pinnacle, now the simple beauty of the forest gladed avenue with its lacework of glittering sunshine. From the frequent bridges, open long vistas of gleaming or foaming water, fretted by boulders, sifted and tangled by luxuriant underbrush."[49] Similarly, Sidney Waldon emphasized artistic features in describing the view of Lake Tahoe. "And then we came out into the basin beyond and held our breath at this new view," he wrote. "For far below, and in a setting of heavily-wooded mountains, was Tahoe—fairest gem of the Sierras—azure blue in the noonday distance. Oh, what a marvelous thing is water in a landscape! Water is surely nature's finest adornment. . . . A lake seems always to be in sympathy with nature's changeful moods and to give them their most beautiful expression."[50] References to pastoral imagery, natural design, along with color, mood, and form allowed tourists to equate viewing nature with viewing art, implying the education and refined sensibility one needed to fully appreciate natural scenes. In this way, the tourist landscape was further associated with an extended axis of respectability and cultivation linking cosmopolitan tourists with high culture and its associated ideas and institutions—art museums, opera houses, and concert halls. As one historian has argued, "The new tourism helped foster PMC [professional-managerial class] consciousness by flattering its consumers that they had the emotional depth required for the quasi-religious experience of what John Sears calls 'sacred places'; by giving them authentic, visual experience of sites already marked in advertising and travel literature as culturally significant; and by affording them cognitive and esthetic familiarity with a world in which only those with decent incomes and education freely moved."[51]

Through this detached tourist gaze, elite tourists further positioned and distinguished themselves by commenting on the work, culture, and behavior of others they encountered on their journeys, most notably Native Americans, African Americans, Mexican Americans, Chinese Americans, and Mormons. From the perspective of elite tourists, these social others became an extension of the tourist spectacle, further allowing tourists to define and distinguish their social status. A. A. Butler was captivated by the black stevedores while traveling for pleasure on a Mississippi Riverboat. "It was amusing to watch the darky deck-hands, coming and going in single file, in opposite directions, and all the time on a dog-trot, a rolling mechanical motion, more like a dumb animal than an intelligent man," he wrote. "The mate ordered them as though they were dogs and they went and came in packs."[52] Through this commentary, Butler implicitly reflected on his own identity— his position of leisure, his whiteness, his intelligence. Similarly, Augustus Tripp described the inhabitants of Santa Fe as "largely comprised of Mexicans and Indians, a rough looking people and said to be vicious and reckless." He went on to note that "their customs and habits are of a primitive order and there is little of American Civilixation [sic], life or language there."[53] In characterizing Mexicans and Indians as primitive others, Tripp implied not only a racially defined, hierarchical social order in which American civilization represented the highest stage of development but also his own position as part of that elite American civilization.

During the late nineteenth century, elite tourist diaries reveal that Chinese, Indians, and Mormons emerged as standard tourist attractions embodying exotic social others. In commenting on the appearance, manners, and customs of these groups, elite tourists reaffirmed their own sense of refinement, culture, status, and American-ness. Early tourist diaries reveal that Raymond and Whitcomb parties were often taken to the "Chinese Quarters" in San Francisco as part of their city tour. They toured Chinese churches and theaters, tea houses and shops, as well as gambling houses and opium dens. Amy Bridges noted that "one of the party gave a Chinaman two bits (25cts) to smoke [opium] for us and we watched him with interest." She included a detailed description of the encounter. Bridges commented on the strangeness of the Chinese and the dirt and unpleasant odors.[54] Augustus Tripp recounted his party's excursion to Chinatown taken "under the escort of a Police guide."[55] Using descriptive words more characteristic of insects than humans, he conveyed his low opinion of their culture:

> First we entered some of the Chinese shops and inspected their peculiar wares and merchandise. These shops were swarming with Chinamen engaged in their various pursuits—merchants, grocers, silversmiths, barbers, &c. We entered a Chinese drug store and obtained a sample of their medicines, consisting of dried reptiles, insects and various barks, all of which seemed more curious than desirable. Next we crawled through dark passage ways underground to opium dens, where Chinamen were packed as thickly as they could well be on shelves in low unventilated rooms, smoking their opium pipes, the fumes of which were dense, suffocating and disgusting to us, but to them, apparently enjoyable. But for our guide, who was evidently well known to the Chinamen as guide and policeman, we would not have dared to enter the dark places he led us into.[56]

Not all elite tourists were so disgusted with the Chinese. Stephen Merritt commented in his diary after their tour through Chinatown that he found the Chinese "a quiet, orderly, temperate, industrious, and well behaved set of people, all and always at work," concluding that he thought they "deserve[d] well of us Americans."[57] Yet whether condemning the Chinese or complimenting them, tourists used them as foils against which they could distinguish themselves as cultured and refined Americans.

Elite tourists described Indians in similar terms. However, whereas Chinese were foreign and exotic, smoking opium and gambling, Indians were primitive and uncivilized, living in squalor and idleness. During her stay in Riverside, California, Amy Bridges and her family took a day trip to see some Digger Indians. She described the two Indian women she saw as unresponsive, "dejected looking," and old. The Indian boy with them had "a low order face with no expression at all." She continued, "There was nothing in the hut. I saw a few rags and bits of things, nothing at all to make life in the least comfortable not even our necessities. I wonder how human beings can live so. I can not imagine how low in the order of human life they could be, almost animals."[58] Stephen Merritt similarly remarked on the "Esquimau" people in Alaska: "Not given to much work; lives in squalor, idleness and shut out from the world; has no refinement or culture. They and a host of dogs occupy their curious houses."[59] These demeaning descriptions contrasted sharply with the excessive praise tourists lavished on the plush resort hotels from which they ventured. Whereas the hotels were exquisitely filled with every sort of modern amenity and frequented by refined society, the abodes of Native Americans were sordid "huts," devoid of goods, and the Indians who inhabited them were equally dejected. In responding to Native Americans in such negative terms, elite tourists further outlined the boundaries of refined and civilized upper-middle-class American culture, connecting consumer goods, social graces, and racial purity with social position. In juxtaposing the civilized and the savage, tourists naturalized their own sense of social identity while marginalizing ethnic others.

Mormons played a similar role in the early tourist experience, adding a moral aspect to this process of identity formation. Amy Bridges characterized the people she saw at the Mormon Tabernacle in Salt Lake City as "a low class," noting further that she "hated to walk among them."[60] C. D. Irwin, however, was much more specific in his condemnation of the Mormons he saw while stopping in Salt Lake. "From all we have seen and learned today, we might well think we had found here a little chunk of perdition, sugared over and dropped in a valley of Paradise!" he wrote. "The Mormons make up the former and the situation is the later." He went on to describe his tourist encounter: "On our way home from the depot last night we were on the lookout for men of many wives and were rewarded by seeing a colored gentleman out walking with a dusky dame on one arm and either a white wife or whitewashed mulatoo on the other! Thus does the 15th amendment give equal rights to black and white." He went on to tour the Tabernacle, and after these brief encounters he observed, "the whole system is an absolute monarchy organized and controlled by a few sensual men who have just knowledge enough to impose upon a mass of ignorant people, and fatten their own purses by the operation." He concluded, "There is no need of rehearsing the many ridiculous, disgusting, treasonable and damnable doings of these Latter Day Sinners! The whole concern is a vile compound of ignorance, avarice, theft, lust, license and murder which smells to heaven whenever it is stirred up."[61] According to Irwin, Mormons were not only polygamous and blasphemous but also engaged in miscegenation and political corruption, all for personal pleasure and private profit. In other words, they transgressed acceptable social, political, religious, and moral boundaries. For elite tourists these transgressions opposed and thus delineated acceptable upper-middle-class moral and social behavior.

Elite tourists did not define the boundaries of upper-middle-class, highbrow culture simply through negative encounters with social others, however. They also distinguished themselves from daytrippers and picnickers and the places they frequented, revealing invisible class lines within the experience of tourism. Recounting an excursion to Cliff House in San Francisco, Amy Bridges remarked that it was "a dirty old place I think for poor city people's excursions and full of peanut and popcorn stalls."[62] Similarly, C. D. Irwin described Cliff House as a "Coney Island for 'Frisco.' It has several large restaurants, dance halls, side-shows and a 'coaster' with other orthodox attractions." He went on to note that "it is now accessible to the masses by means of a railroad which runs across the sand hills from the city limits."[63] Through their characterization of Cliff House, Bridges and Irwin revealed the vast distinction they perceived between amusement parks and highbrow tourist attractions and the class of people that frequented each. The excursionists they encountered were "city people," a part of the growing mass of urban workers and immigrants who could not afford to venture far from the city center for the more exclusive enclaves of upper-middle-class culture.

Elite tourists did not simply categorize tourists sites according to class constituencies; they also distanced themselves from what they perceived as uneducated, lower-class behavior. A. A. Butler, who traveled to Colorado at the turn of the century, made a point of distancing his experiences from the crass behavior and superficial appreciation of daytrippers and excursionists. Describing a trip to Manitou, he wrote, "Went with L. soon after our arrival over to Manitou, which is about 6 miles away by electric car. It has a fine situation and its surroundings are beautiful, but I do not like the place. It is filled with show hotels and pretentious boarding houses. ... It has been called the Saratoga of Colorado but one thinks of S—as a city of magnificent hotels and splendid elm-shaded [streets] of M—as a city of small catch penny shops and donkeys. ... No one who has been there can sense the association. It is all very well to use them [the donkeys] to go up the canons [*sic*], but when it comes to having one's picture taken astride a donkey, as many people do, I must beg to be excused." He illustrated his commentary with two tourist images: one showed a well-dressed mother with her young child strolling down a tree-lined avenue labeled "Recollections of Saratoga," the other revealed a group of people sitting astride beleaguered donkeys labeled "Recollections of Manitou." Later, describing a day trip to North Cheyenne Canyon, he detailed a long hike up the canyon, noting, "It is just this wildness which makes these upper parts so attractive. Below the crowd have come and gone and with their going has disappeared every wild flower and fern in sight, only the great massive beauty of the earth and sky and stream is all that is left. But as soon as one leaves the beaten track he begins to see the more delicate beauty and beautiful forms of vegetable life." Butler found fault with "the crowds," who literally consumed nature, explaining the difference between refined appreciation and thoughtless destruction or superficial appreciation. He noted that "in most cases [one] is content to see and leave these [flowers and ferns] for those who follow after to see also; not that he does not pick specimens of all he sees, but he does not pick armfuls as I have seen people do, and throw them away because they wilted before the city was reached." Picnickers and daytrippers "tramped under foot everything on land and litter[ed] up with rubbish everything in the water." The uninitiated sought amusement and escape through the tourist experience, whereas the refined tourist sought educational enlightenment. Describing a trip to the Garden of the Gods, Butler remarked, "The only drawback to the enjoyment of the trip was the driver who thought that he must entertain us, and one of the party suggested that his tongue moved at both ends. He saw a bird or beast or man in every strangely formed rock in the landscape and we had hard work to hear what we wished to say to one another. But we finally made him understand that we wanted to see the landscape not the ridiculous associations of ignorant visitors." For Butler, these transgressions reflected larger class divisions, and he lamented the intrusion of the lower classes into the natural attractions that surrounded Manitou. Commenting on a hike he took up Cascade Canyon, he wrote, "The next station above Cascade is Green Mountain Falls, a lovely spot which I have visited many times but now I am sorry to see is becoming a great Sunday resort which means the destruction of all its beauty from the class of people that will attend small excursions."[64]

Beyond their class critique of daytrippers, elite tourists also questioned the promotion of tourist attractions, suggesting that excessive marketing diminished the experience of "scared places."[65] Tourists complained that at times the prescriptive tourist literature and images promising sublime and picturesque views created exaggerated expectations that made the real thing seem flat and disappointing. Stephen Merritt remarked, "We were wearied when the announcement was made 200 yards more and we will be at Inspiration Point. We were in great expectation. The pictures we had seen, the descriptions we had read, had caused me to expect an overburst of enthusiasm on my own part as well as on the part of the others as the sight burst upon our view—but we did not enthuse." In comparison with the dramatic scenes he had already experienced, the packaged descriptions and images had created false promises. "We had seen such grand things of which no mention had been made, or photographs taken, that when the scene presented itself to our view it did not meet my expectation," he explained. "It was dwarfed. It was grand,—the grandest I had ever seen; but fell short, flat as to what I had expected."[66] Amy Bridges characterized her view of the Golden Gate in San Francisco Bay in a similar manner, writing, "We had quite a long ride in the ferry boat and saw San Francisco as it seemed upon a hill in the midst of the waters. A fog partly obscured our view. They tell me the waters to the right were the Golden Gate. When a child reading or listening to accounts of it, I thought it must be an entrance between rocks which were lofty and sparked with gold that the water was a beautiful blue and beyond, the sky always wore the golden glory of sunset. But it is not so, and indeed the harbor seemed only ordinary."[67] In expressing their disappointment, tourists such as Bridges and Merritt implicitly rejected the excessive popularization of tourist landscapes, suggesting that tourism required a certain refinement that existed beyond the market and thus further linking tourism with a aura of exclusivity.

In describing the genteel social spaces of exclusive tours and resort hotels, in evoking the sublime, the beautiful, and the picturesque to characterize the tourist landscape, in surveying social others, and in distinguishing the tourist experience from that of daytrippers, picnickers, and excursionists, elite tourists implicitly and explicitly sought to link tourism with an extended upper-middle-class terrain of exclusive suburbs, social clubs, and cultural institutions that had begun to take shape around the turn of the century. In doing so, they participated in the larger process of social reproduction and class formation, distancing themselves from the growing polyglot of city dwellers and the urban-industrial culture in which they circulated. Around the turn of the century, as the national tourist industry took shape, tourism offered one more opportunity for the expanding upper middle class to separate and differentiate themselves from the growing numbers of the laboring classes comprising the rising numbers of rural migrants and foreign immigrants who threatened to inundate urban areas and destabilize their social position through the democratizing force of commercial culture. Around the turn of the century tourism offered another opportunity for the upper middle class to seek identity and distinction through the expanding consumer culture.

In both embracing the consumer aspects of tourism and adapting tourism to the needs of class and identity formation, elite tourists expressed an ambivalent response to modern corporate society in their diaries. Tourism, in providing an escape from the workaday world, expressed an idealized critique of urban industrial culture. Yet it also depended on the larger process of incorporation that reorganized space, redefined nature, and reconfigured human relations.[68] The emerging upper middle class spawned by this new corporate culture, in responding to both the opportunities and limitations of corporate capitalism, turned to tourism, among other forms of consumption, to assess and confirm their new position in American society. In the process they linked the experience of tourism and the landscape of tourism with highbrow culture and genteel social space, positioning it along an extended axis of respectability that overtly defined the boundaries of upper-middle-class identity. At a point at which the expanding national infrastructure was feeding the growth of corporate urban-industrial culture while also facilitating the development of a national tourism, elite tourists used the tourist experience to articulate social position, but they also sought to overtly link the tourist landscape with an extended upper-middle-class terrain as well as respectable forms of behavior and refinement.

The recollections and representations contained in the mementos of later tourists are more difficult to decipher. The increasing popularity and affordability of the automobile, the growing interest in physical recreation, and the expansion of the tourist infrastructure transformed the tourist experience during the early decades of the twentieth century. Many tourists began to venture out on their own, no longer feeling the need to depend on the services of exclusive tourist agencies. A slew of guidebooks, travel maps, tourists brochures, and travel information published in popular periodicals encouraged tourists to choose their own destinations. Simultaneously, the automobile freed tourists from rigid train schedules and predetermined routes. The handful of resort hotels quickly gave way to a plethora of tourist accommodations ranging from the log palaces in the nation's national parks to roadside cabins and camping sites that sprang up to accommodate the tourist trade.[69] And a diverse array of novel attractions emerged to attract the tourist's attention. The tourist experience became much more diversified and individualized. Just at the moment that tourism began to emerge as a popular pastime, tourists increasingly turned away from written accounts to visual imagery to memorialize their tours. Tourist diaries became scrapbooks and snapshot albums, suggesting that tourists embraced George Eastman's advertising entreaties that they document their travels with a Kodak. Despite the fact that the tourist experience and tourist mementos were becoming increasingly commercialized, scrapbooks and snapshot albums still hint at the ways in which tourists interpreted and appropriated the tourist experience.

Scrapbooks and snapshot albums compiled by later tourists, like the diaries that preceded them, presented a narrative of the tourist experience, revealing both the various sites and scenes of the tourist journey and those experiences tourists found most memorable. And although the narrative strategy manifested in scrapbooks and snapshot albums displaced the written tourist narrative onto photographs and tourist ephemera, creating a much more subjective and singular story, these mementos still engaged in the larger discourse concerning the relationship between tourism and modern consumer culture.

The scrapbooks produced by Mildred E. Baker offer a particularly rich source for understanding the shift in perspective from an earlier group of elite tourists to later middle-class tourists. Baker's elaborate scrapbooks convey the essence of her tourist experience. More than just records of the tourist landscape, they reveal the cultural ideals and expectations that shaped her conception of that landscape. The representations and recollections they contain suggest that, unlike earlier elite tourists, Baker increasingly took issues of class formation and the affirmation of middle-class status for granted, instead focusing more on issues of self-realization and personal reaffirmation.

Baker was an active participant in Ernest Thompson Seton's woodcraft movement and an avid birder. References throughout her scrapbooks suggest that the proto-environmentalist concerns articulated in the concepts nature study, the Arts and Crafts movement, and the American Woodcraft League strongly influenced her tourist experiences. As a number of historians have explained, the Arts and Crafts revival and the related enthusiasm for outdoor recreation, both of which had an impact on the popularization of tourism, emerged in the early decades of the twentieth century as an ambiguous antimodernist response to the increasing fragmentation and rationalization of modern urban-industrial living. Middle-class Americans increasingly sought "authentic" experience, "real" life, and self-fulfillment through hand craftsmanship, romantic nature, and more "primitive" ethnic others. These forays into an idealized premodern past served as a palliative for the ills of urban-industrial society. As one historian has explained, "Nature study often displayed this primitivist cast, emphasizing holistic experience over the fragmentation of the city and insisting that to feel nature one had to journey back in time to a simpler life, grasp the experience, and then return, richer but unable to articulate what this psuedomystical encounter had been all about."[70] Similarly, scholars of tourism have argued that many tourists "visit a place in order to rediscover in themselves an identity which they cannot find in their everyday lives."[71] For a single female office worker such as Baker, who might have had some financial independence and perhaps nominal prestige in her job but little social status or power in the male-dominated society of Buffalo, the imaginary geography of the tourist landscape offered an ideal setting in which to escape the humdrum of everyday routine and temporarily refashion or reimagine herself.

Baker's scrapbooks intermingle promotional literature with personal travelogue, connecting literary allusion with real-life experience in a collage of visual and verbal imagery. Snapshots and postcards, maps and brochures are mixed together to illustrate the chronicle of her journeys. At times the line between the promotional and the personal becomes blurred as Baker narrates her experiences. The concluding remarks about her first trip to the Southwest, for example, assumed the tone of a tourist brochure:

This Navajo Empire through which we just passed is the last domain in the United States where Wilderness and Wildness reign supreme. It is a semi-arid grazing area larger than the States of Massachusetts and Connecticut combined, with a total population of 35,000 pastoral, nomadic Indians, plus a handful of white men—traders and members of the Indian Service. It is a region unspoiled by civilization, where the only wholly self-supporting tribe of Indians in the United States live a happy and industrious life.[72]

Snapshots and illustrations also mimicked promotional material. Illustrating her ride through Red Bud Pass, Baker juxtaposed a snapshot of the group on the trail with a promotional image. The snapshot is captioned, "Through Red Bud Pass from Cliff Canyon. A very narrow defile, part of which had been blasted out to permit pack animals to pass through." The caption on the tourist image is almost identical: "Climbing down the trail in Redbud Pass. It took four days to blast a way with dynamite, black powder, and T.N.T through one of the three vertical rock ledges."[73] On one level, Baker's scrapbooks read, at times, like booster literature, suggesting that she bought into marketed tourist images, yet this promotional material is constantly subsumed by the larger collage.

Baker did more than simply copy the visual and verbal imagery used by tourist promoters. She borrowed established narrative strategies used by tourist promoters and popular western fiction to frame her own journey. Her narratives played on themes of adventure, discovery, and escape and invoked the well-established tourist metaphors of exploration, conquest, and romance. Baker's touring narratives do not simply chronicle her journeys but provide a cultural framework that allows her experiences to be both personally and culturally meaningful.[74] In narrating and illustrating her travels, in translating her experiences into book form, and in arranging and binding these visual and verbal memories into a coherent product with a beginning and an end, a build up and a climax, Baker was consciously and unconsciously borrowing from, responding to, imitating, and adding to a wide array of cultural texts and stories that intersected in the tourist landscape.[75]

Baker's narratives are steeped in the literature of romanticism, western fiction, and popular ethnography. Clearly literature, as much as experience, influenced her conceptualization of the tourist experience. She sprinkled her scrapbooks with quotations and references to Zane Grey's westerns, Henry

Van Dyke's poetry, and George Wharton James's guidebooks, among references to other western booster literature. Commenting on the beauty of Surprise Valley during her first pack trip to Rainbow Bridge, she noted, "Sheer cliffs shut in the vale to the east and west, while on the north between the cliffs, one gazes over immense boulders down the valley ... to the red rocks of the Colorado and the looming mass of Wild Horse Mesa. No wonder Zane Grey made this the home of Lassiter and Jane in his 'Riders of the Purple Sage' and 'the Rainbow Trail.'"[76] This literary West was the antithesis of the mundane, urban-industrial, overly civilized East. It was a West of untouched wilderness, noble savages, and frontier justice, a romantic frontier populated by cowboys and Indians, frontiersmen and outlaws.

This mythological western frontier provided a wide array of stories and predictable settings for tourists to appropriate, and Baker tapped into this imagery to explain and envalue her tourist experiences. Prefacing one of her trips to Rainbow Bridge, she wrote, "This pack-trip is the key to the wilderness. It is a lesson in self-reliance, in the rare companionship of faint trails and campfires. It is royal sport for anyone with red blood, good health and even a speaking acquaintance with horsemanship. And it brings glorious memories that will abide forever as a hedge against the troubles of civilization."[77] In celebrating wilderness, adventure, and individualism, Baker represented herself as a modern-day pioneer—a rugged individualist braving the challenges and uncertainties of the western frontier. Numerous references throughout her scrapbooks reinforced this imagery. She not only drew attention to the dangerous trails "where one mis-step is the end of all misery" but also characterized her various pack trips as forays into uncharted territory.[78] In describing ruins or land forms seen on various rides, she repeatedly remarked that she and her party were "probably the first white people to enter much of the territory covered."[79] Despite the fact that she was participating in a tourist experience that by then was available to a wide cross-section of middle-class Americans, she used the language and metaphor of discovery to suggest that she was confronting uncharted terrain, mapping new ground.

Adopting the standard tourist trope of the sublime, Baker also scripted her tourist journeys as romantic wilderness experiences—solitary encounters with untouched nature. "To few people is given the privilege of life in the wilds in these days of supercivilization," Baker wrote in the opening sentences describing her first trip to Rainbow Bridge.[80] Sublime nature offered a sense of therapeutic escape as well as an antidote to the ills of urban-industrial culture. Describing their arrival in Alaska Basin in Grand Teton National Park in Wyoming, she wrote, "We had the peculiar sensation of being utterly alone in the world, for the clouds completely hid all of the surrounding mountains and we could see only our own little meadow or basin with its green lake."[81] Dramatic western scenery inspired Baker in the same way it did earlier elite tourists. Viewing the Grand Canyon from the Colorado River, she wrote, "This is the beginning of the Grand Canyon, and to say that I was thrilled because I was down in the Canyon is putting it mildly. Words are utterly useless in trying to describe how I felt. . . . Surely in all the wide world there is no more glorious sight than these canyon walls. I wanted to cry because of the beauty of it all—a land 'whose beauty takes the breath like pain.'" Similarly, she depicted a night in camp along the Colorado River: "I had the feeling of a protecting sky closely enfolding me, with the whole world below and the stars within arm's reach. These glorious nights, although we did not sleep well, were worth the whole trip, the glow of moonlight on the canyon walls, the glittering stars, the mysterious wilderness were incomparably beautiful."[82] Numerous snapshots of vast panoramic vistas devoid of people reveal her attempts to capture these dramatic views in the same manner that nineteenth-century painters and photographers and their twentieth-century imitators had depicted sublime wilderness. Like earlier tourists who evoked the sublime, Baker also glorified the experience of viewing the dramatic natural landscapes in terms of spiritual renewal. "We thank the Lord, for such spots of peace as this, where the soul finds strength and healing," she wrote after viewing the Rainbow Bridge by moonlight.[83] From the vantage point of the solitary observer, romantic nature offered intense, emotional, authentic experiences in contrast to the artificiality of modern existence.

References to the mythology of the Wild West further added to these metaphors of discovery and renewal. Providing a context for her trip to the Double S Ranch, she wrote, "This whole region is a storied land of romance—and romance that is not so very old at that." She went on to recount the legends of Geronimo and his infamous cattle raids, and Billy the Kid and his murderous escapades, noting, "It was a wild and turbulent country and

Snapshot from Mildred E. Baker's scrapbook, "Memorable Days on the
Teton Trail" (1934). Photographic Collections. (Reproduced by permission
of the Huntington Library, San Marino, California)

still is wild and unsettled. A gun is still regarded like a shirt or hat as an ordinary detail of costume."[84] One snapshot of Baker on her trip to Wyoming labeled "'Tough Guy'—ready to kill with Cloy's revolver, Alaska Basin," showed her in chaps, vest, and cowboy hat holding a revolver, suggesting that she was self-consciously aware of playing cowboy. Comments linking the scenery to "movie scenes of western country" also imply that Baker imagined her experience in the context of popular western adventure films.[85]

Baker also described her travels in educational terms. She linked her experiences to salvage anthropology and popular ethnography and assumed a scientific tone in documenting her tourist observations.[86] In viewing, photographing, and consuming both Indians and nature, Baker suggested that she was in some way engaged in a form of scientific or scholarly pursuit. During her trip to the Grand Canyon she quoted from George Wharton James's *In and Around the Grand Canyon*, a popular guide to the canyon providing ethnographic and geological information, and then noted of her own experience, "In going and coming on this trip we passed a hewa or hogan of an old Indian woman who claims to be 107 years old. She still makes baskets too, and while she looks old, she certainly does not seem as ancient as that. The young women too are making baskets again and I bought a small tray made of willow and cat's claw made by Mecca Uquella."[87] Describing the drive from Kayenta to Monument Valley she similarly recounted, "We packed our camera equipment, for of all places where you want plenty of film, this is one of the best. In the afternoon we came to a Navajo's summer hogan where we had a photographer's paradise of picture-taking of the older women weaving, spinning and carding wool, grinding corn etc."[88] Snapshots and tourist images pasted in her scrapbooks served to illustrate her observations. Informative captions such as "Looking into the home of an ancient cliff dweller" or "Ladder leading to the ruins of communal dwellings at top of Puyé Cliff" explained the significance of her snapshots. These images were juxtaposed with tourist images with labels such as "In a 'modern' pueblo where one may catch archeology alive."[89] In this way, Baker scripted her consumption of Indians through the tourist spectacle as part of the scholarly and scientific process of discovery and exploration in which she imagined herself.

Similarly, Baker embraced this scientific perspective in describing landscape and wildlife. In effect, she positioned herself as an amateur practitioner of geology, ornithology, and botany. Each of her scrapbooks is appended with a list of the birds, plants, and animals she encountered on her trips. She also sprinkled her narratives with observations of animal behavior, geologic formations, and botanical notes. For example, on her raft trip down the Colorado and Green Rivers, describing the passage from Chokecherry Draw to Flaming Gorge, which she identified as "the gateway to the canyons," she noted, "The color is, as one would assume, red but not more so than any of the other canyons and there is some displacement of strata running up about six or seven hundred feet. Above there were Douglass Fir, Western Yellow Pine and Juniper, while along the water's edge there were willows and alder thickets." Or commenting on the wildlife, she wrote, "Again bird life was abundant. A red-tail hawk was being molested by two swallows, evidently having come too close to their nests for their comfort. The cliff swallows nests were plastered all along the cliffs. Many robins were singing happily, while in the stream ahead of us I saw my first western grebe."[90] The narrative goes on to comment on sightings of Canada geese, rabbits, and great blue herons. Her scrapbook from the Double S Ranch trip included remnants of flowers and grasses, with such labels as "piece of Gamma Grass" or "Specimen of Red Gum," pressed between the pages, revealing her penchant for "botanizing."[91] Tourist images of various plant and animal species also illustrated her narratives. Through this language and imagery of scientific and scholarly observation, Baker transformed the tourist experience from a middle-brow consumer experience to a highbrow cultural experience.

Yet Baker's scrapbooks were not simply seamless webs of celebratory prose and pictures. Specifically, her characterizations of Indians and the wilderness experience reveal contention in the narratives. Although her scrapbooks convey a fascination with the tourist Indians, the depictions of her encounters with real Indians exhibit a certain uneasiness. Although Navajos served as assistants and guides on many of her Rainbow Lodge pack trips and Baker named and photographed them in her scrapbooks as part of the larger southwestern tourist experience, she often expressed dissatisfaction with or distrust toward her guides. On a pack trip to Navajo Canyon she noted that at one point the two guides had to leave the party to find another guide because they were uncertain about the trails. Baker grew concerned about water and safety. "We really did not relish being left alone here with so many Navajos wandering freely around, but there seemed no help for it," she wrote.[92] To photograph and interact with domesticated tourist Indians who were usually women was one thing; to depend on Navajo men as guides and equals was quite another. Baker's unease with Navajos "wandering freely" exposed the charade of the tourist fantasy. Only captive or domesticated Indians were safe. Picturesque and exotic tourist Indians who willingly collaborated in the staged authenticity of the tourist experience were acceptable and appealing because they were, in effect, willing prisoners of the tourist spectacle.[93] As objects on display, they became aestheticized consumer products.[94] The real Navajo—the "interior Indians, those within American social boundaries"—on the other hand, represented capricious ethnic others who threatened the predictability of the tourist spectacle and challenged the tourist's control of the tourist experience, while revealing problematic issues of race and class that underlay the tourist spectacle.[95]

Baker's appreciation of the tourist landscape also depended on a specific social and cultural conception of the nature experience. She understood the dramatic landscapes and the flora and fauna of the West in both reverential and educational terms. The wilderness experience was meant to inspire the soul and uplift the mind. Any deviation from this romantic view spoiled the allure of nature. The many tours and pack trips she took supported this perspective. The rustic accommodations combined with the full-service pack trips allowed tourists like Baker to rough it in style. On one of her pack trips to Rainbow Bridge, for example, she noted that the party camped at a permanent camp in the natural amphitheater near the bridge. There the guides "brought out our cots with real mattresses and spread our bed rolls on them under the stars."[96] With all of their needs cared for, tourists were free to focus solely on the wonders of nature. Like the tourist Indians, nature was domesticated through the production of the tourist spectacle, and this wilderness tourist fantasy depended on the comforts of full service.

Most of Baker's experiences on her travels resulted in romantic encounters with the western landscape. However, at times, nature or guides did not cooperate, spoiling her wilderness adventure. Baker's record of her raft trip down the Colorado and Green Rivers with the Nevill Expedition in 1940 revealed these fissures in her wilderness fantasies. This was the most physically challenging of her documented tourist excursions and the furthest removed

Wilder + his sample mule.

Snapshot from Mildred E. Baker's scrapbook, "Peace of Rainbow and Canyon" (1938). Photographic Collections. (Reproduced by permission of the Huntington Library, San Marino, California)

from the standardized western tourist experience of the period. As a member of the crew, Baker was not afforded the luxuries of roughing it in style. She was instead expected to do her share of the work of maintaining the boats and setting up camp. She explained later that she had agreed to help with the cooking in exchange for an allowance to discount the cost of the trip, but that she never received it.[97] Although she tried to narrate her experiences using the standard tourist tropes of adventure, discovery, and romance, veiled complaints and quarrels fractured these formulaic narratives. Issues of gender and class constantly intruded on her tourist fantasy. For example, extolling the possibilities for bird watching, she noted, "What a chance for an ornithological expedition down these rivers! The willow thickets along the shores were alive with birds, which would fly ahead as we approached." Yet she lamented, "As I was in the last boat, I never did get a good look at them." She also complained of bad headaches that were exacerbated by rocks and rapids. As one entry recounted, "We hit many rapids today, some two-liners, which did not help a bad headache that was bothering me. We hit rocks continually, and in one of the rapids when we whammed up against a rock, a most violent pain shot through my head, the first direct re-action."[98] Recollecting the trip, she commented, "It turned out I worked my way down the canyons. I'd work like mad. . . . The men did nothing to help in cooking the whole trip. . . . Sometimes I was so dead tired from constant work at night—our camps were no pleasure."[99] Wet clothes and gear, dish duty, and competition among the men in the party resulted in dissatisfaction.

She grew particularly cross with Norm Nevill, the leader of the expedition. She disliked his grandstanding and felt that he viewed the trip as a mere publicity stunt rather than as a scientific expedition or wilderness adventure. His lack of reverence for the wilderness experience particularly galled her. At one point she noted in her diary that he was "incapable of slowing down to enjoy the scenery. Describing a hike from the river to Rainbow Bridge, she revealed her displeasure. "We went at a rapid pace without stopping except for a pause at a spring," she commented irritably. "All the time Norm either singing at the top of his not-too-good voice, or spouting inane chatter, when I so wanted to enjoy the peace and quiet of that to me—well-nigh holy spot." Norm's irreverence disturbed the sanctity of the nature experience, as did his lack of chivalry. He failed to assist her with the torn sole of her shoe and only lent a helping hand on a difficult part of the trail after she had to ask. She even intimated that Norm put her and the two other women on the trip in danger when climbing up the bridge. She recounted, "Norm decided we should not use the rope, which we had brought along, despite the fact that Hugh had previously advised me not to attempt it without the rope. There is an iron ring fastened above to secure the rope, but Norm thought we would make a better record if we did not use the rope. He made Doris, who had a bum leg at the time, climb down and up without the rope, but Anne and I refused point-blank to risk a broken leg in the wilderness for any whim of Norm's, so when it finally dawned on him that we meant it, he held the rope for Anne and myself."[100] She later commented that "Norm was really unbearable."[101] Clearly, Norm did not measure up to her previous guides, who were quick to assist at any sign of difficulty or discomfort. Norm wanted to conquer nature, Baker wanted to revere it. Baker wanted Natty Bumpo, but she got a crass river runner. Consequently, Norm's bravado spoiled Baker's enchanted view of Rainbow Bridge.

These moments of complaint and contention reveal that Baker's understanding and appreciation of the tourist's West depended on a culturally and individually prescribed interpretation of the nature experience. Baker embraced what one scholar has called the romantic form of the tourist gaze, "in which the emphasis is upon solitude, privacy and a personal, semi-spiritual relationship with the object of the gaze."[102] From this perspective the tourist could contemplate the self in spiritual terms, she could imagine her life in creative ways, far removed from the seemingly unauthentic, humdrum of the modern world. Although Baker's narratives used the established tourist tropes of discovery and adventure to celebrate the frontier West, she rejected any notion of conquest or triumph in connection with the nature experience. Any challenge to the romantic view of nature as sanctuary or laboratory seemed blasphemous in her view. Norm's behavior disturbed her because it sullied her ideal of pristine nature with issues of class, commercialism, and sexism. Baker implicitly and explicitly criticized Norm for his lack of education, his crassness, his selfishness, his arrogance, and his propensity for self-promotion. From her perspective, Norm did not understand his place in nature. She insinuated that Norm was not a gentleman because he did not approach nature with the proper respect and reverence. Consequently, he shattered the illusion of Baker's tourist fantasy. But Baker's criticisms also reveal the underlying assumptions and limitations of her romantic view of nature. She embraced an elitist and exclusionary view of nature, a view that served to mask and even obfuscate the social and commercial realities that underlay the tourist experience. In other words, Baker embraced an understanding of the tourist landscape as an extension of refined middle-class terrain just as her turn of the century counterparts did.

In using the metaphors of discovery and adventure to describe her tourist experiences, in evoking the established tourist trope of the sublime, in framing her observations in scientific and scholarly terms, and in recording fraught encounters with Indians and guides, Baker's scrapbooks, like the mementos of earlier elite tourists, reveal an ambivalent connection to the larger consumer culture. Her wholehearted acceptance of the commercial imagery of tourism as revealed in her display of tourist ephemera and snapshots suggests that she embraced tourism as an integral part of the larger consumer culture. Antimodernist allusions to the frontier West, however, suggest a more fraught response to modern corporate society. Baker imagined the tourist experience as a temporary but necessary escape from the workaday routine of modern urban-industrial culture—a chance for physical and mental regeneration and personal reaffirmation. Tourism offered her the opportunity to flee the social confines of Buffalo and reimagine herself as a modern-day pioneer. Although dependent on corporate, urban-industrial capitalism, tourism also served as an implicit critique of that culture. However, as access to the tourist experience widened with the growing popularity and affordability of the automobile, tourists like Baker still worked to differentiate the tourist experience from common amusement. Although Baker no longer felt the need to overtly link tourism with refined middle-class spaces and identity as turn-of-the-century elite tourists did, she did feel the need to legitimize tourism as a highbrow experience and distinguish herself from the social others who did not embrace or support her refined understanding of the tourist experience. For Baker, tourism existed within the world of modern consumer culture but did not partake of it.

Baker's scrapbooks are singularly accessible because she included a detailed written travel narrative in her visual collage. Other tourist mementos from the nineteen teens through the thirties are not so explicit. They tended

Tourist snapshots often depicted tourists posed in front of their automobiles. Snapshot from Niagara Falls Scrapbook (c. 1927). (Collection of the author)

to rely predominantly on snapshots, postcards, and other tourist ephemera and sometimes included short labels or journal entries. Despite the fact that the expression of personal meaning was displaced onto commercialized images in these mementos, as meticulously compiled visual narratives of individual tourist journeys, they suggest that, like Baker, other middle-class tourists envalued the tourist experience as more than just a consumer experience. Many tourist scrapbooks displayed page after page of snapshots depicting dramatic natural landscapes devoid of people, suggesting a continued acceptance of the sublime perspective.[103] Others included informational brochures and newspaper clippings along with carefully labeled images suggesting that they embraced the tourist experience as an educational experience—a chance to learn something about the world beyond their own community.[104] Frequently scrapbooks included a variety snapshots depicting tourists posed with their automobiles along the roadside, at campsites, or in front of scenic views. These types of images suggest that tourists sought to identify themselves through their connection to the automobile. Like earlier descriptions of resort hotels and Pullman Palace cars, these images served to link tourists to an extended terrain of middle-class culture, where automobile ownership and the time necessary to enjoy a long-distance automobile trip signified a certain level of social status. Overall the form and content of scrapbooks and snapshot albums—the carefully ordered collage of images or the meticulously labeled array of photographs—suggest that middle-class tourists embraced tourism as an opportunity to narrate their own identities. In other words, tourism allowed middle-class Americans to reimagine themselves as active agents within the tourist landscape.

BOUNDED FANTASIES

Tourists mementos, both elite and popular, reveal that tourism represented a cultural dialectic in which tourists invested the marketed experience with their own culturally defined dreams and memories.[105] The allure of the tourist experience resulted from a dynamic interplay among individual desires, associated meanings derived from cultural texts and images, and marketed fantasy. Tourists, in buying, embracing, and, one might even say, collaborating with the staged authenticity of tourism, shared in the production of the tourist experience. They engaged in bounded fantasies, setting their quest for authentic experience and a larger sense of individual meaning and identity within a scripted landscape shaped and defined by cultural texts and commercial aims.[106]

Both early elite tourists and later middle-class tourists were drawn to the tourist experience because of its predictable yet intriguing narratives. The scripted tourist landscapes offered comprehensible stories in which the individual (the tourist) could participate in an ongoing drama. Tourist sites act as stage sets.[107] Through the mechanisms of tourism, places are transformed into scenery and spectacle. As spectator, voyeur, actor, and consumer, the tourist stands at the center, empowered by the all-encompassing tourist gaze not only to possess the tourist landscape but also to weave a totalizing narrative. Predictable tourist narratives gave tourists the opportunity to temporarily reimagine themselves in creative ways and thus transcend the confines of their everyday social identities. In this way tourism provided a welcome contrast to the shifting social boundaries and meanings of corporate, urban-industrial culture and the sense of anonymity, powerlessness, inauthenticity, and fragmentation that characterized the monotonous routine of modern existence.

Elite tourists predominantly embraced or turned to the romantic notion of the sublime to enact personal dramas of spiritual transcendence in the tourist landscape. The tenets of the sublime offered an ideal framework for elite tourists to articulate the bounded fantasies offered by the tourism. Amy Bridges described one such experience which deserves to be quoted in full. Sitting on the verandah of the Raymond Hotel, gazing out at the San Gabriel Mountains, she recounted,

> I wish you could be with me some afternoon on the western piazza—my favorite one—sitting in the big easy rocking chairs they have on the piazzas. . . . The hotel is at the summit of a little hill, below us then is the lovely valley, the town of Pasadena spread out amid it trees and greenery, the cultivated grounds amid scattered houses; or sloping hillsides, so beautiful. The ground rises. There are little hills like our own rising higher and higher behind each other. Then come the wonderful mountains, rising so abruptly from the valley you think you could put your finger on the very line from which they rise. Wrinkled, jagged, broken, some summits with traces of snow. Shadowy canons, bleak overhanging rocks.

The light and shade are wonderful upon them. There is so much awe—authority about them—"the everlasting hills!" I take long breaths as I look up at them—so sure—so grand. Nothing *little* can stand in their presence. The wonderful, wonderful power of God speaks from them—so silently, so overwhelmingly—"From everlasting to everlasting I am God." They bring such peace and rest to me I cannot tell. All this wonderful scene rises apparently so near to you so very distinctly before you because of the clear air that I often think it is painted upon a canvas as some immense drop curtain at a theater. You know how often they are painted with tropical scenes and grand mountains only this more lovely than human hand could paint. So I sit and look and look or with closed eyes till there is no more Amy Bridges but a small sweet truth of happiness and peace—a light that seems a new glory—no sin—no death in the world—nothing but the moment of sacred pleasure. Then soft and sweet from the dance hall near by come the notes of the orchestra—the music of the afternoon concert. Sometimes so sweet and sad the deepest melancholy comes over you but you would not for the world have it go away, though it is a kind of pain to you. And again it is so glad you think the happiness of the whole world is condensed into it. And always your heart is in it—it is bent to it—to be merry or sad. And the sun sets quickly—the glorious colors brighten all the western sky and are reflected from the opposite mountains. A chill creeps up from the valley—cold blue shadows steal up the mountain sides and the outlines of every mountain and hill are more distinct than ever. It is the loveliest view of all, but the music has ceased. It is quite time to go inside for the chill is dangerous that comes with sunset. Reluctantly, I go.[108]

Although this represents just one example, Bridges and other elite tourists recorded these moments of transcendence in their diaries, revealing that the tourist experience inspired them to reaffirm their spirituality in a world increasingly given over to worldly concerns.[109] These transcendent fantasies extended from and reinforced the Protestant culture of salvation, which was increasingly coming under threat by the emergent consumer culture.[110] In using the sublime to validate one's individuality in spiritual terms, elite tourists appropriated a well-worn tourist trope to articulate a sense of individual worth and identity that existed beyond the market.

Later tourists took advantage of a wider array of cultural imagery and drama to play out their bounded fantasies in the tourist landscape. Sidney Waldon prefaced his privately printed account of a 1919 transcontinental auto trip with a poem entitled "The God of the Open Air," which captured the allure of the tourist landscape:

> A gray ribbon of dust runs westward
> into the land of the setting sun,
> And many's the great adventure
> that this winding ribbon has spun.
> The pony express once followed it
> and seekers after gold,
> And earlier still the Indians
> and the buffalo of old.
>
> It passes by many a mansion,
> by many a simple hut;
> Through peaceful valleys and barren planes.
> A ribbon of dust? Yes! but
> To me it's a wonderful highway,
> straight and smooth and fair,
> For it carries me out to do homage to
> The God of the Open Air.
>
> For the lure of the silent places
> and the mountains bleak and bare,
> the mirage that's faintly shimmering
> in the desert's midday glare,
> The one lone bird in a cloudless sky
> and the vastness that's out there,
> Are calling me to do homage to
> The God of the Open Air.
>
> I stand in the morning light
> when the sun peeps o'er the rim,
> and be freed of all that's small and base
> and worthy to worship Him
> Who fashioned the great wide wilderness,
> and the silent places where
> Men might go to do homage to
> The God of the Open Air.[111]

The mythological West of buffalo, Indians, pioneers, and vast open spaces provided an array of romantic stories for tourists to appropriate. Although this is just one example, other middle-class tourists also characterized their journeys in similar terms.

Mildred Baker's scrapbooks reveal the West, with its formulaic stories of western adventure, picturesque Indians, and scientific discovery, as a particularly alluring dreamscape for tourists who sought a temporary respite from urban industrial society. In narrating the tourist experience as a process of discovering uncharted territory and communing with nature, Baker tried to revive and act out the American ideal of rugged individualism on the western frontier. She left behind her home and job, with all the associated social and cultural expectations for a world of fantasy where she could reimagine herself as a heroic figure. Western drama transformed tourism from an experience of passive consumption into an encounter of active agency. Dramatic desert and mountain landscapes combined with the remnants of preindustrial Indian cultures offered an ideal stage set for tourists to refashion themselves by playing cowboy or Indian, ethnographer or pioneer. In the western tourist landscape Baker was no longer a mere secretary from Buffalo; she became a western adventurer—a cohort of Zane Grey's Lassiter and Jane, a colleague of George Wharton James, a companion of John Wesley Powell. But more important, she became the narrator, in control of her own story.

Other middle-class tourist mementos suggest that it was not only the West that offered tourists the opportunity to reimagine themselves. Tourists also followed the footsteps of history and paid homage to literary shrines, associating themselves with heroic historical figures as well as fictional characters and settings throughout the country. They, too, used these cultural sites to temporarily play out new identities beyond the confines of everyday life.

Tourist mementos suggest that both elite and middle-class tourists used the tourist experience as an opportunity to engage in bounded fantasies, using the scripted tourist landscape to narrate their own identities. The shift in these fantasies from the romantic trope of sublime transcendence to the more modern trope of self-realization reveals the larger transformation taking place in American society, from a culture defined by a Protestant ethic of respectability and salvation to a culture of therapeutic self-fulfillment.[112] In using the tourist experience to position themselves in relation to the larger

Tourists connected the allure of the open road with a mythological image of the frontier West. From Sidney Waldon's privately published touring narrative, "Sagebrush and Sequoia" (1919). Photographic Collections. (Reproduced by permission of the Huntington Library, San Marino, California)

The Indian in me coming out at last.

Betatakin

Tourists used the tourist experience to reimagine themselves and play "American."
Snapshot from Mildred E. Baker's scrapbook, "Peace of Rainbow and Canyon" (1938).
Photographic Collections. (Reproduced by permission of the Huntington Library, San
Marino, California)

culture, elite tourists embraced an older ideal of republican virtue and Protestant salvation, using the sublime to articulate their worth in spiritual
terms. Middle-class tourists adopted the tenets of liberal individualism,
seeking authenticity and real life, and defining their identity through the language of the therapeutic ethos. Despite their differences, both elite and middle-class tourists were responding in ambivalent ways to the emerging
corporate, urban-industrial culture. The mementos they produced and the

recollections and representations conveyed through them suggest that the social, economic, and cultural framework of consumption imbued the tourist experience with meaning.

In using the tourist experience to respond to and position oneself in the emerging consumer culture, tourists were implicated in the larger discourse of citizenship that pervaded the prescriptive tourist material. Although tourists might have eschewed the overtly nationalist associations marketed and sold by tourist industries, and although they did not refer directly to tourism as a ritual of citizenship as tourist promoters did, they were integrally engaged with issues of identity and status that were central to the shifting notions of citizenship that underlay the emerging corporate, urban-industrial nation-state.[113]

As a number of historians have argued, the transformation of America to a modern corporate consumer culture corresponded with a decline in popular politics and political participation and shifting ideas about the meaning of consumption. Starting in the 1890s, voter turnout began a precipitous decline as Americans took less and less interest in the political battles of the day.[114] Simultaneously, advertisers and industries began to promote products in political terms. The marketplace was defined as a democracy of goods, and consumption emerged as an act of citizenship.[115] Advertisers and industries not only equated consumption with voting but also defined the commonwealth in terms of the marketplace, linking geographical mobility and access to markets and consumers with the rights of citizenship and the democratic polity.[116] In this way the discourse of citizenship shifted away from vocabulary of political rights or social identity toward a more limited notion of citizenship defined in terms of access to consumer goods, geographical mobility, and purchasing power.

Tourist industries and promoters picked up on this paradigmatic shift, defining tourism in nationalist terms as a ritual of citizenship. Tourist mementos, too, suggest that tourists engaged in this discourse in their attempts to situate themselves both socially and personally within the larger consumer culture. In this way, both tourist industries and tourists participated in promoting this new notion of mobile citizenship that further underscored the changing social relations manifested in the modern corporate nation-state. In promoting the idea of mobile citizenship, both tourist industries and tourists reduced civic responsibility and action to individual desire as it was played out across social spaces. The rights of citizenship were conflated with the ability to consume, and the public sphere was reduced to the marketplace. Public spaces became personalized spaces in the tourist landscape, and the rights of citizenship were implicitly defined in exclusive terms. Tourism privileged seeing over speaking, purchasing over voting, traveling over participating. Participatory democracy became a more passive, individualized experience acted out along an extended axis of mobility. In the process social difference was compressed into geographical diversity and the national polity was represented as an exclusive cohort of mobile middle-class consumers. The implications are that only those who could afford to have access to the tourist landscape—who had the time, money, technology, and imaginative framework—could participate in this ritual of citizenship and validate their identity as Americans. In this way national tourism, both the industry and the tourists themselves participated in the construction of an image of the nation and an ideal of citizenship that reaffirmed the social, cultural, technological, and political relations of modern consumer culture.

The period between 1880 and 1940 marked the heyday of national tourism in the United States. As a national transportation and communication network manifested a national territory, as mass production and mass distribution created a national market, and as the process of incorporation redefined political, social, and economic relations in national terms, an "imagined community" embodied by the modern nation-state solidified in the United States. In paradoxical ways, tourists and tourist industries were integrally involved in reimagining and reaffirming this modern nation-state. Burgeoning tourist industries marketed tourism as a ritual of citizenship, constructing a canon of brand-name American tourist attractions and inscribing a shared national history and culture across the American landscape. Tourists, in turn, took to the road to discover and consume America, positioning themselves as modern individuals and engaging in a larger dialogue about personal and national identity. National tourism depended on this corporate, urban-industrial infrastructure. Yet tourist industries and tourists created and consumed a nostalgic ideal of America as "nature's nation." National tourism as a form of patriotic consumption sought to reconcile this organic nationalism, which celebrated nature, democracy, and liberty with the urban-industrial nation-state that depended on extraction, consumption, and hierarchy. Thus, as the emergence of a modern consumer culture reshaped the social and cultural boundaries of the United States, national tourism helped to imbue the nation with form and substance by imagining and legitimizing America as a modern nation. The post–World War II boom and the emergence of a mass consumer culture transformed the underlying premises of the modern nation in complex and complicated ways. Consequently, the rise of a postmodern outlook and experience that came to dominant American culture in the post–World War II era marked the demise of this distinct form of national tourism.

EPILOGUE

$\mathcal{I}$N 1946, AS TRIUMPHANT American GIs returned to civilian life and American industry shifted from the needs of wartime production toward the satisfaction of pent-up consumer desires, General Motors (GM) developed a new advertising jingle to promote its new line of Chevrolet automobiles: the Fleetmaster, the Fleetline, and the Styleline. Tapping into the patriotic fervor that swept the nation in the aftermath of the allied victory and capitalizing on dramatically increased production capacity, the company encouraged Americans to "See the USA in your Chevrolet." The catchy jingle, sung by such noted singers as Pat Boone and Dinah Shore, became one of the most longstanding and popular advertising campaigns developed in the postwar era. Running from 1946 to 1963 on radio and television, GM sought to stimulate sales by reviving and expanding on the ideal of national tourism.[1]

GM was not alone in seeking to reestablish the link between tourism and nationalism in the postwar era. As the United States began to define and position itself as a world superpower, presidents from Dwight D. Eisenhower to Lyndon B. Johnson looked to tourism as a means of celebrating and supporting the American economy and national identity.[2] In the winter of 1965, at the height of American postwar prosperity and power, President Johnson delivered a special message to Congress on the status of the American economy. He reported that the state of the dollar on the world market was strong, but he expressed concern about the international imbalance of payments and the outflow of American dollars to foreign countries.[3] Johnson had come before Congress to address this issue, and tourism played a central role in his economic plan.[4] "The growing interest of our citizens in foreign lands, and the steady rise in their incomes, have greatly increased American vacation travel abroad," he explained. "Foreign travel should be encouraged when we can afford it," he noted, "but not while our payments position remains urgent. Today, our encouragement must be directed to travel in the United States, both by our own citizens and by our friends from abroad." He asked for the assistance of "the tourist industry to strengthen and broaden the appeal of American vacations to foreign and domestic travelers," stating that he would support its efforts through the "See the U.S.A." program.[5]

See the U.S.A., also referred to by the press as the administration's See America First campaign, took shape as a government sponsored program to develop the tourist potential of the United States for both domestic and overseas travelers.[6] While the U.S. Travel Service in the Department of Commerce worked to facilitate foreign travel to America, the administration wavered over how to entice Americans to stay at home. Amid heated debate over travel restrictions, head taxes, and reduction of the duty-free allowance, Johnson appointed Vice President Hubert Humphrey to head a Cabinet task force to organize and unite corporations in the travel industry behind the cause of domestic travel.[7] In the spring of 1965, Humphrey helped organize a "quasi-official agency aimed at promoting domestic travel attractions."[8] This new entity, called Discover America, Inc., was a privately funded and operated "non-profit public service corporation" run by volunteer directors drawn from corporate executives within the tourist industry.[9] "Its going concern," noted the New York Times, was "dedicated to persuading American private enterprise to spend its own dollars to persuade the American people to travel within their own country, the purpose being to spread dollars inside the nation and to make more Americans better acquainted with their own land."[10]

Between 1965 and 1968, Discover America worked with the backing of the administration to develop and promote the possibilities of domestic travel. In the spring of 1967, it launched its first national campaign, announcing Discover America Vacation Planning Week and the slogan for its cooperative advertising campaign: "Discover America—It's 3,000 Smiles Wide."[11] For the 1967 campaign the corporation paid for the erection of forty-five hundred Discover America billboards, a slew of Discover America buttons, and more than fifty thousand Discover America posters to be placed on U.S. Postal Service trucks. It also developed and disseminated a Discover America theme song, sponsored a Discover America sweepstakes, and backed a film on American tourist attractions. In addition, private companies such as United Airlines and Hertz Rental Car joined the campaign by using the Discover America slogan in their company advertisements.[12] In 1968, as American military involvement overseas became increasingly more contested, Discover America intensified its promotional campaign, allocating $100,000 for their program "to acquaint Americans with travel opportunities at home."[13]

The activities and programs sponsored by Discover America in the mid-1960s revived the idea of national tourism in a new guise. As did earlier interwar national tourist campaigns, this new attempt to encourage Americans to tour America expressed an economic nationalism that linked increased domestic tourism with national prosperity. However, just as pre-Depression advocates of See America First and national tourism used the rhetoric of economic nationalism to express their anxieties and ideals about America, so did those promoting Discover America reveal their concerns and convictions about national identity and national unity.

Discover America's mission to entice Americans to travel at home expressed official cold war concerns about the nation's status and identity as a superpower. As President Johnson explained in an address to members of the See the U.S.A. Committee, "Ours is really an open land, an open society with no walls around it, nothing to hide within it, and we want the world and Americans themselves to see the U.S.A. For to see it, I think, is to understand better why we Americans all love peace and why we love freedom so much, and why we would like for all the people of the world to love it as we do."[14] The emphasis on reducing the balance of payments deficit through domestic travel expressed an economic nationalism based on the idea that America needed to sustain a strong economy in order to lead the free world. As Vice President Humphrey noted in a speech to the directors of Discover America, "With every American that is persuaded to see first-hand more of his own country, and with every foreign citizen who is persuaded to come into our midst as a visitor, we create just a bit more understanding and enlightenment. And at the same time, we protect the integrity of the American dollar."[15] The message conveyed through the Discover America publicity campaign also reaffirmed the validity and the legitimacy of American history, culture, and tradition in opposition to a defeated Europe, thus legitimizing America's claim to world leadership. Drawing on the established rhetoric of national tourism, Secretary of the Interior Stuart Udall said in a promotional statement for the Discover America campaign, "When it comes to the search for history, we have our own castles, kingly places, and even ancient cathedrals. . . . Our Spanish missions and Indian villages also have an antiquity transcending Europe's."[16] Not only would domestic travel help maintain America's strong economic position in the world and reaffirm the status of American history and culture, but also, according to Humphrey and others, domestic tourism offered the potential for creating a more unified America. As with earlier campaigns promoting national tourism, the implied message was that by seeing and knowing America, American citizens might be able to overcome the conflict and tensions that were polarizing American society. Referring to the possibilities of tourism, Humphrey argued that "the understanding of people for one another is the greatest thing we have to gain through our promotion of travel. For it is only through such mutual understanding that we may hope to build in time a more just and peaceful world for all men."[17]

Despite these official and commercial attempts to revive national tourism as a patriotic ritual of citizenship in the postwar era, widespread prosperity along with shifting social, economic, and political relations had dramatically transformed the experience and implications of leisure in American society as well as the messages and meanings embedded in the tourist landscape. Tourism emerged as a mass leisure activity in the postwar decades. At the same time, the automobile came to symbolize both access to and escape from the American dream. In the process, tourism became a more complex and complicated cultural experience, making it much more difficult for the government and tourist industries to sell tourism purely in national and patriotic terms.

During the postwar boom years, American tourists inundated highways, resorts, and roadside attractions. In 1949 6.3 million new motor vehicles came off American assembly lines.[18] By 1950 there were more than 40 million automobiles registered in the United States—approximately one car for every three people.[19] In 1948 a little over half of American families owned one or more automobiles. By 1965 more than three-quarters of American families owned one or more automobiles.[20] While automobile use and ownership increased, so did the construction of new roads. In 1945 the federal highway system encompassed approximately 300,000 miles; by 1965 the number of miles had tripled to more than 900,000.[21] In an effort to promote and expand the development of national interstate highways, Congress passed the Interstate Highway Act, which provided federal funding for the construction of 41,000 miles of national highways.[22] Meanwhile, work time was decreasing while vacation time was increasing. In 1950 American workers spent approximately 40 hours per week on the job; a decade later those hours had decreased to 37.5.[23] In addition, American companies increasingly began to institutionalize the paid vacation. Almost half of American wage earners had some form of paid vacation plan by the early 1940s. Despite the fact that paid vacations remained a privilege rather than an entitlement after World War II, by 1949, 93 percent of all union contracts included some provision for a paid holiday.[24]

With increased automobile use and ownership along with federally funded highway construction, and with the expansion of leisure time, tourism emerged as a central social and economic force in the postwar era. In Southern California, for example, where tourism provided the second largest source of income behind the aircraft industry, tourists spent approximately $457 million dollars in 1949.[25] Between 1950 and 1960, in San Diego County alone, tourist revenues more than doubled, rising from $60 million to more than $150 million.[26] And tourist revenues in places such as southern California only continued to increase as the tourist infrastructure expanded during the postwar decades.

Unprecedented prosperity and the expansion and transformation of the white middle class in the decades after World War II paved the way for tourism as a mass leisure activity and simultaneously complicated the messages and meaning of the tourist experience. As European American ethnics moved out of established urban neighborhoods to new residential suburbs increasingly segregated along racial lines, the boundaries of white, middle-class identity expanded and blurred, shifting and complicating the desires and ideals associated with American middle-class culture.[27] The upper middle class that had solidified during the interwar years no longer embodied the divergent social and economic character of this expanding postwar middle class. Large corporations adopted strategies of market segmentation and embraced the ideal of a pluralistic buying public in an effort to capitalized on the diverse desires of this expanding middle class. As one historian has argued, "The landscape of mass consumption created a metropolitan society in which people were no longer brought together in central marketplaces and the parks, streets and public buildings that surrounded them but, rather, were separated by class, gender, and race in differentiated commercial sub-entities."[28] Just as residential suburbs and the public marketplace became more segmented along class and racial lines, so the tourist landscape shifted from a predominantly white, middle-class space to a series of distinct landscapes and places catering to diverse constituencies. The established canon of tourist attractions, including national parks, historic sights, and vacation resorts, that had emerged during the early decades of the twentieth century now had to compete with an extensive variety of tourist destinations, including theme parks, roadside attractions, and rising numbers of ski resorts and seaside getaways.[29] Places such as Disneyland, which opened in Anaheim, California, in 1955, epitomized a new form of tourist destination that catered predominantly to amusement rather than cultural uplift or identity.[30] Recreational and entertainment tourism embodied in places such as Aspen, Vail, and Steamboat Springs, Colorado, as well as Las Vegas and Disneyland, came to dominate the tourist industry.[31] Simultaneously, widespread prosperity better enabled local and regional interests to vie with national corporations for the tourist dollar. Places such as Wall Drug, which began to flourish along what would become U.S. Highway 80 in the postwar era, offered a novel local attraction for automobile tourists who became bored by the monotony of long-distance highway driving. What one historian has described as the roadside colossus—gigantic statues and buildings in the shape of animals, giants, teepees, and igloos, among other novel forms—emerged as novel local tourist attractions in the postwar era.[32] Through this process national tourism gave way to a much more complicated and diverse melange of tourist experiences that catered more to individual desires than national ideals.

The rise of mass tourism finalized the transformation of tourism from a cultural experience to a more recreational and therapeutic experience. At the same time, the messages and meanings embedded in the tourist landscape also shifted. As the automobile emerged as the dominant form of transportation, the highway became the central venue for travel of all kinds. Long-distance driving came to embody much more than a tourist opportunity; the road came to symbolize the potential for both escape and pursuit. It offered the promise of individual mobility. It manifested an ideal of freedom and retreat. As such, the American road became both an American icon and a countercultural refuge. The notion of the cross-country tour as a patriotic ritual of American citizenship became increasingly more problematic as Americans took to the road in search of and to escape from the American dream.

"Lord, I'm going down the road feeling bad," began a Woody Guthrie song that sought to draw attention to the plight of thousands of Dustbowl refugees who had been forced off their farms in the 1930s. One historian has estimated that "almost a million plains people left their farms in the first half of the decade, and 2.5 million left after 1935."[33] Crippled by excessive mortgages and widespread soil erosion brought on by mechanized cash-crop agriculture devastated by drought, farm families across the Great Plains loaded old cars and trucks with what belongings they could carry and took to the road in search of a chance to start over. Roadside and municipal camp grounds that had once been the enclaves of middle-class automobile tourists and various professional travelers, were transformed into overcrowded drought refugee camps commonly known as "Hoovervilles." California, which had actively promoted itself as a tourist paradise, attracted hundreds of thousands of Dustbowl refugees who sought to begin their lives anew in the land of sunshine but ended up as poorly paid migrant workers beholden to the agricultural industry. Okies, as they were commonly known, ultimately turned to the road for some of the same reasons as earlier tourists: they sought its freedom. In so doing, however, they transformed the messages and meanings of the tourist

Photograph by Dorothea Lange, *Untitled* (c. 1937). Farm Security Administration/
Office of War Information Photographic Collection, LC-USF 34-018620-CDLC.
(Courtesy of the Library of Congress)

landscape and the tourist experience. Whereas middle-class tourists sought a
temporary escape from workaday routines and relied on specialized gadgets
and gear to enhance their travel experience, Dustbowl refugees, forced to
abandon their farms, sought a chance to begin again. They turned to the road
as a last resort, and many broke down, ran out of money and gas, or lost hope
without ever reaching a final destination. For them roadside camping was a
necessity rather than an amusement. No longer an extension of controlled
middle-class space, the road now became a refuge for those who could not afford the promises of middle-class culture. Dustbowl migrants and other Depression era casualties left a lasting legacy in transgressing what had been the
confines of the tourist landscape; the road became more than a venue for discovering the American dream. Now it also became a place of escape from a
failed American dream.

On 17 July 1947, Jack Kerouac, a Columbia University dropout who had spent two months in basic training, served in the merchant marine, weathered a rocky marriage, and taken to heavy drinking and Benzedrine use with his "beat" friends in New York City, set out from Bearsville, New York, to hitchhike across the country first to Denver and then on to California. He spent his first day stranded in the rain and ended up taking a Greyhound back to New York City and on to Chicago before he actually succeeded in hitchhiking from Joliet, Illinois, to Denver. Still, Kerouac eventually got "on the road," and between 1947 and 1950 he traveled across country and back four separate times, ranging between New York, Denver, San Francisco, Los Angeles, New Orleans, and Mexico City, with many stops in between. He spent his time searching for "kicks," hooking up with friends, working odd jobs, picking up girls, and observing the people and places of America. His novel cum memoir, *On the Road*, captures the allure of the road and the automobile for a generation numbed by the malaise and blandness of postwar suburban culture. As one literary historian has argued, "It is the infectious enthusiasm of his hitchhiking accounts that encouraged thousands of young people to follow him down that road" in the postwar era.[34] For Kerouac the road offered the chance to observe the real America of pool halls and cheap hotel rooms, cornfields and prairie, Greyhound bus stations and passed-over small towns. He presented a view of American from a speeding automobile. For the children of the postwar era, *On the Road* revealed the promise of escape from the restricting conformity of middle-class suburbs and the routine monotony of mainstream workaday America. As a personal rite of passage, Kerouac's journey was far removed from the ideal of tourism as a patriotic ritual of citizenship. Rather than celebrating the triumphs of American culture, Kerouac embraced downtrodden farmers and workers, social outcasts and deviants; he sought out and documented the underside of America. He built on the legacy of escape that had been laid by Dustbowl refugees and transformed it into a quest for personal freedom that tapped into the alienation and restlessness of white suburban youth. In so doing, he helped transform the road into a liminal countercultural space at odds with the marketed tourist landscape and mainstream American culture.

In many ways *On the Road* signaled the end of national tourism. Although tourist industries and government proponents would seek to revive the ideal of national tourism during the postwar era, the emergence of mass tourism, with its emphasis on recreational and therapeutic escape, combined with the developing image of the road as both commercial strip and countercultural space, eclipsed the ideal of national tourism. Amid widespread prosperity and increasing emphasis on personal self-realization, tourism emerged as more of a rite of passage than a ritual of citizenship. Although these tendencies were in the making during the nineteen teens and twenties, it would take the unprecedented economic boom of the postwar era to finalize the emergence of a mass consumer culture in the United States and completely transform the touring experience. Widespread automobile ownership, standardized interstate highways, franchised motels and restaurants, affordable jet service, and a host of other travel amenities facilitated a new type of travel experience. Tourism was no longer a romantic middle-class journey shaped by a dialogue about national identity and personal discovery. Postwar tourists no longer felt the need to connect with a national ideal of collective memory and tradition. Rather, tourism emerged as the ultimate quest for self-indulgent individual pleasure and hedonistic personal freedom in a culture of mass consumption that revolved around spectacle, fantasy, and desire. Building on and adding to the postwar promises of television, widespread automobile ownership, and suburbanization, tourism now combined the possibilities of abundance with the desire for escape. Embodying the contradictions of the postmodern age, it simultaneously reaffirmed the triumph of mass consumer culture and provided an antidote to it.

ACKNOWLEDGMENTS

I am tempted to trace my interest in the American tourist landscape to a long drive from Cincinnati, Ohio, to Aspen, Colorado, that my family took in the mid-1970s. As the youngest passenger, I was relegated to the hatchback space of an ailing AMC Hornet and took in a backward view of the midwestern landscape of Indiana, Illinois, Missouri, Kansas, and Colorado as it unfolded along Interstate 70. I missed that first dramatic view of the snow-clad Rocky Mountain peaks shimmering over the prairie. In some ways this project and the many trips I have taken along the way have been an attempt to compensate for that missed view. However, if that childhood journey captured my imagination, my work in the Program in American Civilization at Harvard University under the direction of John R. Stilgoe and Werner Sollors allowed me to transform that latent curiosity into a program of scholarly research and interest that has sustained this project as it has evolved from dissertation to book.

Along this intellectual journey I have benefited immeasurably from the work, knowledge, and support of many individuals and institutions. Financial support from the Summer Travel Fund of the Program in American Civilization, the Smithsonian Institution's National Museum of American History, the Program in Landscape Architecture at Dumbarton Oaks, and the James J. Hill Reference Library in St. Paul, Minnesota, provided access to research material and allowed me to complete my dissertation. A Summer Research Grant from the University of North Carolina at Wilmington and a Dorothy Collins Brown and Fletcher Jones Foundation Fellowship from the Huntington Library, San Marino, California, helped me to reframe and expand my research for the book. A year-long Mellon Post Doctoral Research Fellowship from the Huntington Library provided the needed research and writing time to complete the revised manuscript.

I owe considerable thanks to many archivists, curators, and librarians who have helped me throughout the course of this project. I extend special thanks to the staffs at the Archives Center and the library at the National Museum of American History; Dumbarton Oaks; the Library of Congress; the National Archives; the Special Collections Department at the Perkins Library at Duke University; the James J. Hill Reference Library; the Minnesota Historical Society, St. Paul; the Special Collections Department at the Bancroft Library at the University of California, Berkeley; and the Huntington Library. In particular, I would like to thank Peter Blodgett, Fath Ruffins, Jennifer Watts, and Roger White for alerting me to materials relevant to the project in their respective collections and for keeping a constant eye out for new and novel sources.

The intellectual debt accrued during the course of this project has been extensive. I am grateful to William Deverell, Charles McGovern, and Hal Rothman, who have provided crucial guidance and support throughout this project; to Peter Blodgett and Roger White, who shared their own research on tourism; and to Peter Blodgett, Susan Davis, Phoebe Kropp, and Terrence Young, who read parts of the manuscript and provided insightful comments. I also thank Leah Dilworth, Carolyn Goldstein, Mark Harvey, Doug Rossinow, Timothy Spears, Mark Spence, Jeffrey Stine, Paul Sutter, Elizabeth White, and Joachim Wolschke-Bullman for reading various parts of the thesis at various stages of the project; and Frances McMillen, Sharon Vriend, and

Ann Margaret Webb for research assistance. I thank my colleagues at Miami University in Oxford, Ohio, Andrew Cayton and Peter Williams, for reading the completed draft of the manuscript and helping me get it off to the press. The editorial staff at the Smithsonian Institution Press, Mark Hirsch and Mary De Young, have also helped smooth the transition from manuscript to book. In particular I would like to thank Mark Hirsch for his continued encouragement and Karin Kaufman for her copy-editing acumen. Finally, I thank Mark Hilgendorf for his longstanding inspiration.

I have presented various portions of this research at numerous conferences, and this book has greatly benefited from the numerous comments and provocative discussions provided by these scholarly forums. In addition, a version of chapter 3 entitled "Seeing the *Nature* of America: The National Parks as National Assets, 1914–1929" has been published in *Being Elsewhere: Tourism, Consumer Culture and Identity in Modern Europe and North America*, edited by Shelly Baranowski and Ellen Furlough (Ann Arbor: University of Michigan Press, 2001); and a version of chapter 6 entitled "Seeing America First: The Search for Identity in the Tourist Landscape" has been published in *Seeing and Being Seen*, edited by Patrick T. Long and David M. Wrobel (Lawrence: University of Kansas Press, 2001).

Rooted in the lasting memory of a family vacation, this project has extended from and depended on the encouragement and support of my family. In her life my grandmother, Elizabeth Blake Shaffer, provided unqualified support of my education. I would also like to thank my parents, Peggy and Dick Palmer, who always told me to press on, and my sisters, Blake Gustafson and Mary Palmer, who egged me on. Most of all I thank my husband, Ben Jacks. This book would not exist without him. As many tourists lamented the inability to put their feelings and experiences into words, I am acutely aware that no simple line of thanks could ever convey my love and gratitude. I dedicate this book to him and our daughter Callie in the hope that we will have many happy journeys to come.

NOTES

INTRODUCTION

1. Stephen Merritt, "From Ocean to Ocean or Across and Around the Country. Being an account of the Raymond and Whitcomb Pacific, North West and Alaska, Excursion of 1892. Including the Yosemite Valley and the Yellowstone Park," typewritten travel journal, 1892, pt. 1, p. 1, Western Manuscript Collections, Huntington Library, San Marino, California (hereafter cited as Western Manuscript Collections).

2. Merritt, "From Ocean to Ocean," 17.

3. Jack Kerouac, *On the Road* (New York: Viking, 1957), 3.

4. John Sears provides an assessment of this nineteenth-century form of secular pilgrimage to the "sacred places" of America. See John Sears, *Sacred Places: American Tourist Attractions in the Nineteenth Century* (New York: Oxford, 1989).

5. See Henri Levebrve, *The Production of Space*, trans. Donald Nicholson-Smith

(Cambridge, Mass.: Blackwell, 1991), for the ways in which culture is mapped onto the landscape.

6. The concepts of nation and nationalism as they were worked out in the United States raise a number of complicated issues that scholars are still in the process of sorting out. Throughout their history, Americans have been engaged in the cultural invention of the United States as a unified nation. In the early years of the Republic, political and cultural nationalism were tied to the Revolutionary principles and practices of democracy. However, as the nation-state began to expand, national consciousness and the concept of the nation became more complicated. Shifting territorial boundaries, an influx of diverse immigrants seeking citizenship, a growing commercial infrastructure, and the development of a more centralized federal government added new dimensions to the idea of the nation and the ideologies of nationalism. The political notion of the United States as a nation formed and sustained by democratic contract became intertwined with a more romantic ideal of the nation grounded on the traditions and mythologies of a unified culture rooted in common traditions and a bounded territory. For surveys of American nationalism, see Merle Curti, *The Roots of American Loyalty* (New York: Columbia University Press, 1946); Michael Kammen, *Mystic Chords of Memory: The Transformation of Tradition in American Culture* (New York: Vintage, 1993); and Hans Kohn, *American Nationalism: An Interpretive Essay* (New York: Macmillan, 1957). See also John Higham, *Strangers in the Land: Patterns of American Nativism, 1860–1925* (New York: Atheneum, 1985), 194–233; Philip Gleason, "American Identity and Americanization," in *Concepts of Ethnicity* (Cambridge: Belknap Press, 1982), 80–109. My own ideas about nation and nationalism have been shaped predominantly by the following scholarly works: Benedict Anderson, *Imagined Communities: Reflections on the Origin and Spread of Nationalism*, rev. ed. (New York: Verso, 1991); Homi K. Bhabha, ed., *Nation and Narration* (New York: Routledge, 1990); Ernest Gellner, *Nations and Nationalism* (Ithaca, N.Y.: Cornell University Press, 1983; Eric Hobsbawm and Terence Ranger, eds., *The Invention of Tradition* (New York: Cambridge University Press, 1983); Patrick Wright, *On Living in an Old Country: The National Past in Contemporary Britain* (New York: Verso, 1985); and Wilbur Zelinsky, *Nation into State: The Shifting Symbolic Foundations of American Nationalism* (Chapel Hill: University of North Carolina Press, 1988).

7. George Lipsitz, *Time Passages: Collective Memory and American Popular Culture* (Minneapolis: University of Minnesota Press, 1990), 8.

8. For the idea of "nature's nation," see Perry Miller, "The Romantic Dilemma in American Nationalism and the Concept of Nature," in *Nature's Nation*, by Perry Miller (Cambridge: Belknap Press, 1967), 197–207. See also Gellner, *Nations and Nationalism*, for a discussion of the ways in which the nation is inscribed "in the nature of things" (49).

9. Dean MacCannell, *The Tourist: A New Theory of the Leisure Class* (New York: Schocken Books, 1976), 24.

10. The scholarship on these topics—the search for American identity, the development of a national consumer culture, and the emergence of the United States as modern, urban-industrial nation-state—is too vast to cite in one brief footnote. For recent scholarship addressing the search for American identity, see David Thelen and Frederick E. Hoxie, eds., *Discovering American: Essays on the Search for an Identity* (Urbana: University of Illinois Press, 1994). For the historiography of the rise of consumer culture, see Jean-Christophe Agnew, "Coming Up for Air: Consumer Culture in Historical Perspective," in *Consumption and the World of Goods*, ed. John Brewer and Roy Porter (New York: Routledge, 1993), and Daniel Miller, ed., *Acknowledging Consumption: A Review of New Studies* (New York: Routledge, 1995). For a classic study of the emergence of the United States as a modern nation-state, see Alan Trachtenberg, *The Incorporation of America: Culture and Society in the Gilded Age* (New York: Hill & Wang, 1982).

11. My conceptualization of this shift from public space to marketplace and republican citizen to patriotic consumer grows out of my readings of the following works: Jürgen Habermas, *The Structural Transformation of the Public Sphere: An Inquiry into a Category of Bourgeois Society*, trans. Thomas Burger (Cambridge: MIT Press, 1991); Levebrve, *Production of Space*; Graham Murdock, "Citizens, Consumers, and Public Culture," in *Media Cultures: Reappraising Transnational Media*, ed. Michael Skovmand and Kim Christian Schroder (New York: Verso, 1992), 17–41; Raymond Williams, "Advertising: The Magic System," in *Problems in Materialism and Culture: Selected Essays*, by Raymond Williams (New York: Verso, 1980), 170–95; and Raymond Williams, *Television: Technology and Cultural Form* (New York: Shocken, 1977).

I. THE CONTINENT SPANNED

1. Samuel Bowles, *Across the Continent: A Summer's Journey to the Rocky Mountains, the Mormons, and the Pacific States with Speaker Colfax* (New York: Hurd & Houghton, 1865), 1–2.

2. In his seminal essay "From Traveler to Tourist: The Lost Art of Travel," Daniel Boorstin defines tourism as "a pseudo-event," in opposition to the more authentic and educational experience of nineteenth-century travel, thus distinguishing tourism from travel. See Daniel J. Boorstin, "From Traveler to Tourist: The Lost Art of Travel," in *The Image: A Guide to Pseudo-Events in America* (New York: Atheneum, 1980), 79. I disagree with the underlying dualism and class implications of this framework. From my perspective, tourism represents a particular type of travel in which one journeys from place to place for the pleasures of sightseeing.

3. Bowles, *Across the Continent*, ix.

4. For a contextual overview of Bowles's journey, see Anne Farrar Hyde, *An American Vision: Far Western Landscape and National Culture, 1820–1920* (New York: New York University Press, 1990), 67–70.

5. Samuel Bowles, *Our New West: Records of Travel Between the Mississippi River and the Pacific Ocean* (Hartford, Conn.: Hartford Publishing, 1869), vi. Note that *Our New West*, and other guides published by Bowels, including *The Switzerland of America*, reprint much of the information published in *Across the Continent*.

6. Bowles, *Our New West*, vi, xi, and ix–x.

7. Ibid., 195, 31, 45, 50, 11, 57, 63, 67, and 73.

8. Ibid., 96, 99, 385, and 523.

9. Ibid., 195.

10. Samuel Bowles, *The Pacific Railroad—Open* (Boston: Fields, Osgood, 1869), 116–17.

11. *The Oxford English Dictionary*, 2d ed. (Oxford: Clarendon Press, 1989), 18:304. See also Boorstin, "From Traveler to Tourist," 85.

12. For example, historian Hal K. Rothman has argued that tourism is a "modern and postmodern endeavor" that did not begin to emerge until the nineteenth century. See Hal K. Rothman, *Devil's Bargains: Tourism in the Twentieth-Century American West* (Lawrence: University of Kansas Press, 1998), 30. Cindy S. Aron argues that tourism is "a type of vacation rather than a synonym for vacationing" (Cindy S. Aron, *Working at Play: A History of Vacations in the United States* [New York: Oxford, 1999], 128).

13. *Oxford English Dictionary* 18:306.

14. For a history of the Grand Tour of Europe, see Jeremy Black, *The British Abroad: The Grand Tour in the Eighteenth Century* (New York: St. Martin's Press, 1992).

15. *Oxford English Dictionary* 18:306.

16. Dona Brown, *Inventing New England: Regional Tourism in the Nineteenth Century* (Washington, D.C.: Smithsonian Institution Press, 1995), 16–23.

17. Timothy Dwight, *Travels in New England and New York, 1821–22*, ed. Barbara Miller Solomon (Cambridge: Harvard University Press, 1969).

18. For a history of nineteenth-century tourism in the United States, see Aron, *Working at Play*, 127–55; Brown, *Inventing New England*; Hans Huth, *Nature and the American: Three Centuries of Changing Attitudes*, rev. ed. (Lincoln: University of Nebraska Press, 1990), 71–86; and Sears, *Sacred Places*.

19. For a history of picturesque tours, see Judith Alder, "Origins of Sightseeing," *Annals of Tourism Research* 16, no. 1 (1989): 7–29; Gina Crandall, *Nature Pictorialized: "The View" in Landscape History* (Baltimore: Johns Hopkins University Press, 1993); John Dixon Hunt, *Gardens and the Picturesque: Studies in the History of Landscape Architecture* (Cambridge: MIT Press, 1992), 5; and Barbara Maria Stafford, *Voyage into*

Substance: Art, Science, Nature and the Illustrated Travel Account, 1760–1840 (Cambridge: MIT Press, 1984), 3–13.

20. For a discussion of the role of artists and intellectuals in articulating an ideal of scenic nationalism, see Huth, *Nature and the American*, 30–53; Joni Kinsey, *Thomas Moran and the Surveying of the American West* (Washington, D.C.: Smithsonian Institution Press, 1992); David Lowenthal, "The Place of the Past in the American Landscape," in *Geographies of the Mind*, ed. David Lowenthal and Martyn J. Bow (New York: Oxford University Press, 1976), 89–117; Angela Miller, *The Empire of the Eye: Landscape Representation and American Cultural Politics, 1825–1875* (Ithaca, N.Y.: Cornell University Press, 1993); Miller, "Romantic Dilemma in American Nationalism," 197–207; Roderick Nash, *Wilderness and the American Mind,* 3d ed. (New Haven, Conn.: Yale University Press, 1982), 44–95; Barbara Novak, *Nature and Culture: American Landscape and Painting, 1825–1875* (New York: Oxford, 1980); Earl Pomeroy, *In Search of the Golden West: The Tourist in Western America* (Lincoln: University of Nebraska Press, 1990), 31–72; and Alfred Runte, *National Parks: The American Experience,* 3d ed. (Lincoln: University of Nebraska Press, 1997), 11–32.

21. Brown, *Inventing New England,* 24–25; Huth, *Nature and the American,* 71–86; Sears, *Sacred Places,* 3–4.

22. Aron, *Working at Play,* 127–55; Brown, *Inventing New England;* and Sears, *Sacred Places.*

23. Sears, *Scared Places;* see also Aron, *Working at Play,* 143.

24. Trachtenberg, *Incorporation of America;* see also Susan Strasser, *Satisfaction Guaranteed: The Making of the American Mass Market* (Washington, D.C.: Smithsonian Institution Press, 1995); Martin J. Sklar, *The Corporate Reconstruction of American Capitalism, 1890–1916: The Market, the Law and Politics* (Cambridge: Cambridge University Press, 1988); and Wilber Zelinsky, *Nation into State: The Shifting Symbolic Foundations of American Nationalism* (Chapel Hill: University of North Carolina Press, 1988).

25. Stephen Kern, *The Culture of Time and Space, 1880–1918* (Cambridge: Harvard University Press, 1983).

26. Robert G. Athearn, *The Mythic West in Twentieth-Century America* (Lawrence: University of Kansas Press, 1986); Rothman, *Devil's Bargains,* 39–44; Richard Slotkin, *The Fatal Environment: The Myth of the Frontier in the Age of Industrialization* (New York: Atheneum, 1985); Henry Nash Smith, *Virgin Land: The American West as Symbol and Myth.* (Cambridge: Harvard University Press, 1970); and William Truettner, ed., *The West as America: Reinterpreting Images of the Frontier* (Washington, D.C.: Smithsonian Institution Press, 1991).

27. For example, southern resorts started to become popular with northerners who sought to escape the growing masses at northeastern resorts. See C. Brenden Martin, "Selling the Southern Highlands: Tourism and Community Development in the Mountain South" (Ph.D. diss., University of Tennessee, 1997), and Nina Sil-

ber, *The Romance of Reunion: Northerners and the South, 1865–1900* (Chapel Hill: University of North Carolina Press, 1993) 66–92.

28. Pomeroy, *In Search of the Golden West*, 7–10; Hyde, *American Vision*, 108.

29. George A. Crofutt, *Great Trans-Continental Railroad Guide* (Chicago: Geo. A. Crofutt, 1869), title page. J. Valerie Fifer argues that Crofutt was instrumental in popularizing the term "transcontinental." See J. Valerie Fifer, *American Progress: The Growth of The Transport, Tourist, and Information Industries in the Nineteenth-Century West* (Chester, Conn.: Globe Pequot Press, 1988), 168–73.

30. Crofutt, *Great Trans-Continental Railroad Guide*, title page.

31. Ibid., n.p.

32. Fifer, *American Progress*, 151–90. Note that Crofutt's guide was revised and reissued as Crofutt's *New Overland Tourist* from 1878 to 1884.

33. George A. Crofutt, *New Overland Tourist and Pacific Coast Guide* (Chicago: Overland Publishing, 1878), n.p.

34. Fifer, *American Progress*, 210–11.

35. Crofutt, *New Overland Tourist*, 304.

36. For an overview of western guidebooks, see Robert G. Waite, "Over the Ranges to the Golden Gate: Tourist Guides to the West, 1880–1920," *Journal of the West* 31 (April 1992): 103–13.

37. Crofutt, *Great Trans-Continental Railroad Guide* (1869), 18.

38. Stanley Wood, *Over the Range to the Golden Gate: A Complete Tourist's Guide to Colorado, New Mexico, Utah, Nevada, California, Oregon, Puget Sound, and the Great Northwest* (Chicago: R. R. Donnelley & Sons, 1904), 5.

39. John F. Stover, *American Railroads*, 2d ed. (Chicago: University of Chicago Press, 1997), 61–95.

40. For the history of early touring agencies and guidebooks, see Fifer, *American Progress*, 183, 301, 331–32; and Pomeroy, *In Search of the Golden West*, 13–30. For a history of the Fred Harvey/Santa Fe partnership, see Leah Dilworth, *Imagining Indians in the Southwest: Persistent Visions of a Primitive Past* (Washington, D.C.: Smithsonian Institution Press, 1996), 77–124; and Marta Weigle and Barbara Babcock, eds., *The Great Southwest of the Fred Harvey Company and the Santa Fe Railway* (Phoenix: Heard Museum, 1996). For a history of the Denver and Rio Grande's publicity campaigns, see Richard G. Athearn, *Rebel of the Rockies: A History of the Denver and Rio Grande Western Railway* (New Haven, Conn.: Yale University Press, 1960), 187. For a history of railroad promotion, see Carlos A. Schwantes, *Railroad Signatures across the Pacific Northwest* (Seattle: University of Washington Press, 1993), "Landscapes of Opportunity: Phases of Railroad Promotion of the Pacific Northwest," *Montana* 43 (1993): 38–51; and "Tourists in Wonderland: Early Railroad Tourism in the Pacific Northwest," *Columbia* 7 (1993/94), 22–30.

41. For a history of Thomas Cook, see Edmund Swinglehurst, *The Romantic Journey: The Story of Thomas Cook and Victorian Travel* (New York: Harper and Row, 1974). See also Fifer, *American Progress*, 205–7, 301–14; and Hugh DeSantis, "The Democratization of Travel: The Travel Agent in American History," *Journal of American Culture* 1 (Spring 1978): 1–17.

42. There is no complete history of the Raymond and Whitcomb. See Fifer, *American Progress*, 293–94, 305, 311–14; Pomeroy, *In Search of the Golden West*, 13–17; and DeSantis, "Democratization of Travel."

43. Raymond and Whitcomb, *Raymond's Vacation Excursions: Four Grand Winter Trips to California* (Boston, 1886), 8–9.

44. Raymond and Whitcomb, *Vacation Excursions: Five Grand Summer Trips for July 1882* (Boston, 1882), 3–4.

45. For a description of the site of the new hotel and the landscape, see Raymond and Whitcomb, *Raymond and Whitcomb Vacation Excursions Grand Trip to Colorado, California and the Pacific Northwest* (Boston, 1884), 15. See also Fifer, *American Progress*, 293–94.

46. Raymond and Whitcomb, *A Winter Trip to California with a Sojourn of Five Months at the Famous Winter Health and Pleasure Resort of the Pacific Coast, the Elegant Hotel Del Monte, Monterey, Cal.* (Boston, 1883), title page.

47. Raymond and Whitcomb, *Raymond's Vacation Excursions: A Winter in California* (Boston, 1888).

48. For example, see Raymond and Whitcomb, *Raymond's Vacation Excursions: Three Spring and Early Summer Tours* (Boston, 1891).

49. Raymond and Whitcomb, *Raymond's Vacation Excursions: Three Spring and Early Summer Tours* (Boston, 1891), 5.

50. Merritt, "From Ocean to Ocean," 24–25. For accounts focusing on the social aspects of Raymond and Whitcomb excursions, see Amy Bridges, "Journal Kept on a Raymond Excursion from Massachusetts to California and Return Including a Three Month Stay at the Raymond Hotel in South Pasadena, the Del Monte, and San Francisco, etc. 1886–1887," diary, Western Manuscript Collections; and Augustus F. Tripp, "Notes of an Excursion to California in the Winter and Spring of 1893," diary, 1893, Western Manuscript Collections.

51. "Editorial Comments," *Harper's Weekly*, 2 December 1905, 1731.

52. For the promotion and development of scenic wonders in the West, see Fifer, *American Progress*; William H. Goetzmann, *Exploration and Empire: The Explorer and the Scientist in the Winning of the American West* (New York: Knopf, 1966); William H. Goetzmann and William N. Goetzmann, *The West of the Imagination* (New York: Norton 1989); Peter B. Hales, *William Henry Jackson and the Transformation of the American Landscape* (Philadelphia: Temple University Press, 1988); Huth, *Na-*

ture and the American, 105–91; Hyde, *American Vision;* Nash, *Wilderness and the American Mind,* 108–60; Pomeroy, *In Search of the Golden West* and *The Pacific Slope: A History of California, Oregon, Washington, Idaho, Utah, and Nevada* (New York: Knopf, 1965), 334–52; Alfred Runte, *Trains of Discovery: Western Railroads and the National Parks* (Flagstaff, Ariz.: Northland Press, 1984); Alfred Runte, "Promoting Wonderland: Western Railroads and the Evolution of National Park Advertising," *Journal of the West* 31 (January 1992): 43–48; Runte, *National Parks;* Schwantes, *Railroad Signatures;* Sears, *Sacred Places,* 122–81; and Truettner, *West as America,* 237–343.

53. Huth, *Nature and the American,* 155–58; and Pomeroy, *In Search of the Golden West,* 51–52.

54. Pomeroy, *In Search of the Golden West,* 60–72; Hyde, *American Vision,* 147–90; Huth, *Nature and the American,* 148–64; Nash, *Wilderness and the American Mind,* 141–60.

55. Pomeroy, *In Search of the Golden West,* 59–60, discusses increased accessibility of western scenery.

56. Runte, *Trains of Discovery,* 24–26, 30–31, and 40.

57. Hyde, *American Vision,* 108; and Pomeroy, *Pacific Slope,* 351–52, and *In Search of the Golden West,* 7–10, discuss the expense of tourist travel.

58. "Real Work Has Only Now Begun," *Salt Lake Tribune,* 28 January 1906.

59. "Governors, Delegates Welcome!" *Salt Lake Tribune,* 26 January 1906.

60. Marguerite S. Shaffer, "'See America First': Re-Envisioning Nation and Region through Western Tourism," *Pacific Historical Review* 65 (November 1996): 559–81.

61. Clipping, *Salt Lake City Telegram,* 24 October 1905, Scrapbook 3, and Salt Lake City Commercial Club to Whomever, 24 October 1905, Scrapbook 3, Fisher Sanford Harris Papers, Special Collections, Perkins Library, Duke University, Durham, N.C. (hereafter cited as Harris Papers). For a history of Fisher Harris's use of "See America First," see Shaffer, "See America First."

62. C. F. Carter to Salt Lake City Commercial Club, 19 October 1905, Scrapbook 2, 1905–1906, Harris Papers.

63. Salt Lake City Commercial Club, *The "See America First" Conference, Salt Lake City, Utah, January 25–26, 1906* (Salt Lake City: Tribune Job Printing 1906) (quotations are on 5–6, 9, and 11–13).

64. There were mixed responses to the plan adopted at the conference. Some felt that the plans ratified by the delegates were too vague (see "See America's Convention," *Salt Lake Tribune,* 28 January 1906). Others felt that it would be impossible to convince strong-willed and wealthy Americans to travel in the West (see "Editorial Scores: 'See America First,'" *New York Times,* 1 April 1906; and editorial, *Nation* 82 [25 January 1906]: 58).

65. "To Crowd Work of 'See America First,'" *Salt Lake Tribune,* 8 February 1906.

66. "Fisher Harris Is Back from the East," *Salt Lake Tribune*, 5 April 1906, Scrapbooks 1 and 2, Harris Papers, include memorabilia and clippings from his trip.

67. "Fisher Harris Is Back from the East."

68. For a brief overview of Southern Pacific Railroad's *Sunset* magazine, see Frank Luther Mott, *A History of American Magazines, 1885–1905* (Cambridge: Harvard University Press, 1957), 4:105, and Theodore Peterson, *Magazines in the Twentieth Century* (Urbana: University of Illinois Press, 1956), 343–42.

69. Mott, *History of American Magazines* 4:77, discusses urban weeklies. Salt Lake City's urban weekly was originally called *Truth*. It began publication in 1903 and was edited by John W. Huges until January 1908. Parley P. Jensen took over as editor in March 1908, and in May 1908 the magazine's name was changed to *Western Weekly*. In December 1908, the magazine became the official organ of the See America First League and adopted a new name, *Western Monthly*, which reflected its new monthly format.

70. See the *Union List of Serials* for the complete publication history of the *Western Monthly*. See also Parely P. Jenson, "Current Comments and Announcements," *Western Monthly*, December 1908, 87, for the announcement that the magazine was becoming the "Official Organ of the See America First League."

71. For Harris's illness, see clipping, *Salt Lake Herald*, 8 July 1907, Clippings 1907–1925, Harris Papers. See also Tom Richardson to Fisher Harris, 4 October 1907, and Charles F. Burton to Fisher Harris, 12 July 1906, Harris Papers.

72. For a complete history of the See America First slogan, see Marguerite S. Shaffer, "See American First: Tourism and National Identity, 1905–1930" (Ph.D. diss., Harvard University, 1994) and "Negotiating National Identity: Western Tourism and "See America First," in *Reopening the American West: Environment and Culture in the Western Past and Present*, ed. Hal K. Rothman (Tucson: University of Arizona Press, 1998), 122–51.

73. "See America First Association" pamphlet enclosure with letter M. L. H. Odea to Louis W. Hill, 24 June 1912, President's Office Subject Files: Advertising, 1903–1916, File 3903, Great Northern Railway Records, Minnesota Historical Society, St. Paul (hereafter cited as GNRR).

74. "See America First Association," enclosure M. L. H. Odea to Louis W. Hill, 24 June 1912, President's Office Subject Files: Advertising, 1903–1916, File 3903, GNRR.

75. "See America First Strongly Indorsed," *See America First*, March 1912, 24.

76. "Mission of SEE AMERICA FIRST," *See America First*, March 1912, 2.

77. Trans-Mississippi Commercial Congress, *Offficial Proceedings of the Twenty-Third Annual Session of the Trans-Mississippi Commercial Congress* (Kansas City: Edwin J. Becker, 1912), 110–11, and 113. For more information on the Trans-Mississippi Commercial Congress, see Robert W. Rydell, "The Trans-Mississippi and Inter-

national Exposition: To Work Out the Problem of Universal Civilization," *American Quarterly* 33 (Winter 1981): 587–607.

78. Trans-Mississippi Commercial Congress, *Offficial Proceedings of the Twenty-Third Annual Session*, 114, 117, and 125.

79. "In the Lion's Den," *West Coast Magazine*, August 1912, 609.

80. Lummis was cognizant of the See America First slogan before 1912 and had previously identified himself as the originator of the general idea in 1905, when the Salt Lake City Commercial Club began to promote the See America First Conference. In his monthly column in *Out West Magazine* he mentioned his call for Americans to see and know the wonders of the Southwest and wrote, "The newest apostle of this good propaganda is the Commercial Club of Salt Lake City, a corporation whose motto is 'See Europe if you will, but see America first.'" After summarizing the Commercial Club's argument and promotional ideas, he went on to acknowledge, "The movement is a laudable one." Unlike his 1912 assertion, he did not imply that he had authored the slogan. See "Wakening a Sober Patriotism," *Out West Magazine*, December 1905, 592.

81. As proof of this assertion, he quoted the original introduction: "We live in the most wonderful of lands; and one of the most wonderful things in it is that we as Americans find so little to wonder at. . . . There is a part of America,—a part even of the United States—of which Americans know as little as they do of inner Africa, and of which too many of them are much less interested to learn. . . . I hope to live to see Americans proud of knowing America, and ashamed not to know it; and it is to my countrymen that I look for the patriotism to effect so needed a change" (Charles F. Lummis, *Some Strange Corners of Our Country: The Wonderland of the Southwest* [Tucson: University of Arizona Press, 1989], 1–2).

82. John A. Jakle, *The Tourist: Travel in Twentieth Century North America* (Lincoln: University of Nebraska Press, 1985), 102.

83. For an overview of the Panama-Pacific International Exposition, see Burton Benedict, *The Anthropology of World's Fairs: San Francisco's Panama Pacific International Exposition of 1915* (Berkeley, Calif.: Scholar Press, 1983), and Robert W. Rydell, *All the World's a Fair* (Chicago: University of Chicago Press, 1984).

84. Charles C. Moore, "San Francisco and the Exposition: The Relation of the City to the Nation as Regards the World's Fair," *Sunset*, February 1912, 198.

85. Union Pacific Railroad, *California and the Expositions, 1915* (Union Pacific System, 1915), 16–19, Reel 169, No. 6, Panama-Pacific International Exposition, Worlds Fairs Microfilm Collection, National Museum of American History, Smithsonian Institution, Washington, D.C. (hereafter cited as Worlds Fairs).

86. For descriptions of the various railroad exhibits at the fair, see Robert A. Reid, *The Blue Book: A Comprehensive Official Souvenir View Book of the Panama-Pacific Interna-*

tional Exposition at San Francisco, 2d ed. (Panama-Pacific Exposition Company, 1915), 312, Reel 169, No. 4, Worlds Fairs; Guy Richard Kingsley, "Progress of America's Great Panama Canal Celebration," *Overland Monthly*, October 1914, 6; Hamilton Wright, "The Panama-Pacific Exposition in Its Glorious Prime," *Overland Monthly*, October 1915, 297; and Rydell, *All the World's a Fair*, 227–28.

87. Rydell, *All the World's a Fair*, 219.
88. Gaines M. Foster, *Ghosts of the Confederacy: Defeat, the Lost Cause, and the Emergence of the New South 1865 to 1913* (New York: Oxford University Press, 1987).
89. Andrew R. L. Cayton and Peter S. Onuf, *The Midwest and the Nation: Rethinking the History of America Region* (Bloomington: Indiana University Press, 1990).
90. For a discussion of western regionalism, see Athearn, *Mythic West*; Walter Prescott Webb, *The Great Plains* (Boston: Ginn, 1959); and Donald Worster, "New West, True West: Interpreting the Region's History," *Western Historical Quarterly* 18 (April 1987): 141–56. For a discussion of the myth of the West, see Slotkin, *Fatal Environment*; Smith, *Virgin Land*; and Truettner, *West as America*.
91. For a discussion of the economic relationship between the West and the nation, see William G. Robbins, *Colony and Empire: The Capitalist Transformation of the American West* (Lawrence: University of Kansas Press, 1994).
92. "Great Move to Promote the West," *Salt Lake Tribune*, 5 April 1906.
93. Fisher Harris, "Are the People of the East Growing Effete?" *Western Monthly*, June 1909, 8.
94. Fisher Harris, "Europe vs. America," *Western Monthly*, December 1908, 15.
95. Clipping, *Los Angeles Arrowhead*, December 1905, Scrapbook 3, Harris Papers.
96. Dorothy Ross has argued that republican theory and rhetoric continued to be used to define an ideal of America into the twentieth century. She defines the decades surrounding the turn of the century as a moment of crisis when the balance between the notions of virtue and corruption were threatened by political corruption, plutocracy, social unrest, immigration, economic depression, and the apparent closing of the frontier. See Dorothy Ross, "The Liberal Tradition Revisited and the Republican Tradition Addressed," in *New Directions in American Intellectual History*, ed. John Higham and Paul Conkin (Baltimore: Johns Hopkins University Press, 1977), 116–31. T. J. Jackson Lears has extended this analysis of republicanism by suggesting that it was replaced by the more self-oriented therapeutic ethos. See T. J. Jackson Lears, *No Place of Grace: Antimodernism and the Transformation of American Culture, 1880–1920* (New York: Pantheon, 1981), and "From Salvation to Self-Realization: Advertising and the Therapeutic Roots of the Consumer Culture, 1880–1930," in *The Culture of Consumption: Critical Essays in American History, 1880–1980*, ed. Richard Wightman Fox and T. J. Jackson Lears (New York: Pantheon, 1983), 3–38. The language used by Fisher Harris to define and promote the See America First idea suggests he was

caught up in the transition from the republican ideal to the therapeutic ethos. Not only did he use the language of virtue and corruption characteristic of republicanism to define the See America First ideal, but he also used the language of personal salvation and self-realization characteristic of the therapeutic ethos. This wavering back and forth suggests that he was seeking a way to celebrate the ideal of a republican empire while capitalizing on the newly emerging consumer society.

2. CORPORATE DOMINION

1. "To Advertise Glacier National Park," *St. Paul Pioneer Press Dispatch*, 26 May 1910.
2. Clipping, Herbert J. Smith, "Booming a New National Park," *Printer's Ink*, enclosure of letter H. A. Noble to L. W. Hill, 17 June 1910, President's Office Subject Files: Publicity, File 4325, GNRR.
3. "To Advertise Glacier National Park."
4. The packaging and promotion of tourist attractions by transcontinental railroads followed the same strategies used by other corporations to develop recognizable, or brand name, products that could take advantage of the emerging national market. For a history of these marketing strategies, see Pamela Walker Laird, *Advertising Progress: American Business and the Rise of Consumer Marketing* (Baltimore: Johns Hopkins University Press, 1998); T. J. Jackson Lears, *Fables of Abundance: A Cultural History of Advertising in America* (New York: Basic Books, 1994); Roland Marchand, *Advertising the American Dream: Making Way for Modernity 1920–1940* (Berkeley and Los Angeles: University of California Press, 1985); Roland Marchand, *Creating the Corporate Soul: The Rise of Public Relations and Corporate Imagery in American Big Business* (Berkeley and Los Angeles: University of California Press, 1998); Michael Schudson, *Advertising the Uneasy Persuasion: Its Dubious Impact on American Society* (New York: Basic Books, 1984); and Strasser, *Satisfaction Guaranteed*.
5. See Alfred D. Chandler, *The Visible Hand: The Managerial Revolution in American Business* (Cambridge: Harvard University Press, 1977), 81–187.
6. Brown, *Inventing New England*, 49.
7. Huth, *Nature and the American*, 71–86. See also Sears, *Sacred Places*, and Eric Purchase, *Out of Nowhere: Disaster and Tourism in the White Mountains* (Baltimore: Johns Hopkins University Press, 1999).
8. See Hyde, *American Vision*, 77–130, for promotion of western landscapes. See also Schwantes, *Railroad Signatures*. For early western resorts, see Hyde, *American Vision*, 147–90.
9. Hyde, *American Vision*, quote from page 165; description of hotel, 168–70.
10. Hyde argues that the success of the Del Monte extended from its imitation of European resorts.
11. For the history of the development of Yellowstone, see Mark Daniel Barringer, "Pri-

vate Empire, Public Land: The Rise and Fall of the Yellowstone Park Company" (Ph.D. diss., Texas Christian University, 1997); Richard A. Bartlett, *Yellowstone: A Wilderness Besieged* (Tucson: University of Arizona Press, 1985); Aubrey L. Haines, *The Yellowstone Story: A History of Our First National Park,* 2 vols. (Yellowstone National Park, Wyo.: Yellowstone Library and Museum Association in Cooperation with Colorado University Press, 1977); and Chris J. Magoc, *Yellowstone: The Creation and Selling of an American Landscape, 1870–1903* (Albuquerque: University of New Mexico Press, 1999).

12. N. P. Langford, "The Wonders of the Yellowstone," *Scribner's Monthly,* June 1871, 128.

13. *Scribner's* loaned Moran another five hundred dollars and Moran repaid Cooke with sixteen water colors of Yellowstone landscapes. (See Kinsey, *Thomas Moran,* 51; Runte, *National Parks,* 39; and Runte, *Trains of Discovery,* 17–18.)

14. U.S. Statutes at Large, 17 (1872), 32–33, quoted in Runte, *National Parks,* 46.

15. Runte, *National Parks,* 46.

16. Magoc, *Yellowstone,* 61–63; Bartlett, *Yellowstone,* 125–55; Barringer, "Private Empire, Public Land," 16–24.

17. Magoc, *Yellowstone,* 112–19; Bartlett, *Yellowstone,* 137–209; Barringer, "Private Empire, Public Land," 25–97.

18. For the work of Robert C. Reamer, see David Leavengood, "A Sense of Shelter: Robert C. Reamer in Yellowstone National Park," *Pacific Historical Review* 54 (November 1985): 495–513.

19. Rustic architecture drew on the late-nineteenth-century precedents of the great camps of the Adirondacks, the work of Charles and Henry Greene in Southern California, as well as the Work of Bernard Maybeck in the San Francisco Bay area. See Linda Flint McClelland, *Building the National Parks: Historic Landscape Design Construction* (Baltimore: Johns Hopkins University Press, 1998, 91–120).

20. Olin D. Wheeler, *Wonderland 1904* (St. Paul, Minn.: Northern Pacific Railway, 1904), 57.

21. Haines, *Yellowstone Story* 2:120.

22. Thomas Murphy, *Three Wonderlands of the American West* (Boston: Page, 1913), 11.

23. See Hyde, *American Vision,* 255–62, for an assessment of the significance of the Old Faithful Inn.

24. Northern Pacific Railway, *Yellowstone National Park, America's Only Geyser Land* (Buffalo, N.Y.: Matthews Northrup Works, 1913), n.p.

25. Leavengood notes that Reamer designed over twenty-five structures in Yellowstone and Montana. See Leavengood, "Sense of Shelter," 511.

26. Hiram Martin Chittenden, *The Yellowstone National Park: Historical and Descriptive* (Norman: University of Oklahoma Press, 1964), 238.

27. Barringer, "Private Empire, Public Land," 37–49, and Haines, *Yellowstone Story* 2:100–159.

28. Haines, *Yellowstone Story* 2:104.

29. There is no detailed history of Northern Pacific promotional activities. For information on Charles S. Fee, see Edward W. Nolan, *Northern Pacific Views: The Railroad Photography of F. Jay Haynes, 1876–1905* (Helena: Montana Historical Society Press, 1983), 14–22. For overviews of Northern Pacific promotion, see Schwantes, *Railroad Signatures*, and Robin W. Winks, *Frederick Billings: A Life* (New York: Oxford University Press, 1991), 284–86.

30. Olin D. Wheeler, *6000 Miles Through Wonderland: Being a Description of the Marvelous Region Traversed by the Northern Pacific Railroad* (St. Paul, Minn.: Northern Pacific Railway, 1893), 65.

31. Langford, "Wonders of the Yellowstone," *Scribner's Monthly*, May 1871, 1–17, and June 1871, 113–28. Langford refers to the wonders of Yellowstone throughout his essay, but in no place does he describe the area as wonderland.

32. See Magoc, *Yellowstone*, chap. 1, 194 n. 5.

33. Harry J. Norton, *Wonder-Land Illustrated; or Horseback Rides through the Yellowstone National Park* (Virginia City, Mont: Harry J. Norton, 1873), 11.

34. Edwin J. Stanley, *Rambles in Wonderland; or, The Yellowstone* (New York: D. Appleton, 1878).

35. In 1886 the Northern Pacific published Lt. Frederick Schwatka and John Hyde, *Wonderland; or Alaska and the Inland Passage* (St. Paul, Minn.: Northern Pacific Railroad, 1886). The title page notes that John Hyde was the author of two other Northern Pacific Brochures: "The Wonderland Route to the Pacific Coast," and "Alice's Adventures in the New Wonderland." Hyde described the area as an "enchanted realm where the most extravagant creations of the fancy appear trivial and commonplace beside the more extraordinary works of Nature" (John Hyde, *Alice's Adventures in Wonderland* [St. Paul, Minn.: Northern Pacific Railway, n.d.] 3). See also W. C. Riley, *Official Guide to the Yellowstone National Park: A Manual for Tourists, Being a Description of . . . the New Wonderland*, rev. ed. (St. Paul, Minn.: Northern News, 1888) (revised by John Hyde; first edition came out in 1886).

36. Wheeler, *Wonderland 1904*, 33.

37. Olin D. Wheeler, *Wonderland 1901* (St. Paul, Minn.: Northern Pacific Railway, 1901), 74.

38. Wheeler, *6000 Miles Through Wonderland*, 75.

39. Olin D. Wheeler, *Wonderland 1902* (St. Paul, Minn.: Northern Pacific Railway, 1902), 86.

40. For a discussion of the cultural meaning of the miniature and the monumental, see Susan Stewart, *On Longing: Narratives of the Miniature, the Gigantic, the Souvenir, the Collection* (Durham, N.C.: Duke University Press, 1993).

41. Olin D. Wheeler, *Wonderland '97* (St. Paul, Minn.: Northern Pacific Railway, 1897),

62; Wheeler, *6000 Miles Through Wonderland*, 65; Wheeler, *Wonderland 1902*, 83 and 86. For a discussion of the patriotic imagery used to promote Yellowstone, see Joan Michele Zenzen, "Promoting the National Parks: Images of the West in the American Imagination, 1864–1972" (Ph.D. diss., University of Maryland, College Park, 1997), 220. For a discussion of imaginary geography, see Rob Shields, *Places on the Margins: Alternative Geographies of Modernity* (New York: Routledge, 1991).

42. For the history of the Santa Fe/Harvey promotion of the Southwest, see Dilworth, *Imagining Indians in the Southwest;* Kathleen L. Howard and Diana F. Pardue, *Inventing the Southwest: The Fred Harvey Company and Native American Art* (Phoenix: Heard Museum, 1996); T. C. McLuhan, *Dream Tracks: The Railroad and the American Indian, 1890–1930* (New York: Harry N. Abrams, 1985); Scott Norris, ed., *Discovered Country: Tourism and Survival in the American West* (Albuquerque: Stone Ladder Press, 1994); Mark Neumann, *On the Rim: Looking for the Grand Canyon* (Minneapolis: University of Minnesota Press, 1999); Marta Weigle, "From Desert to Disney World: The Santa Fe Railway and the Fred Harvey Company Display the Indian Southwest," *Journal of Anthropological Research* 45 (1989): 115–37; Marta Weigle, "Southwest Lures: Innocents Detoured, Incensed Determined," *Journal of the Southwest* 32 (1990): 499–540; Marta Weigle, "Exposition and Mediation: Mary Colter, Erna Fergusson, and the Santa Fe/Harvey Popularization of the Native Southwest, 1902–1940," *Frontiers: A Journal of Women Studies* 12 (Summer 1991): 117–50; and Weigle and Babcock, *Great Southwest*.

43. Keith L. Bryant, Jr., *History of the Atchison, Topeka and Santa Fe Railway* (New York: Macmillan, 1974), 327–28; and Marta Weigle and Kathleen L. Howard, "'To Experience the Real Grand Canyon': Santa Fe/Harvey Panopticism, 1910–1935," in Weigle and Babcock, *Great Southwest*, 13–14.

44. Kinsey, *Thomas Moran*, 128, and Hales, *William Henry Jackson*, 187.

45. Weigle and Howard, "To Experience the Real Grand Canyon," 13–23.

46. J. Donald Hughes, *In the House of Stone and Light: A Human History of the Grand Canyon* (Grand Canyon, Ariz.: Grand Canyon Natural History Association, 1978), 57.

47. Hyde, *American Vision*, 272.

48. W. H. Simpson, *El Tovar: A New Hotel at the Grand Canyon of Arizona* (Chicago: Rand McNally, 1905), 9, Atchison, Topeka, and Santa Fe Railway, Railroads, Warshaw Collection, National Museum of American History Archives, Smithsonian Institution, Washington, D.C. (hereafter cited as Warshaw).

49. Hyde, *American Vision*, 274–76.

50. Simpson, *El Tovar*, 7.

51. Murphy, *Three Wonderlands*, 116.

52. Note that the Grand Canyon was set aside as a forest reserve in 1893. In 1906 President Theodore Roosevelt designated the canyon as a national game reserve. In 1908

it was upgraded to a national monument. Not until 1919 did the Grand Canyon gain national park status. (See Hughes, *In the House of Stone and Light*, 66). For an overview of the National Park Service's concessionaire policy, see Peter J. Blodgett, "Striking a Balance: Managing Concessions in the National Parks, 1916–1933," *Forest and Conservation History* 34 (April 1990): 60–68.

53. Matilda McQuaid and Karen Bartlett, "Building an Image of the Southwest: Mary Colter, Fred Harvey Company Architect," in Weigle and Babcock, *Great Southwest*, 26; and Virginia L. Grattan, *Mary Colter: Builder upon the Red Earth* (Flagstaff, Ariz.: Northland Press, 1980), 14–19.

54. Simpson, *El Tovar*, 21.

55. Ibid., 23.

56. McQuaid and Bartlett, "Building an Image of the Southwest," 28; and Grattan, *Mary Colter*, 25–32.

57. Hughes, *In the House of Stone and Light*, 70; and Weigle and Howard, "To Experience the Real Grand Canyon," 18.

58. "Trails, Drives and Saddle Horses" (Grand Canyon, Ariz.: Fred Harvey, c. 1906), Arkansas/Arizona, Warshaw. See also Hughes, *In the House of Stone and Light*, 67–68. Note that the Bright Angel Hotel was bought by Santa Fe Harvey in 1901 and then closed and reopened in 1905 as Bright Angel Camp.

59. For competing interests at the Grand Canyon, see Rothman, *Devil's Bargains*, 50–80.

60. C. A. Higgins, *Grand Canyon of Arizona* (Chicago: Passenger Department, Santa Fe Railway, 1902), 10–11, Arkansas/Arizona, Warshaw.

61. Fred Harvey Company, *California and the Grand Canyon of Arizona* (Los Angeles: Fred Harvey, 1914), n.p.

62. Mark Neumann, "The Commercial Canyon," in Norris, *Discovered Country*, 196–209; and Neumann, *On the Rim*.

63. Fred Harvey Company, *California and the Grand Canyon of Arizona*, n.p.

64. C. A. Higgins, *Titan of Chasms: The Grand Canyon of the Arizona* (Chicago: Passenger Department of the Santa Fe Railway, 1906), 5.

65. Simpson, *El Tovar*, 23.

66. Dilworth, *Imagining Indians in the Southwest*, 82. See also Marta Weigle, "Exposition and Mediation: Mary Colter, Erna Fergusson, and the Santa Fe/Harvey Popularization of the Native Southwest, 1902–1940," 117–50; and Weigle and Babcock, *Great Southwest*.

67. Barbara Babcock, "Mudwomen and Whitemen," in Norris, *Discovered Country*, 187.

68. Leah Dilworth, "Discovering Indians in Fred Harvey's Southwest," in Weigle and Babcock, *Great Southwest*, 163; and Dilworth, *Imagining Indians in the Southwest*, 103–17.

69. Louis Hill was president of the Great Northern from 1907 to 1912. In 1912 he became chairman of the board until his resignation in 1929.

70. Rufus Steele, "The Son Who Showed His Father," *Sunset Magazine*, March 1915, 479.

71. Ralph W. Hidy, Muriel E. Hidy, and Roy V. Scott, with Don L. Hofsommer, *The Great Northern Railway: A History* (Cambridge: Harvard University Press, 1988), 108, 124. Louis Warren Hill was born in 1872 and groomed by his father, James J. Hill, to take on a leading role in the management of the Great Northern. After graduating from Yale's Sheffield Scientific School in 1893, Hill started working for the Great Northern "at the bottom of the ladder" as a clerk in the accounting department. After serving in a variety of departments, apparently without remuneration, including the stores of the company roadmaster's office, the local freight office in Duluth, Minnesota, the car accountants office, and the travel department, Hill was appointed assistant to the President in 1899. He then advanced to the position of vice president and then president of the Eastern Minnesota Railroad between 1899 and 1903. In 1903 he became vice president of the Great Northern Railway Company, ascending to the presidency four years later on the retirement of his father James J. Hill. Louis Hill served as president until 1912 and then assumed the position of chairman of the board, remaining in that position until 1929. (There is no biography of Louis Hill. For an overview of Louis Hill's career with Great Northern, see "Louis W. Hill Is Promoted to President," *St. Paul Pioneer Press Dispatch*, 3 April 1907; and information provided by the James J. Hill Reference Library, St. Paul, Minnesota.)

72. Hill monitored Yellowstone publicity material distributed by the Northern Pacific, and he repeatedly asked his staff for copies of Yellowstone folders. See President's Office Subject Files: Publicity 1903–1916, File 3903, GNRR. See also L. W. Hill to S. J. Ellison, 27 November 1909, President's Office Subject Files: Publicity, File 4325, GNRR.

73. For further discussion of Northern Pacific's promotion of Yellowstone, see Runte, *Trains of Discovery*, 19–31, and Kinsey, *Thomas Moran*.

74. There is much disagreement about Louis W. Hill's role in the creation of Glacier National Park. For two opposing accounts, see James W. Sheire, *Glacier National Park: Historic Resource Study* (Washington, D.C.: National Park Service, Office of History and Historic Architecture Eastern Service Center, 1970), and Alan S. Newell, David Walterm, and James R. McDonald, *Historic Resource Study, Glacier National Park and Historic Structures Survey* (Denver: National Park Service, Denver Service Center, 1980). Sheire argues that Hill was integrally involved in the creation of the Park. Newell argues that this was a myth promoted by the Great Northern after they began to develop the park. Most recently Michael G. Schene in "The Crown of the Continent: Private Enterprise and Public Interest in the Early Development of Glacier National Park, 1910–1917," *Forest and Conservation History* 34

(April 1990): 69–75, has noted "careful examination of the recently opened Louis Warren Hill papers in the James J. Hill Reference Library, St. Paul, Minnesota, has failed to produce any material relating to the younger Hill's involvement in the political process dealing with the legislation establishing Glacier National Park. Correspondence, especially encoded telegrams, in the President's Subject Files, Records of the Great Northern Railway, Minnesota Historical Society, St. Paul, Minnesota ... indicates that Louis Hill was involved in the park legislation, but these documents do not clarify his role. A contemporary Montana politician, Charles N. Pray, reportedly told Louis W. Hill Jr. in 1957 that the Great Northern faction avoided disclosing its lobbying efforts for the Glacier Park bill because they feared that knowledge of railroad interest might prevent the act from passing. Louis W. Hill, Jr. 'Memo—Louis W. Hill Papers and Creation of the Glacier National Park,' Louis W. Hill Papers" (Schene, "Crown of the Continent," 74 n. 1). In surveying the Louis W. Hill Papers at the James J. Reference Library the Great Northern Papers at the Minnesota Historical Society, and the Records of the National Park Service on Glacier National Park, I have found no evidence that Hill was actively lobbying for the creation of Glacier Park until the spring of 1909. His first trip through the proposed park took place in August 1909. See "Finish in Montana," *St. Paul Pioneer Press Dispatch*, 26 August 1909; "Irrigation in Montana," *St. Paul Pioneer Press Dispatch*, 29 August 1909; and "Hill Quits Rockies," *St. Paul Pioneer Press Dispatch*, 30 August 1909.

75. "New Playground for Americans," *St. Paul Pioneer Press Dispatch*, 17 April 1910.

76. Michael J. Ober, "Enmity and Alliance: Park Service-Concessioner Relations in Glacier National Park, 1892–1916" (Master's thesis, University of Montana, 1973); Sheire, *Glacier National Park*; and Newell, Walterm, and McDonald, *Historic Resource Study*, provide the most complete overviews of park development.

77. Ober, "Enmity and Alliance," 54–55.

78. Great Northern Railway, *Hotels and Tours: Glacier National Park* (St. Paul, Minn.: Great Northern Railway, 1914), 6, Great Northern Railway, Railroads, Warshaw.

79. *Glacier National Park* (St. Paul, Minn.: Great Northern Railway, 1915), n.p., Glacier National Park Company: Histories and Related Records, File 5, GNRR.

80. For a description of the hotel, see John Willy, "A Week in Glacier National Park," *Hotel Monthly*, August 1915, 45–48. See also Hyde, *American Vision*, 281–93.

81. *What to Wear in Glacier National Park: A Few Suggestions for the Tourists Planning an Outing in the American Alps* (St. Paul, Minn.: Great Northern Railway, 1912), President's Office Subject Files: Publicity, File 4325, GNRR.

82. H. A. Noble to L. W. Hill, 10 August 1912, President's Office Subject Files: Publicity, File 4325, GNRR.

83. I am indebted to Dr. W. Thomas White, curator of the James J. Hill Reference Library, for pointing out that the Louis W. Hill Papers contain numerous hunting

and fishing licenses and gardening catalogs, and for noting Hill's interest in painting and photography.

84. For a more complete discussion of the growing fascination with wilderness, see Nash, *Wilderness and the American Mind,* 141–60; and Peter J. Schmitt, *Back to Nature: The Arcadian Myth in Urban America* (Baltimore: Johns Hopkins University Press, 1990). See also Jackson Lears, *No Place of Grace.*

85. See President's Office Subject Files: Glacier Park Tourists, 1913–1961, File 5827, GNRR.

86. "Park Visitors, 1919," enclosure with letter H. H. Parkhouse to L. W. Hill, 7 July 1919, President's Office Subject Files: Glacier Park Tourists, 1913–1961, File 5827, GNRR.

87. L. W. Hill to W. B. Acker, 1 August 1914, President's Office Subject Files: Publicity, File 4325, GNRR.

88. Louis W. Hill to Andrew Schoch, 10 July 1919; L. W. Hill to H. A. Noble, telegram, 12 July 1919; L. W. Hill to H. A. Noble, telegram, 17 July 1919, President's Office Subject Files: Glacier Park Tourists, 1913–1961, File 5827, GNRR.

89. Louis W. Hill to Samuel Rea, 15 July 1916, President's Office Subject Files: Glacier Park Tourists, 1913–1961, File 5827, GNRR.

90. "Service Regulations and Information for Employees" (Glacier Park Hotel Company, n.d.), Louis W. Hill Papers, James J. Hill Reference Library, St. Paul Minnesota (hereafter cited as the L. W. Hill Papers).

91. David Thelen, "Memory and American History," *Journal of American History* 75 (March 1989): 1117–29. For further discussion of this issue, see Eric Hobsbawm, "Introduction: Inventing Traditions," in Hobsbawm and Ranger, *Invention of Tradition,* and Lowenthal, "Place of the Past in the American Landscape."

92. See Mark David Spence, *Dispossessing the Wilderness: Indian Removal and the Making of the National Parks* (New York: Oxford University Press, 1999), 71–82. See also Brian Reeves and Sandy Peacock, *"Our Mountains Are Our Pillows": An Ethnographic Overview of Glacier National Park* (Denver: National Park Service, Denver Service Center, 1995), and Sheire, *Glacier National Park,* 3–34.

93. Great Northern Railway, *Hotels and Tours,* 25, Great Northern Railway, Railroads, Warshaw.

94. "A Report on Glacier National Park for Season 1913," from J. A. Shoemaker to L. W. Hill, C. R. Gray, W. P. Kenney, 7 October 1913, President's Office Subject Files: Chairman's File Glacier Park Publicity, File 4, GNRR.

95. L. W. Hill to W. P. Kenney, 3 June 1914, President's Office Subject Files: Publicity, File 4325, GNRR.

96. *Walking Tours: Glacier National Park* (St. Paul, Minn.: Great Northern Railway, 1914), n.p., Great Northern Railway, Warshaw.

97. Great Northern Railway, *Hotels and Tours*, 3.

98. Willy, "Week in Glacier National Park," 45.

99. Great Northern Railway, *Hotels and Tours*, 5.

100. Louis Hill received photographs of chalets from Switzerland and read about the design of Swiss chalets in America. See Fred K. Leland to Louis W. Hill, 27 March 1911; Fred K. Leland to Louis Hill, 16 February 1911; Robert C. Auld, "The Alpine House: Distinctive Type in Spite of Many Mangled Reproductions in this Country," *Arts and Decoration,* enclosure with letter, Walter A. Johnson to James B. Hill, 21 March 1911, President's Office Subject Files: Advertising 1903–1916, all File 3903, GNRR.

101. Great Northern Railway, *Hotels and Tours*, 17.

102. "A Trip Through Glacier National Park, 'Switzerland of America,'" *New York Press*, 2 August 1914, vol. 2, Roll 6, Frame 130, Great Northern Railway Company, Advertising and Publicity Department, Magazine and Newspaper Articles and Other Publicity, 1911–1943, Microfilm Edition, Minnesota Historical Society, St. Paul (hereafter cited as GN Publicity).

103. *See America First: The Great Northern Annotated Time Table* (St. Paul, Minn.: Great Northern Railway, 1916), 63, Advertising and Publicity Department: Advertising Literature, File 4551, GNRR.

104. Ober, "Enmity and Alliance"; Sheire, *Glacier National Park;* and Newell, Walterm, and McDonald, *Historic Resource Study,* provide the most complete discussion of Glacier Park facilities constructed by the Great Northern. See also Hyde, *American Vision,* 281–93, for a discussion of the Glacier Park Hotel and the Many Glacier Hotel in the context of other National Park Hotels.

105. For more information on the relationship between American landscape and national identity see Huth, *Nature and the American,* 30–53; Kinsey, *Thomas Moran;* Lowenthal, "Place of the Past in the American Landscape"; Miller, "Romantic Dilemma in American Nationalism," 197–207; Nash, *Wilderness and the American Mind,* 67–83; Novak, *Nature and Culture;* Pomeroy, *In Search of the Golden West,* 31–72; and Runte, *National Parks,* 11–32.

106. For a discussion of Great Northern trade with Asia and the development and promotion of the Oriental Limited, see Hidy et al., *Great Northern Railway,* 121–22; and Emily S. Rosenberg, *Spreading the American Dream: American Economic and Cultural Expansion, 1890–1945* (New York: Hill & Wang, 1982), 16–18.

107. The company encouraged newspapers and magazines with which they had contracts to editorialize the See America First idea. Clipping, "'See America First' Is Good Advice for Americans," 22 April 1912. Penciled note to Louis Hill on clipping states, "Significantly first! Pretty good cooperation?" President's Office Subject Files: Advertising 1903–1916, File 3903, GNRR.

108. H. A. Noble to W. P Kenney, 8 August 1911, President's Office Subject Files: Advertising, 1903–1916, File 3903, GNRR.

109. L. W. Hill to W. P. Kenney, On Line, 17 August 1912, President's Office Subject Files: Advertising, 1903–1916, File 3903, GNRR.

110. For examples of Hoke Smith articles, see Vols. 1–2, Roll 6, GN Publicity.

111. L. W. Hill to Hoke Smith, On Line, 3 September 1912; Hoke Smith to Louis W. Hill, 26 September 1911; both in President's Office Subject Files: Publicity, File 4325, GNRR.

112. Hoke Smith, "America's New Wonderland—Glacier National Park," *Seattle Post Intelligencer*, 20 April 1913, Vol. 1, Roll 6, Frame 12, GN Publicity. For additional Hoke Smith publicity articles, see President's Office Subject Files: Glacier Park Advertising, File 7872, GNRR.

113. "Montana Indians Refuse to Live in Gotham Hotel," 27 March 1913, Vol. 1, Roll 6, Frame 87, GN Publicity. For further descriptions of the Indians in New York, see newspaper clippings, Vols. 1–2, Roll 6, GN Publicity, along with Report, J. A. Shoemaker to L. W. Hill, C. R. Gray, W. P. Kenney, 1 April 1913, President's Office Subject Files: Publicity, File 4325, GNRR.

114. "'America First,' Lesson of Big Vacation Show," *New Jersey Evening Telegram*, 21 March 1913, Vol. 1, Roll 6, Frame 87, GN Publicity.

115. Report, J. A. Shoemaker to L. W. Hill, C. R. Gray, W. P. Kenney, 1 April 1913, President's Office Subject Files: Publicity, File 4325, GNRR.

116. "Wild Indians Dance in the Heart of the City," *World*, 19 March 1913, Vol. 1, Roll 6, Frame 87, GN Publicity.

117. John C. Van Dyke to Louis W. Hill, 1 October 1910; Louis W. Hill to W. H. Cowles, 16 September 1911; Edw. Frank Allen to Lewis [sic] W. Hill, 28 August 1912; all in President's Office Subject Files: Publicity, File 4325, GNRR. These letters reveal the various ways in which Hill courted writers.

118. Robert D. Heinl, "The Man Who Is Building a National Park," *Leslie's Illustrated Weekly*, 7 March 1912, 260, 275.

119. Robert D. Heinl to L. W. Hill, 20 August 1912; Hoke Smith to L. W. Hill, 24 August 1912; L. W. Hill to J. M. Cathcart, 27 August 1912; all in President's Office Subject Files: Publicity, File 4325, GNRR.

120. Mary Roberts Rinehart, "Through Glacier National Park with Howard Eaton," *Collier's*, 22 April 1916, 11–13, and 29 April 1916, 20–21.

121. Mary Roberts Rinehart, *Through Glacier Park: Seeing America First with Howard Eaton* (Boston: Houghton Mifflin, 1916), 8–9.

122. Mary Roberts Rinehart, *My Story: A New Edition and Seventeen New Years* (New York: Arno Press, 1980), 205.

123. Louis W. Hill to Mary Roberts Rinehart, 4 December 1915, President's Office Subject File: Advertising 1903–1916, File 3903, GNRR.

124. See the following by Mary Roberts Rinehart: *Tenting Tonight* (Boston: Houghton Mifflin, 1918); *The Out Trail* (New York: George H. Doran, 1923); "On the Trail in Wonderland II," *Wide World*, November 1916, 59–68; "My Country Tish of Thee," *Saturday Evening Post*, 1 April 1916, 3–6, 54–55, 58–59, 62, 65–66; 8 April 1916, 19–22, 43, 47, 50–51; and "The Family Goes A-Gypsying," *Outlook*, 12 June 1918, 263–66.

125. For more information on Rinehart's characterization of her Glacier excursion, see Shaffer, "Tourism and National Identity, 1905–1930," 131–42.

126. The President's Office Subject Files, GNRR, and the Louis W. Hill Papers reveal ample evidence of Great Northern's support for writers. See also Newell, Walterm, and McDonald, *Historic Resource Study*, 82; and Sheire, *Glacier National Park*, 200.

127. Ober, "Enmity and Alliance," 23. See also "Glacier National Park, Montana, Called Artists' Mecca: Railroad Establishes 'Swiss Chalet' for Summer Colony," *Minneapolis Sunday Tribune*, 25 June 1911, Vol. 1, Roll 6, Frame 7, GN Publicity.

128. W. P. Kenney to L. W. Hill, 10 July 1913, President's Office Subject Files: Glacier Park Tourists, 1913–1961, File 5827, GNRR.

129. W. R. Mills to J. A. Shoemaker, 9 June 1914, President's Office Subject Files: Publicity, File 4325, GNRR.

130. L. W. Hill to Clement S. Ucker, 28 November 1910, President's Office Subject Files: Publicity, File 4325, GNRR.

131. L. W. Hill to Major W. R. Logan, 29 November 1910, President's Office Subject Files: Publicity, File 4325, GNRR.

132. Kiser was a noted member of the Portland Mountain Climbing Club, the Mazamas. In 1906 he gained fame as a mountain climber by successfully guiding a small group of Mazamas up the north face of Mount Baker for the first time. For background history on Kiser and his work, see *Kiser Brother's Pacific Coast Pictures* (Portland, Oreg., 1904); Fred H. Kiser, *Official Photographs of the Louis and Clark Exposition* (Portland, Oregon, 1905); Thomas Robinson, *Oregon Photographers; Biographical History and Directory, 1952–1917* (Portland, Oreg.: Published by author, 1992); Ellen S. Thomas, "Scooping the Local Field: Oregon's Newsreel Industry," *Oregon Historical Quarterly* 90 (Fall 1989): 229–81; Kiser-Dodson Letters, William D. B. Dodson Papers, University of Oregon Special Collections, Eugene; Kiser Files and Photographs, Oregon Historical Society, Portland, and See America First Exhibit, Crater Lake National Park Museum and Library, Crater Lake, Oregon. Kiser claimed that he was "one of the first scenic photographers in the United States to apply opaque oil colors to the emulsion of the photograph and develop a system of producing hand-colored-in-oil photographs for volume distribution." (See F. H. Kiser to Board of Geographical Names, Department of the Interior, 16

November 1947, Central Classified Files, 1907–1949, Records of the National Park Service, RG 79, National Archives, College Park, Maryland [hereafter cited as NA, Maryland]. I am indebted to Crater Lake Historian Stephen R. Mark for xeroxing this letter from the See America First Exhibit materials.)

133. L. W. Hill to Francis B. Clarke, 5 January 1909, L. W. Hill Papers.

134. Louis W. Hill to F. H. Kiser, 6 February 1909; W. W. Broughton to W. P. Kenney, 8 February 1909; both in President's Office Subject File: F. H. Kiser Contract for Photographing Scenery, File 4507, GNRR; and "Show of Fine Photographs," *St. Paul Pioneer Press Dispatch*, 7 February 1909, and "Photos Are Marvels," *St. Paul Pioneer Press Dispatch*, 8 February 1909.

135. F. H. Kiser to Louis W. Hill, 12 February 1909, President's Office Subject File: F. H. Kiser Contract for Photographing Scenery, File 4507, GNRR.

136. Louis W. Hill to Mr. F. H. Kiser, 23 February 1909, President's Office Subject File: F. H. Kiser Contract for Photographing Scenery, File 4507, GNRR.

137. Louis W. Hill to A. L. Craig, 10 April 1909, President's Office Subject File: F. H. Kiser Contract for Photographing Scenery, File 4507, GNRR.

138. L. W. Hill to Kiser, 23 August 1909, President's Office Subject File: F. H. Kiser Contract for Photographing Scenery, File 4507, GNRR.

139. For background on Kiser's career accomplishments, see F. H. Kiser to board of Geographical Names, 16 November 1947. See America First Exhibit, Crater Lake National Park Museum, Crater Lake, Oregon.

140. F. H. Kiser to J. L. Galen, 28 August 1914, RG 79, Records of the National Park Service, Central Files, Glacier National Park: Privileges, F. H. Kiser, NA, Maryland (hereafter cited as Privileges, F. H. Kiser).

141. H. A. Noble to Stephen Mather, 28 March 1921, Privileges, F. H. Kiser.

142. H. A. Noble to L. W. Hill, 16 June 1910, President's Office Subject Files: Advertising, 1903–1916, File 3903, GNRR.

143. L. W. Hill to H. A. Noble, 17 June 1910, President's Office Subject Files: Advertising, 1903–1916, File 3903, GNRR.

144. Quoted in a letter from W. P. Kenney to L. W. Hill, 31 March 1914, President's Office Subject Files: Publicity, File 4325, GNRR.

145. Newell, Walterm, and McDonald, *Historic Resource Survey*, 81–82; Schene, "Crown of the Continent," 70; W. O. Chapman, *Diary of an Amateur Explorer in Glacier National Park* (St. Paul, Minn.: Great Northern Railway, 1911); A. C. Brokaw, *Glacier National Park: Where Fighting Trout Leap* (Great Northern Railway, 1912); Tom Dillon, *Over the Trails of Glacier National Park* (Great Northern Railway, 1912), Great Northern Railway, Railroads, Warshaw.

146. Chapman, *Diary of an Amateur Explorer*, 2–4.

147. Ibid.; Brokaw, *Where Fighting Trout Leap*; Dillon, *Over the Trails*. Tom Dillon,

"Over the Trails of Glacier National Park," *Seattle Post Intelligencer*, 17 September 1911, Vol. 2, Roll 6, Frame 119; Clarence L. Speed, "Uncle Sam's Last Wild Domain," *Chicago Record Herald*, 10 September 1911, Vol. 2, Roll 6, Frame 123; Jay Cairns, "In Uncle Sam's Newest Playground," *Chicago Inter-Ocean*, 10 September 1911, Vol. 2, Roll 6, Frame 125; A. C. Brokaw, "'Hitting the Trail' Through Glacier National Park," *Minneapolis Tribune*, 19 November 1911, Vol. 2, Roll 6, Frame 129; "Scenic Grandeur From the New Glacier Park," *Minneapolis Journal*, 10 September 1911, Vol. 2, Roll 6, Frame 136; all in GN Publicity.

148. In the summer of 1912 the Great Northern hosted a number of newspaper parties through the park, including a southwestern party, an eastern party, and a western party. W. P. Kenney to L. W. Hill, 4 September 1912, President's Office Subject Files: Publicity, File 4325, GNRR.

149. See publicity articles, Vol. 1, Roll 6, GN Publicity, for the articles generated from this trip.

150. Speed, "Uncle Sam's Last Wild Domain."

151. Brokaw, *Where Fighting Trout Leap.*

152. Dillon, *Over the Trails.*

153. Chapman, *Diary of an Amateur Explorer*, 2.

154. Ibid., 14–15.

155. Dillon, *Over the Trails*, 11.

156. Speed, "Uncle Sam's Last Wild Domain."

157. John Muir quoted in Freeman Tilden, *The National Parks: What They Mean to You and Me* (New York: Alfred A. Knopf, 1951), 18.

158. Lears, *No Place of Grace*, 4–5.

159. Brokaw, *Where Fighting Trout Leap*, 10; Dillon, *Over the Trails*, 11, 15.

160. Lears, *No Place of Grace*, 4–5.

161. See G. Edward White, *The Eastern Establishment and the Western Experience* (New Haven, Conn.: Yale University Press, 1968), 31–51, 60–67, 79–93, for formation of Roosevelt's world view. For Roosevelt's views on race see Richard Slotkin, "Nostalgia and Progress: Theodore Roosevelt's Myth of the Frontier," *American Quarterly* 33 (Winter 1981): 608–38.

162. Slotkin, "Nostalgia and Progress," 615.

163. Ibid., 633.

164. Theodore Roosevelt, *The Strenuous Life: Essays and Addresses* (New York: Century, 1902), 20–21.

165. White, *Eastern Establishment and the Western Experience*, 185.

166. Speed, "Uncle Sam's Last Wild Domain."

167. Emily Bayne Bosson to Louis Hill, 21 August 1921, L. W. Hill Papers.

168. E. L. Lindley to L. W. Hill, 15 April 1912, President's Office Subject Files: Advertising, 1903–1916, File 3903, GNRR.

3. THE NATIONAL PARKS AS NATIONAL ASSETS

1. Department of the Interior, *Report of the General Superintendent and Landscape Engineer of National Parks to the Secretary of the Interior, 1915* (Washington, D.C.: GPO, 1915), 6.

2. Wai-Teng Leong, "Culture and the State: Manufacturing Traditions for Tourism," *Critical Studies in Mass Communications* 6 (December 1989): 357.

3. Yosemite National Park (1890), Sequoia National Park (1890), General Grant National Park (1890), Mount Rainier National Park (1899), Crater Lake National Park (1902), Wind Cave National Park (1903), Sullys Hill National Park (1904), Platt National Park (1904), Mesa Verde National Park (1906), and Glacier National Park (1910).

4. Allen Chamberlain, "Scenery as a National Asset," *Outlook,* 28 May 1910, 159, 162, 165, 166, 169.

5. Department of the Interior, *Annual Report of the Secretary of the Interior for the Fiscal Year Ended June 30, 1915* (Washington, D.C.: GPO, 1915), 122. Note that Robert B. Marshall in his report to the secretary of the interior for 1910 commended the idea of establishing a separate bureau. "A national park," he argued, "preserved in all its beauty and at the same time made accessible to the public for all time, is as grand a heritage as it is possible to leave to future generations and too much thought and care can not be given to its preservation; at the same time provision should be made for its fullest use by the people of to-day" (2). He concluded, "Your plan to establish a bureau of parks is the first practical one that has been suggested and, to my mind, is the only way to provide for the proper administration of this important matter" (5). See R. B. Marshall to Secretary of the Interior, 30 November 1910, Record of the National Park Service, Central Files, Entry 6, General, Reports General, Part 1: November 30, 1910 to September 27, 1926, RG 79, NA, Maryland. For a history of the debate, see Alfred Runte, *National Parks,* 97–101.

6. Quoted in Department of the Interior, *Annual Report of the Secretary of the Interior for the Fiscal Year Ended June 30, 1915,* 122.

7. Clipping "Advertising the National Parks," Denver *Republican,* 29 October 1911, in RG 79, Entry 6, General, Miscellaneous, Part 6: October 28, 1911 to January 15, 1912, NA, Maryland.

8. W. P. Acker to Miss Medora J. Simpson, 4 November 1911; and Clement Ucker to Mr. Chas. S. Fee, 20 November 1911; both in Entry 6, General, Miscellaneous, Part 6: October 28, 1911 to January 15, 1912, RG 79, NA, Maryland.

9. Memorandum from L. S. Schmeckebier attached to Memorandum for the Secretary from Clement Ucker, 19 March 1913, Entry 6, General, Miscellaneous, January 15, 1913 to May 12, 1913, RG 79 NA, Maryland.

10. Wm. W. Forsyth to Secretary of the Interior, 26 February 1912. See also the following letters of response: H. W. Hutchings to Secretary of the Interior, 20 February 1912; T. M. Brell to Secretary of the Interior, 21 February 1912; Edward S. Hall to Secretary of the Interior, 21 February 1912; and General Passenger Agent Great Northern Railroad to Mr. H. J. Brock, 13 April 1912, all in Entry 6, General, Moving Pictures, Part 1: February 9, 1912 to June 3, 1912, RG 79, NA, Maryland.

11. Clipping, 25 May 1912, Entry 6, General, Moving Pictures, Part 1: February 9, 1912 to June 3, 1912, RG 79, NA, Maryland.

12. Clement Ucker to Geo. W. Hibbard, 28 May 1912, Entry 6, General, Moving Pictures, Part 1: February 9, 1912 to June 3, 1912, RG 79 NA, Maryland.

13. L. F. Schmeckebier, "Our National Parks," *National Geographic*, June 1912, 531–79. Other contributors of photographs included George R. King, W. S. Berry, Haynes, A. H. Barnes, Asahel Curtis, J. T. Boysen, H. C. Best, W. L. Huber, and Pen-Dike Studio.

14. Clement Ucker to E. L. Bevington, 18 July 1912, Entry 6, General, Miscellaneous, 22 April 1912 to 9 August 1912, RG 79, NA, Maryland. See also Stephen T. Mather, *Progress in the Development of the National Parks* (Washington, D.C.: GPO, 1916), 36–37.

15. William Harper Dean, "Advertising America: Uncle Sam Tells His People about Their National Parks," *Outing*, August 1916, 464.

16. Schmeckebier, "Our National Parks," 531.

17. Keith W. Olson, *Biography of a Progressive: Franklin K. Lane, 1864–1921* (Westport, Conn.: Greenwood Press, 1979), 53 and 71.

18. For discussion of American nationalism during World War I, see Higham, *Strangers in the Land*, 194–233; Gleason, "American Identity and Americanization," 80–109; and David M. Kennedy, *Over Here: The First World War and American Society* (New York: Oxford University Press, 1980). For a discussion of the relationship between consumption and nationalism, see Charles F. McGovern, "Sold American: Inventing the Consumer, 1890–1940" (Ph.D. diss., Harvard University, 1993).

19. For a history of the relationship between railroads and the development of tourism, see Fifer, *American Progress*; Alfred Runte, "Pragmatic Alliance: Western Railroads and the National Parks," *National Parks and Conservation Magazine* 48 (April 1974): 14–21; Runte, *Trains of Discovery*; Runte, "Promoting Wonderland," 43–48; Schwantes, "Tourists in Wonderland," 22–30; and Schwantes, "Landscapes of Opportunity," 38–51.

20. For the history of the good roads movement, see Peter J. Hugill, "Good Roads and

the Automobile in the United States, 1880–1929," *Geography Review* 72, no. 3 (1982): 327–49; and Philip Parker Mason, "The League of American Wheelmen and the Good Roads Movement, 1880–1905" (Ph.D. diss., University of Michigan, 1957). For a history of the Lincoln Highway Association, see Drake Hokanson, *The Lincoln Highway: Main Street across America* (Iowa City: University of Iowa Press, 1988).

21. For a discussion of the Panama-Pacific International Exposition and its impact on domestic tourism, see Shaffer, "Tourism and National Identity, 1905–1930," 168–77.

22. In the fall of 1914, following the outbreak of World War I, *Collier's* magazine ran a series of editorials advocating commercial patriotism, and domestic tourism was promoted as a means of supporting the American economy. See "Free Trade for Americans—With Americans," *Collier's*, 3 October 1914, n.p.; "A Billion Dollar Sentiment," *Collier's*, 10 October 1914, n.p.; "Giving the American Label Its Due," *Collier's*, 17 October 1914, n.p.; "Patriotism that Pays," *Collier's*, 24 October 1914, n.p.; "See America First," *Collier's*, 31 October 1914, n.p.; and "U.S. Spells US," *Collier's*, 7 November 1914, n.p.

23. For a discussion of the ideal of "nature's nation," see Miller, "Romantic Dilemma in American Nationalism," 196–207. See also Huth, *Nature and the American*, 30–53; Nash, *Wilderness and the American Mind*, 67–83; Runte, *National Parks*, 11–32; Novak, *Nature and Culture*; and Lowenthal, "Place of the Past in the American Landscape," 89–117.

24. Gellner, *Nations and Nationalism*, 49. Emphasis added.

25. Robert Sterling Yard, "Historical Basis of National Parks Standards," *National Parks Bulletin*, November 1929, 3, Stephen Tyng Mather Papers, Bancroft Library, University of California, Berkeley (hereafter cited as Mather Papers). Note that a version of this material examining the Park Service publicity campaign developed between 1914 and 1918 has been published in an essay examining the history of the "See America First" slogan. See Shaffer, "Negotiating National Identity."

26. Olson, *Biography of a Progressive*, 13. For Lane's ideal of the parks, see Stephen T. Mather, "Report to the Secretary of the Interior," 1–2, 1 December 1916, in RG 79, Entry 6, General, Miscellaneous, 29 June 1916 to January 1917, NA, Maryland.

27. Robert Shankland, *Steve Mather of the National Parks*, 3d ed. (New York: Knopf, 1970) provides a comprehensive overview of Mather's career as director of the national parks. In addition, Donald C. Swain, *Wilderness Defender: Horace M. Albright and Conservation* (Chicago: University of Chicago Press, 1970), Horace M. Albright and Robert Cahn, *The Birth of the National Park Service: The Founding Years, 1913–33* (Chicago: Howe Brothers, 1985), John Ise, *Our National Park Policy: A Critical History* (Baltimore: Johns Hopkins Press, 1961), and Hal K. Rothman, *Preserving Different Pasts: The American National Monuments* (Chicago: University of Illinois

Press, 1989), 89–118, also provide information on Mather's work for the Park Service. I am also indebted to Peter J. Blodgett for sharing his history of national park publicity during the Mather/Albright era. See Peter J. Blodgett, "Selling Scenery: Advertising and the National Parks, 1916–1933," in *Seeing and Being Seen,* ed. David Wrobel and Patrick Long (Lawrence: University of Kansas Press, 2001). A small collection of Mather's papers, most notably scrapbooks covering his career and obituaries overviewing his life, are held by the Bancroft Library, University of California, Berkeley. A few of Mather's papers are scattered throughout the National Park Service Records, RG 79, NA, Maryland. However, the Park Service Records contain no organized collection of his papers.

28. "Testimonial to Awarded 'Father of National Park,'" Stephen Tyng Mather Clippings, Carton 1, Mather Papers.

29. Stephen Tyng Mather, "The National Parks on a Business Basis," *American Review of Reviews,* April 1915, 429.

30. *Proceedings of the National Parks Conference, Berkeley, California, March 11, 12, and 13, 1915* (Washington: GPO, 1915), 11, 79. "Heads of National Parks Are to Meet," *San Francisco Examiner,* 15 February 1915; "To Make the Parks People's Own," *Los Angeles Times,* 8 March 1915; "National Park Chief Opens Sessions To-Day"; and "Steps Taken to Make U.S. Parks More Accessible," *Christian Science Monitor,* 18 March 1915, all in Scrapbook, Vol. 4, Clippings Re: Public Official Career, 1915–1916, Mather Papers.

31. Robert Sterling Yard, "Historical Basis of National Parks Standards," 3, U.S. National Park Service, Carton 1, Mather Papers.

32. See Robert Sterling Yard, *The Publisher* (Boston: Houghton Mifflin, 1913). Yard was hired at a salary of $30.00 per month by U.S. Geological Survey and given a small office in the Bureau of Mines. Mather supplemented his salary by five thousand dollars per year. Shankland, *Steve Mather,* 59. For an examination of Yard's role in wilderness advocacy see Paul Shriver Sutter, "Driven Wild: The Intellectual and Cultural Origins of Wilderness Advocacy during the Interwar Years" (Ph.D. diss., University of Kansas, 1997), 155–230.

33. *Proceedings of the National Parks Conference, Berkeley* (Washington, D.C.: GPO, 1915), 151.

34. Horace M. Albright, "Making the Parks Known to the People," *Living Wilderness,* December 1945, 6, S. T. Mather Clippings, Carton 1; "World Will Be Told of State's Wonder," *Rocky Mountain News,* 3 September 1915, Scrapbook, Vol. 9, Personal Clippings, 1915–1929, all in Mather Papers. See also Stephen T. Mather, "Report to the Secretary of the Interior," 2–3.

35. National Park Service, *The National Parks Portfolio* (New York: Scribner's, 1916), and *Glimpses of Our National Parks* (Washington, D.C.: GPO, 1916).

36. Mather donated five thousand dollars to finance the publishing of the book and secured the additional forty-three thousand dollars from seventeen western railroads. Yard arranged to have Scribner's put out the first edition. See Ise, *Our National Park Policy*, 196; Shankland, *Steve Mather*, 97–98; and Swain, *Wilderness Defender*, 57–58.

37. Albright, "Making the Parks Known to the People"; Ise, *Our National Park Policy*, 196; Shankland, *Steve Mather*, 97–98; Swain, *Wilderness Defender*, 57–58. A second edition of the *National Parks Portfolio* was issued by the Government Printing Office in 1917. For more information on later editions see RG 79, Entry 7, Portfolio of the National Parks, NA, Maryland.

38. Quotations from National Park Service, *National Parks Portfolio*, n.p.

39. Kenneth A. Erickson, "Ceremonial Landscapes of the American West," *Landscape* 22 (Autumn 1977): 39–41 provides an interesting discussion of "ceremonial landscapes." Also Sears, *Sacred Places*, 5, suggests that nineteenth-century American tourist attractions were depicted as "ceremonial landscapes," arguing that they "assumed some of the functions of sacred places in traditional societies."

40. National Park Service, *National Parks Portfolio*, n.p.

41. For an extended discussion of the commercial justification for national park preservation see Runte, *National Parks*, 82–105. It should be noted, however, that Runte's argument, which suggests that the See America First campaign was the product of a select group of preservationists seeking to justify the National Park idea in opposition to utilitarian conservationists, overlooks the fact that See America First was a growing popular movement that existed beyond the concerns of preservationists.

42. National Park Service, *Glimpses of Our National Parks*, 3, 7–8, and 45.

43. See clippings in Scrapbook, Vols. 4–7, Mather Papers. It should be noted that Mather suffered a nervous breakdown in the winter of 1917, which put him out of commission for eighteen months, during which time Horace Albright became acting director of national parks. For more information on Mather's illness, see Shankland, *Steve Mather*, and Swain, *Wilderness Defender*.

44. "Colorado—A Game Sanctuary," *Rocky Mountain News*, 26 March 1915, and "Trying to Turn Travel to Wonderlands of the U.S." Scrapbook, Vol. 4, Clippings Re: Public Official Career, 1915–1916, Mather Papers.

45. In the spring of 1916, when the National Park Service bill was being debated in congress, Grosvenor devoted the April issue of *National Geographic* to American scenery. He wrote the only feature article, "Land of the Best," which was illustrated with over one hundred photographs of American sites and scenery. Lorimer also actively supported the parks not only by printing editorials discussing park issues but also by constantly featuring articles on the parks by such writers and park enthusiasts as Emerson Hough, Herbert Quick, Hal Evarts, and Mary Roberts Rinehart. The national park articles produced by these various writers for the *Sat-*

urday Evening Post covered a wide array of topics ranging from descriptions of specific parks to wildlife and nature study to tourism to park administrative issues. For an overview of the park publicity provided by the *Saturday Evening Post,* see Scrapbook, Vols. 4–7, especially Vol. 5, Clippings Re: Public Official Career, 1916–1919, Mather Papers. See also Shankland, *Steve Mather,* 85–92. Note that correspondence between Hal Evarts and Mather reveals that Mather kept Evarts abreast of park issues, provided him with information, and included him in park events. In 1920, when President Harding traveled to Yosemite, Mather invited Evarts to join the party. See Hal G. Evarts/Stephen Tyng Mather correspondence, Hal G. Evarts Papers, 1919–51, University of Oregon, Eugene, Oregon. Both Shankland and Swain suggest that Herbert Quick and Emerson Hough were also in close contact with the Park Service. See Shankland, *Steve Mather,* and Swain, *Wilderness Defender.*

46. Department of the Interior, *Annual Report of the Secretary of the Interior, 1918* (Washington, D.C.: GPO, 1918), 119, 122. Note that John Ise suggests that Mather probably drafted the letter for Secretary Lane. See Ise, *Our National Park Policy,* 195.

47. For a discussion of the ways in which western landscapes were represented as quintessential American landscapes, see Hyde, *American Vision.*

48. Clipping, "Development of the National Parks," *Chicago Tribune,* 18 January 1916, Scrapbook, Vol. 4, Clippings Re: Public Official Career, 1915–1916, Mather Papers.

49. Mark Daniels, "Scenic Resources in the United States," *California Forestry* 1 (May 1917): 12.

50. Department of Interior, *Report of the Director of the National Park Service to the Secretary of the Interior for the Fiscal Year Ended June 30, 1917* (Washington, D.C.: GPO, 1917), 15.

51. Ibid., 17–18.

52. Note that 335,299 people visited the parks in 1915 and 358,006 in 1916, as compared with 487,368 in 1917 according to Park Service estimates. Ibid., 190.

53. Stephen T. Mather to P. C. Spencer, 15 April 1918, Entry 6, General, Tours, Miscellaneous, 10 April 1917 to 10 November 1919, RG 79, NA, Maryland.

54. Stephen T. Mather, "Memorandum for the Secretary," 30 April 1918, and Edward Chambers to R. H. Aishton, 29 April 1918, Entry 6, General, Western Lines Bureau of Service, Part 1: April 30, 1918 to November 11, 1918, RG 79, NA, Maryland.

55. Edward Chambers to R. H. Aishton, 29 April 1918, Entry 6, General, Western Lines Bureau of Service, Part 1: April 30, 1918 to November 11, 1918, RG 79, NA, Maryland.

56. Horace M. Albright to Stephen T. Mather, telegram, 2 July 1918, Entry 6, General, Western Lines Bureau of Service, Part 1: April 30, 1918 to November 11, 1918, RG 79, NA, Maryland.

57. Howard H. Hayes to P. S. Eustis, 29 May 1918, Entry 6, General, Western Lines

Bureau of Service, Part 1: April 30, 1918 to November 11, 1918, RG 79, NA, Maryland.

58. Howard H. Hayes to P. S. Eustis, 29 May 1918, Entry 6, General, Western Lines Bureau of Service, Part 1: April 30, 1918 to November 11, 1918, RG 79, NA, Maryland.

59. For the various publicity strategies used by the Bureau of Service, see Howard H. Hays to Stephen T. Mather, 25 June 1918; Stephen T. Mather to Howard H. Hays, 27 June 1918; "Statement on Handling Correspondence about National Parks and Monuments Originating from Inquiries Received by Western Lines," n.d.; Howard H. Hays to Stephen T. Mather, 17 July 1918; and memorandum, 17 September 1918, all in Entry 6, General, Western Lines Bureau of Service, Part 1: April 30, 1918 to November 11, 1918, RG 79, NA, Maryland.

60. For an overview of the promotional activities undertaken by the Bureau of Service see Howard H. Hays, "Bureau of Service Resume, June 1 to September 30, 1918," Entry 6, General, Western Lines Bureau of Service, Part 1: April 30, 1918 to November 11, 1918, RG 79, NA, Maryland.

61. See Howard H. Hays, "Bureau of Service Resume, June 1 to September 30, 1918," Entry 6, General, Western Lines Bureau of Service, Part 1: April 30, 1918 to November 11, 1918, RG 79; and Howard H. Hays to Stephen T. Mather, 15 November 1918, Entry 6, General, Western Lines Bureau of Service, Part 2: November 14, 1918 to April 14, 1919, RG 79, NA, Maryland.

62. Howard H. Hays to Horace M. Albright, 17 December 1918, and Horace M. Albright to Howard H. Hays, 20 December 1918, Entry 6, General, Western Lines Bureau of Service, Part 2: November 14, 1918 to April 14, 1919, RG 79, NA, Maryland.

63. Howard H. Hayes to Stephen T. Mather, 1 February 1919, Entry 6, General, Western Lines Bureau of Service, Part 2: November 14, 1918 to April 14, 1919, RG 79, NA, Maryland.

64. Walter P. Hines to Ticket Agent, 15 May 1919, Entry 6, General, Western Lines Bureau of Service, Loose Papers, RG 79, NA, Maryland.

65. Circular No. 86, "Promotive Advertising of National Parks and Principal Western Resort Regions," 10 May 1919, Entry 6, General, Western Bureau of Service, RG 79, NA, Maryland.

66. "Bureau of Service Resume, January 1st to September 30, 1919," Entry 6, General, Western Bureau of Service Lines, Part 4, RG 79, NA, Maryland.

67. For a discussion of the ideal of scenic monumentalism, see Runte, *National Parks*, 11–47.

68. For post–World War I restrictions on Park Service publicity, see Stephen T. Mather to H. H. Hunkins, 5 April 1920, Entry 6, General, Western Bureau of Service Lines, Part 4, RG 79, NA, Maryland.

69. Franklin K. Lane, "A Mind's Eye Map of America," *National Geographic,* June 1920, 479 and 510.

70. Clipping, Stephen T. Mather, "National Parks in War Time," *Bulletin of the American Game Protective Association,* April 1918, in Scrapbook, Vol. 5, Clippings Re: Public Official Career, 1916–1919, Mather Papers.

71. John B. Patton, "National Parks Banquet," Entry 6, General, Publicity: Far Western Travelers Association, 23 June 1919 to 3 April 1920, RG 79, NA, Maryland.

72. A. B. Cammerer to C. R. Richards, 16 September 1919, Entry 6, General, Publicity: Far Western Travelers Association, 23 June 1919 to 3 April 1920, RG 79, NA, Maryland. Cammerer noted that he was sending a copy of the article on national parks for the forthcoming yearbook. See also attached "The National Parks, Our Scenic Wonderlands," Entry 6, General, Publicity: Far Western Travelers Association, 23 June 1919 to 3 April 1920, RG 79, NA, Maryland.

73. Huston Thompson, "Our National Parks," [Address of Hon. Houston A. Thompson Vice Chairman of the Federal Trade Commission Formerly Assistant Attorney General of the United States, Before the Far Western Traveler's Association at Hotel Plaza, New York City, 7 February 1920], Entry 6, General, Publicity: Far Western Travelers Association, 23 June 1919 to 3 April 1920, RG 79, NA, Maryland.

74. Press release, "Why the Far Western Travelers are Sending a Party of Boy Scouts to the West," 3 April 1920, Entry 6, General, Publicity: Far Western Travelers Association, 23 June 1919 to 3 April 1920, RG 79, NA, Maryland.

75. Thompson, "Our National Parks," 4.

76. "The National Parks, Our Scenic Wonderlands," 5, Entry 6, General, Publicity: Far Western Travelers Association, 23 June 1919 to 3 April 1920, RG 79 NA, Maryland.

77. See Blodgett, "Striking a Balance," 60–68.

78. Clipping, "National Park-to-Park Highway Association," Scrapbook, Vol. 4, Clippings Re: Public Official Career, 1915–1916, Mather Papers.

79. "Memorandum of the Press," 16 May 1919, Entry 6, General, Tours: Brooklyn Daily Eagle Tour, Part 1, RG 79, NA, Maryland.

80. The ideal of an inaugural run was specifically suggested by H. V. Kaltenborn, assistant managing editor and tour director of the *Brooklyn Daily Eagle.* See H. V. Kaltenborn to Chauncey, copy of letter, 20 May 1919, Entry 6, General, Tours: Brooklyn Daily Eagle Tour, Part 1, RG 79, NA, Maryland. For the details of promoting and organizing the tour, see Stephen T. Mather to Mr. H. W. Child, 24 May 1919; Horace M. Albright to Howard H. Hays, 27 May 1919; Horace M. Albright to H. H. Hunkins, 27 May 1919; and Horace M. Albright to H. W. Child, 4 June 1919. For the naming of the road, see Horace M. Albright to M. Max Goodsill, 28 May 1919, Entry 6, General, Tours: Brooklyn Daily Eagle Tour, Part 1, RG 79, NA, Maryland.

81. Gus Holmes to Librarian, Bureau of Public Roads, 22 December 1921, and attached pamphlet, "The National Park to Park Highway," Vertical Files, U.S. Department of Transportation Library, Washington, D.C.; and clipping, "Road

Sponsors Closed Sessions," *Salt Lake Tribune*, 18 July 1921, Entry 6, General, Maps: Second Annual Convention, National Park to Park Highway Association, Salt Lake City, Utah, 16–17 June 1921, RG 79, NA, Maryland.

82. Clipping, "State Parks: For the Beauty of America," *National Republican*, 22 March 1924, Scrapbook, Vol. 9, Personal Clippings, 1915–1929, Mather Papers.

83. Arno B. Cammerer to Abbott Lowell, 23 February 1923; see also letters to colleges and universities making the same request in General, Tours: Universities and Colleges, Part 1, 23 February to 12 June 1923, RG 79, NA, Maryland.

84. Franklin K. Lane to Stephen T. Mather, 13 May 1918, Entry 6, General, Manual, Loose Papers, RG 79, NA, Maryland. See also Hubert Work, "Statement of National Park Policy," 11 March 1925, Entry 7, General Administration and Personnel Policy, RG 79, NA, Maryland.

85. R. S. Yard to Howard H. Hays, 7 April 1919, Entry 6, General, Western Lines, Bureau of Service, Part 2: November 14, 1918 to April 14, 1919, RG 79, NA, Maryland.

86. Announcement, "Help Us Save the National Parks," Entry 6, General, National Parks Association, RG 79, NA, Maryland.

87. John C. Miles, *Guardians of the Parks: A History of the National Park and Conservation Association* (Washington, D.C.: Taylor and Francis, 1995).

88. Arno B. Cammerer, "Memorandum for Mr. Yard," 2 May 1923, Entry 6, General, National Parks Association, RG 79, NA, Maryland.

89. Arno B. Cammerer, "The National Parks, Our Out-of-Door Classrooms," 2, Entry 6, General, Publicity: Far Western Travelers Association, Part 2: April 8, 1920 to December 30, 1922, RG 79, NA, Maryland.

90. Executive Committee to the Members of the National Parks Association, 24 November 1920, Entry 6, General, National Parks Association, RG 79, NA, Maryland.

91. Announcement, "Annual Dinner of the Travel Club of America," 21 January 1922, Entry 6, General, Exhibits, Part 1: 21 September 1920 to 30 March 1922, RG 79, NA, Maryland. Note Robert Sterling Yard reiterated these comments verbatim in promotional material for the National Parks Association. See Robert Sterling Yard, "Essential Facts Concerning the War on the National Parks," n.d., Entry 6, General, National Parks Association, RG 79, NA, Maryland.

92. Richard Handler, "Authenticity," *Anthropology Today* 2 (February 1986), 2, 4. For an examination of the fascination with authenticity in American culture, see Kammen, *Mystic Chords of Memory*, and Miles Orvell, *The Real Thing: Imitation and Authenticity in American Culture, 1880–1940* (Chapel Hill: University of North Carolina Press, 1989).

93. Lionel Trilling, *Sincerity and Authenticity* (Cambridge: Harvard University Press, 1971), 93; quoted in Handler, "Authenticity," 3.

94. Handler, "Authenticity," 4. Note that Handler bases this idea of possession on the work of C. B. Macpherson and his theory of "possessive individualism" characteriz-

ing the modern ideology derived from Locke which links individualism to the possession of private property. See C. B. Macpherson, *The Political Theory of Possessive Individualism: Hobbs to Locke* (New York: Oxford University Press, 1962).

95. Robert S. Yard, "Economic Aspects of Our National Parks Policy," *Scientific Monthly*, April 1923, 387.

96. Roger W. Toll, "National Park Development Without Over-Development," Entry 6, General, Minutes, Sixth National Parks Conference, 1922, RG 79, NA, Maryland.

97. Robert Sterling Yard, "The People and the National Parks," *Survey Graphic*, August 1922, 547. Note that Yard develops and reiterates this argument in Yard, "Economic Aspects of Our National Parks Policy."

98. Yard, "People and the National Parks," 547–48 and 550.

99. Ibid., 583.

100. Ibid., 552.

101. "Accommodations for Colored People," Entry 6, General, Minutes, Sixth National Parks Conference, 1922, RG 79, NA, Maryland.

102. John Wesley Hill, "Extract from a Speech Delivered at the Opening of Yellowstone National Park, June 20, 1923," 3, 6, and 8, Entry 6, General, Dr. John Wesley Hill, Part 1, 26 May 1923 to 20 September 1923, RG 79, NA, Maryland.

103. Ibid., 9–11.

104. Ibid., 14.

105. Smith, *Virgin Land*. For further discussion of the republican ideal of the American nation, see J. G. A. Pocock, *The Machiavellian Moment: Floretine Political Thought and the Atlantic Republican Tradition* (Princeton, N.J.: Princeton University Press, 1975), and Ross, "Liberal Tradition Revisited," 116–31.

106. Gellner, *Nations and Nationalism*, 49.

4. A NATION ON WHEELS

1. Newton A. Fuessle, "The Lincoln Highway—A National Road," *Travel*, February 1915, 26–29; March 1915, 30–33, 57; April 1915, 30–33.

2. Fuessle, "Lincoln Highway—A National Road," 26.

3. John B. Rae, *The American Automobile: A Brief History* (Chicago: University of Chicago Press, 1965), 1–11. Despite the significance of the automobile in American culture, the scholarly literature is relatively sparse. For introductory surveys, see John B. Rae, *The Road and the Car in American Life* (Cambridge: MIT Press, 1971); Rae, *American Automobile*; and James J. Flink, *The Car Culture* (Cambridge: MIT Press, 1975), *America Adopts the Automobile, 1895–1910* (Cambridge: MIT Press, 1970), *The Automobile Age* (Cambridge: MIT Press, 1988), and "Three Stages of American Automobile Consciousness," *American Quarterly* 24 (October 1972): 451–73. For surveys addressing the cultural issues raised by the automobile, see Warren James

Belasco, *Americans on the Road: From Autocamp to Motel, 1910–1945* (Cambridge: MIT Press, 1981); Michael L. Berger, *The Devil Wagon in God's Country: The Automobile and Social Change in Rural America, 1893–1929.* (Hamden, Conn.: Archon Books, 1979); B. Bruce-Briggs, *The War against the Automobile* (New York: E. P. Dutton, 1977); Kathleen Franz, "Narrating Automobility: Travelers, Tinkerers, and Technological Authority in the Twentieth Century" (Ph.D. diss., Brown University, 1999); Cynthia Golomb Dettelbach, *In the Driver's Seat: The Automobile in American Literature and Popular Culture* (Westport, Conn.: Greenwood Press, 1976); Joseph Anthony Interrante, "A Movable Feast: The Automobile and the Spatial Transformation of American Culture, 1890–1940" (Ph.D. diss., Harvard University, 1983); David L. Lewis and Laurence Goldstein, eds., *The Automobile and American Culture* (Ann Arbor: University of Michigan Press, 1980); Clay McShane, *Down the Asphalt Path: American Cities and the Coming of the Automobile* (New York: Columbia University Press, 1994); Virginia Scharff, *Taking the Wheel: Women and the Coming of the Motor Age* (New York: Free Press, 1991); Reynold M. Wik, *Henry Ford and Grass Roots America* (Ann Arbor: University of Michigan Press, 1973).

4. Rae, *American Automobile*, 17. Peter J. Hugill, "The Rediscovery of America: Elite Automobile Touring," *Annals of Tourism Research* 12, no. 3 (1985): 435–447.

5. Hugill, "Good Roads and the Automobile," 327–49.

6. For the history of the development of automobile touring, see Belasco, *Americans on the Road*; Hugill, "Rediscovery of America"; Interrante, "Moveable Feast"; Jakle, *Tourist*, 101–19; and Rothman, *Devil's Bargains*, 143–67.

7. For an example of books promoting auto touring in Europe, see Francis Miltoun, *The Automobilist Abroad* (Boston: Page, 1907); Thomas Dowler Murphy, *British Highways and Byways from a Motor Car* (Boston: Page, 1908); and Edith Wharton, *The Motor Flight Through France* (New York: Scribner's, 1909). For an overview of the periodical literature promoting touring, see *American Motorist* 1909–1913.

8. Rae, *Road and the Car*, 34.

9. Carey S. Bliss, *Autos across America: A Bibliography of Transcontinental Automobile Travel, 1903–1940* (New Haven: Jekins & Reese, 1982), 1.

10. For an overview of some of the early transcontinental tours, see "Touring Across the Continent," *American Motorist*, May 1911, 261–64; Darwin S. Hatch, "Transcontinental Treks of Other Days," *Motor Age*, 25 February 1915, 36–40; Bliss, *Autos across America*.

11. For an overview of the Glidden Tours, see Jakle, *Tourist*, 106–7.

12. Hatch, "Transcontinental Treks of Other Days.".

13. Bliss, *Autos across America*, 22–23; Darwin S. Hatch, "Transcontinental Treks of Other Days," *Motor Age*, 25 February 1915; and Victor Eubank, "Log of an Auto

Prairie Schooner: Motor Pioneers on the 'Trail to Sunset,'" *Sunset,* February 1912, 188–95.

14. Hatch, "Transcontinental Treks of Other Days."

15. "'Personally Conducted' Transcontinental Tour," *American Motorist,* September 1911, 526–27.

16. Rae, *American Automobile,* 59–61 and 66.

17. Although there has been a vast amount of material written about the development of roads in the United States, there is relatively little critical scholarship on the topic. For a concise overview of the history of roads in the United States see Rae, *Road and the Car,* 3–86. For a more popular history, see Phil Patton, *Open Road: A Celebration of the American Highway* (New York: Simon & Schuster, 1986). For a history of the development of an interstate highway system and the Bureau of Public Roads, see Bruce E. Seely, *Building the American Highway System: Engineers as Policy Makers* (Philadelphia: Temple University Press, 1987). For the influence of the bicycle and the development of the Good Roads movement, see Mason, "League of American Wheelmen." For surveys addressing the cultural issues of the development of roads in the United States, see Jean Labatut and Wheaton J. Lane, eds., *Highways in Our National Life: A Symposium* (Princeton, N.J.: Princeton University Press, 1950); Chester H. Liebs, *Main Street to Miracle Mile: American Roadside Architecture* (Boston: Little, Brown, 1985); Karal A. Marling, *Colossus of Roads: Myth and Symbol along the American Highway* (Minneapolis: University of Minnesota Press, 1984); and Thomas J. Schlereth, *U.S. 40: A Roadscape of the American Experience* (Indianapolis: Indiana Historical Society, 1985).

18. Seely, *Building the American Highway System,* 9–66.

19. For a comprehensive overview of good roads rhetoric, see American Automobile Association, *Federal Aid for Good Roads, Proceedings of First National Convention* (Washington, D.C.: American Automobile Association, 1912). See also Mason, "League of American Wheelmen," 83–105.

20. Mary Eloise de Garmo to Robert P. Hooper, 10 January 1912, reprinted in American Automobile Association, *Federal Aid for Good Roads,* 20.

21. Mason, "League of American Wheelmen," 124–49; and Seely, *Building the American Highway System,* 36–45.

22. Quoted in Richard Weingroff, "The National Old Trails Road," unpublished manuscript in possession of author, 1989, 1. In addition to giving me a copy of his unpublished manuscript on the history of the National Old Trails Road, I am indebted to Richard Weingroff of the Department of Transportation for discussing the history of early roads with me, and for allowing me to examine his personal files related to the history of road development in the United States.

23. "Transcontinental Highway Organizations," "Trail Organizations," "Routes," "Organized Highways of National Importance," Named Roads, Vertical Files, U.S. De-

partment of Transportation Manuscripts, Department of Transportation Library, Washington, D.C. (hereafter cited as DOT MSS).

24. "The Old Trails Road: The National Highway as a Monument to the Pioneer Men and Women" (Elizabeth Butler Gentry, 1911), 5, National Old Trails Road, Vertical Files, DOT MSS.

25. Note that Boone's Lick Road is also spelled Boon's Lick Road in some places, and Kearny is spelled Kearney. For the sake of consistency I have used Boone and Kearny throughout the chapter.

26. "The Old Trails Road: The National Highway as a Monument," 9 and 11.

27. For a discussion of the rising popular interest in American history and Americana see Kammen, *Mystic Chords of Memory*, 338–41.

28. Weingroff, "National Old Trails Road," 2–4.

29. "Vast Road System," *Better Roads*, September 1911, 29.

30. Mrs. T. A. Cordry, *The Story of the Marking of the Santa Fe Trail* (Topeka, Kans.: Crane, 1915), 13.

31. Cordry, *Story of the Marking of the Santa Fe Trail*; J. M. Lowe, *The National Old Trails Road: The Great Historic Highway of America* (Kansas City: Published by author, 1924), 3; and Marc Simmons, *Following the Santa Fe Trail: A Guide for Modern Travelers* (Santa Fe, N.M.: Ancient City Press, 1984), 9–12.

32. For a comprehensive history of the National Old Trails Road, see Weingroff, "National Old Trails Road."

33. For an overview of the dispute, see ibid., 41–44.

34. "Good Roads Notes Gathered Here and There," *Southern Good Roads*, January 1912, 21–23.

35. "National Old Trails Road Convention," *Better Roads*, June 1912, 66–88.

36. "National Old Trails Road Association," *Better Roads and Streets*, September 1915, 41.

37. Weingroff, "National Old Trails Road," 29–30.

38. A. L. Westgard, "Motor Routes to the California Expositions" (National Highways Association, 1915), 2, DOT MSS.

39. Weingroff, "National Old Trails Road," 32.

40. "National Old Trails Road," *Better Roads*, August 1912, 58, 56, and 57.

41. National Old Trails Association, *Proceedings of the First National Old Trails Road Convention, Held at the Commercial Club Room, Kansas City, Missouri, April 17, 1912* (Kansas City: National Old Trails Association, 1920), 86–93.

42. "Address by Mrs. Hunter M. Merriwether," *Better Roads*, June 1912, 70.

43. "One of the Many Reasons Why You Should See America First," *American Motorist*, February 1913, 144–45; March 1913, 232–33; and May 1913, 390.

44. W. D. Rishel, "What Transcontinental Touring Really Means," *American Motorist*, May 1913, 395, 396, and 398.

45. James T. McCleary, "What Shall the Lincoln Memorial Be?" Lincoln Memorial Road, Vertical Files, DOT MSS. See also "Lincoln Memorial Highway Bill Pending," *American Motorist*, February 1911, 108; "Address of Hon. William P. Borland of Missouri," in American Automobile Association, *Federal Aid for Good Roads*, 81–84; and Hokanson, *Lincoln Highway*, 9. Little has been written about the history of parkways. For a comprehensive overview with an emphasis on the Mount Vernon Memorial Parkway see Timothy Mark Davis, "Mt. Vernon Memorial Highway and the Evolution of the American Parkway" (Ph.D. diss., University Texas, Austin, 1997). See also Christian Zapatka, "The American Parkways: Origins and Evolution of the Park Road," *Quarterly Architectural Review* (Winter 1984): 113–21.

46. McCleary, "What Shall the Lincoln Memorial Be?" 15, 16–17, and 21.

47. Quoted in Hokanson, *Lincoln Highway*, 9.

48. Fisher wrote to the Lincoln Memorial Road Association after Congress had voted down McCleary's proposal and asked if they would turn the name over to his group to use for their idea of a coast-to-coast highway. See Lincoln Highway Association, *The Lincoln Highway: The Story of a Crusade that Made Transportation History* (New York: Dodd, Mead, 1935), 24.

49. Quoted in Hokanson, *Lincoln Highway*, 11. For a complete overview of the Lincoln Highway and its history see Hokanson, *Lincoln Highway*. For an official history, see Lincoln Highway Association, *Lincoln Highway*. It should be noted that the incredible amount of publicity generated and disseminated by the Lincoln Highway Association has made it the most popular of the named transcontinental roads, and much of what has been written about the highway assumes that it was the first transcontinental highway to be proposed and constructed. As the material on the National Old Trails Road reveals, this was not the case. Although these issues are not the focus of this chapter, it should be noted that there is ample opportunity for additional scholarship on the history of the Lincoln Highway and the development of early long-distance roads. For an overview of the publicity tactics used by the association, see Lincoln Highway Association, *Lincoln Highway*, 91–107.

50. For the official proclamation of the route, see Lincoln Highway Association, *Lincoln Highway*, 61–64.

51. Hokanson, *Lincoln Highway*, 17.

52. "Following the Path of Progress" (Detroit: Lincoln Highway Association, 1914), DOT MSS. Although the author's name is not listed on this pamphlet, selections of this essay were reprinted in the *American Motorist* and attributed to A. R. Pardington. See A. R. Pardington, "Following the Path of Progress," *American Motorist*, January 1915, 28–29.

53. Ibid., 2.

54. Lincoln Highway Association, *The Complete Official Road Guide of the Lincoln Highway* (Detroit: Lincoln Highway Association, 1915), 25–26.

55. For an overview of the issues raised in this debate, see Mason, "League of American Wheelmen," 90–105, and 124–49.

56. William Stull Holt, *The Bureau of Public Roads: Its History, Activities and Organization* (Baltimore: Johns Hopkins University Press, 1923), 14.

57. For an assessment of the issues of federal aid, see Seely, *Building the American Highway System*; Holt, *Bureau of Public Roads*; and "U.S. Bureau of Public Roads and its Work," 30 June 1930, DOT MSS.

58. C. H. Claudy, *The National Highways Association* (N.p.: National Highways Association, 1914), 1, DOT MSS.

59. For biographical background on Davis, see "Charles Davis, 86, Retired Engineer," *New York Times*, 4 June 1951; Claudy, *National Highways Association*, 33; Allan Sinsheimer, "Father of the National Highways Association, Charles Henry Davis," reprinted from *Motor Age*, 31 August 1916, National Highways Association, Vertical Files, DOT MSS; L. C. Hall, "Charles Henry Davis and National Highways," reprinted from *Cape Cod Magazine*, September 1916, National Highways Association, Vertical Files, DOT MSS; "The National Highways Association: Its Aims and Purposes," reprinted from *Automobile Journal*, September 1913, National Highways Association, Vertical Files, DOT MSS.

60. Claudy, *National Highways Association*; and "National Highways Association: Its Aims and Purposes."

61. For a list of Good Roads organizations associated with the National Highways Association, see Claudy, *National Highways Association*, 18.

62. "National Highways Association: Its Aims and Purposes," 7–8. For an autobiographical account of Westgard's role as a pathfinder, see A. L. Westgard, *Tales of a Pathfinder* (New York: Author, 1920).

63. Claudy, *National Highways Association*, 10.

64. "The National Old Trails Road," reprinted from *Travel*, May 1915, 1, DOT MSS.

65. Hugill, "Good Roads and the Automobile," 332.

66. "Illustrated Arguments for and against National Highways Versus Federal Aid" (National Highways Association, 1913), 12, DOT MSS.

67. "National Highways Association: Its Aims and Purposes," 4.

68. Charles Henry Davis, "Good Roads Everywhere," 3, 5, 18, and 9; address delivered before the Annual Convention of the North Carolina Good Roads Association, 31 July, 1 August 1913, reprinted in National Highways Association Publications, Vol. 2, DOT MSS.

69. Charles Henry Davis, "The National Old Trails Road: Perpetuating the Historic

Highways of America's Pioneers—The Value of the Old Trails Road in the 'See America' Movement," 5, reprinted from *Travel*, May 1915, DOT MSS.

70. Charles Henry Davis, *National Highways*, 14, 2, and 3, National Highways Publications, Vol. 2, DOT MSS.

71. Davis, *National Highways*, 1.

72. For further discussion of automobile tourism as experience, see Rothman, *Devil's Bargains*, 148.

73. For a discussion of the effect of World War I on the transportation network in the United States, see Rae, *Road and the Car*, 37–38.

74. Flink, *Automobile Age*, 38.

75. Rae, *Road and the Car*, 50.

76. For an overview of the popularization of automobile touring, see Belasco, *Americans on the Road*. Although Belasco implies, as do the tourists narratives that he analyzes, that touring was a democratic pastime, the time and expenses demanded for an automobile tour suggest that it remained a relatively exclusive pastime into the 1920s and beyond. In 1921 an estimated 20,000 Americans out of a population of 100 million Americans, approximately .02 percent of the total population, made transcontinental tours. (For estimated number of transcontinental tourists see page 72. For population estimates in 1921, see *Historical Statistics of the United States, Colonial Times to 1970* [Washington, D.C.: GPO, 1975], pt. 1, 9.) Granted a transcontinental motor tour was the most expensive and time consuming type of tour, and thus drew only a limited number of tourists. When compared to the number of people estimated to have traveled abroad in 1921—294,000 people—the exclusivity of automobile touring becomes more apparent. (For the number of people traveling abroad, see *Historical Statistics*, pt. 1, 404.) Although Belasco notes that in 1919 there were 6.7 million cars registered in the United States which increased to 17.5 million in 1925, arguing, "It seems reasonable that the number of autocampers increased proportionally," with some agencies suggesting that during the 1920s there were between 10 and 20 million autocampers on the road each year, what one needs to consider is that all those who might have used automobile camps were not tourists (see Belasco, *Americans on the Road*, 74). Many of the touring narratives published suggest that auto tourists took to the road for a month or sometimes more with a daily cost per person ranging between $1.00 and $5.00, not including repairs, and initial costs of equipment. Thus, a month-long tour at the least might cost between $30.00 and $150.00, which accounted for between 2 and 10 percent of the average clerical workers yearly income of $1,505. Even Belasco notes that "a $100.00 trip was beyond the range of the average family with an annual income under $1,500." (For the cost of touring, see Belasco, *Americans on the Road*, 42–43. For the average yearly income of clerical workers, see *Historical Statistics*, pt. 1, 321.)

In addition, a depiction of the class of people who toured also depends on how the idea of touring is defined. I believe that the experience of touring meant much more than just spending the night on the road with an automobile. It was a vacation of more than one day or night spent on the road and directed toward the leisure possibilities offered along the road. Although automobile touring was presented as a much more democratic form of leisure, it was not until after World War II that this became a reality. See also Franz, "Narrating Automobility," 95–100.

77. "Federal-State Highway Board Starts Work Recommending Simplicity and Uniformity in Marking," Department of Agriculture press release, 21 April 1925, United States Numbered Highways, Vertical Files, DOT MSS.

78. For an overview of the resolutions agreed upon by the Joint Board, see "Uniform Road Marker System Planned," *Colorado Highways*, May 1925, 11.

79. "Uniform Road Marker System Planned," *Colorado Highways*, May 1925, 11.

80. See Department of Agriculture press releases, United States Numbered Highways and United States Routes, Vertical Files, DOT MSS.

81. "Complete U.S. Highway System Now Designated and Approved," U.S. Department of Agriculture, Press Release, 2 January 1927, U.S. Routes, Vertical Files, DOT MSS. See American Association of State Highway Officials, *Manual and Specifications for the Manufacture, Display and Erection of U.S. Standard Road markers and Signs*, 1st ed. (N.p.: N.p, 1927), for the standard system of signage adopted.

82. "Passing of the 'Paper' Highways," press release, U.S. Routes, Vertical Files, DOT MSS.

83. "Ohio Method of Marking Highways Offers Best Suggestion," clipping, U.S. Numbered Routes, Vertical Files, DOT MSS.

84. Quoted in "Ohio Method of Marking Highways Offers Best Suggestion."

85. "United States Route No. 1 Is a Highway of History," 9 October 1927, U.S. Department of Agriculture, press release, U.S. Routes, Vertical Files, DOT MSS; "United States Route 40—Great East-and-West Motorway—Traces Paths of Pioneers," 29 April 1928, U.S. Department of Agriculture, Press Release; "From A. C. to Astoria," 7 October 1928, U.S. Department of Agriculture, Press Release; "Longest Stretch of Improved Road," 16 December 1928, U.S. Department of Agriculture, Press Release, U.S. Routes, Vertical Files, DOT MSS; "Two Southern Highways Available for Coast-to-Coast Motoring," 1 September 1929, U.S. Department of Agriculture, Press Release; "Scenic and Historic Highway Connects North and South," 30 March 1930, U.S. Department of Agriculture, Press Release; "U.S. Highway No. 66 from Chicago to West Coast Is All-Year Route," 21 June 1931, U.S. Department of Agriculture, Press Release, U.S. Routes, Vertical Files, DOT MSS.

86. "United States Route No. 1 Is a Highway of History."

87. "Longest Stretch of Improved Road."

88. "United States Route 40—Great East-and-West Motorway—Traces Paths of Pioneers," 29 April 1928, Department of Agriculture, Press Release, U.S. Routes, Vertical Files, DOT MSS.

89. William Ullman, "Springtime Is Motoring Time: A Medley of Thoughts," *American Motorist*, April 1916, 10.

90. Ullman, "Springtime Is Motoring Time," 17.

91. Robert Bruce, "Named and Marked Roads," *American Motorist*, April 1917, 9.

92. *American Motorist*, May 1924, contents page.

93. Stanley G. Thompson, "Scenic Tour of the Blue Grass," *American Motorist*, July 1926, 38.

94. "The Trail of the Lonesome Pine," *American Motorist*, July 1926, 36.

95. Eva Barr, "The Redwood Empire," *American Motorist*, July 1926, 88.

96. Otto W. Jones, "By the Waters of the Turbulent Columbia," *American Motorist*, July 1926, 55.

97. Elon Jessup, "Those Amazing Northeastern States," *American Motorist*, July 1926, 20.

98. For a brief discussion of the relationship between the development of tourism in the United States and the dissemination of popular conceptions about American tradition and history, see Kammen, *Mystic Chords of Memory*, 338–41.

99. For an analysis of the growing interest in self-fulfillment and "real" experience during the Progressive era, see Lears, *No Place of Grace*.

100. Dr. William Joseph Showalter, "Washington the Mecca of Vacation Touring," *American Motorist*, March 1927, 9.

101. *American Motorist*, September 1924, table of contents page.

5. NARRATING THE NATION

1. Federal Works Agency, Work Projects Administration, "WPA Announces Guide Week November 10 to 16," Folder 6, Miscellaneous Procedure, Box 2, Instructions 13–18, Miscellaneous, Alsberg Letters, etc., Entry 11, Manuals and Instructions, 1935–1939, Works Project Administration, Records of the Federal Writers' Project, Records of the Central Office, RG 69, NA, Maryland (hereafter cited as RG 69, NA, Maryland). Note that subsequent citations from RG 69 are formatted in the following manner: document, folder, box, entry, record group. Titles of boxes and folders will be provided (hereafter box numbers and folder numbers will be omitted).

2. Roosevelt's letter of endorsement quote in "American Guide Week Planned for November 10th–16th," *Publishers Weekly*, 11 October 1941, 1463.

3. Federal Works Agency, Work Projects Administration, "WPA Announces Guide Week November 10 to 16."

4. Roosevelt's letter of endorsement quoted in "American Guide Week Planned for November 10th–16th," 1463.
5. Little has been written about the literature of travel guides in the United States. For a discussion of George A. Crofutt's guides, see Fifer, *American Progress,* and Waite, "Over the Ranges," 103–13. For discussion of the Baedeker guide to the United States, see Larzer Ziff, *The American 1890s: Life and Times of a Lost Generation* (New York: Viking Press, 1966), 4–8.
6. *Appleton's Hand-Book Through the United States* (New York: D. Appleton, 1846); Wellington Williams, *Appleton's New and Complete United States Guidebook for Travelers: Embracing the Northern, Eastern, Southern and Western States, Canada, Nova Scotia, New Brunswick, etc.* (New York: D. Appleton, 1850); T. Addison Richards, *Appleton's Illustrated Hand-Book of American Travel* (New York: D. Appleton, 1857); Edward H. Hall, *Appleton's Hand-Book of American Travel: The Northern Tour* (New York: D. Appleton, 1867); Edward H. Hall, *Appleton's Hand Book of American Travel: The Southern Tour* (New York: D. Appleton, 1866); *Appleton's Hand-Book of American Travel: The Western Tour* (New York: D. Appleton, 1873).
7. *Appleton's Hand-Book Through the United States,* title page, v, xiv, and vi. For an overview of the tourist opportunities of the mid-nineteenth century in the United States, see Aron, *Working at Play;* Brown, *Inventing New England;* William Irwin, *The New Niagara: Tourism, Technology, and the landscape of Niagara Falls, 1776–1917* (University Park: Pennsylvania State University Press, 1996); Elizabeth McKinsey, *Niagara Falls: Icon of the American Sublime* (New York: Cambridge University Press, 1985); and Sears, *Sacred Places.*
8. Williams, *Appleton's New and Complete United States Guide Book,* 4.
9. Richards, *Appleton's Illustrated Hand-Book of American Travel,* 5, 13, 23, and 6.
10. Hall, *Appleton's Hand-Book of American Travel: The Northern Tour.* Note that the northern tour was organized by state and included New York, Connecticut, Rhode Island, Massachusetts, New Hampshire, Vermont, Maine, New Jersey, Delaware, Pennsylvania, Ohio, Indiana, Illinois, Missouri, Iowa, Minnesota, Wisconsin, Michigan, Kansas, Nebraska, California, Oregon, Washington, Arizona, New Mexico, Nevada, Utah, Idaho, Montana, Colorado, and Dacotah [*sic*]. Hall, *Appleton's Hand-Book of American Travel: The Southern Tour.* Note that the southern tour included Maryland, the District of Columbia, Virginia, North Carolina, South Carolina, Georgia, Florida, Alabama, Mississippi, Louisiana, Texas, Arkansas, Tennessee, and Kentucky. *Appleton's Hand-Book of American Travel: Western Tour.* Note that the western tour included Ohio, Indiana, Illinois, Iowa, Michigan, Wisconsin, Minnesota, Missouri, Kansas, Nebraska, Colorado, Nevada, California, Oregon, and the territories of Dakota, Wyoming, Montana, Idaho, Utah, Washington, and Alaska.
11. Hall, *Appleton's Hand-Book of American Travel: The Northern Tour,* xi.

12. Joshua Shaw, *Picturesque Views of American Scenery* (Philadelphia: M. Carey & Son, 1820), Nathaniel Parker Willis, *American Scenery; or Land, Lake, and River Illustrations of Transatlantic Nature* (London: George Virtue, 1840). See Huth, *Nature and the American*, 52–54.

13. *The Scenery of the United States Illustrated in a Series of Forty Engravings* (New York: D. Appleton, 1855), v, 12, and 14.

14. William Cullen Bryant, ed., *Picturesque America; or, The Land We Live In* (New York: D. Appleton, 1872), vol. 1, pt. 1, iii.

15. Advertisement in Bryant, *Picturesque America*, vol. 1, pt. 1, n.p.

16. See Huth, *Nature and the American*, 152.

17. Advertisement in Bryant, *Picturesque America*, vol. 1, pt. 1, n.p.

18. For a discussion of the picturesque, see William Gilpin, *Three Essays on Picturesque Beauty* (Westmead, England: Gregg International Publishers, 1972); Hunt, *Gardens and the Picturesque*, 5; Stafford, *Voyage into Substance*, 3–13; and Alder, "Origins of Sightseeing," 7–29. For an interesting discussion of the ways in which the picturesque influenced ways of seeing, see Gina M. Crandall, "When Art Challenges Beauty," *Landscape* 29 (1986): 10–16, and *Nature Pictorialized*.

19. John Towner, "The Grand Tour: A Key Phase in the History of Tourism," *Annals of Tourism Research* 12, no. 3 (1985): 297–334. For a concise history of the Grand Tour, see Jeremy Black, *British Abroad*, especially 14–85.

20. Note that not all eighteenth-century travel focused on the picturesque. For a discussion of the differences between picturesque travel and voyages of exploration, see Stafford, *Voyage into Substance*.

21. Bryant, *Picturesque America*, vol. 1, pt. 1, iii; vol. 1, pt. 1, 14; vol. 2, pt. 1, 3; vol. 1, pt. 1, iii; and vol. 2, pt. 1, 2.

22. For an analysis of the tourist gaze in relation to contemporary tourist sites, see John Urry, *The Tourist Gaze: Leisure and Travel in Contemporary Society* (London: Sage Publications, 1990).

23. Bryant, *Picturesque America*, vol. 1, pt. 1, 8; and vol. 1, pt. 1, 10.

24. For a discussion of the visual emphasis in tourism, see Edward M. Bruner, "The Ethnographer/Tourist Is Indonesia," in *International Tourism: Identity and Change*, ed. Marie-Françoise Lanfant, John B. Allcock, and Edward M. Bruner (London: Sage, 1995), 224–41.

25. Bryant, *Picturesque America*, vol. 1, pt. 2, 424.

26. Ibid., vol. 1, pt. 2, 347, and vol. 1, pt. 2, 562.

27. For the concept of sacred places see Sears, *Sacred Places*.

28. Bryant, *Picturesque America*, vol. 1, pt. 2, 320, and vol. 2, pt. 1, 27.

29. I am indebted to Leah Dilworth for pointing out the importance of spectacle in the construction of the tourist experience. See Dilworth, *Imagining Indians in the Southwest*.

30. D. W. Meinig, "Symbolic Landscapes: Models of American Community," in *The Interpretation of Ordinary Landscapes: Geographical Essays*, ed. D. W. Meinig (New York: Oxford University Press, 1979), 164.

31. For a brief history of the Page Company, see John Tebbel, *A History of Book Publishing in the United States* (New York: R. R. Bowker, 1975), 2:400–402, 509, 598, 653; 3:42, 545. See also Raymond Lincoln Kilgour, *Estes and Lauriat: A History, 1872–1898* (Ann Arbor: University of Michigan Press, 1957), and "Page Company Absorbs Dana Estes and Co.," *Publishers Weekly*, 28 March 1914, 1098–1100. Founded in 1897, the company continued to publish through the 1950s, when it was bought out by Farrar, Straus and Giroux. Note that when originally established, the company was called L. C. Page and Company, after its president and general manager, Lewis Coues Page. In 1914, when the company acquired the Estes and Lauriat publishing house, the name was shortened to the Page Company. Throughout this chapter the company will be referred to by its later name.

32. See America First series advertisement. George Wharton James, *California Romantic and Beautiful* (Boston: Page, 1914), front piece. Note that these advertisements for the series were updated for every subsequent volume in the series.

33. Charles Edwin Hopkins, *Ohio the Beautiful and Historic* (Boston: Page, 1931), ix.

34. Edward Mendelson, "Baedeker's Universe," *Yale Review* 74 (April 1985): 386–403, provides a concise overview of the style used by Baedeker guides. For a brief discussion of Baedeker's guide to the United States, see Ziff, *American 1890s*, 4–8. Quotation from James, *California Romantic and Beautiful*, xvii.

35. Hopkins, *Ohio the Beautiful and Historic*, x.

36. James was a popular advocate for the American Southwest. His writings covered a wide array of topics which included the geography of California and the Southwest, California missions and their Hispanic origins, as well as southwestern and Californian Indians and their ceremonies and crafts. After exiling himself from California, James spent two years in Chicago, where he continued lecturing and wrote *Chicago's Dark Places* (1891), which, in the spirit of Progressive reform, exposed the plight of the Chicago slums. He then returned to southern California in 1892 and began a new career as a tour guide for Professor Thaddeus S. C. Lowe's Echo Mountain Railway and Hotel. In addition James began writing and lecturing about the wonders of Southern California and the Southwest. In 1893 he published *Scenic Mount Lowe and its Wonderful Railway*, which was followed by *The Tourist Guide Book to Southern California* (1895). In the following five years he wrote a number of books detailing the tourist attractions of California and the Southwest covering such topics as California scenery, Spanish missions, and the wonders of the Grand Canyon, including *Old Missions and Mission Indians of California* (Los Angeles: B. R. Baumgardt, 1895), *Picturesque Southern California* (Los Angeles, 1898), and *In and Around the Grand Canyon*

(Boston: Little, Brown, 1900). The Grand Canyon book attracted national attention and established James as an authority on tourism in the Southwest. This book was followed by a number of successful titles on related topics, including *Indian Basketry* (New York: H. Malkan, 1901), *Indians of the Painted Desert Region* (Boston: Little, Brown, 1903), *In and Out of the Old Missions of California* (Boston: Little, Brown, 1905), *Wonders of the Colorado Desert* (Boston: Little, Brown, 1906), and *Through Ramona's Country* (Boston: Little, Brown, 1908). By 1914 James had become a well-established authority on southern California and southwestern culture and a noted travel writer. He was the obvious choice to write the California guide, which would debut the See America First series. For biographical information and a broad overview of his career, see *Masterkey*, Spring 1986, special issue on "George Wharton James: Writer, Collector, Photographer." Articles include Stephen G. Maurer, "In the Heart of the Great Freedom: George Wharton James and the Desert Southwest," 4–10; Paul R. Arreola, "George Wharton James and the Indians," 11–18; and Enrique Cortes, "Advocate for the Golden State: George Wharton James in California," 19–25. See also Joseph Bourdon, "George Wharton James, Interpreter of the Southwest" (Ph.D. diss., University of California, Los Angeles, 1965), and Kevin Starr, *Inventing the Dream: California through the Progressive Era* (New York: Oxford University Press, 1985), 109–12.

37. James, *California, Romantic and Beautiful*; Murphy, *Three Wonderlands*; Frank Hutchins and Cortelle Hutchins, *Houseboating on a Colonial Waterway* (Boston: Page, 1914); Forbes Lindsay, *Panama and the Canal Today* (Boston: Page, 1910); and Charles L. G. Anderson, *Old Panama and the Castillo Del Oro* (Boston: Page, 1914). Page Company advertisement, *Publishers Weekly*, 26 September 1914, 1085. A survey of the Page Company advertisements in *Publishers Weekly* from January 1912 to December 1914 revealed no advertisements for the See America First series previous to the aforementioned James advertisement. Although Bourdon in his biography of James suggests that *California Romantic and Beautiful* was the second volume in the series, he provides no citation to verify this statement (see Bourdon, "George Wharton James, Interpreter of the Southwest," 226). Reviews of the James book also suggest that *California Romantic and Beautiful* was not the first See America First series publication (see "Books on California," *Nation*, 17 December 1914, 714). As stated, the Page Company included a number of previously published books in the announcement of their See America First series to fill out the series. However, the survey of *Publishers Weekly* suggests that James's volume on California was actually the first volume commissioned specifically for the series.

38. See the review of James, *California Romantic and Beautiful*, in "Other Books Worth While," *Literary Digest*, 16 January 1915, 107, 109.

39. James, *California Romantic and Beautiful*, xvii.

40. John Higham, *History: Professional Scholarship in America* (Baltimore: Johns Hopkins University Press, 1983), 173. For further discussion of the notion of Progressive history, see Richard Hofstadter, *The Progressive Historians: Turner, Beard, Parrington* (New York: Knopf, 1968).

41. For a discussion of the rational view characteristic of the Progressive era, see Robert H. Wiebe, *The Search for Order, 1877–1920* (New York: Hill & Wang, 1967), 145–63; Cecelia Tichi, *Shifting Gears: Technology, Literature, Culture in Modernists America* (Chapel Hill: University of North Carolina Press, 1987); and Martha Banta, *Taylored Lives: Narrative Productions on the Age of Taylor, Veblen and Ford* (Chicago: University of Chicago Press, 1993).

42. For an overview of post-Darwinist thought popular in the Progressive era, see Richard Hofstadter, *Social Darwinism in American Thought*, rev. ed. (New York: George Braziller, 1959), and Wiebe, *Search for Order*, 133–63.

43. After exiling himself from California in 1889, James spent two years in Chicago, where he lectured and wrote *Chicago's Dark Places*, which, in the spirit of progressive reform, sought to expose the plight of the Chicago slums.

44. Born in Iowa, Murphy first established himself as a newspaper editor. In 1895 he organized the Thomas Dowler Murphy Company, which manufactured and sold art calendars displaying reproductions of paintings by famous European and American artists. By 1904 he had expanded his business to England. Murphy's travel writing grew out of his interest in automobiling, and his early guides recounted the tours he had taken through England and the western United States (See *The National Cyclopedia of American Biography* (New York: James T. White, 1918), 16:26–27.

45. It was only with the publication of James's *California Romantic and Beautiful* in 1914 that the Page Company announced the See America First series and included Murphy's *Three Wonderlands* on the list, making it the earliest book in the series.

46. See Murphy, *British Highways and Byways*, and Thomas Dowler Murphy, *In Unfamiliar England* (Boston: Page, 1910). For picturesque tours, see Crandal, *Nature Pictorialized*.

47. William Copeman Kitchin, *A Wonderland of the East Comprising the Lake and Mountain Region of New England and Eastern New York* (Boston: Page, 1920), vii.

48. See America First series advertisement. Thomas D. Murphy, *Seven Wonderlands of the American West* (Boston: Page, 1925), n.p.

49. My understanding of the See America First series as a constructed narrative that functioned as a panoptic apparatus emerged from my readings of the following sources: Michel Foucault, *Discipline and Punish: The Birth of the Prison* (New York: Vintage Books, 1979); Donald Preziosi, "The Panoptic Gaze and the Anamorphic Archive," in *Rethinking Art History: Meditations on a Coy Science* (New Haven, Conn.: Yale University Press, 1989), 54–79; Donald Horne, *The Great Museum: The Repre-*

sentation of History (London: Pluto Press, 1984); and Dilworth, *Imagining Indians in the Southwest.*

50. Hopkins, *Ohio the Beautiful and Historic*, 4.

51. Murphy, *Seven Wonderlands*, 44.

52. George Wharton James, *Arizona the Wonderland* (Boston: Page, 1917), 5–6.

53. James, *California the Romantic and Beautiful*, 115.

54. Murphy, *Three Wonderlands*, preface.

55. George Wharton James, *New Mexico: The Land of the Delight Makers* (Boston: Page, 1920), 4.

56. Mae Lacy Baggs, *Colorado, the Queen Jewel of the Rockies* (Boston: Page, 1918), 27.

57. For recent scholarship on the popular representation of Native Americans, see Dilworth, *Imagining Indians in the Southwest*, and Philip J. Deloria, *Playing Indian* (New Haven: Yale University Press, 1998).

58. For tourist appropriation of Native Americans, see Deloria, *Playing Indian*, 95–127.

59. James, *Arizona the Wonderland*, 9–10.

60. James, *California Romantic and Beautiful*, 196–97, and 198.

61. For an overview of the history of the conservation and preservation movements in the United States, see Nash, *Wilderness and the American Mind*, 96–181, Samuel Hays, *Conservation and the Gospel of Efficiency: The Progressive Conservation Movement, 1890–1920* (Cambridge: Harvard University Press, 1959), and *Forest and Conservation History* 34 (April 1990), special issue on conservation, preservation and the National Parks. For a discussion of the cultural construction of nature and the preservationist ideal, see William Cronon, "The Trouble with Wilderness; or, Getting Back to the Wrong Nature," in *Uncommon Ground: Rethinking the Human Place in Nature*, ed. William Cronon (New York: W. W. Norton, 1996), 69–90.

62. James, *New Mexico*, 21.

63. James, *Arizona the Wonderland*, 147.

64. Kitchin, *Wonderland of the East*, 145.

65. Nevin O. Winter, *Florida, the Land of Enchantment* (Boston: Page, 1918), 178.

66. Thomas Dowler Murphy, *On Sunset Highways: A Book of Motor Rambles in California* (Boston: L. C. Page, 1912), 160.

67. For a discussion of the artifacts of the past in the landscape, see David Lowenthal, "Age and Artifact: Dilemmas of Appreciation," in Meinig, *Interpretation of Ordinary Landscapes*, 103–28; and David Lowenthal, *The Past Is a Foreign Country* (New York: Cambridge University Press, 1985).

68. Murphy, *On Sunset Highways*, 160 and 67–68.

69. Nevin O. Winter, *Texas, the Marvelous* (Boston: Page, 1916), 115.

70. James, *Arizona the Wonderland*, 335.

71. Murphy, *On Sunset Highways*, 356.

72. Winter, *Florida, the Land of Enchantment*, 187.

73. Frank Hutchins and Cortelle Hutchins, *Virginia: The Old Dominion* (Boston: Page, 1921), 85.

74. Hutchins and Hutchins, *Virginia*, 49.

75. Thomas Dowler Murphy, *New England Highways and Byways from a Motor Car* (Boston: Page, 1924), 75–76.

76. Kitchin, *Wonderland of the East*, 48–49.

77. Lawrence Buell, "The Thoreauvian Pilgrimage: The Structure of an American Cult," *American Literature* 61 (May 1989): 175–99. Buell's article provides one example of the role of literary pilgrimage in canon formation. He argues that pilgrimage to Walden was integral the process of Thoreau's inclusion in the established canon of American literature. Beyond that, literary pilgrimage offered tangible proof of the existence of an American literary tradition.

78. Murphy, *New England Highways*, 187 and 193–94.

79. For an extensive overview of post-Darwinist theories popular during the Progressive era, see Hofstadter, *Social Darwinism in American Thought*, and Wiebe, *Search for Order*, 133–63.

80. See C. Vann Woodward, *The Strange Career of Jim Crow*, 3d rev. ed. (New York: Oxford University Press, 1974), and John Higham, *Strangers in the Land: Patterns of American Nativism, 1860–1925* (New York: Atheneum, 1985).

81. Thomas Dowler Murphy, *Oregon the Picturesque* (Boston: Page, 1917), 285–86. Note that a tour of the Petrified Forest was included at the end of this Oregon tour, which is why Murphy comments on the Roosevelt Dam.

82. Baggs, *Colorado*, 215.

83. Murphy, *New England Highways*, 208.

84. For a discussion of the technological sublime see David E. Nye, *American Technological Sublime* (Cambridge: MIT Press, 1994). For an overview of the popular notions of progress during the turn of the century, see Henry Nash Smith, *Popular Culture and Industrialism, 1865–1890* (New York: Anchor Books, 1967). See also Lears, *No Place of Grace*, 7–26.

85. Ross, "Liberal Tradition Revisited," 126. For a discussion of the role of Republican theory in the United States, see Pocock, *Machiavellian Moment*.

86. Christine Bold, *The WPA Guides: Mapping America* (Jackson: University of Mississippi Press, 1999), 9.

87. A total of 276 volumes and 791 pamphlets were published documenting the American Scene (see Kammen, *Mystic Chords of Memory*, 475).

88. Lewis Mumford, "Writers' Project," *New Republic*, 20 October 1937, 306–8.

89. Warren I. Susman, "The Culture of the Thirties," in *Culture as History: The Transformation of American Society in the Twentieth Century* (New York: Pantheon Books, 1984), 154.

90. Alfred Haworth Jones, "The Search for a Usable American Past in the New Deal," *American Quarterly* 23 (December 1971): 710; and Alfred Kazin, *On Native Grounds: An Interpretation of American Prose Literature* (New York: Reynal and Hitchcock, 1942), 486.

91. Bold, *WPA Guides*, 23–25; and Monty Noam Penkower, *The Federal Writers' Project: A Study in Government Patronage of the Arts* (Urbana: University of Illinois Press, 1977), 18–21.

92. Henry G. Alsberg to Mr. Baker, memorandum, 27 November 1935; Reed Harris to Mr. Oliver Griswold, memorandum, 15 February 1936; Reed Harris to Col. Lawrence Westbrook, memorandum, 25 February 1936; Bruce McLure to Mrs. Godwin, memorandum, 27 February 1936; Memoranda, 1935–1936; Memoranda; Entry 5, Administrative Memoranda, 1935–38, RG 69, NA, Maryland. See also Christine Bold, "The View from the Road: Katherine Kellock's New Deal Guidebooks," *American Studies* 29 (1988): 5–29; and *WPA Guides*, 25. See also Penkower, *Federal Writers' Project*, 22–23.

93. Reed Harris to All Central Staff Personnel, memorandum, 16 September 1935, Instructions (Folder 2), Instructions, Entry 3, American Guide Instructions, RG 69, NA, Maryland. See also Penkower, *Federal Writers' Project*, 30–54; and Bold, *WPA Guides*, 19–36,

94. See Penkower, *Federal Writers' Project*, 36–37.

95. See Bold, *WPA Guides* for an overview of the contentious production of the guides.

96. "The American Guide Manual," October 1935, 31, American Guide Manual box, Vol. 1, Entry 11, Manuals and Instructions, 1935–1939, RG 69, NA, Maryland.

97. The specific boundaries of each region were as follows: (1) Maine, Vermont, New Hampshire, Massachusetts, Rhode Island, Connecticut, New York, Pennsylvania, New Jersey, Delaware, Ohio, Indiana, Michigan, Illinois, Wisconsin; (2) Maryland, District of Columbia, West Virginia, Virginia, Kentucky, North Carolina, South Carolina, Tennessee, Arkansas, Louisiana, Mississippi, Alabama, Georgia, Florida; (3) Idaho, Montana, Wyoming, North Dakota, South Dakota, Nebraska, Minnesota, Iowa; (4) Arizona, Colorado, New Mexico, Texas, Oklahoma, Kansas, Missouri; and (5) California, Nevada, Utah, Oregon, Washington ("American Guide Manual," October 1935, 31).

98. Memorandum, "Tentative Plans for Regional Guides," 16 February 1937, Miscellaneous Procedure, Instructions 13–18, Miscellaneous, Alsberg letters, etc., Entry 11, Manuals and Instructions, 1935–1939, RG 69, NA, Maryland.

99. "Notes of the Federal Writers' Projects with Special Reference to the American Guide," 17 September 1936, Memoranda 1935–1936, Memoranda, Entry 5, Administrative Memoranda, 1935–1938, RG 69, NA, Maryland.

100. Penkower, *Federal Writers' Project*, 30–31.

101. In 1949 Hastings House published a one-volume guide to America edited by Als-
     berg and others. See Henry G. Alsberg, ed., *The American Guide: A Source Book and
     Complete Travel Guide for the United States* (New York: Hastings House, 1949).
102. Penkower, *Federal Writers' Project*, 31; and Bold, *WPA Guides*, 37.
103. "American Guide Manual," October 1935, 4 and 23.
104. "Supplementary Instructions #2 to The American Guide Manual," 10 December
     1935, Instructions—American Guide 1–4, American Guide Manual Instructions
     1–12, Entry 11, Manuals and Instructions, 1935–1939, RG 69, NA, Maryland.
105. "Supplementary Instructions #11 to The American Guide Manual," 1 April 1936, 1,
     Instructions 11B, American Guide Manual Instructions 1–12, Entry 11, Manuals
     and Instructions, 1935–1939, RG 69, NA, Maryland.
106. Henry G. Alsberg to Mr. John B. Derby, 18 May 1837, Connecticut State Guide
     Tours, Connecticut, Entry 13, Editorial Correspondence, 1936–39, RG 69, NA,
     Maryland.
107. "Supplementary Instructions #11 to The American Guide Manual," 1 April 1936, 12.
108. Washington Office to Mrs. Dot Kennan, 10 November 1937, Arkansas State
     Guide Cities, Arizona-Arkansas, Entry 13, Editorial Correspondence, 1936–39,
     RG 69, NA, Maryland.
109. "Preparation of an American Guide, and Collection of New Research Material on
     Matters of Local, Historical, Art and Scientific Interest in the United States," In-
     structions (Folder 2), Instructions, Entry 3, Records of George W. Cronyn, 1935–
     1939, RG 69, NA, Maryland.
110. "Information Concerning the Federal Writers Project," Progress Reports, 1937–
     38, Records of Henry Alsberg, Entry 2, Records of Henry G. Alsberg, September
     1935–June 1939, RG 69, NA, Maryland.
111. "Supplementary Instructions #11-C to American Guide Manual," 19 September
     1936, 5, Instructions 11–12, American Guide Manual Instructions 1–12, Entry 11,
     Manuals and Instructions, 1935–1939, RG 69, NA, Maryland.
112. [Harry Hopkins], Untitled Project Overview, 1936?, Misc. (Folder 4), Records of
     Henry Alsberg, Entry 2, Records of Henry G. Alsberg, September 1935–June 1939,
     RG 69, NA, Maryland.
113. Bold, *WPA Guides*, 36. Bold provides a detailed analysis of the contested produc-
     tion of the WPA guides and their representation of national identity.
114. For regionalism, see Robert L. Dorman, *Revolt of the Provinces: The Regionalist Move-
     ment in America, 1920–1945* (Chapel Hill: University of North Carolina Press, 1993);
     for documentary, see William Stott, *Documentary Expression and Thirties America*
     (Chicago: University of Chicago Press, 1986); for the principles of the New Deal,
     see Alan Brinkley, *The End of Reform: New Deal Liberalism in Depression and War*
     (New York: Knopf, 1995).

115. Federal Writers' Project, *Kansas: A Guide to the Sunflower State* (New York: Viking, 1939), 3; *North Carolina: A Guide to the Old North State* (Chapel Hill: University of North Carolina Press, 1939), 3.

116. "Notes of the Federal Writers' Projects with Special Reference to the American Guide," 17 September 1936, Memoranda 1935–1936, Memoranda, Entry 5, Administrative Memoranda 1935–1938, RG 69, NA, Maryland.

117. Henry G. Alsberg to Mr. William C. Young, Michigan State Guide Tours, Michigan, Entry 13, Editorial Correspondence, 1936–39, RG 69, NA, Maryland.

118. "Supplementary Instructions #11 to the American Guide Manual, Appendix A," 5 May 1936, 2, Instructions 11B, American Guide Manual Instructions 1–12, Entry 11, Manuals and Instructions 1935–1938, RG 69, NA, Maryland.

119. "Supplementary Instructions #16 to American Guide Manual," 21 October 1936, 9, Instructions 16, Instructions 13–18, Miscellaneous, Alsberg Letters, etc., Entry 11, Manuals and Instructions 1935–1939, RG 69, NA, Maryland.

120. "Supplementary Instructions #11-C to American Guide Manual," 19 September 1936, 3.

121. "Supplementary Instructions #11 B (replacing #11) to American Guide Manual," 25 July 1936, 5, Instructions 11B, American Guide Manual Instructions 1–12, Entry 11, Manuals and Instructions 1935–1939, RG 69, NA, Maryland.

122. George Cronyn to Mr. James Egan, 25 June 1937, Washington State Guide Essays, Washington, Entry 13, Editorial Correspondence, 1936–39, RG 69, NA, Maryland.

123. "Supplementary Instructions #11 to the American Guide Manual," 1 April 1936, 17–18.

124. "Supplementary Instructions 11 B, Appendix 1 (Revised) to the American Guide Manual," 22 May 1937, 1, Instructions 11B, American Guide Manual Instructions 1–12, Entry 11, Manuals and Instructions, 1935–1939, RG 69, NA, Maryland.

125. "Supplementary Instructions #11-E to The American Guide Manual," rev. 6 January 1939, 3, Instructions 11–12, American Guide Manual Instructions 1–12, Entry 11, Manuals and Instructions, 1935–1939, RG 69, NA, Maryland.

126. Henry G. Alsberg to Mr. D. E. Williamson, 17 September 1938, Nevada State Guide Tours, Nevada, Entry 13, Editorial Correspondence, 1936–39, RG 69, NA, Maryland.

127. "Supplementary Instructions #11-E to The American Guide Manual," rev. 6 January 1939, 3.

128. Henry G. Alsberg to Miss Anne E. Windhusen, 23 February 1939, Washington State Guide Tours, Washington, Entry 13, Editorial Correspondence, 1936–39, RG 69, NA, Maryland.

129. Henry G. Alsberg to Mr. Bryon Crane, 9 March 1938, Montana State Tours, Montana, Entry 13, Editorial Correspondence, 1936–39, RG 69, NA, Maryland.

130. Henry G. Alsberg to Mrs. Dot Kennan, 1 November 1938, Arkansas State Guide Tours, Arizona-Arkansas, Entry 13, Editorial Correspondence, 1936–39, RG 69, NA, Maryland.

131. Katherine A. Kellock to Dana N. Doten, 26 January 1937, Vermont State Guide Tours, Vermont, Entry 13, Editorial Correspondence, 1936–39, RG 69, NA, Maryland.

132. Henry G. Alsberg to Mr. James Hopper, 30 October 1937, California State Guide Tours, California, Entry 13, Editorial Correspondence, 1936–39, RG 69, NA, Maryland.

133. Henry G. Alsberg, "The American Guide," Miscellaneous (Folder 2), Records of Henry Alsberg, Entry 2, Records of Henry G. Alsberg, September 1935–June 1939, RG 69, NA, Maryland.

134. "Supplementary Instructions #9 to the American Guide Manual," 12 March 1936, 1, Instructions 8–9, American Guide Manual Instructions 1–12, Entry 11, Manuals and Instructions, 1935–1939, RG 69, NA, Maryland.

135. Henry G. Alsberg to Mr. J. Harris Gable, 15 August 1936, Nebraska State Guide Tours, Nebraska, Entry 13, Editorial Correspondence, 1936–39, RG 69, NA, Maryland.

136. "Supplementary Instructions #9 to the American Guide Manual," 12 March 1936, 1.

137. For quotation, see "Supplementary Instructions #9-C to the American Guide Manual," 4 August 1936, 11, Instructions 9C–9F, American Guide Manual Instructions 1–12, Entry 11, Manuals and Instructions 1935–1939. For Indian lore, see "Supplementary Instructions #5 to the American Guide," 3 January 1936, Instructions 5–7, American Guide Manual Instructions 1–12, Entry 11, Manuals and Instructions 1935–1939. For former slaves, see "Supplementary Instructions #9-E to the American Guide Manual," 22 April 1937, Instructions 9C–9F, American Guide Manual Instructions 1–12, Entry 11, Manuals and Instructions 1935–1939, RG 69, NA, Maryland.

138. Jared Putnam, "Massachusetts: A Guide to Its Places and People—$2.50—To Be Published Summer 1937," quoted in Bold, *WPA Guides*, 9.

139. George W. Cronyn to Mrs. Carita Doggett Corse, 13 February 1936, Florida Sate Guide Miscellaneous, Florida, Entry 13, Editorial Correspondence, 1936–39, RG 69, NA, Maryland.

140. Henry G. Alsberg to Mr. John T. Frederick, 19 August 1938, Illinois State Guide Cities, Illinois, Entry 13, Editorial Correspondence, 1936–39, RG 69, NA, Maryland.

141. "Supplementary Instructions #11 B (replacing #11) to American Guide Manual," 25 July 1936, 7.

142. See Jerre G. Mangione, *The Dream and the Deal: The Federal Writers' Project, 1935–1943* (Boston: Little, Brown, 1972), 201–208; Bold, *WPA Guides*, 37–63.

143. Ray Allen Billington to Mr. Henry G. Alsberg, 21 April 1937, Massachusetts State

Guide Essays, Massachusetts, Entry 13, Editorial Correspondence, 1936–39, RG 69, NA, Maryland.

144. See Penkower, *Federal Writers' Project*, 140–43.

145. Edwin Bjorkman to Henry G. Alsberg, 1 September 1938, Federal Writers' Project, Couch Papers, quoted in Bold, *WPA Guides*, 134.

146. Thompson to Cunningham, 16 May 1938, quoted in Penkower, *Federal Writers' Project*, 142.

147. Penkower, *Federal Writers' Project*, 142.

148. Bold, *WPA Guides*, 136.

149. See Mangione, *Dream and the Deal*, 3–23; and Penkower, *Federal Writers' Project*, 215–37.

150. "Supplementary Instructions #11 B (replacing #11) to American Guide Manual," 25 July 1936, 4.

151. "The American Guide Manual," October 17, 1935, American Guide Manual, Vol. 1, Entry 11, Manuals and Instructions 1935–1939, RG 69, NA, Maryland.

152. Kammen, *Mystic Chords of Memory*, 444–80.

153. For a discussion of heritage, see David Lowenthal, *The Heritage Crusade and the Spoils of History* (Cambridge: Cambridge University Press, 1998).

154. Anderson, *Imagined Communities*, see also W. T. J. Mitchell, ed., *Landscape and Power* (Chicago: University of Chicago Press, 1994).

155. Bold, *WPA Guides*, 118.

6. TOURIST ENCOUNTERS

1. Despite the vast amount of scholarship on Sinclair Lewis and his fiction, there has been relatively little scholarship on *Free Air*. For a brief discussion of *Free Air* as one of Lewis' serialized novels, see Martin Bucco, "The Serialized Novels of Sinclair Lewis," in *Modern Critical Views: Sinclair Lewis*, ed. Harold Bloom (New York: Chelsea House, 1987), 63–70. For an overview of the biographical circumstances behind the narrative, see Mark Schorer, *Sinclair Lewis: An American Life* (New York: McGraw-Hill, 1961), 235–39 and 253–61.

2. Sinclair Lewis, *Free Air* (1919; reprint, Lincoln: University of Nebraska Press, 1993), 13.

3. Lewis, *Free Air*, 45.

4. Nelson H. H. Graburn, "Tourism: The Sacred Journey," in *Hosts and Guests: The Anthropology of Tourism*, ed. Valene L. Smith (Philadelphia: University of Pennsylvania Press, 1989), 21–36. See also Victor Turner and Edith Turner, *Image and Pilgrimage in Christian Culture: Anthropological Perspectives* (New York: Columbia University Press, 1978).

5. For a discussion of the relationship between travel and narrative, see David E.

Nye, *Narratives and Spaces: Technology and the Construction of American Culture* (New York: Columbia University Press, 1997), and Mary Louise Pratt, *Imperial Eyes: Travel Writing and Transculturation* (New York: Routledge, 1992).

6. Pomeroy, *In Search of the Golden West*, 15. Although there is no scholarly monograph detailing the history of the literature of travel and tourism as it developed in the United States, a number of works on the history of tourism in America provide a selective overview of some of that literature. In addition to Pomeroy, see Belasco, *Americans on the Road*; Brown, *Inventing New England*; Jakle, *Tourist*; and Sears, *Sacred Places*.

7. Bowles, *Across the Continent*; Horace, Greeley, *An Overland Journey from New York to San Francisco in the Summer of 1859* (New York: C. M. Saxton, Barker, 1860); Henry James, *The American Scene* (London: Chapman and Hall, 1907); Mark Twain, *Roughing It* (Hartford, Conn.: American Publishing, 1872). These represent some of the more famous published narratives out of many which used the travel experience to document American life.

8. See Belasco, *Americans on the Road*, 19–39, for the differences tourists found between travel by train and travel by automobile.

9. Ibid., 7–8.

10. Because I believe that the automobile essentially defined the popular touring experience as it emerged in the United States during the early twentieth century, I rely solely on automobile touring narratives for this chapter.

11. Lewis, *Free Air*, 38, 46, and 47.

12. Ibid., 140.

13. Post, *By Motor to the Golden Gate*, 6 and 23.

14. Vernon McGill, *Diary of a Motor Journey from Chicago to Los Angeles* (Los Angeles: Grafton Publishing, 1922), 31.

15. Beatrice Massey, *It Might Have Been Worse: A Motor Trip from Coast to Coast* (San Francisco: Harr Wagner, 1920), forward; and Mary Crehore Bedell, *Modern Gypsies: The Story of a Twelve Thousand Mile Motor Camping Trip Encircling the United States* (New York: Brentano's, 1924), 262.

16. Effie Price Gladding, *Across the Continent by the Lincoln Highway* (New York: Brentano's, 1915), ix.

17. Letitia Stockett, *America: First, Fast and Furious* (Baltimore: Norman-Remington, 1930), vi.

18. Dallas Lore Sharp, *The Better Country* (Boston: Houghton Mifflin, 1928), 36.

19. See also Myrtle Barrett, *Our Wonderous Trip* (N.p.: Published by author, 1914); Hoffman Birney, *Roads to Roam* (Philadelphia: Penn Publishing, 1930); Daniel Smith Crowningshield, *The Jolly Eight: Coast to Coast and Back* (Boston: Richard G. Badger, 1929); Winifred Hawkridge Dixon, *Westward Hoboes: Ups and Downs of Frontier Motoring* (New York: Charles Scribner's Sons, 1921); James Flagg, *Boulevards*

All the Way—Maybe (New York: Doran, 1925); Kathryn Hulme, *How's the Road?* (San Francisco: Published by author, 1928); Caroline Rittenberg, *Motor West* (New York: Harold Vinal, 1926); Gula Sabin, *California by Motor* (Milwaukee: Published by author, 1926); Ted Salmon, *From Southern California to Casco Bay* (San Bernardino, Calif.: San Bernardino Publishing, 1930); Paul E. Vernon, *Coast to Coast by Motor* (London: A. & C. Black, 1930); Clara Walker Whiteside, *Touring New England on the Trail of the Yankee* (Philadelphia: Penn Publishing, 1926); and Andrew Wilson, *The Gay Gazel: An Adventure in Auto Biography* (Published by author, 1926) for a selection of touring narratives addressing at various levels the issues of seeing America.

20. For a discussion of the origins of these feelings of powerlessness, weightlessness, and anonymity and the reactions to these feelings, see Lears, *No Place of Grace*.

21. Frederic F. Van de Water, *The Family Flivvers to Frisco* (New York: D. Appleton, 1927), 5–6. For a biographical sketch of Van de Water's writing career, see Stanley J. Kunitz, ed., *Twentieth Century Authors*, first supplement (New York: H. W. Wilson, 1955), 1023–24.

22. Van de Water, *Family Flivvers to Frisco*, 8, 9, and 173.

23. Ibid., 293 and 71.

24. Ibid., 137. For a discussion of the values and ideals associated with the small town, see Wiebe, *Search for Order*.

25. Van de Water, *Family Flivvers to Frisco*, 71.

26. Ibid., 45.

27. For the notion of Imperialist nostalgia, see Renato Rosaldo, "Imperialist Nostalgia," *Representations* 26 (1989): 107–22.

28. Van de Water, *Family Flivvers to Frisco*, 240.

29. Ibid., 83–86 and 12.

30. Belasco, *Americans on the Road*, 92–103.

31. For a discussion of who could afford the luxury of automobile touring, see Franz, "Narrating Automobility," 95–100. See also chapter 4, note 76.

32. For a discussion of the agrarian myth and the ideal of the middle landscape, see Smith, *Virgin Land*, and Leo Marx, *The Machine in the Garden: Technology and the Pastoral Ideal in America* (New York: Oxford University Press, 1964).

33. Stockett, *America*, 44.

34. Hulme, *How's the Road?* 9.

35. For a broad overview of the social, ethnic, and racial realities of the West, see Patricia Nelson Limerick, *The Legacy of Conquest: The Unbroken Past of the American West* (New York: W. W. Norton, 1987). For a discussion of the urban character of the West, see Pomeroy, *Pacific Slope*.

36. Whiteside, *Touring New England*, ix, 1–2, 170, 4, 82, and 83.

37. Ibid., 295.

38. Wiebe, *Search for Order*.
39. Despite the vast amount of scholarship on Dreiser and his fiction, there has been relatively little scholarship on *Hoosier Holiday*. For an overview of the biographical circumstances behind the narrative, see Richard Lingeman, *Theodore Dreiser: An American Journey, 1908–1945* (New York: G. P. Putnam's Sons, 1990), 115–118.
40. Theodore Dreiser, *A Hoosier Holiday* (1916; reprint, Westport, Conn.: Greenwood Press, 1974), 48, 49, and 69.
41. Dreiser, *A Hoosier Holiday*, 27, 58, 171, 177, and 65.
42. Ibid., 128 and 512.
43. Ibid., 101.
44. Ibid., 78.
45. Ibid., 113 and 510.
46. John Bodnar, *Remaking America: Public Memory, Commemoration and Patriotism in the Twentieth Century* (Princeton, N.J.: Princeton University Press, 1992), 15.
47. Lewis, *Free Air*, 31–32, 87, 50, and 338–39.
48. MacCannell, *Tourist*, 24.
49. For a discussion of the tourist gaze in contemporary Western culture, see Urry, *Tourist Gaze*.
50. Graburn, "Tourism," 22 and 25.
51. For a discussion of the freeing possibilities of leisure activities, see Kathy Peiss, *Cheap Amusements: Working Women and Leisure in New York City, 1880 to 1920* (Philadelphia: Temple University Press, 1986), and Roy Rosenzweig, *Eight Hours for What We Will: Workers and Leisure in an Industrial City, 1870–1920* (New York: Cambridge University Press, 1983); in relation to amusement parks see John F. Kasson, *Amusing the Million: Coney Island at the Turn of the Century* (New York: Hill & Wang, 1978); in relation to movie theaters see Lary May, *Screening Out the Past: The Birth of Mass Culture and the Motion Picture Industry* (New York: Oxford University Press, 1980).
52. Lipsitz, *Time Passages*, 8.
53. Turner and Turner, *Image and Pilgrimage in Christian Culture*.
54. Kasson, *Amusing the Million*.
55. Sharp, *Better Country*, 5, 6, 13, and 11.
56. Ibid., 127, 109, and 113.
57. Ibid., 114.
58. Birney, *Roads to Roam*, 268–69, 287, and 295.
59. Harvey Green, *Fit for America: Health, Fitness, Sport and American Society* (New York: Pantheon Books, 1986), 219–58. See also John Higham, "The Reorientation of American Culture in the 1890s," in *Writing American History: Essays on Modern Scholarship* (Bloomington: Indiana University Press, 1970), 73–102.
60. Dreiser, *Hoosier Holiday*, 506, 232, and 283–84.

61. For a discussion of the importance of dreaming in Dreiser's fiction, see Philip Fisher, *Hard Facts: Setting and Form in the American Novel* (New York: Oxford University Press, 1985), 128–78.

62. Dreiser, *Hoosier Holiday,* 425.

63. For a discussion of the theme of decline as related to *Sister Carrie,* see Fisher, *Hard Facts,* 169–78.

64. Dreiser, *Hoosier Holiday,* 184.

65. Lears, *No Place of Grace,* 32.

66. Ibid., 98–139. Although Lears does not actually address the wilderness experience as an antimodernist phenomenon, his analysis of the martial impulse suggests that touring and the possible wilderness experience it encompassed embodied similar antimodernist desires and anxieties. See Also David E. Shi, *The Simple Life: Plain Living and High Thinking in American Culture* (New York: Oxford University Press, 1985).

67. Lears, "From Salvation to Self-Realization," 11.

68. Lewis, *Free Air,* 11, 14–15, 33, and 45.

69. Ibid., 143.

70. For a discussion of the gendered experience of driving, see Interrante, "Moveable Feast"; Franz, "Narrating Automobility," 34–88; and Scharff, *Taking the Wheel.*

71. For a discussion of the image of the New Woman, see Carol Smith-Rosenberg, "The New Woman as Androgyne: Social Order and Gender Crisis, 1870–1936," in *Disorderly Conduct: Visions of Gender in Victorian America* (New York: Knopf, 1985), 245–96; Estelle Friedman, "The New Woman: Changing Views of Women in the 1920s," *Journal of American History* 61 (1974): 373–93; and Ellen Wiley Todd, *The "New Woman" Revised: Painting and Gender Politics on Fourteenth Street* (Berkeley and Los Angeles: University of California Press, 1993), 1–38.

72. Hulme, *How's the Road?* 1.

73. Ibid., 2. See Belasco, *Americans on the Road,* 35–36, for a discussion of the medieval connotations of Reggie, Hulme's car.

74. See Smith-Rosenberg, "New Woman as Androgyne," for a provocative discussion of the New Woman of the 1920s.

75. Hulme, *How's the Road?* 16, 96, and 97.

76. Ibid., 35, 43, and 19.

77. Ibid., 13 and 32.

78. Ibid., 9 and 40–41.

79. Lewis Atherton, *Main Street on the Middle Border* (Bloomington: Indiana University Press, 1954), 33–64.

80. For a history of the traveling salesman and his symbolic significance in American culture, see Timothy B. Spears, *100 Years on the Road: The Traveling Salesman in American Culture* (New Haven, Conn.: Yale University Press, 1995), and "'All Things to

All Men': The Commercial Traveler and the Rise of Modern Salesmanship," *American Quarterly* 45 (December 1993): 524–55.

81. Hulme, *How's the Road?* 63.

82. MacCannell, *Tourist*, 56–76.

83. Post, *By Motor to the Golden Gate*; Dixon, *Westward Hoboes*; Stockett, *America*. For other examples, see Barrett, *Our Wonderous Trip*; Bedell, *Modern Gypsies*; Rittenberg, *Motor West*; Sabin, *California by Motor*. Note that some women traveled with their husbands and many did not comment specifically on their experience in gendered terms. However, the mere number of published narratives written by women suggests that touring offered a particularly novel experience for women traditionally hemmed in by the ideology of the domestic sphere.

84. Dixon, *Westward Hoboes*, 87. See Scharff, *Taking the Wheel*, 135–64.

85. See Smith-Rosenberg, "New Woman as Androgyne," for an interesting discussion of how some women novelists of the twenties borrowed male language to define the identity of the New Woman.

86. For a broader discussion of these issues see Wiebe, *Search for Order*; Lears, *No Place of Grace*; Trachtenberg, *Incorporation of America*; and Higham, *Strangers in the Land*.

87. Higham, "Reorientation of American Culture," 79–80.

7. TOURIST MEMENTOS

1. Amy Bridges, "Journal Kept on 4th Raymond Excursion [from Massachusetts to California and Return]" (1882), Western Manuscripts Collection.

2. Mildred E. Baker, "Navajo Mountain," 5, Mildred E. Baker Collection, Album 237, Vol. 5, Huntington Library Photographic Collections, Huntington Library, San Marino, California (hereafter cited as Huntington Photo).

3. Warren I. Susman, *Culture as History: The Transformation of American Society in the Twentieth Century* (New York: Pantheon Books, 1984), xx. For the historiography of consumer culture studies, see Agnew, "Coming Up for Air," and Miller, *Acknowledging Consumption*.

4. For a historical overview of the transformation of America to a consumer culture, see Strasser, *Satisfaction Guaranteed*.

5. For the symbolic meaning attached to consumer goods, see Lears, *No Place of Grace*, 68–75, and "From Salvation to Self-Realization," 3–38. See also William Leach, *Land of Desire: Merchants, Power, and the Rise of a New American Culture* (New York: Pantheon Books, 1993); and Colin Campbell, *The Romantic Ethic and the Spirit of Modern Consumption* (Oxford: Basil Blackwell, 1987).

6. For an overview of leisure in American culture, see Lipsitz, *Time Passages*; David Nasaw, *Going Out: The Rise and Fall of Public Amusements* (New York: Basic Books, 1993); Peiss, *Cheap Amusements*; and Rosenzweig, *Eight Hours for What We Will*. In

relation to amusement parks, see Kasson, *Amusing the Million;* in relation to movie theaters, see May, *Screening Out the Past.*

7. For a discussion of tourism as consumption, see Rothman, *Devil's Bargains,* 10–28.

8. For a discussion of the urban upper middle class and an extended axis of respectability, see Richard M. Ohmann, *Selling Culture: Magazines, Markets, and Class at the Turn of the Century* (London: Verso, 1996).

9. Little scholarly work has been done on tourist mementos. On souvenirs, see Joe Benson and Rob Silverman, "Tourist Photographs as Souvenirs," *Prospects* 11 (1987): 261–72. On family photograph albums, see Richard Chalfen, *Turning Leaves: The Photographic Collections of Two Japanese American Families* (Albuquerque: University of New Mexico Press, 1991).

10. Towner, "Grand Tour," 297–334. For a concise history of the Grand Tour, see Jeremy Black, *British Abroad,* especially 14–85. See also Gilpin, *Three Essays on Picturesque Beauty;* Hunt, *Gardens and the Picturesque,* 5; Stafford, *Voyage into Substance,* 3–13; Alder, "Origins of Sightseeing," 7–29.

11. Henry Ford Museum, *Americans on Vacation* (Dearborn, Mich.: Henry Ford Museum and Greenfield Village, 1990), 84–85.

12. Reese V. Jenkins, "Technology and the Market: George Eastman and the Origins of Mass Amateur Photography," *Technology and Culture* 16 (January 1975): 1–19.

13. Advertisement from *Town and Country,* April 1905, reprinted in Strasser, *Satisfaction Guaranteed,* 103.

14. Quoted in Julie K. Brown, "'Seeing and Remembering': George Eastman and the World's Columbian Exposition, Chicago 1893," *Image* 39, nos. 1–2 (Spring/Summer 1996): 3.

15. Quoted from Kodak No. 1 advertisement reprinted in "From the Collections," *Image* 39, nos. 1–2 (Spring/Summer 1996): 28.

16. Advertisements reprinted in Henry Ford Museum, *Americans on Vacation,* 89–91.

17. Bridges, "Journal Kept on 4th Raymond Excursion," n.p., and "Journal Kept on a Raymond Excursion," n.p.

18. Merritt, "From Ocean to Ocean," pt. 1, p. 106, and pt. 2, p. 174.

19. My assessment of tourist scrapbooks is based on an examination of the following scrapbooks: Mildred E. Baker Scrapbooks (1931–1942), Huntington Photo; A. A. Butler and C. W. Butler, "Colorado Outings" (c. 1898), Western Manuscripts Collection; Mary Foster Scrapbook (1871) and Mildred Cramer Srapbooks (1930 and 1931), Henry Ford Museum Archives, Dearborn, Michigan; Miriam A. Musgrave Scrapbook (1933); Clarence Schumacher Scrapbook (1938); Elizabeth Blake Scrapbook (1922–23); Viola Schumacher Scrapbook (1937); Daroll Pershing Scrapbook (1929); Ethel Yocom, Pauline Burns, and Gilbert C. Yocom Scrapbook (1938); Pennsylvania to California Scrapbook (1941); Niagara Falls Scrapbook (c. 1927);

Maine to Quebec Scrapbook (1924); Wyoming to Boston Scrapbook (c. 1940), collection of the author. These sources are difficult to find. Library and archives are only beginning to collect and preserve them. However, I believe this small collection of sources provides a representative sample of how tourists preserved and memorialized their experiences.

20. Bridges, "Journal Kept on 4th Raymond Excursion," n.p.
21. Tripp, "Notes of an Excursion," 26, also 46, 65, Huntington MS.
22. Miriam A. Musgrave Scrapbook, n.p.
23. Baker, "Navajo Mountain," 55.
24. Mildred E. Baker, "Peace of Rainbow and Canyon" (1938), 9 and 18, Album 237, Vol. 10, Huntington Photo.
25. Bridges, "Journal Kept on 4th Raymond Excursion," n.p.
26. Merritt, "From Ocean to Ocean," pt. 2, p. 168, and pt. 2, p. 129.
27. Ethel Richardson Allen, Photograph Album (1921–1923), Album 340, Huntington Photo.
28. Bridges, "Journal Kept on a Raymond Excursion," n.p.
29. Tripp, "Notes of an Excursion," 8.
30. C. D. Irwin, "Diaries of Round-the-World Trip Including some Travel in the United States," vol. 3, "Letter from Australia, New Zealand and the Hawaiian Islands" (1885), 1–3, Western Manuscript Collections.
31. For an overview of the metropolitan corridor, see John R. Stilgoe, *Metropolitan Corridor: Railroads and the American Scene* (New Haven, Conn.: Yale University Press, 1985).
32. Mildred E. Baker, "A Glimpse of the Old West" (1935), 3, Album 237, Vol. 7, Huntington Photo.
33. Merritt, "From Ocean to Ocean," pt. 1, p. 15, pt. 1, pp. 11–12, and pt. 2, p. 146.
34. Bridges, "Journal Kept on 4th Raymond Excursion," n.p.
35. Merritt, "From Ocean to Ocean," pt. 2, p. 178.
36. Richard Ohmann defines this expanding middle class as the professional-managerial class. Although I agree with his characterization of this new social constituency, I find the term "professional-managerial class" to be rather unwieldy, and so I have chosen to refer to this new group as the upper middle class. See Ohmann, *Selling Culture*, 118–19.
37. Bridges, "Journal Kept on a Raymond Excursion," n.p.
38. Merritt, "From Ocean to Ocean," pt. 2, pp. 27–28.
39. For a discussion of the tourist landscape as a new kind of public space, see Ohmann, *Selling Culture*, 157; and Catherine Cocks, *Doing the Town: The Rise of Urban Tourism in the United States, 1850–1915* (Berkeley and Los Angeles: University of California Press, 2001).

40. Bridges, "Journal Kept on 4th Raymond Excursion," n.p.

41. Bridges, "Journal Kept on a Raymond Excursion," n.p.

42. For a discussion of the construction of highbrow culture, see Lawrence Levine, *Highbrow/Lowbrow: The Emergence of Cultural Hierarchy in America* (Cambridge: Harvard University Press, 1988).

43. For a history of the sublime, the beautiful, and the picturesque, see Crandall, *Nature Pictorialized.*

44. For a discussion of tourists' appropriation of the sublime, see McKinsey, *Niagara Falls.*

45. Bridges, "Journal Kept on a Raymond Excursion," n.p.

46. Merritt, "From Ocean to Ocean," pt. 2, pp. 8–9.

47. Ibid., pt. 2, p. 107.

48. Bridges, "Journal Kept on 4th Raymond Excursion," n.p.

49. Butler and Butler, "Colorado Outings," n.p.

50. [Sidney Waldon], "Sagebrush and Sequoia" (1919), photograph album and travel journal, Album 388, Huntington Photo.

51. Ohmann, *Selling Culture,* 158.

52. Butler and Butler, "Colorado Outings," n.p.

53. Tripp, "Notes of an Excursion," 11–12.

54. Bridges, "Journal Kept on 4th Raymond Excursion," n.p.

55. Tripp, "Notes of an Excursion," 49.

56. Ibid., 49–50.

57. Merritt, "From Ocean to Ocean," pt. 2, p. 41.

58. Bridges, "Journal Kept on a Raymond Excursion," n.p.

59. Merritt, "From Ocean to Ocean," pt. 2, p. 101.

60. Bridges, "Journal Kept on a Raymond Excursion," n.p.

61. Irwin, "Diaries of Round-the-World Trip," 4, 5, and 9–10.

62. Bridges, "Journal Kept on a Raymond Excursion," n.p.

63. Irwin, "Diaries of Round-the-World Trip," 40.

64. Butler and Butler, "Colorado Outings," n.p.

65. Sears, *Sacred Places.*

66. Merritt, "From Ocean to Ocean," pt. 2, pp. 7–8.

67. Bridges, "Journal Kept on 4th Raymond Excursion," n.p.

68. Richard Ohmann addresses this process in connection with suburbanization. See Ohmann, *Selling Culture,* 136.

69. See Belasco, *Americans on the Road,* and Jakle, *Tourist,* 152–68.

70. Deloria, *Playing Indian,* 102.

71. Marie-Françoise Lanfant, John B. Allcock, and Edward M. Bruner, eds., *International Tourism: Identity and Change* (London: Sage, 1995), 9.

72. Baker, "Navajo Mountain," 46.

73. Ibid., 16.

74. Hayden White has characterized historical narratives as "extended metaphors," arguing that they do not simply reproduce events, but rather "tell us in what direction to think about events and charge our thought about the events with different emotional valences." Baker's touring narratives can be understood in similar terms. See Hayden White, "The Historical Text as Literary Artifact," in *The Writing of History: Literary Form and Historical Understanding*, ed. Robert H. Canary and Henry Kozicki (Madison: University of Wisconsin Press, 1978), 52, 53.

75. For a discussion of the ways in which individual narratives are shaped surrounding cultural texts, see Jay Clayton and Eric Rothstein, eds., *Influence and Intertextuality in Literary History* (Madison: University of Wisconsin Press, 1991).

76. Baker, "Navajo Mountain," 35.

77. Mildred E. Baker, "Turquoise Skies and Copper Canyons" (1942), 1, Album 237, Vol. 13, Huntington Photo.

78. Baker, "Navajo Mountain," 34.

79. Baker, "Turquoise Skies and Copper Canyons," 29.

80. Baker, "Navajo Mountain," 5.

81. Mildred E. Baker, "Memorable Days on the Teton Trail" (1934), 8, Album 237, Vol. 6, Huntington Photo.

82. Mildred E. Baker, "Rough Water: Down the Colorado and Green Rivers" (1940), 82 and 28–29, Album 237, Vol. 10, Huntington Photo.

83. Baker, "Peace of Rainbow and Canyon," 13.

84. Baker, "Glimpse of the Old West," 4 and 5.

85. Baker, "Memorable Days on the Teton Trail," n.p. and 13.

86. For a discussion of the tourist experience as an extension of salvage anthropology and popular ethnography, see Weigle and Babcock, *Great Southwest*, 1–8.

87. Baker, "Peace of Rainbow and Canyon," 9.

88. Baker, "Turquoise Skies and Copper Canyons," 12–13.

89. Baker, "Navajo Mountain," 57, 67 and 66.

90. Baker, "Rough Water," 12 and 10.

91. Baker, "Glimpse of the Old West," n.p.

92. Baker, "Turquoise Skies and Copper Canyons," 32.

93. For a discussion of staged authenticity, see MacCannell, *Tourist*, 91–107.

94. As Leah Dilworth argues, "In the touristic encounter with Indians, the tourist is always the receiver of information; the Indian is always the object of the gaze, a commodity to be consumed visually" (Dilworth, "Discovering Indians in Fred Harvey's Southwest," 163).

95. Deloria, *Playing Indian*, 103.

96. Baker, "Peace of Rainbow and Canyon," 13.

97. Mildred E. Baker Journal, 1940, Notes, Otis Marston Papers, Huntington Library, San Marino, California (hereafter cited as Marston Papers).

98. Baker, "Rough Water," 23 and 32.

99. Notes, Otis Marston interview with Mildred E. Baker, 15 April 1948, Letters—Comments, 1948–1949, Marston Papers.

100. Baker, "Rough Water," 28, 67, and 68.

101. Notes, Marston interview with Baker, 15 April 1948, Marston Papers.

102. John Urry, Consuming Places (New York: Routledge, 1995), 137.

103. For example, see Elizabeth Blake Scrapbook and Wyoming to Boston Scrapbook, collection of the author.

104. See Miriam A. Musgrave Scrapbook, Mildred E. Baker Scrapbooks, Mary Foster Scrapbook, and Mildred Cramer Scrapbooks.

105. Defining a theory of modern consumption, Colin Campbell argues that "many cultural products offered for sale in modern societies are in fact consumed because they serve as aids to the construction of day dreams." He goes on to note, "Fragments of stories or images taken from books or films are often used as the foundation stories for these continually extended dream edifices" (Campbell, Romantic Ethic, 92–93).

106. This notion of tourism as a form of bounded fantasy grows out of Pierre Bourdieu's notion of "regulated improvisation." See Pierre Bourdieu, The Logic of Practice, trans. Richard Nice (Stanford, Calif.: Stanford University Press, 1990), 52–65.

107. For a discussion of staged authenticity, see MacCannell, Tourist, 91–107.

108. Bridges, "Journal Kept on a Raymond Excursion," n.p.

109. See Merritt, "From Ocean to Ocean," pt. 2, pp. 145–49, for another excellent expression of this form of transcendent fantasy that took place in the tourist landscape.

110. Lears, No Place of Grace, 68–75, and "From Salvation to Self-Realization," 3–38.

111. [Waldon], "Sagebrush and Sequoia," n.p.

112. Lears, "From Salvation to Self-Realization," 3–5.

113. For the ways in which the emerging consumer culture shifted notions of citizenship, see Charles McGovern, "Consumption and Citizenship in the United States, 1900–1940," in Getting and Spending: European and American Consumer Societies in the Twentieth Century, ed. Susan Strasser, Charles McGovern, and Matthias Judt (New York: Cambridge University Press, 1998); McGovern, "Sold American," 62–155; Murdock, "Citizens, Consumers, and Public Culture," 17–41; and Williams, "Advertising," 170–95.

114. See Michael E. McGerr, The Decline of Popular Politics: The American North, 1865–1928 (New York: Oxford University Press, 1986).

115. See Marchand, Advertising the American Dream, 217–22; and McGovern, "Consumption and Citizenship in the United States" and "Sold American," 62–155.

116. Catherine Gudis provides a provocative examination of the ways in which outdoor advertisers sought to define a new ideal of citizenship by defining the market in geographical terms. See Catherine Gudis, "The Road to Consumption: Outdoor Advertising and the American Cultural Landscape, 1917–1965" (Ph.D. diss., Yale University, 1999).

EPILOGUE

1. For a history of postwar Chevrolet models produced by General Motors, see Beverly Rae Kimes and Robert C. Ackerson, *Chevrolet: A History from 1911* (Princeton, N.J.: Princeton Publishing, 1981), 94–113. For a brief history of the "See the USA in Your Chevrolet" jingle, see David Phillips, "Chevy Sings Old Song: 'See the USA . . . ,'" *Detroit News,* 24 February 1999.

2. Eisenhower instigated the official promotion of the United States as a tourist destination in 1958 when he issued a presidential proclamation calling for "business, labor, agricultural and civic groups, as well as the people of the United States generally to observe 1960 as Visit the United States of America Year with exhibits, ceremonies, and other appropriate activities designed to forward the purpose of international understanding and world peace" (Horace Sutton, "Why They Don't Visit the U.S.A.," *Saturday Review,* 15 October 1960, 48). Eisenhower hoped to transform the United States into a host nation following the example of Great Britain after World War Two and reap the economic benefits generated through the tourist industry. Although the government did not allocate any funds to support the proclamation, a private organization called the National Association of Travel Organizations, better known as NATO, distributed a series of portfolios advertising American tourist attractions to foreign travel agents and tourist bureaus. Otherwise, little was done to support the Visit the USA Year (see Sutton, "Why They Don't Visit the U.S.A.," 48–51). After his election, President Kennedy, following Eisenhower's lead and drawing on a bill being debated in Congress, immediately pledged to "attract more foreign travel" to the United States. He called for legislation to create an office of international travel in the Commerce Department which resulted in the formation of the United States Travel Service. (See "President Looks to Spur Tourism," *New York Times,* 1 February 1961; "Text of President's Message to Congress on U.S. Balance of Payments and on Gold," *New York Times,* 7 February 1961; and "Closing the Tourist Gap," *Time,* 31 March 1961, 84. For an overview of the early activities of the United States Travel Service, see Department of Commerce, *Semi-Annual Report of the Secretary of Commerce on the United States Travel Service, 1961–1965.*) Both Eisenhower and Kennedy were primarily interested in encouraging foreign travel to the United States. However, in 1963 in a message to Congress about the balance of payments, Kennedy stated that he

was going to ask the domestic travel and tourism industry to initiate a unified program "to encourage Americans to learn more about their heritage." He went on to state, "A See America Now program, to be in full operation by the spring of 1964, will make the most of our magnificent resources, and make travel at home a more appealing alternative to travel abroad" ("Special Message to the Congress on Balance of payments, July 18, 1963," John F. Kennedy, *Public Papers of the Presidents of the United States, John F. Kennedy, Containing the Public Messages, Speeches and Statements of the President* [Washington, D.C.: GPO, 1964], 578).

3. "Special Message to the Congress on International Balance of Payments: February 10, 1965," Lyndon B. Johnson, *Public Papers of the Presidents of the United States, Lyndon B. Johnson, Containing the Public Messages, Speeches and Statements of the President* (Washington, D.C.: GPO, 1966), bk. 1, p. 170.

4. The administration argued that the revenues lost through American overseas travel amounted to almost one-third of the balance of payments deficit.

5. "Special Message to the Congress on International Balance of Payments: February 10, 1965," 175–76. See also "President's News Conference, August 15, 1964," Johnson, *Public Papers of the Presidents of the United States,* 964. For a response to the See the USA program, see Anne Chamberlin, "See America First," *Saturday Evening Post,* 28 August 1965, 25–31, 70–74.

6. See "U.S. Tourist Drive Runs into Two Snags," *New York Times,* 5 May 1965; "Despite LBJ Pleas: Boom in Travel Abroad," *U.S. News and World Report,* 29 March 1965, 8; and "Boom in Foreign Travel and in U.S., Too," *U.S. News and World Report,* 29 June 1965, 10.

7. Horace Sutton, "Turning the Red, White, and Blue into Gold," *Saturday Review,* 12 November 1966, 50–51; and Hubert H. Humphrey, "Solving the Nation's Travel Arithmetic," *Saturday Review,* 12 November 1966, 52. For a brief overview of the accomplishments of the cabinet task-force on travel, see "Vice President Reaffirms Freedom-to-Travel Policy," *New York Times,* 4 June 1967.

8. Department of Commerce, *Eighth Semi-Annual Report of the Secretary of Commerce on the United States Travel Service, 1965,* 14. For a brief overview of the history of Discover America, see Department of Commerce, *Travel USA: A Simplified Explanation of the Role of Tourism in the United States Economy* (Washington, D.C.: GPO, 1968), 7–8.

9. Note that originally "See the USA" was proposed, but because of the slogan's association with General Motor's Chevrolet advertising jingle, "See the USA in your Chevrolet," the corporation adopted "Discover America" instead. See "Everybody Out to Discover America," *New York Times,* 9 April 1967. Directorships in the new organization were offered to executives in automobile, railroad and airline companies, hotel chains, oil companies, car rental companies, tire manufactures and representatives from a variety of other transportation and travel industries. Robert E. Short, owner

of the Leamington Hotel in Minneapolis and close friend of Hubert Humphrey, was named as chairman. Donald Y. McCoy who had been associated with the petroleum industry was appointed executive director. See "Everybody Out to Discover America" and "Johnson Picks Tourism Aide," *New York Times,* 3 May 1965.

10. "Everybody Out to Discover America."

11. Ibid. See also "Advertising: Year for Discovering America," *New York Times,* 10 March 1967.

12. "Everybody Out to Discover America" and "Advertising: Year for Discovering America."

13. "Field of Travel: Springtime Will Be Trip-Planning Time," *New York Times,* 24 December 1967.

14. "Remarks to the Members of the See the U.S.A. Committee, August 11, 1965," in Johnson, *Public Papers of the Presidents of the United States,* bk. 2, p. 874.

15. "Vice President Reaffirms Freedom-to-Travel Policy."

16. "Udall Urges U.S. Travelers to See America First," *New York Times,* 24 February 1965.

17. Humphrey, "Solving the Nation's Travel Arithmetic," 52.

18. Flink, *Car Culture,* 131.

19. Rae, *Road and the Car,* 50.

20. "Percent Distribution of Automobile Ownership, and Financing, 1947–1970," *Historical Statistics of the United States: Colonial Times to 1970* (Washington, D.C.: GPO, 1975), pt. 2, 717.

21. "Mileage and Cost of Federal Aid Highway Systems, 1917 to 1970," *Historical Statistics of the United States,* pt. 2, 711.

22. Rae, *Road and the Car,* 187–88.

23. Jakle, *Tourist,* 186.

24. Gary S. Cross, *Time and Money: The Making of Consumer Culture* (New York: Routledge, 1993), 96.

25. Jakle, *Tourist,* 188.

26. Susan G. Davis, "Landscapes of Imagination: Tourism in Southern California," *Pacific Historical Review* 68 (May 1999): 173–92, quoted on page 177–78 and footnote 11.

27. For a discussion of the expansion of the white middle class during the postwar era, see George Lipsitz, "The Possessive Investment in Whiteness: Racialized Social Democracy and the 'White' Problem in American Studies," *American Quarterly* 47 (September 1995): 369–87.

28. Lizbeth Cohen, "From Town Center to Shopping Center: The Reconfiguration of Community Marketplaces in Postwar America," *American Historical Review* 101 (October 1996): 1079.

29. For the expansion of postwar tourist opportunities in the American West, see Rothman, *Devil's Bargains*.

30. On Disneyland, see Karal Ann Marling, ed., *Designing Disney's Theme Parks: The Architecture of Reassurance* (New York: Flammarion, 1997); Michael Sorkin, ed., *Variations on a Theme Park: The New American City and the End of Public Space* (New York: Hill & Wang, 1992); and Eric Smoodin, ed., *Disney Discourse: Producing the Magic Kingdom* (New York: Routledge, 1994).

31. For and overview of recreational and entertainment tourism see Rothman, *Devil's Bargains*, 202–370.

32. Marling, *Colossus of Roads*.

33. Donald Worster, *Dustbowl: The Southern Plains in the 1930s* (New York: Oxford University Press, 1979), 49–50.

34. Barry Miles, *Jack Kerouac, King of the Beats: A Portrait* (New York: Henry Holt, 1998), 112. See also Sven Birkerts, *American Energies: Essays on Fiction* (New York: William Morrow, 1992), 196–202; and Rowland A. Sherrill, *Road-book America: Contemporary Culture and the New Picaresque* (Urbana: University of Illinois Press, 2000).

BIBLIOGRAPHY

MANUSCRIPT COLLECTIONS

Bancroft Library, University of California, Berkeley
    Mather, Stephen Tyng. Papers.
    Panama-Pacific International Exposition Records.
Crater Lake National Park Museum and Library, Crater Lake, Oregon
    See America First Exhibit Files.
Huntington Library, San Marino, California
    Allen, Ethel Richardson. Photograph album. 1921–23. Photographic Collections.
    Baker, Mildred E. "A Glimpse of the Old West." Scrapbook. 1935. Photographic Collections.
    ———. "Memorable Days on the Teton Trail." Scrapbook. 1934. Photographic Collections.
    ———. "Navaho Mountain." Scrapbook. 1931. Photographic Collections.

———. "Peace of Rainbow and Canyon." Scrapbook. 1938. Photographic Collections.

———. "Rough Water: Down the Colorado and Green Rivers." Scrapbook. 1940. Photographic Collections.

———. "Turquoise Skies and Copper Canyons. Scrapbook. 1942. Photographic Collections.

Bridges, Amy. "Journal Kept on 4th Raymond Excursion [from Massachusetts to California and Return]." 1882. Diary. Western Manuscript Collections.

———. "Journal Kept on a Raymond Excursion from Massachusetts to California and Return Including a Three Month Stay at the Raymond Hotel in South Pasadena, the Del Monte, and San Francisco, etc. 1886–1887." Diary. Western Manuscript Collections.

Butler, A. A., and C. W. Butler. "Colorado Outings." c. 1898. Western Manuscript Collections.

Fall, Albert Bacon. Collection.

Gunnison, Andrew Charles. Sketchbook. 1887. Western Manuscript Collections.

Irwin, C. D. "Diaries of Round-the-World Trip Including some Travel in the United States." Vol. 3, "Letter from Australia, New Zealand and the Hawaiian Islands." 1885. Western Manuscript Collections.

Marston, Otis. Papers.

Merritt, Stephen. "From Ocean to Ocean or Across and the Around the Country. Being an account of the Raymond and Whitcomb Pacific, North West and Alaska, Excursion of 1892. Including the Yosemite Valley and the Yellowstone Park." Typewritten travel journal. 1892. Western Manuscript Collections.

Tripp, Augustus F. "Notes of an Excursion to California in the Winter and Spring of 1893." Diary. 1893. Western Manuscript Collections.

"Trips to Colorado, Yosemite and Throughout the Grand Canyon." Anonymous photograph album. 1921–24. Photographic Collections.

[Waldon, Sidney.] "Sagebrush and Sequoia." Photograph album and travel journal. 1919. Photographic Collections.

James J. Hill Reference Library. St. Paul, Minnesota
    Hill, Louis W. Papers.

J. William Marriott Library, University of Utah, Salt Lake City
    Special Collections.

Lake County Museum, Wauconda, Illinois
    Curt Teich Postcard Archives.

Minnesota Historical Society, St. Paul
    Great Northern Railway Company. Advertising and Publicity Department. Magazine and Newspaper Articles and Other Publicity, 1911–1943. Microfilm edition.
    Great Northern Railway Records.

National Archives II, College Park, Maryland
  Office of the Secretary of the Interior. Records. Record Group 48.
  National Park Service. Records. Record Group 79.
  Works Projects Administration. Records of the Federal Writers' Project, Records of
    the Central Office. Records. Record Group 69.
National Museum of American History, Smithsonian Institution, Washington, D.C.
  Blenkle, Victor A. Postcard Collection. Archives Center.
  Division of Technology. Miscellaneous Collections.
  Warshaw Collection of Business Americana. Archives Center.
  Worlds Fairs Microfilm Collection.
National Parks and Conservation Association, Washington, D.C.
  National Parks Association. Miscellaneous Papers.
Oregon Historical Society, Portland
  Kiser, Fred H. Files and Photographs.
Perkins Library, Duke University, Durham, North Carolina
  Harris, Fisher Sanford. Papers, 1865–1909. Special Collections Department.
University of Oregon, Eugene
  Dodson, William Daniel Boone. Papers. Special Collections.
  Evarts, Hal G. Papers, 1919–1951. Special Collections.
U.S. Department of Transportation Library, Washington, D.C.
  United States Department of Transportation. Miscellaneous Papers.
Utah State Historical Society, Salt Lake City
  Miscellaneous Collections.

BOOK, ARTICLES, DISSERTATIONS, AND GOVERNMENT DOCUMENTS

Abbott, Carl. *Boosters and Businessmen: Popular Economic Thought and Urban Growth in the
  Antebellum Middle West.* Westport, Conn: Greenwood Press, 1981.
"A Billion Dollar Sentiment." *Collier's,* 10 October 1914.
"Address by Mrs. Hunter M. Merriwether." *Better Roads,* June 1912.
Adler, Judith. "Origins of Sightseeing." *Annals of Tourism Research* 16, no. 1 (1989): 7–29.
————. "Youth on the Road: Reflection on the History of Tramping." *Annals of Tour-
  ism Research* 12, no. 3 (1985): 335–54.
"Advertising: Year for Discovering America." *New York Times,* 10 March 1967.
Agnew, Jean-Christophe. "Coming up for Air: Consumer Culture in Historical Perspec-
  tive." In *Consumption and the World of Goods,* edited by John Brewer and Roy Porter,
  19–39. New York: Routledge, 1993.
Albright, Horace M., and Robert Cahn. *The Birth of the National Park Service: The Founding Years, 1913–33.* Chicago: Howe Brothers, 1985.

Alsberg, Henry G., ed. *The American Guide: A Source Book and Complete Travel Guide for the United States.* New York: Hastings House, 1949.

American Association of State Highway Officials. *Manual and Specifications for the Manufacture, Display and Erection of U.S. Standard Road Markers and Signs.* N.p.: N.p, 1927.

American Automobile Association. *Federal Aid for Good Roads: Proceedings of First National Convention.* Washington D.C.: American Automobile Association, 1912.

"American Guide Week Planned for November 10th–16th." *Publishers Weekly,* 11 October 1941.

"A Motorist's Creed." *American Motorist,* June 1917.

Anderson, Benedict. *Imagined Communities: Reflections on the Origin and Spread of Nationalism.* Rev. ed. New York: Verso, 1991.

Anderson, Charles L. G. *Old Panama and the Castilla del Oro.* Boston: Page, 1914.

Appleton's Hand-Book of American Travel: The Western Tour. New York: D. Appleton, 1873.

Appleton's Hand-Book Through the United States. New York: D. Appleton, 1846.

Aron, Cindy S. *Working at Play: A History of Vacations in the United States.* New York: Oxford, 1999.

Arreola, Paul R. "George Wharton James and the Indians." *Masterkey* 60 (Spring 1986): 11–18.

Athearn, Richard G. *The Mythic West in Twentieth-Century America.* Lawrence: University of Kansas Press, 1986.

————. *Rebel of the Rockies: A History of the Denver and Rio Grande Western Railway.* New Haven, Conn.: Yale University Press, 1960.

Atherton, Lewis. *Main Street on the Middle Border.* Bloomington: Indiana University Press, 1954.

Babcock, Barbara. "Mudwomen and Whitemen." In Norris, *Discovered Country,* 180–95.

Baggs, Mae Lacy. *Colorado, the Queen Jewel of the Rockies.* Boston: Page, 1918.

Bakhtin, Mikail M. "Discourse in the Novel." In *The Dialogic Imagination: Four Essays by M. M. Bakhtin,* edited by Michael Hoquist, 259–422. Austin: University of Texas Press, 1981.

Banta, Martha. *Taylored Lives: Narrative Productions in the Age of Taylor, Veblen and Ford.* Chicago: University of Chicago Press, 1993.

Barr, Eva. "The Redwood Empire." *American Motorist,* July 1926.

Barrett, Myrtle. *Our Wonderous Trip.* N.p.: Published by author, 1914.

Barringer, Mark Daniel. "Private Empire, Public Land: The Rise and Fall of the Yellowstone Park Company." Ph.D. diss., Texas Christian University, 1997.

Bartlett, Richard A. *Nature's Yellowstone.* Albuquerque: University of New Mexico Press, 1974.

————. *Yellowstone: A Wilderness Besieged.* Tucson: University of Arizona Press, 1985.

Bedell, Mary Crehore. *Modern Gypsies: The Story of a Twelve Thousand Mile Motor Camping Trip Encircling the United States*. New York: Brentano's, 1924.

Belasco, Warren James. *Americans on the Road: From Autocamp to Motel, 1910–1945*. Cambridge: MIT Press, 1979.

Bell, Archie. *Sunset Canada: British Columbia and Beyond*. Boston: Page, 1918.

Benedict, Burton. *The Anthropology of World's Fairs: San Francisco's Panama Pacific International Exposition of 1915*. Berkeley, Calif.: Scholar Press, 1983.

Benson, Joe, and Rob Silverman. "Tourist Photographs as Souvenirs." *Prospects* 11 (1987): 261–72.

Berger, Michael L. *The Devil Wagon in God's Country: The Automobile and Social Change in Rural America, 1893–1929*. Hamden, Conn.: Archon Books, 1979.

Berkhofer, Robert F., Jr. *The White Man's Indian: Images of the American Indian from Columbus to the Present*. New York: Vintage Books, 1979.

Bettis, William Charles. *A Trip to the Pacific Coast by Automobile Across the Continent, Camping all the Way*. N.p.: Published by author, 1922.

Bhabha, Homi K., ed. *Nation and Narration*. New York: Routledge Press, 1990.

Birney, Hoffman. *Roads to Roam*. Philadelphia: Penn Publishing, 1930.

Birkerts, Sven. *American Energies: Essays on Fiction*. New York: William Morrow, 1992.

Black, Jeremy. *The British Abroad: The Grand Tour in the Eighteenth Century*. New York: St. Martin's Press, 1992.

Bliss, Carey S. *Autos across America: A Bibliography of Transcontinental Automobile Travel: 1903–1940*. New Haven, Conn.: Jekins & Reese, 1982.

Blodgett, Peter J. "Selling Scenery: Advertising and the National Parks, 1916–1933." In *Seeing and Being Seen*, edited by David Wrobel and Patrick Long. Lawrence: University of Kansas Press, 2001.

———. "Striking a Balance: Managing Concessions in the National Parks, 1916–33." *Forest and Conservation History* 34 (April 1990): 60–68.

Bodnar, John. *Remaking America: Public Memory, Commemoration and Patriotism in the Twentieth Century*. Princeton, N.J.: Princeton University Press, 1992.

Bold, Christine. "The View from the Road: Katherine Kellock's New Deal Guidebooks." *American Studies* 29 (1988): 5–29.

———. *The WPA Guides: Mapping America*. Jackson: University of Mississippi Press, 1999.

"Books on California." *Nation*, 17 December 1914.

"Boom in Foreign Travel and in U.S., Too." *U.S. News and World Report*, 29 June 1965.

Boorstin, Daniel. *The Americans: The National Experience*. New York: Vintage, 1965.

———. "From Traveler to Tourist: The Lost Art of Travel." In *The Image: A Guide to Pseudo-Events in America*, by Daniel Boorstin, 77–117. New York: Atheneum, 1980.

Bourdieu, Pierre. *The Logic of Practice*. Translated by Richard Nice. Stanford, Calif.: Stanford University Press, 1990.

Bourdon, Roger Joseph. "George Wharton James, Interpreter of the Southwest." Ph.D. diss., University of California, Los Angeles, 1965.

Bowden, Martyn J. "The Great American Desert in the American Mind: The Historiography of a Geographical Notion." In *Geographies of the Mind*, edited by David Lowenthal and Martyn J. Bow, 119–47. New York: Oxford University Press, 1976.

Bowles, Samuel. *Across the Continent: A Summer's Journey to the Rocky Mountains, the Mormons, and the Pacific States with Speaker Colfax.* New York: Hurd & Houghton, 1865.

———. *Our New West: Records of Travel Between the Mississippi River and the Pacific Ocean.* Hartford, Conn.: Hartford Publishing, 1869.

———. *The Pacific Railroad—Open.* Boston: Fields, Osgood, 1869.

Brimmer, F. E. *Motor Camp Craft.* New York: Macmillan, 1923.

Brinkley, Alan. *The End of Reform: New Deal Liberalism in Depression and War.* New York: Knopf, 1995.

Brown, Dona. *Inventing New England: Regional Tourism in the Nineteenth Century.* Washington, D.C.: Smithsonian Institution Press, 1995.

Brown, Julie K. "'Seeing and Remembering': George Eastman and the World's Columbian Exposition, Chicago 1893." *Image* 39, nos. 1–2 (Spring/Summer 1996): 1–30.

Bruce, Robert. "Named and Marked Roads." *American Motorist*, April 1917.

Bruce-Briggs, B. *The War against the Automobile.* New York: E. P. Dutton, 1977.

Bryant, Keith L., Jr. *History of the Atchison, Topeka and Santa Fe Railway.* New York: Macmillan, 1974.

Bryant, William Cullen, ed. *Picturesque America; or, The Land We Live In.* Vols. 1 and 2. New York: D. Appleton, 1872–74.

Bucco, Martin. "The Serialized Novels of Sinclair Lewis." In *Modern Critical Views, Sinclair Lewis,* edited by Harold Bloom, 63–70. New York: Chelsea House, 1987.

Buell, Lawrence. "The Thoreauvian Pilgrimage: The Structure of an American Cult." *American Literature* 61 (May 1989): 175–99.

Burr, Agnes Rush. *Alaska, Our Beautiful Northland of Opportunity.* Boston: Page, 1919.

"California Takes Stock of its Fair." *Literary Digest,* 25 December 1915.

Campbell, Colin. *The Romantic Ethic and the Spirit of Modern Consumption.* Oxford: Basil Blackwell, 1987.

Carr, Ethan. *Wilderness by Design: Landscape Architecture and the National Park Service.* Lincoln: University of Nebraska Press, 1998.

Cayton, Andrew R. L., and Peter S. Onuf. *The Midwest and the Nation: Rethinking the History of America Region.* Bloomington: Indiana University Press, 1990.

Chalfen, Richard. *Turning Leaves: The Photographic Collections of Two Japanese American Families.* Albuquerque: University of New Mexico Press, 1991.

Chamberlain, Allen. "Scenery as a National Asset." *Outlook,* 28 May 1910.

Chamberlin, Anne. "See America First." *Saturday Evening Post,* 28 August 1965.

Chandler, Alfred D. *The Visible Hand: The Managerial Revolution in American Business.* Cambridge: Harvard University Press, 1977.

"Charles Davis, 86, Retired Engineer." *New York Times*, 4 June 1951.

Chittenden, Hiram Martin. *The Yellowstone National Park: Historical and Descriptive.* Norman: University of Oklahoma Press, 1964.

Clayton, Jay, and Eric Rothstein, eds. *Influence and Intertextuality in Literary History.* Madison: University of Wisconsin Press, 1991.

Clifford, James. *The Predicament of Culture: Twentieth-Century Ethnography, Literature and Art.* Cambridge: Harvard University Press, 1988.

"Closing the Tourist Gap." *Time*, 31 March 1961.

Cocks, Catherine. *Doing the Town: The Rise of Urban Tourism in the United States, 1850–1915.* Berkeley and Los Angeles: University of California Press, forthcoming 2001.

Cohen, Lizbeth. "From Town Center to Shopping Center: The Reconfiguration of Community Marketplaces in Postwar America." *American Historical Review* 101 (October 1996): 1050–81.

Cohn, Jan. *Improbable Fiction: The Life of Mary Roberts Rinehart.* Pittsburgh: University of Pittsburgh Press, 1980.

Commager, Henry Steele. "The Search for a Usable Past." In *The Search for a Usable Past and Other Essays on Historiography*, by Henry Steele Commanger, 3–27. New York: Knopf, 1967.

Cordry, Mrs. T. A. *The Story of the Marking of the Santa Fe Trail.* Topeka, Kans.: Crane, 1915.

Cortes, Enrique. "Advocate for the Golden State: George Wharton James in California." *Masterkey* 60 (Spring 1986): 19–25.

Cosgrove, Denis, and Stephen Daniel. *The Iconography of Landscape.* Cambridge: Cambridge University Press, 1988.

Crandall, Gina M. *Nature Pictorialized: "The View" in Landscape History.* Baltimore: Johns Hopkins University Press, 1993.

———. "When Art Challenges Beauty." *Landscape* 29 (1986): 10–16.

Crofutt, George A. *Great Trans-Continental Railroad Guide.* Chicago: Geo. A. Crofutt, 1869.

———. *Great Trans-Continental Railroad Guide.* Chicago: Geo. A. Crofutt, 1870.

———. *New Overland Tourist and Pacific Coast Guide.* Chicago: Overland, 1878.

Cronon, William. *Nature's Metropolis: Chicago and the Great West.* New York: Norton, 1991.

———. "The Trouble with Wilderness; or, Getting Back to the Wrong Nature." In *Uncommon Ground: Rethinking the Human Place in Nature*, edited by William Cronon, 69–90. New York: W. W. Norton, 1996.

Cross, Gary S. *Time and Money: The Making of Consumer Culture.* New York: Routledge, 1993.

Crowningshield, Daniel Smith. *The Jolly Eight: Coast to Coast and Back.* Boston: Richard G. Badger, 1929.

Crunden, Robert M. *Ministers of Reform: The Progressives' Achievement in American Civilization, 1889–1920.* New York: Basic Books, 1982.

Curti, Merle. *The Roots of American Loyalty.* New York: Columbia University Press, 1946.

Davis, Susan G. "Landscapes of Imagination: Tourism in Southern California." *Pacific Historical Review* 68 (May 1999): 173–92.

Davis, Timothy Mark. "Mt. Vernon Memorial Highway and the Evolution of the American Parkway." Ph.D. diss., University of Texas, Austin, 1997.

Dean, William Harper. "Advertising America: Uncle Sam Tells His People about Their National Parks." *Outing,* August 1916.

Deloria, Philip J. *Playing Indian.* New Haven, Conn.: Yale University Press, 1998.

DeSantis, Hugh. "The Democratization of Travel: The Travel Agent in American History." *Journal of American Culture* 1 (Spring 1978): 1–17.

"Despite LBJ Pleas: Boom in Travel Abroad." *U.S. News and World Report,* 29 March 1965.

Dettelbach, Cynthia Golomb. *In the Driver's Seat: The Automobile in American Literature and Popular Culture.* Westport, Conn.: Greenwood Press, 1976.

Diggins, John Patrick. "Republicanism and Progressivism." *American Quarterly* 37 (Fall 1985): 572–98.

Dilworth, Leah. *Imagining Indians in the Southwest: Persistent Visions of a Primitive Past.* Washington, D.C.: Smithsonian Institution Press, 1996.

Dixon, Winifred Hawkridge. *Westward Hoboes: Ups and Downs of Frontier Motoring.* New York: Charles Scribner's Sons, 1921.

Dole, Nathan Haskell, and Irwin Leslie Gordon. *Maine of the Sea and Pines.* Boston: Page, 1928.

Dorman, Robert L. *Revolt of the Provinces: The Regionalist Movement in America, 1920–1945.* Chapel Hill: University of North Carolina Press, 1993.

Dreiser, Theodore. *A Hoosier Holiday.* Westport, Conn.: Greenwood Press, 1974.

Duncan, James, and Derek Gregory, eds. *Writes of Passage: Reading Travel Writing.* London: Routledge, 1999.

Dwight, Timothy. *Travels in New England and New York, 1821–22.* Edited by Barbara Miller Solomon. Cambridge: Harvard University Press, 1969.

Editorial. *Nation,* 25 January 1906.

Editorial Comments. *Harper's Weekly,* 2 December 1905.

"Editorial Scores: 'See America First.'" *New York Times,* 1 April 1906.

Erickson, Kenneth A. "Ceremonial Landscapes of the American West." *Landscape* 22 (Autumn 1977): 39–41.

Eubank, Victor. "Log of an Auto Prairie Schooner: Motor Pioneers on the 'Trail to Sunset.'" *Sunset,* February 1912.

"Everybody Out to Discover America." *New York Times,* 9 April 1967.

Ewald, Donna, and Peter Clute. *San Francisco Invites the World: The Panama-Pacific International Exposition of 1915.* San Francisco: Chronicle Books, 1991.

Ewing, Alfred M. *Seeing America First.* N.p.: Published by author, 1932.

Federal Writers' Project. *Kansas: A Guide to the Sunflower State.* New York: Viking, 1939.

———. *North Carolina: A Guide to the Old North State.* Chapel Hill: University of North Carolina Press, 1939.

"Field of Travel: Springtime Will be Trip-Planning Time." *New York Times,* 24 December 1967.

Fifer, J. Valerie. *American Progress: The Growth of Transport, Tourist, and Information Industries in the Nineteenth Century West.* Chester, Conn.: Pequot Press, 1988.

"Finish in Montana." *St. Paul Pioneer Press Dispatch,* 26 August 1909.

"Fisher Harris Is Back from the East." *Salt Lake Tribune,* 5 April 1906.

Fisher, Philip. *Hard Facts: Setting and Form in the American Novel.* New York: Oxford University Press, 1985.

Flagg, James. *Boulevards All the Way—Maybe.* New York: Doran, 1925.

Flink, James J. *America Adopts the Automobile, 1895–1910.* Cambridge: MIT Press, 1970.

———. *The Automobile Age.* Cambridge: MIT Press, 1988.

———. *The Car Culture.* Cambridge: MIT Press, 1975.

———. "Three Stages of American Automobile Consciousness." *American Quarterly* 24 (October 1972): 451–73.

Foresta, Ronald A. *America's National Parks and Their Keepers.* Washington, D.C.: Resources for the Future, 1984.

Foster, Gaines M. *Ghosts of the Confederacy: Defeat, the Lost Cause, and the Emergence of the New South 1865 to 1913.* New York: Oxford University Press, 1987.

Foucault, Michel. *Discipline and Punish: The Birth of the Prison.* New York: Vintage Books, 1979.

Fox, Richard Wightman, and T. J. Jackson Lears. *The Culture of Consumption: Critical Essays in American History, 1880–1980.* New York: Pantheon, 1983.

Fox, Stephen R. *The Mirror Makers: A History of American Advertising and its Creators.* New York: William Morrow, 1984.

Franz, Kathleen. "Narrating Automobility: Travelers, Tinkerers, and Technological Authority in the Twentieth Century." Ph.D. diss., Brown University, 1999.

Fred Harvey Company, *California and the Grand Canyon of Arizona.* Los Angeles: Fred Harvey, 1914.

"Free Trade for Americans—With Americans." *Collier's,* 3 October 1914.

Friedman, Estelle. "The New Woman: Changing Views of Women in the 1920s." *Journal of American History* 61 (1974): 373–93.

"From the Collections." *Image* 39, nos. 1–2 (Spring/Summer 1996).

Fuessle, Newton A. "The Lincoln Highway—A National Road." *Travel*, February–April 1915.

Fussell, Paul. *Abroad: British Literary Traveling between the Wars*. New York: Oxford University Press, 1980.

Gellner, Ernest. *Nations and Nationalism*. Ithaca, N.Y.: Cornell University Press, 1983.

Gilpin, William. *Three Essays on Picturesque Beauty*. Westmead, England: Gregg International, 1972.

"Giving the American Label Its Due." *Collier's*, 17 October 1914.

Gladding, Effie Price. *Across the Continent by the Lincoln Highway*. New York: Brentano's, 1915.

Glassberg, David. *American Historical Pageantry: The Uses of Tradition in the Early Twentieth Century*. Chapel Hill: University of North Carolina Press, 1990.

Gleason, Philip. "American Identity and Americanization." In *Concepts of Ethnicity*, edited by William Peterson, Michael Novak, and Philip Gleason, 57–143. Cambridge: Belknap Press, 1982.

Goetzmann, William H. *Exploration and Empire: The Explorer and the Scientist in the Winning of the American West*. New York: W. W. Norton, 1966.

Goetzmann, William H., and William N. Goetzmann. *The West of the Imagination*. New York: W. W. Norton, 1989.

"Good Roads Notes Gathered Here and There." *Southern Good Roads*, January 1912.

Gordon, Dudley C. *Charles F. Lummis: Crusader in Corduroy*. Los Angeles: Cultural Assets Press, 1972.

"Governors, Delegates Welcome!" *Salt Lake Tribune*, 26 January 1906.

Graburn, Nelson H. H. "The Anthropology of Tourism." *Annals of Tourism Research* 10, no. 1 (1983): 9–33.

———. "Tourism: The Sacred Journey." In *Hosts and Guests: The Anthropology of Tourism*, edited by Valene Smith, 21–36. Philadelphia: University of Pennsylvania Press, 1989.

Grattan, Virginia L. *Mary Colter: Builder upon the Red Earth*. Flagstaff, Ariz.: Northland Press, 1980.

"The Great Fair and Our Country: See Your Own Country and the World as Mirrored by the Panama-Pacific Exposition." *Delineator*, February 1915.

"Great Move to Promote the West." *Salt Lake Tribune*, 5 April 1906.

Greeley, Horace. *An Overland Journey from New York to San Francisco in the Summer of 1859*. New York: C. M. Saxton, Barker, 1860.

Green, Harvey. *Fit for America: Health, Fitness, Sport and American Society*. New York: Pantheon Books, 1986.

Grosvenor, Gilbert H. "The Land of the Best." *National Geographic Magazine*, April 1916.

Gudis, Catherine. "The Road to Consumption: Outdoor Advertising and the American Cultural Landscape, 1917–1965." Ph.D. diss., Yale University, 1999.

Gutheim, Frederick. "America in Guide Books." *Saturday Review of Literature*, 14 June 1941.

Habermas, Jürgen. *The Structural Transformation of the Public Sphere: An Inquiry into a Category of Bourgeois Society*. Translated by Thomas Burger. Cambridge: MIT Press, 1991.

Haines, Aubrey L. *The Yellowstone Story: A History of Our First National Park*, 2 vols. Yellowstone National Park, Wyo.: Yellowstone Library and Museum Association in Cooperation with Colorado University Press, 1977.

Hales, Peter B. *William Henry Jackson and the Transformation of the American Landscape*. Philadelphia: Temple University Press, 1988.

Hall, Edward H. *Appleton's Hand-Book of American Travel: The Northern Tour*. New York: D. Appleton, 1867.

———. *Appleton's Hand-Book of American Travel: The Southern Tour*. New York: D. Appleton, 1866.

Handler, Richard. "Authenticity." *Anthropology Today* 2 (February 1986): 2–4.

———. *Nationalism and the Politics of Culture in Quebec*. Madison: University of Wisconsin Press, 1988.

———. "On Having a Culture: Nationalism and the Preservation of Quebec's Patrimonie." In *Objects and Others: Essays on Museums and Material Culture*, edited by George W. Stocking, 192–215. Madison: University of Wisconsin Press, 1985.

Haraway, Donna. *Primate Visions: Gender, Race and Nature in the World of Modern Science*. New York: Routledge, 1989.

Harris, Fisher. "Are the People of the East Growing Effete?" *Western Monthly*, June 1909.

———. "Europe vs. America." *Western Monthly*, December 1908.

Hatch, Darwin S. "Transcontinental Treks of Other Days." *Motor Age*, 25 February 1915.

Hays, Samuel. *Conservation and the Gospel of Efficiency: The Progressive Conservation Movement, 1890–1920*. Cambridge: Harvard University Press, 1959.

Heinl, Robert D. "The Man Who Is Building a Great National Park." *Leslie's Illustrated Weekly*, 7 March 1912.

Henry Ford Museum. *Americans on Vacation*. Dearborn, Mich.: Henry Ford Museum and Greenfield Village, 1990.

Hiestand, Orville O. *See America First*. Chicago: Regan Printing House, 1922.

Hidy, Ralph W., Muriel E. Hidy, and Roy V. Scott, with Don L. Hofsommer. *The Great Northern Railway: A History*. Boston: Harvard University Press, 1988.

Higgins, C. A. *Titan of Chasms: The Grand Canyon of the Arizona*. Chicago: Passenger Department of the Santa Fe Railway, 1906.

Higham, John. *History: Professional Scholarship in America*. Baltimore: Johns Hopkins University Press, 1983.

———. "The Reorientation of American Culture in the 1890s." In *Writing American History: Essays on Modern Scholarship*, by John Higham, 73–101. Bloomington: Indiana University Press, 1970.

————. *Strangers in the Land: Patterns of American Nativism, 1860–1925.* New York: Atheneum, 1985.

"Hill Quits Rockies." *St. Paul Pioneer Press Dispatch,* 30 August 1909.

Hobsbawn, E. J., and Terence Ranger, eds. *The Invention of Tradition.* Cambridge: Cambridge University Press, 1983.

————. *Nations and Nationalism Since 1870: Programme, Myth, Reality.* Cambridge: Cambridge University Press, 1990.

Hofstadter, Richard. *The Age of Reform: From Bryan to F. D. R.* New York: Vintage Books, 1955.

————. *The Progressive Historians: Turner, Beard, Parrington.* New York: Knopf, 1968.

————. *Social Darwinism in American Thought.* Rev. ed. New York: George Braziller, 1959.

Hokanson, Drake. *The Lincoln Highway: Main Street across America.* Iowa City: University of Iowa Press, 1988.

Holt, William Stull. *The Bureau of Public Roads: Its History, Activities and Organization.* Baltimore: Johns Hopkins University Press, 1923.

Hopkins, Charles Edwin. *Ohio the Beautiful and Historic.* Boston: Page, 1931.

Howard, Kathleen L., and Diana F. Pardue. *Inventing the Southwest: The Fred Harvey Company and Native American Art.* Phoenix: Heard Museum, 1996.

Horne, Donald. *The Great Museum: The Representation of History.* London: Pluto Press, 1984.

Hughes, J. Donald. *In the House of Stone and Light: A Human History of the Grand Canyon.* Grand Canyon, Ariz.: Grand Canyon Natural History Association, 1978.

Hugill, Peter J. "Good Roads and the Automobile in the Untied States, 1880–1929." *Geography Review* 72, no. 3 (1982): 327–49.

————. "The Rediscovery of America: Elite Automobile Touring." *Annals of Tourism Research* 12, no. 3 (1985): 435–47.

Hulme, Katherine. *How's the Road?* San Francisco: Published by author, 1928.

Humphrey, Hubert H. "Solving the Nation's Travel Arithmetic." *Saturday Review,* 12 November 1966.

Hunt, John Dixon. *Gardens and the Picturesque: Studies in the History of Landscape Architecture.* Cambridge: MIT Press, 1992.

Hutchins, Frank, and Cortelle Hutchins. *Virginia: The Old Dominion.* Boston: Page, 1921.

Huth, Hans. *Nature and the American: Three Centuries of Changing Attitudes.* Rev. ed. Lincoln: University of Nebraska Press, 1990.

Hyde, Anne Farrar. *An American Vision: Far Western Landscape and National Culture, 1820–1920.* New York: New York University Press, 1990.

Hyde, John. *Alice's Adventures in Wonderland.* St. Paul, Minn.: Northern Pacific Railway, n.d.

Interrante, Joseph Anthony. "A Movable Feast: The Automobile and the Spatial Transformation of American Culture, 1890–1940." Ph.D. diss., Harvard University, 1983.

"Irrigation in Montana." *St. Paul Pioneer Press Dispatch,* 29 August 1909.

Irwin, William. *The New Niagara: Tourism, Technology, and the Landscape of Niagara Falls, 1776–1917.* University Park: Pennsylvania State University Press, 1996.

Ise, John. *Our National Park Policy: A Critical History.* Baltimore: Johns Hopkins University Press, 1961.

Jakle, John. *The Tourist in Twentieth-Century North America.* Lincoln: University of Nebraska Press, 1985.

James, George Wharton. *Arizona the Wonderland.* Boston: Page, 1917.

———. *California Romantic and Beautiful.* Boston: Page, 1914.

———. *In and Around the Grand Canyon.* Boston: Little, Brown, 1900.

———. *In and Out of the Old Missions of California.* Boston: Little, Brown, 1905.

———. *Indian Basketry.* New York: H. Malkan, 1901.

———. *Indians of the Painted Desert Region.* Boston: Little, Brown, 1903.

———. *The Land of the Sky, Lake Tahoe.* Boston: Page, 1928.

———. *New Mexico: The Land of the Delight Makers.* Boston: Page, 1920.

———. *Old Missions and Mission Indians of California.* Los Angeles: B. R. Baumgardt, 1895.

———. *Picturesque Southern California.* Los Angeles, 1898.

———. *Through Ramona's Country.* Boston: Little, Brown, 1908.

———. *Utah, The Land of Blossoming Valleys.* Boston: Page, 1922.

———. *Wonders of the Colorado Desert.* Boston: Little, Brown, 1906.

Jehlen, Myra. "The American Landscape as Totem." *Prospects* 6 (1981): 17–36.

Jenkins, Reese V. "Technology and the Market: George Eastman and the Origins of Mass Amateur Photography." *Technology and Culture* 16 (January 1975): 1–19.

Jenks, Cameron. *The National Park Service: Its History, Activities and Organization.* New York: Appleton, 1922.

Jenson, Parely P. "Current Comments and Announcements." *Western Monthly,* December 1908.

Jessup, Elon. *The Motor Camping Book.* New York: G. P. Putnam's Sons, 1921.

———. "Those Amazing Northeastern States." *American Motorist,* July 1926.

Johnson, Lyndon B. *Public Papers of the Presidents of the United States, Lyndon B. Johnson, Containing the Public Messages, Speeches and Statements of the President, Book I and II–1965.* Washington, D.C.: GPO, 1966.

"Johnson Picks Tourism Aide." *New York Times,* 3 May 1965.

Jones, Alfred Haworth. "The Search for a Usable American Past in the New Deal." *American Quarterly* 23 (December 1971): 710–24.

Jones, Otto W. "By the Waters of the Turbulent Columbia." *American Motorist,* July 1926.

Jowett, Garth S. "The Emergence of the Mass Society: The Standardization of American Culture, 1830–1920." *Prospects* 7 (1982): 207–28.

Kammen, Michael. *Mystic Chords of Memory: The Transformation of Tradition in American Culture.* New York: Vintage Books, 1993.

Kasson, John F. *Amusing the Million: Coney Island at the Turn of the Century.* New York: Hill & Wang, 1978.

Kazin, Alfred. *On Native Grounds: An Interpretation of American Prose Literature.* New York: Reynal and Hitchcock, 1942.

Kennedy, David M. *Over Here: The First World War and American Society.* New York: Oxford University Press, 1980.

Kennedy, H. J. "Railway Exhibits at the Panama-Pacific Exposition." *Scientific American Supplement,* 24 July 1915.

Kennedy, John F. *Public Papers of the Presidents of the United States, John F. Kennedy, Containing the Public Messages, Speeches and Statements of the President, January 1 to November 22, 1963.* Washington, D.C.: GPO, 1964.

Kern, Stephen. *The Culture of Time and Space, 1880–1918.* Cambridge: Harvard University Press, 1983.

Kilgour, Raymond Lincoln. *Estes and Lauriat: A History, 1872–1898.* Ann Arbor: University of Michigan Press, 1957.

Kimes, Beverly Rae, and Robert C. Ackerson. *Chevrolet: A History from 1911.* Princeton, N.J.: Princeton Publishing, 1981.

Kingsley, Guy Richard. "Progress of America's Great Panama Canal Celebration." *Overland Monthly,* October 1914.

Kinsey, Joni. *Thomas Moran and the Surveying of the American West.* Washington, D.C.: Smithsonian Institution Press, 1992.

Kirkland, Edward Chase. *Industry Comes of Age: Business, Labor and Public Policy, 1860–1897.* Chicago: Quadrangle Books, 1967.

Kiser Brother's Pacific Coast Pictures. Portland, Oreg., 1904.

Kiser, Fred H. *Official Photographs of the Louis and Clark Exposition.* Portland, Oreg., 1905.

Kitchin, William Copeman. *A Wonderland of the East Comprising the Lake and Mountain Region of New England and Eastern New York.* Boston: Page, 1920.

Kohn, Hans. *American Nationalism: An Interpretive Essay.* New York: Macmillan, 1957.

Kritzman, Lawrence D., ed. *Michel Foucault: Politics, Philosophy, Culture: Interviews and Other Writings, 1977–1984.* New York: Routledge, 1988.

Labatut, Jean, and Wheaton J. Lane, eds. *Highways in Our National Life: A Symposium.* Princeton, N.J.: Princeton University Press, 1950.

Laird, Pamela Walker. *Advertising Progress: American Business and the Rise of Consumer Marketing.* Baltimore: Johns Hopkins University Press, 1998.

Lanfant, Marie-Françoise, John B. Allcock, and Edward M. Bruner, eds. *International Tourism: Identity and Change.* London: Sage, 1995.

Langford, N. P. "The Wonders of the Yellowstone." *Scribner's Monthly,* May 1871. (Part 1.)

————. "The Wonders of the Yellowstone." *Scribner's Monthly*, June 1871. (Part 2.)

Leach, William. *Land of Desire: Merchants, Power, and the Rise of a New American Culture.* New York: Pantheon Books, 1993.

Lears, T. J. Jackson. *Fables of Abundance: A Cultural History of Advertising in America.* New York: Basic Books, 1994.

————. *No Place of Grace: Antimodernism and the Transformation of American Culture, 1880–1920.* New York: Pantheon, 1981.

————. "The Rise of American Advertising." *Wilson Quarterly* 7 (Winter 1983): 156–67.

————. "Some Versions of Fantasy: Toward a Cultural History of American Advertising, 1880–1930." *Prospects* 9 (1984): 349–405.

Leavengood, David. "A Sense of Shelter: Robert C. Reamer in Yellowstone National Park." *Pacific Historical Review* 54 (November 1985): 495–513.

Leed, Eric J. *The Mind of the Traveler: From Gilgamesh to Global Tourism.* New York: Basic Books, 1991.

Leiss, William, Stephen Kline, and Sut Jhally. *Social Communication in Advertising: Persons, Products and Images of Well Being.* 2d ed. Scarborough, Ont.: Nelson Canada, 1990.

Leong, Wai-Teng. "Culture and The State: Manufacturing Traditions for Tourism." *Critical Studies in Mass Communication* 6 (December 1989): 355–75.

Levebrve, Henri. *The Production of Space.* Translated by Donald Nicholson-Smith. Cambridge, Mass: Blackwell, 1991.

Levine, Lawrence. *Highbrow/Lowbrow: The Emergence of Cultural Hierarchy in America.* Cambridge: Harvard University Press, 1988.

Lewis, David L., and Laurence Goldstein, eds. *The Automobile and American Culture.* Ann Arbor: University of Michigan Press, 1980.

Lewis, Sinclair. *Free Air.* Lincoln: University of Nebraska Press, 1993.

Liebs, Chester H. *Main Street to Miracle Mile: American Roadside Architecture.* Boston: Little, Brown, 1985.

Limerick, Patricia Nelson. *The Legacy of Conquest: The Unbroken Past of the American West.* New York: W. W. Norton, 1987.

Lincoln Highway Association. *The Complete Official Road Guide of the Lincoln Highway.* Detroit: Lincoln Highway Association, 1915.

————. *The Lincoln Highway: The Story of a Crusade that Made Transportation History.* New York: Dodd, Mead, 1935.

Lindsay, Forbes. *Panama and the Canal Today.* Boston: L. C. Page, 1910.

Lingeman, Richard. *Theodore Dreiser: An American Journey, 1908–1945.* New York: G. P. Putnam's Sons, 1990.

Lipsitz, George. "The Possessive Investment in Whiteness: Racialized Social Democracy and the 'White' Problem in American Studies." *American Quarterly* 47 (September 1995): 369–87.

————. *Time Passages: Collective Memory and American Popular Culture.* Minneapolis: University of Minnesota Press, 1990.

Long, J. C., and John D. Long. *Motor Camping.* New York: Dodd, Mead, 1923.

"Louis W. Hill Is Promoted to President." *St. Paul Pioneer Press Dispatch,* 3 April 1907.

Lowe, J. M. *The National Old Trails Road: The Great Historic Highway of America.* Kansas City: Published by author, 1924.

Lowenthal, David. "Age and Artifact: Dilemmas of Appreciation." In *The Interpretation of Ordinary Landscapes: Geographical Essays,* edited by D. W. Meinig, 103–27. New York: Oxford University Press, 1979.

————. *The Heritage Crusade and the Spoils of History.* Cambridge: Cambridge University Press, 1998.

————. *The Past Is a Foreign Country.* Cambridge: Cambridge University Press, 1985.

————. "The Place of the Past in American Landscape." In *Geographies of the Mind,* edited by David Lowenthal and Martyn J. Bow, 89–117. New York: Oxford University Press, 1976.

Lummis, Charles F. "In the Lions Den." *West Coast,* August 1912, 609.

————. *Some Strange Corners of Our Country: The Wonderland of the Southwest.* Tucson: University of Arizona Press, 1989.

————. "Wakening a Sober Patriotism." *Out West Magazine,* December 1905.

MacCannell, Dean. *The Tourist: A New Theory of the Leisure Class.* New York: Schocken Books, 1976.

Macpherson, C. B. *The Political Theory of Possessive Individualism: Hobbs to Locke.* Oxford: Oxford University Press, 1962.

Magoc, Chris J. *Yellowstone: The Creation and Selling of an American Landscape, 1870–1903.* Albuquerque: University of New Mexico Press, 1999.

Mangione, Jerre G. *The Dream and the Deal: The Federal Writers' Project, 1935–1943.* Boston: Little, Brown, 1972.

Marchand, Roland. *Advertising the American Dream.* Berkeley and Los Angeles: University of California Press, 1985.

————. *Creating the Corporate Soul: The Rise of Public Relations and Corporate Imagery in American Big Business.* Berkeley and Los Angeles: University of California Press, 1998.

————. "The Fitful Career of Advocacy Advertising: Political Protection, Client Cultivation, and Corporate Morale." *California Management Review* 29 (Winter 1987): 128–56.

Marling, Karal A. *Colossus of Roads: Myth and Symbol along the American Highway.* Minneapolis: University of Minnesota Press, 1984.

————, ed. *Designing Disney's Theme Parks: The Architecture of Reassurance.* New York: Flammarion, 1997.

Martin, C. Brenden. "Selling the Southern Highlands: Tourism and Community Development in the Mountain South." Ph.D. diss., University of Tennessee, 1997.

Marx, Leo. *The Machine in the Garden: Technology and the Pastoral Ideal in America.* New York: Oxford University Press, 1964.

Mason, Philip Parker. *A History of American Roads.* Chicago: Rand McNally, 1967.

———. "The League of American Wheelmen and the Good-Roads Movement, 1880–1905." Ph.D. diss., University of Michigan, 1957.

Massey, Beatrice. *It Might Have Been Worse: A Motor Trip from Coast to Coast.* San Francisco: HarrWagner, 1920.

Mather, Stephen Tyng. "The National Parks on a Business Basis." *American Review of Reviews,* April 1915.

———. *Progress in the Development of the National Parks.* Washington, D.C.: GPO, 1916.

Maurer, Stephen G. "In the Heart of the Great Freedom: George Wharton James and the Desert Southwest." *Masterkey* 60 (Spring 1986): 4–10.

May, Lary. *Screening Out the Past: The Birth of Mass Culture and the Motion Picture Industry.* New York: Oxford University Press, 1980.

McClelland, Linda Flint. *Building the National Parks: Historic Landscape Design Construction.* Baltimore: Johns Hopkins University Press, 1998.

McGerr, Michael E. *The Decline of Popular Politics: The American North, 1865–1928.* New York: Oxford University Press, 1986.

McGill, Vernon. *Diary of a Motor Journey from Chicago to Los Angeles.* Los Angeles: Grafton Publishing, 1922.

McGovern, Charles F. "Consumption and Citizenship in the United States, 1900–1940." In *Getting and Spending: European and American Consumer Societies in the Twentieth Century,* edited by Susan Strasser, Charles McGovern, and Matthias Judt, 37–58. New York: Cambridge University Press, 1998.

———. "Sold American: Inventing the Consumer, 1890–1940." Ph.D. diss., Harvard University, 1993.

McKinsey, Elizabeth. *Niagara Falls: Icon of the American Sublime.* Cambridge: Cambridge University Press, 1985.

McLuhan, T. C. *Dream Tracks: The Railroad and the American Indian, 1890–1930.* New York: Harry N. Abrams, 1985.

McQuaid, Matilda, and Karen Bartlett. "Building an Image of the Southwest: Mary Colter, Fred Harvey Company Architect." In Weigle and Babcock, *Great Southwest,* 24–35.

McShane, Clay. *Down the Asphalt Path: American Cities and the Coming of the Automobile.* New York: Columbia University Press, 1994.

Meinig, D. W. "Symbolic Landscapes: Some Idealizations of American Communities." In *The Interpretation of Ordinary Landscapes: Geographical Essays,* edited by D. W. Meinig, 164–92. New York: Oxford University Press, 1979.

Mendelson, Edward. "Baedeker's Universe." *Yale Review* 74 (April 1985): 386–403.

Miles, Barry. *Jack Kerouac, King of the Beats: A Portrait.* New York: Henry Holt, 1998.

Miles, John C. *Guardians of the Parks: A History of the National Parks and Conservation Association.* Washington, D.C.: Taylor and Francis, 1995.

Miller, Angela. *The Empire of the Eye: Landscape Representation and American Cultural Politics, 1825–1875.* Ithaca, N.Y.: Cornell University Press, 1993.

Miller, Daniel, ed. *Acknowledging Consumption: A Review of New Studies.* New York: Routledge, 1995.

Miller, Perry. "The Romantic Dilemma in American Nationalism and the Concept of Nature." In *Nature's Nation,* by Perry Miller, 197–207. Cambridge: Belknap Press, 1967.

Miltoun, Francis. *The Automobilist Abroad.* Boston: L. C. Page, 1907.

"Mission of SEE AMERICA FIRST." *See America First,* March 1912.

Mitchell, Lee Clark. *Witnesses to a Vanishing America: The Nineteenth-Century Response.* Princeton, N.J.: University of Princeton Press, 1981.

Mitchell, W. T. J., ed. *Landscape and Power.* Chicago: University of Chicago Press, 1994.

Moore, Charles C. "San Francisco and the Exposition: The Relation of the City to the Nation as Regards the World's Fair." *Sunset,* February 1912.

Mott, Frank Luther. *A History of American Magazines, 1885–1905.* Vol. 4. Cambridge: Harvard University Press, 1957.

Mumford, Lewis. "Writers' Project." *New Republic,* 20 October 1937.

Murdock, Graham. "Citizens, Consumers, and Public Culture." In *Media Cultures: Reappraising Transnational Media,* edited by Michael Skovmand and Kim Christian Schroder, 17–41. New York: Verso, 1992.

Murphy, Thomas Dowler. *British Highways and Byways from a Motor Car.* Boston: L. C. Page, 1908.

———. *In Unfamiliar England.* Boston: Page, 1910.

———. *New England Highways and Byways from a Motor Car.* Boston: Page, 1924.

———. *On Sunset Highways: A Book of Motor Rambles in California.* Boston: L. C. Page, 1912.

———. *Oregon the Picturesque.* Boston: Page, 1917.

———. *Seven Wonderlands of the American West.* Boston: Page, 1925.

———. *Three Wonderlands of the American West.* Boston: L. C. Page, 1912.

Nasaw, David. *Going Out: The Rise and Fall of Public Amusements.* New York: Basic Books, 1993.

Nash, Roderick. "The American Invention of National Parks." *American Quarterly* 22 (Fall 1970): 726–35.

———. "The Exporting and Importing of Nature: Nature Appreciation as a Commodity, 1850–1980." *Perspectives in American History* 12 (1979): 517–60.

———. *Wilderness and the American Mind.* 3d ed. New Haven, Conn.: Yale University Press, 1982.

National Old Trails Association. *Proceedings of the First National Old Trails Road Convention, Held at the Commercial Club Room, Kansas City, Missouri, April 17, 1912.* Kansas City: National Old Trails Association, 1920.

"National Old Trails Road." *Better Roads,* August 1912.

"National Old Trails Road Association." *Better Roads and Streets,* September 1915.

"National Old Trails Road Convention." *Better Roads,* June 1912.

National Park Service [Robert Sterling Yard]. *Glimpses of Our National Parks.* Washington, D.C.: GPO, 1916.

————. *The National Parks Portfolio.* New York: Scribner's, 1916.

Neumann, Mark. "The Commercial Canyon." In Norris, *Discovered Country,* 196–209.

————. *On the Rim: Looking for the Grand Canyon.* Minneapolis: University of Minnesota Press, 1999.

"New Playground for Americans." *St. Paul Pioneer Press Dispatch,* 17 April 1910.

Newell, Alan S., David Walterm, and James R. McDonald. *Historic Resource Study, Glacier National Park and Historic Structures Survey.* Denver: National Park Service, Denver Service Center, 1980.

Nolan, Edward W. *Northern Pacific Views: The Railroad Photography of F. Jay Haynes, 1876–1905.* Helena: Montana Historical Society Press, 1983.

Norris, Scott, ed. *Discovered Country: Tourism and Survival in the American West.* Albuquerque: Stone Ladder Press, 1994.

Northern Pacific Railway. *Yellowstone National Park, America's Only Geyser Land.* Buffalo: Matthews Northrup Works, 1913.

Norton, Harry J. *Wonder-Land Illustrated; or Horseback Rides through the Yellowstone National Park.* Virginia City, Mont.: Harry J. Norton, 1873.

Novak, Barbara. *Nature and Culture: American Landscape Painting, 1825–1875.* New York: Oxford University Press, 1980.

Nye, David E. *American Technological Sublime.* Cambridge: MIT Press, 1994.

————. *Image Worlds: Corporate Identities at General Electric, 1890–1930.* Cambridge: MIT Press, 1985.

————. *Narratives and Spaces: Technology and the Construction of American Culture.* New York: Columbia University Press, 1997.

Ober, Michael J. "Enmity and Alliance: Park Service-Concessioner Relations in Glacier National Park, 1892–1916." Master's thesis, University of Montana, 1973.

Ohmann, Richard M. *Selling Culture: Magazines, Markets, and Class at the Turn of the Century.* London: Verso, 1996.

Olneck, Michael R. "Americanization and the Education of Immigrants, 1900–1925: An Analysis of Symbolic Action." *American Journal of Education* 97 (August 1989): 398–423.

Olson, Keith W. *Biography of a Progressive: Franklin K. Lane, 1864–1921.* Westport, Conn.: Greenwood Press, 1979.

"One of the Many Reasons Why You Should See America First." *American Motorist,* February 1913.

Orvell, Miles. *The Real Thing: Imitation and Authenticity in American Culture, 1880–1940.* Chapel Hill: University of North Carolina Press, 1989.

"Other Books Worth While." *Literary Digest,* 16 January 1915.

"Page Company Absorbs Dana Estes and Co." *Publisher's Weekly,* 28 March 1914.

Pardington, A. R. "Following the Path of Progress." *American Motorist,* January 1915.

"Patriotism that Pays." *Collier's,* 24 October 1914.

Patton, Phil. *Open Road: A Celebration of the American Highway.* New York: Simon & Schuster, 1986.

Peiss, Kathy. *Cheap Amusements: Working Women and Leisure in New York City, 1880 to 1920.* Philadelphia: Temple University Press, 1986.

Penkower, Monty Noam. *The Federal Writers' Project: A Study in Government Patronage of the Arts.* Urbana: University of Illinois Press, 1977.

"'Personally Conducted' Transcontinental Tour." *American Motorist,* September 1911.

Peterson, Theodore. *Magazines in the Twentieth Century.* Urbana: University of Illinois Press, 1956.

Phillips, David. "Chevy Sings Old Song: 'See the USA . . .'" *Detroit News,* 24 February 1999.

"Photos Are Marvels." *St. Paul Pioneer Press Dispatch,* 8 February 1909.

Pocock, J. G. A. *The Machiavellian Moment: Florentine Political Thought and the Atlantic Republican Tradition.* Princeton, N.J.: Princeton University Press, 1975.

Pomeroy, Earl. *In Search of the Golden West: The Tourist in Western America.* Lincoln: University of Nebraska Press, 1990.

———. *The Pacific Slope: A History of California, Oregon, Washington, Idaho, Utah, and Nevada.* New York: Knopf, 1965.

Post, Emily. *By Motor to the Golden Gate.* New York: D. Appleton, 1917.

Pratt, Mary Louise. *Imperial Eyes: Travel Writing and Transculturation.* New York: Routledge, 1992.

"President Looks to Spur Tourism." *New York Times,* 1 February 1961.

Preziosi, Donald. "The Panoptic Gaze and the Anamorphic Archive." In *Rethinking Art History: Meditations on a Coy Science,* by Donald Preziosi, 54–79. New Haven, Conn.: Yale University Press, 1989.

Purchase, Eric. *Out of Nowhere: Disaster and Tourism in the White Mountains.* Baltimore: Johns Hopkins University Press, 1999.

Rae, John, B. *The American Automobile: A Brief History.* Chicago: University of Chicago Press, 1965.

———. *The Road and the Car in American Life.* Cambridge: MIT Press, 1971.

Raymond and Whitcomb Company. *Raymond and Whitcomb Vacation Excursions Grand Trip to Colorado, California and the Pacific Northwest.* Boston, 1884.

———. *Raymond's Vacation Excursions: Four Grand Winter Trips to California.* Boston, 1886.

———. *Raymond's Vacation Excursions: Three Spring and Early Summer Tours.* Boston, 1891.

———. *Raymond's Vacation Excursions: A Winter in California.* Boston, 1888.

———. *Vacation Excursions: Five Grand Summer Trips for July 1882.* Boston, 1882.

———. *A Winter Trip to California with a Sojourn of Five Months at the Famous Winter Health and Pleasure Resort of the Pacific Coast, the Elegant Hotel Del Monte, Monterey, Cal.* Boston, 1883.

"Real Work Has Only Now Begun." *Salt Lake Tribune.* 28 January 1906.

Reeves, Brian, and Sandy Peacock. *"Our Mountains Are Our Pillows": An Ethnographic Overview of Glacier National Park.* Denver: National Park Service, Denver Service Center, 1995.

Reiger, John F. *American Sportsmen and the Origins of Conservation.* Norman: University of Oklahoma Press, 1975.

Richards, T. Addison. *Appleton's Illustrated Hand-Book of American Travel.* New York: D. Appleton, 1857.

Riegel, Robert Edgar. *The Story of the Western Railroads: From 1952 through the Reign of the Giants.* Lincoln: University of Nebraska Press, 1964.

Riley, W. C. *Official Guide to the Yellowstone National Park: A Manual for Tourists, Being a Description of . . . the New Wonderland.* Rev. ed. St. Paul, Minn.: Northern News, 1888.

Rinehart, Mary Roberts. "The Family Goes A-Gypsying." *Outlook,* 12 June 1918.

———. "My Country Tish of Thee." *Saturday Evening Post,* 1 April 1916. (Part 1.)

———. "My Country Tish of Thee." *Saturday Evening Post,* 8 April 1916. (Part 2.)

———. *My Story: A New Edition and Seventeen Years.* New York: Arno Press, 1980.

———. "On the Trail in Wonderland II." *Wide World,* November 1916.

———. *The Out Trail.* New York: George H. Doran, 1923.

———. *Tenting Tonight.* Boston: Houghton Mifflin, 1918.

———. "Through Glacier National Park with Howard Eaton." *Collier's,* 22 and 29 April 1916.

———. *Through Glacier Park: Seeing America First with Howard Eaton.* Boston: Houghton Mifflin, 1916.

Rishel, W. D. "What Transcontinental Touring Really Means." *American Motorist,* May 1913.

Rittenberg, Caroline. *Motor West.* New York: Harold Vinal, 1926.

Robbins, William G. *Colony and Empire: The Capitalist Transformation of the American West.* Lawrence: University of Kansas Press, 1994.

Robinson, Thomas. *Oregon Photographers; Biographical History and Directory, 1952–1917.* Portland, Oreg.: Published by author, 1992.

Rogers, Daniel T. "Republicanism: The Career of a Concept." *Journal of American History* 79 (June 1992): 11–38.

———. *The Work Ethic in Industrial America, 1850–1920.* Chicago: University of Chicago Press, 1978.

Roosevelt, Theodore. *The Strenuous Life: Essays and Addresses.* New York: Century, 1902.

Roseberry, William. *Anthropologies and Histories: Essays in Culture, History, and Political Economy.* New Brunswick, N.J.: Rutgers University Press, 1989.

Rosenberg, Emily S. *Spreading the American Dream: American Economic and Cultural Expansion, 1890–1945.* New York: Hill & Wang, 1982.

Rosenzweig, Roy. *Eight Hours for What We Will: Workers and Leisure in an Industrial City, 1870–1920.* New York: Cambridge University Press, 1983.

Ross, Dorothy. "The Liberal Tradition Revisited and the Republican Tradition Addressed." In *New Directions in American Intellectual History,* edited by John Higham and Paul Conkin, 116–31. Baltimore: Johns Hopkins University Press, 1977.

Rothman, Hal K. *Devil's Bargains: Tourism in the Twentieth-Century American West.* Lawrence: University of Kansas Press, 1998.

———. *Preserving Different Pasts: The American National Monuments.* Chicago: University of Illinois Press, 1989.

Runte, Alfred. *National Parks: The American Experience.* 3d ed. Lincoln: University of Nebraska Press, 1997.

———. "Pragmatic Alliance: Western Railroads and the National Parks." *National Parks and Conservation Magazine* 48 (April 1974): 14–21.

———. "Promoting Wonderland: Western Railroads and the Evolution of National Park Advertising." *Journal of the West* 31 (January 1992): 43–48.

———. *Trains of Discovery: Western Railroads and the National Parks.* Flagstaff, Ariz.: Northland Press, 1984.

Rydell, Robert W. *All the World's a Fair.* Chicago: University of Chicago Press, 1984.

———. "The Trans-Mississippi and International Exposition: To Work Out the Problem of Universal Civilization." *American Quarterly* 33 (Winter 1981): 587–607.

Sabin, Gula. *California by Motor.* Milwaukee: Published by author, 1926.

Said, Edward W. *Orientalism.* New York: Vintage Books, 1978.

Salmon, Ted. *From Southern California to Casco Bay.* San Bernardino, Calif.: San Bernardino Publishing, 1930.

Salt Lake City Commercial Club. *The "See America First" Conference, Salt Lake City, Utah, January 25–26, 1906.* Salt Lake: Tribune Job Printing, 1906.

Scharff, Virginia. *Taking the Wheel: Women and the Coming of the Motor Age.* New York: Free Press, 1991.

The Scenery of the United States Illustrated in a Series of Forty Engravings. New York: D. Appleton, 1855.

Schene, Michael G. "The Crown of the Continent: Private Enterprise and Public Interest in the Early Development of Glacier National Park, 1910–1917." *Forest and Conservation History* 34 (April 1990): 69–75.

Schivelbusch, Wolfgang. *The Railway Journey: The Industrialization of Time and Space in the 19th Century.* Berkeley and Los Angeles: University of California Press, 1986.

Schlereth, Thomas J. *U.S. 40: A Roadscape of the American Experience.* Indianapolis: Indiana Historical Society, 1985.

Schmeckebier, L. F. "Our National Parks." *National Geographic,* June 1912.

Schmitt, Peter J. *Back to Nature: The Arcadian Myth in Urban America.* Baltimore: Johns Hopkins University Press, 1990.

Schorer, Mark. *Sinclair Lewis: An American Life.* New York: McGraw-Hill, 1961.

Schudson, Michael. *Advertising the Uneasy Persuasion: Its Dubious Impact on American Society.* New York: Basic Books, 1984.

Schwantes, Carlos A. "Landscapes of Opportunity: Phases of Railroad Promotion of the Pacific Northwest." *Montana* 43 (1993): 38–51.

———. *Railroad Signatures across the Pacific Northwest.* Seattle: University of Washington Press, 1993.

———. "Tourists in Wonderland: Early Railroad Tourism in the Pacific Northwest." *Columbia* 7 (1993/94): 22–30.

Schwatka, Lt. Frederick, and John Hyde. *Wonderland; or Alaska and the Inland Passage.* St. Paul, Minn.: Northern Pacific Railroad, 1886.

Sears, John F. *Sacred Places: American Tourist Attractions in the Nineteenth Century.* New York: Oxford University Press, 1989.

"See America's Convention." *Salt Lake Tribune,* 28 January 1906.

"See America First." *Collier's,* 31 October 1914.

"See America First Strongly Indorsed." *See America First,* March 1912.

"See Europe If You Will, but See America First": An Address delivered by Hon. Herber M. Wells Before the "See America First" Conference at Salt Lake City, January 25, 1906. Denver: Passenger Department, Denver and Rio Grande Railroad, 1906.

Seely, Bruce E. *Building the American Highway System: Engineers as Policy Makers.* Philadelphia: Temple University Press, 1987.

Shaffer, Marguerite S. "Negotiating National Identity: Western Tourism and 'See America First.'" In *Reopening the American West: Environment and Culture in the Western Past and Present,* edited by Hal K. Rothman, 122–51. Tucson: University of Arizona Press, 1998.

———. "'See America First': Re-Envisioning Nation and Region through Western Tourism." *Pacific Historical Review* 65 (November 1996): 559–81.

———. "See American First: Tourism and National Identity, 1905–1930." Ph.D. diss., Harvard University, 1994.

———. "Seeing America First: The Search for Identity in the Tourist Landscape." In *Seeing and Being Seen,* edited by Patrick T. Long and David M. Wrobel. Lawrence: University of Kansas Press, 2001.

————. "Seeing the *Nature* of America: The National Parks as National Assets, 1914–1929." In *Being Elsewhere: Tourism, Consumer Culture and Identity in Modern Europe and North America*, edited by Shelly Baranowski and Ellen Furlough. Ann Arbor: University of Michigan Press, 2001.

Shankland, Robert. *Steve Mather of the National Parks*. 3d ed. New York: Knopf, 1970.

Sharp, Dallas Lore. *The Better Country*. Boston: Houghton Mifflin, 1928.

Sheire, James W. *Glacier National Park: Historic Resource Study*. Washington, D.C.: National Park Service, Office of History and Historic Architecture Eastern Service Center, 1970.

Shepard, Paul. *Man in the Landscape: A Historic View of the Esthetics of Nature*. College Station: Texas A&M University Press, 1991.

Sherrill, Rowland A. *Road-book America: Contemporary Culture and the New Picaresque*. Urbana: University of Illinois Press, 2000.

Shi, David E. *The Simple Life: Plain Living and High Thinking in American Culture*. New York: Oxford University Press, 1985.

Shields, Rob. *Places on the Margins: Alternative Geographies of Modernity*. New York: Routledge, 1991.

"Show of Fine Photographs." *St. Paul Pioneer Press Dispatch*, 7 February 1909.

Showalter, Dr. William Joseph. "Washington the Mecca of Vacation Touring." *American Motorist*, March 1927.

Silber, Nina. *The Romance of Reunion: Northerners and the South, 1865–1900*. Chapel Hill: University of North Carolina Press, 1993.

Simmons, Marc. *Following the Santa Fe Trail: A Guide for Modern Travelers*. Santa Fe: Ancient City Press, 1984.

Simpson, W. H. *El Tovar: A New Hotel at the Grand Canyon of Arizona*. Chicago: Rand McNally, 1905.

Sklar, Martin J. *The Corporate Reconstruction of American Capitalism, 1890–1916: The Market, the Law and Politics*. Cambridge: Cambridge University Press, 1988.

Slotkin, Richard. *The Fatal Environment: The Myth of the Frontier in the Age of Industrialization*. New York: Atheneum, 1985.

————. "Nostalgia and Progress: Theodore Roosevelt's Myth of the Frontier." *American Quarterly* 33 (Winter 1981): 608–38.

Smith, Anthony D. *National Identity*. Reno, Nev.: University of Nevada Press, 1991.

Smith, Henry Nash. *Popular Culture and Industrialism, 1865–1890*. New York: Anchor Books, 1967.

————. *Virgin Land: The American West as Symbol and Myth*. New York: Vintage, 1957.

Smith, Valene, ed. *Hosts and Guests: The Anthropology of Tourism*. Philadelphia: University of Pennsylvania Press, 1989.

Smith-Rosenberg, Carol. "The New Woman as Androgyne: Social Order and Gender

Crisis, 1870–1936." In *Disorderly Conduct: Visions of Gender in Victorian America*, edited by Carol Smith-Rosenberg, 245–96. New York: Knopf, 1985.

Smoodin, Eric, ed. *Disney Discourse: Producing the Magic Kingdom*. New York: Routledge, 1994.

Sorkin, Michael, ed. *Variations on a Theme Park: The New American City and the End of Public Space*. New York: Hill & Wang, 1992.

Spears, Timothy B. *100 Years on the Road: Traveling Salesmen in American Culture*. New Haven, Conn.: Yale University Press, 1995.

———. "'All Things to All Men': The Commercial Traveler and the Rise of Modern Salesmanship." *American Quarterly* 45 (December 1993): 524–55.

Spence, Mark David. *Dispossessing the Wilderness: Indian Removal and the Making of the National Parks*. New York: Oxford University Press, 1999.

Stafford, Barbara Maria. *Voyage into Substance: Art, Science, Nature and the Illustrated Travel Account, 1760–1840*. Cambridge: MIT Press, 1984.

Stanley, Edwin J. *Rambles in Wonderland; or, The Yellowstone*. New York: D. Appleton, 1878.

Starr, Kevin. *Inventing the Dream: California through the Progressive Era*. New York: Oxford University Press, 1985.

Steele, David M. *Vacation Journeys East and West: Descriptive Stories of American Summer Resorts*. New York: G. P. Putnam's Sons, 1918.

Steele, Rufus. "The Son Who Showed His Father." *Sunset Magazine*, March 1915.

Stewart, Susan. *On Longing: Narratives of the Miniature, the Gigantic, the Souvenir, the Collection*. Durham, N.C.: Duke University Press, 1993.

Stilgoe, John R. *Metropolitan Corridor: Railroads and the American Scene*. New Haven, Conn.: Yale University Press, 1983.

Stockett, Letitia. *America: First, Fast and Furious*. Baltimore: Norman-Remington, 1930.

Stott, William. *Documentary Expression and Thirties America*. Chicago: University of Chicago Press, 1986.

Stover, John F. *American Railroads*. 2d ed. Chicago: University of Chicago Press, 1997.

Strasser, Susan. *Satisfaction Guaranteed: The Making of the American Mass Market*. Washington, D.C.: Smithsonian Institution Press, 1995.

Susman, Warren I. *Culture as History: The Transformation of American Society in the Twentieth Century*. New York: Pantheon Books, 1984.

Sutton, Horace. "Turning the Red, White, and Blue into Gold." *Saturday Review*, 12 November 1966.

———. "Why They Don't Visit the U.S.A." *Saturday Review*, 15 October 1960.

Swain, Donald C. *Wilderness Defender: Horace M. Albright and Conservation*. Chicago: University of Chicago Press, 1970.

Swinglehurst, Edmund. *The Romantic Journey: The Story of Thomas Cook and Victorian Travel*. New York: Harper and Row, 1974.

Tebbel, John. *A History of Book Publishing in the United States.* 4 vols. New York: R. R. Bowker, 1975.

Tedlow, Richard S. *Keeping the Corporate Image: Public Relations and Business, 1900–1950.* Greenwich, Conn.: JAI Press, 1979.

"Text of President's Message to Congress on U.S. Balance of Payments and on Gold." *New York Times,* 7 February 1961.

Thelen, David. "Memory and American History." *Journal of American History* 75 (March 1989): 1117–29.

Thelen, David, and Frederick E. Hoxie, ed. *Discovering America: Essays on the Search for an Identity.* Urbana: University of Illinois Press, 1994.

Thomas, Ellen S. "Scooping the Local Field: Oregon's Newsreel Industry." *Oregon Historical Quarterly* 90 (Fall 1989): 229–81.

Thompson, Stanley G. "Scenic Tour of the Blue Grass." *American Motorist,* July 1926.

Tichi, Cecelia. *Shifting Gears: Technology, Literature, Culture in Modernist America.* Chapel Hill: University of North Carolina Press, 1987.

Tilden, Freeman. *The National Parks: What They Mean to You and Me.* New York: Knopf, 1951.

"To Advertise Glacier National Park." *St. Paul Pioneer Press Dispatch,* 26 May 1910.

Tobin, Gary Allan. "The Bicycle Boom of the 1890s: The Development of Private Transport and the Birth of the Modern Tourist." *Journal of Popular Culture* 7 (Spring 1974): 838–49.

"To Crowd Work of 'See America First.'" *Salt Lake Tribune,* 8 February 1906.

Todd, Ellen Wiley. *The "New Woman" Revised: Painting and Gender Politics on Fourteenth Street.* Berkeley and Los Angeles: University of California Press, 1993.

Todd, Frank Morton. *The Story of the Exposition: Being the Official History of the International Celebration Held at San Francisco in 1915 to Commemorate the Discovery of the Pacific Ocean and the Construction of the Panama Canal.* 5 vols. New York: G. P. Putnam's Sons, 1912.

"Touring Across the Continent." *American Motorist,* May 1911.

Towner, John. "Approaches to Tourism History." *Annals of Tourism Research* 15, no. 1 (1988): 47–62.

———. "The Grand Tour: A Key Phase in the History of Tourism." *Annals of Tourism Research* 12, no. 3 (1985): 297–334.

Trachtenberg, Alan. *The Incorporation of America: Culture and Society in the Gilded Age.* New York: Hill & Wang, 1982.

"The Trail of the Lonesome Pine." *American Motorist,* July 1926.

Trans-Mississippi Commercial Congress. *Official Proceedings of the Sixteenth Session of the Trans-Mississippi Commercial Congress.* Portland, Oreg.: Glass & Prudhomme, 1905.

———. *Official Proceedings of the Twenty-Third Annual Session of the Trans-Mississippi Commercial Congress.* Kansas City: Edwin J. Becker, 1912.

Trilling, Lionel. *Sincerity and Authenticity.* Cambridge: Harvard University Press, 1971.

Truettner, William H., ed. *The West as America: Reinterpreting Images of the Frontier, 1820–1920.* Washington, D.C.: Smithsonian Institution Press, 1991.

Tuan, Yi-Fu. *Topophilia: A Study of Environmental Perception, Attitudes, and Values.* New York: Columbia University Press, 1974.

Turner, Frederick Jackson. "The Significance of the Frontier in American History." In *The Frontier in American History,* by Frederick Jackson Turner, 1–38. Tucson: University of Arizona Press, 1986.

Turner, Victor, and Edith Turner. *Image and Pilgrimage in Christian Culture: Anthropological Perspectives.* New York: Columbia University Press, 1978.

"Udall Urges U.S. Travelers to See America First." *New York Times,* 24 February 1965.

Ullman, William. "Springtime Is Motoring Time: A Medley of Thoughts." *American Motorist,* April 1916.

"Uniform Road Marker System Planned." *Colorado Highways,* May 1925.

Urry, John. *Consuming Places.* New York: Routledge, 1995.

———. *The Tourist Gaze: Leisure and Travel in Contemporary Society.* London: Sage Publications, 1990.

U.S. Congress. *International Travel: Hearing before the Committee on Interstate and Foreign Commerce.* Washington, D.C.: GPO, 1961.

U.S. Department of Commerce. *Semi-Annual Report of the Secretary of Commerce on the United States Travel Service.* 1961–65. Washington, D.C.: GPO, 1961–65.

———. *Travel USA: A Simplified Explanation of the Role of Tourism in the United States Economy.* Washington, D.C.: GPO, 1968.

U.S. Department of the Interior. *Annual Report of the Department of the Interior.* 1910–25. Washington, D.C.: GPO, 1910–25.

———. *Annual Report of the Secretary of the Interior.* 1910–25. Washington, D.C.: GPO, 1910–25.

———. *Proceedings of the National Parks Conference, Berkeley, California, March 11, 12 and 13, 1915.* Washington, D.C.: GPO, 1915.

———. *Proceedings of the National Parks Conference, Held at the Auditorium of the New National Museum, Washington D.C., January 2, 3, 4, 5, and 6, 1917.* Washington, D.C.: GPO, 1917.

———. *Proceedings of the National Parks Conference Held at Yellowstone National Park, September 11 and 12, 1911.* Washington, D.C.: GPO, 1912.

———. *Proceedings of the National Parks Conference, Yosemite National Park, October 14, 15 and 16, 1912.* Washington, D.C.: GPO, 1913.

———. *Progress in the Development of the National Parks.* Washington, D.C.: GPO, 1916.

———. *Report of the Director of the National Park Service to the Secretary of the Interior for the Fiscal Year Ended June 30, 1917.* Washington, D.C.: GPO, 1917.

————. *Report of the General Superintendent and Landscape Engineer of National Parks to the Secretary of the Interior, 1915.* Washington, D.C.: GPO, 1915.

U.S. Railroad Administration. *Crater Lake National Park, Oregon.* Chicago: Rathbun-Grant-Heller, 1919.

————. *Glacier National Park, Montana.* St. Paul, Minn.: McGill-Warner, 1919.

————. *Grand Canyon National Park, Arizona.* Chicago: H. O. Shepard, 1919.

————. *Hawaii National Park, Hawaiian Islands.* Chicago: Rathbun-Grant-Heller, 1919.

————. *Hot Springs National Park, Arkansas.* Chicago: W. J. Hartman, 1919.

————. *Mesa Verde National Park, Colorado.* Chicago: W. J. Hartman, 1919.

————. *Mt. Rainier National Park, Washington.* Chicago: Poole Brothers, 1919.

————. *Petrified Forest National Monument, Arizona.* Chicago: W. J. Hartman, 1919.

————. *Rocky Mountain National Park, Colorado.* Chicago: Faulkner-Ryan, 1919.

————. *Sequoia and General Grant National Parks, California.* Chicago: Rathbun-Grant-Heller, 1919.

————. *Yellowstone National Park, Wyoming, Montana, Idaho.* Chicago: Rand, McNally, 1919.

————. *Yosemite National Park, California.* Chicago: Poole Brothers, 1919.

————. *Zion National Monument, Utah.* Chicago: Rathbun-Grant-Heller, 1919.

"U.S. Spells US." *Collier's,* 7 November 1914.

"U.S. Tourist Drive Runs into Two Snags." *New York Times,* 5 May 1965.

Van de Water, Frederic F. *The Family Flivvers to Frisco.* New York: D. Appleton, 1927.

"Vast Road System." *Better Roads,* September 1911.

Vernon, Paul E. *Coast to Coast By Motor.* London: A. & C. Black, 1930.

"Vice President Reaffirms Freedom-to-Travel Policy." *New York Times,* 4 June 1967.

Waite, Robert G. "Over the Ranges to the Golden Gate: Tourist Guides to the West, 1880–1920." *Journal of the West* 31 (April 1992): 103–13.

Webb, Walter Prescott. *The Great Plains.* Boston: Ginn and Company, 1959.

Weigle, Marta. "Exposition and Mediation: Mary Colter, Erna Fergusson, and the Santa Fe/Harvey Popularization of the Native Southwest, 1902–1940." *Frontiers: A Journal of Women Studies* 12 (Summer 1991): 117–50.

————. "From Desert to Disney World: The Santa Fe Railway and the Fred Harvey Company Display the Indian Southwest." *Journal of Anthropological Research* 45 (1989): 115–37.

————. "Southwest Lures: Innocents Detoured, Incensed Determined." *Journal of the Southwest* 32 (1990): 499–540.

Weigle, Marta, and Barbara Babcock, eds. *The Great Southwest of the Fred Harvey Company and the Santa Fe Railway.* Phoenix: Heard Museum, 1996.

Weigle, Marta, and Kathleen L. Howard. "'To *Experience* the Real Grand Canyon': Santa Fe/Harvey Panopticism, 1910–1935." In Weigle and Babcock, *Great Southwest,* 13–23.

Weingroff, Richard. "The National Old Trails Road." Unpublished manuscript in possession of author, 1989.

Westgard, A. L. *Tales of a Pathfinder*. New York: Author, 1920.

Wharton, Edith. *The Motor Flight Through France*. New York: Scribner's, 1909.

Wheeler, Olin D. *6000 Miles Through Wonderland: Being a Description of the Marvelous Region Traversed by the Northern Pacific Railroad*. St. Paul, Minn.: Northern Pacific Railway, 1893.

———. *Wonderland 1901*. St. Paul, Minn.: Northern Pacific Railway, 1901.

———. *Wonderland 1902*. St. Paul, Minn.: Northern Pacific Railway, 1902.

———. *Wonderland 1904*. St. Paul, Minn.: Northern Pacific Railway, 1904.

———. *Wonderland '97*. St. Paul, Minn.: Northern Pacific Railway, 1897.

White, G. Edward. *The Eastern Establishment and the Western Experience*. New Haven, Conn.: Yale University Press, 1968.

White, Hayden. "The Historical Text as Literary Artifact." In *The Writing of History: Literary Form and Historical Understanding*, edited by Robert H. Canary and Henry Kozicki, 41–62. Madison: University of Wisconsin Press, 1978.

Whiteside, Clara Walker. *Touring New England on the Trail of the Yankee*. Philadelphia: Penn Publishing, 1926.

Wiebe, Robert. *The Search for Order, 1877–1920*. New York: Hill & Wang, 1967.

Wik, Reynold M. *Henry Ford and Grass Roots America*. Ann Arbor: University of Michigan Press, 1973.

Williams, Raymond. "Advertising: The Magic System." In Williams, *Problems in Materialism and Culture*, 170–95.

———. *The Country and the City*. New York: Oxford University Press, 1973.

———. *Problems in Materialism and Culture: Selected Essays*. London: Verso, 1980.

———. *Television: Technology and Cultural Form*. New York: Shocken, 1977.

Williams, Wellington. *Appleton's New and Complete United States Guide Book for Travelers: Embracing the Northern, Eastern, Southern, and Western States, Canada, Nova Scotia, New Brunswick, etc.* New York: D. Appleton, 1850.

Willy, John. "A Week in Glacier National Park." *Hotel Monthly*, August 1915.

Wilson, Andre. *The Gay Gazel: An Adventure in Auto Biography*. Author, 1926.

Winks, Robin W. *Frederick Billings: A Life*. New York: Oxford University Press, 1991.

Winter, Nevin O. *Florida, the Land of Enchantment*. Boston: Page, 1918.

———. *Texas, the Marvelous*. Boston: Page, 1916.

Wood, Stanley. *Over the Range to the Golden Gate: A Complete Tourist's Guide to Colorado, New Mexico, Utah, Nevada, California, Oregon, Puget Sound, and the Great Northwest*. Chicago: R. R. Donnelley & Sons, 1904.

Woodward, C. Vann. *The Strange Career of Jim Crow*. 3d rev. ed. New York: Oxford University Press, 1974.

"Work Is Strongly Endorsed by Press." *Salt Lake Tribune*, 26 January 1906.

Worster, Donald. *Dustbowl: The Southern Plains in the 1930s.* New York: Oxford University Press, 1979.

————. "New West, True West: Interpreting the Region's History." *Western Historical Quarterly* 18 (April 1987): 141–56.

Wright, Hamilton. "The Panama-Pacific Exposition in Its Glorious Prime." *Overland Monthly,* October 1915.

Wright, Patrick. *On Living in an Old Country: The National Past in Contemporary Britain.* London: Verso, 1985.

Yard, Robert Sterling. "Economic Aspects of Our National Park Policy." *Scientific Monthly,* April 1923.

————. "The People and the National Parks." *Survey Graphic,* August 1922.

————. *The Publisher.* Boston: Houghton Mifflin, 1913.

Zapatka, Christian. "The American Parkways: Origins and Evolution of the Park Road." *Quarterly Architectural Review* (Winter 1984): 113–21.

Zelinsky, Wilbur. *Nation into State: The Shifting Symbolic Foundations of American Nationalism.* Chapel Hill: University of North Carolina Press, 1988.

Zenzen, Joan Michele. "Promoting the National Parks: Images of the West in the American Imagination, 1864–1972." Ph.D. diss., University of Maryland at College Park, 1997.

Ziff, Larzer. *The American 1890s: Life and Times of a Lost Generation.* New York: Viking Press, 1966.

Index

Boldface page numbers indicate illustrations